D. G. Leahy
and the Thinking Now Occurring

SUNY series in Theology and Continental Thought
———————
Douglas L. Donkel, editor

D. G. Leahy
and the Thinking Now Occurring

Edited by
Lissa McCullough and Elliot R. Wolfson

Published by State University of New York Press, Albany

© 2021 State University of New York

All rights reserved

Printed in the United States of America

No part of this book may be used or reproduced in any manner whatsoever without written permission. No part of this book may be stored in a retrieval system or transmitted in any form or by any means including electronic, electrostatic, magnetic tape, mechanical, photocopying, recording, or otherwise without the prior permission in writing of the publisher.

For information, contact State University of New York Press, Albany, NY
www.sunypress.edu

Library of Congress Cataloging-in-Publication Data

Names: McCullough, Lissa, editor. | Wolfson, Elliot R., editor.
Title: D. G. Leahy and the thinking now occurring / Lissa McCullough and Elliot R. Wolfson, editors.
Description: Albany : State University of New York Press, [2021] | Series: SUNY series in Theology and Continental Thought | Includes bibliographical references and index.
Identifiers: ISBN 9781438485072 (hardcover : alk. paper) | ISBN 9781438485065 (pbk. : alk. paper) | ISBN 9781438485089 (ebook)
Further information is available at the Library of Congress.

10 9 8 7 6 5 4 3 2 1

Do not be conformed to this world
but be transformed by the renewal of your mind . . .

—Paul, Letter to the Romans 12:2 (RSV)

Contents

Preface   xi

Acknowledgments   xiii

Abbreviations   xv

Introduction to D. G. Leahy: A Quick Start Guide for the
Vexed and Perplexed   1
   Lissa McCullough

Part I. History and Time

Chapter 1
History and the Thinking Now Occurring   27
   Charles Stein

Chapter 2
Temporal Diremption and the Novelty of
Genuine Repetition   53
   Elliot R. Wolfson

Chapter 3
A Metaphysics of Enchantment or a Case of Immanentizing
the Eschaton?   97
   Graham James McAleer

Part II. Apocalyptic Actuality

Chapter 4
Apocalypticism in Modern Thinking: Descartes, Hegel, Leahy   111
Thomas J. J. Altizer

Chapter 5
The Shape of Catholic Apocalypse   127
Cyril O'Regan

Chapter 6
The Act of Omnipotence: Abolition of the Mystical Quest   155
Michael James Dise

Part III. A Physical Ethics

Chapter 7
The Ethic of Simplicity   175
Nathan Tierney

Chapter 8
The Vanishment of Evil from the World   189
Todd Carter

Chapter 9
The Transparency of the Good   209
Alina N. Feld

Part IV. The Edge Where Creating Begins

Chapter 10
Concerning the Absolute Edge   237
Edward S. Casey

Chapter 11
To Think the Beginning: The Apocalyptic "I"   251
Sarah Lilly Eaton

Chapter 12
Life at the Edge: Medicine and the New Thinking   271
   Steven B. Hoath, MD

Glossary of Key Terms in D. G. Leahy   287

D. G. Leahy Comprehensive Bibliography   317

D. G. Leahy Biographical Sketch   321

Contributors   323

Index   327

Preface

We hope that this volume engaging D. G. Leahy's philosophical thinking will serve as a starting point and springboard for expanding awareness of his work worldwide, attracting readers far and near to the immense challenge of this new thinking: a post-modern universal particularism that thinks an absolutely actual creative unity—a unicity—in the form of absolute difference. This volume has come to fruition gradually by fits and starts over something like a dozen years. Initially there was only a handful of souls to tap, not a sufficient quorum of contributors to constitute a full-scale volume. But over time individuals who were actively wrangling with Leahy's thinking emerged from the woodwork and expressed interest in taking part. The extended period during which this project was incubating sadly saw the deaths of three of its major contributors: Steven B. Hoath, MD (d. January 2017), Thomas J. J. Altizer (d. November 2018), and David Leahy himself (d. August 2014). Per the original plan, Leahy had committed to offer responses to each of the essays, but alas we must do without them, assimilating and adjudging these critical engagements without the benefit of his input.

In a more personal vein, we editors wish to honor the philosophical legacy of our beloved friend. An epochal thinker and outstanding teacher, David was also the keen, inspiring, good-humored, quick-witted, and empathetic friend who brought joy and blessing to our lives. We will never forget his looming presence, the fullness of his voice, that Brooklyn accent, that laugh—the essence of David Leahy qua actually existing person!

Lissa McCullough and Elliot R. Wolfson
March 2021

Acknowledgments

The editors wish to acknowledge the kind permission granted to publish in revised form selected segments from Lissa McCullough, "D. G. Leahy," in *Palgrave Handbook of Radical Theology*, ed. Christopher D. Rodkey and Jordan E. Miller (New York: Palgrave Macmillan, 2018), 269–80, which are incorporated into the introduction; and a revised and retitled version of Thomas J. J. Altizer, "Apocalypticism and Modern Thinking," *Journal for Christian Theological Research* [www.jctr.org] 2, no. 2 (1997), pars. 1–27, which appears as chapter 4.

Abbreviations

The following abbreviations are used for the works of D. G. Leahy most frequently cited in the text. Full bibliographic details appear in the comprehensive bibliography at the end of the volume.

BS *Beyond Sovereignty: A New Global Ethics and Morality*

F   *Foundation: Matter the Body Itself*

FP *Faith and Philosophy: The Historical Impact*

NM *Novitas Mundi: Perception of the History of Being,* referring to the 1994 reprint by SUNY Press

Leahy was an avid user of italics. All italicizations in the quotations from Leahy's writings are in the original text unless the contributor indicates otherwise.

Introduction to D. G. Leahy

A Quick Start Guide for the Vexed and Perplexed

LISSA McCULLOUGH

The philosophical writings of D. G. Leahy are exceedingly demanding. They are highly technical, hard to read, recondite, often bewildering, even crazy sounding—especially at first when a reader comes to them cold. For the moment this is new territory and there are very few interpretive footsteps to walk in. In view of the exceptional difficulty faced by the novice, this "quick start guide" offers orientations to and prehensions of Leahy's thinking to serve as heuristic footholds where the learning curve is steepest: it is for first-time readers and anyone debating whether or how to begin the effort, as well as intermediate readers seeking to progress further. This guide is especially intended for those who are intrigued but frustrated from the get-go, already finding themselves vexed and perplexed. This guide, supplemented with the "Glossary of Key Terms" in the back of the volume, invites the patient reader to enter in and begin the process of acclimation, reading and rereading (see "Reading Strategies that Work," below) for the sake of the extraordinary benefits that are to be won by thinking this thinking along with Leahy. The twelve essays of the volume provide a diverse array of expository and critical approaches that readers will find differentially helpful from one time to another.

Quick Start Q&A

Q1: *Why read Leahy if it's so difficult? Why bother?*

A1: Certain thinkers are so original in their purpose that the critical question is not so much whether the reader stands in *accord* with the thinking, but whether she or he has genuinely encountered, absorbed, and been transformed by the intellectual and existential challenge that the thinking incites. One need not be wholly convinced or converted to receive the untold benefit of the thinking proposed. Anyone seriously reading the work of Leahy will be provoked out of habituated categories and projected into a "live" new realm of thinking/existing—an achievement most beneficial in our present globalizing era in the new millennium in which fresh, novel, uncanned thinking is more needful than ever. One might be resistant to Leahy's fundamental outlook and balk at accepting it, but one cannot seriously engage his thinking without being jarred alert, shaken out of intellectual complacency, and provoked to contend with the most fundamental matters on which it is possible to think and act today. Indeed, the deepest project of Leahy's essentially new logic and ethics is to provoke readers to think/act anew every moment precisely because every moment is a new creation, and because not to think/act absolutely anew is unethical. There exists an ethical imperative to undertake this thinking in positive terms—as an X in which one has no choice but to participate—rather than mainly in terms of what it brings to an end, displaces, and renders a thinking of the past. A reader who does not (seek to) begin with the positive X will not get there—because it is categorically transformative of all earlier ontological and ethical thinking. That is what makes the challenge overwhelming. We embody the metanoia. The metanoia embodies us.

Q2: *First, how about a simple overview?*

A2: Yes, a functioning intuitive handle is indispensable. The "new world order" delineated in Leahy's works is characterized as an *absolute creativity* in which the creating is "live," a happening occurring *now*, a now that is an infinitely supersaturated polyontological actuality in which *creation begins*. The world is indeed created—but only *beginning now*. The universe is not precreated; its identity is not fixed but essentially new. To begin this thinking, apply your mind to think an absolute exteriority—an otherness than which none more all-inclusive and thoroughgoing can be thought—one so thorough that the very idea of subjectivity or "self" is canceled, driven out, forefended. Think this thought fully, along with all the reasons for which we can suppose that we have in fact arrived at this perception of the actually existing universe. Demonstrably, existence exists. We are *in fact* in this creative abyss of existence that is neither transcendent nor immanent but a unity beyond both, an absolutely actual unicity. The claim is, moreover, that this is not a matter of knowledge per se but of immediate *perception*. Certainly this involves comprehension and intelligibility, but in a manner "otherwise than knowledge," the beginning of the absolute transcendence of knowledge (FP 153). So then, Leahy implies, "don't blame Leahy." He is thinking something that is in fact happening for thinking, not his doing. The thinking now occurring is not Leahy's "own" thinking for the simple reason that (perception of) existence is gift, and it is for us to *receive* this gift via creative-receptive perception, but not to appropriate it as our own. In colloquial terms, the argument is saying, more or less: apply the powers of the mind until you naturally find that this thinking becomes a transparent intelligibility, even a freely acknowledged inevitability; using your mind expansively it becomes, in the colloquial sense, a "no brainer." The fully open mind's eye sees this absolute actuality, not something else. This actuality now manifest is essentially created by the logic (creative perception) that delineates it.

Q3: *What is important about this thinking?*

A3: The thinking now occurring commences an essentially newborn, universal, fully "digitized" actuality that is nothing but newness, novelty, which inherently also implies *nothing but change*. It is absolute change that powers all "seeming to stay the same." The claim of an essentially new reality may sound grandiose—even impossible or absurd—until one understands the logical basis of the claim to *essential* novelty. At issue is not any form of ideality but rather the full pragmatic fact of actuality, materiality, factuality as now fully thinkable in a way that was not heretofore conceivable—not, that is, before various forerunning breakthroughs in and realizations of ontological thought prepared the way. Thought hitherto has been wedded to conventionality, a system of categorizations and presuppositions, a tracing of fixations, a fixing of traces, because language has been conventional, logic has been conventional; logic is a social construct and a communal good. Anyone who feels attached to a rational/intellectual/scientific status quo, its conventional logics and categories, will be disinclined to welcome or embrace this deep dive into an anticonventional "change of mind" (*metanoia*) at work. By contrast, any who believe that humanity could do with a quantum leap beyond the thrall of modern and postmodern fixations should attempt to hear and understand this thinking for which the stases of conventionality are eliminated wholesale; a thinking that refuses to be conditioned by paradigms, categories, species, genera, walls, bridges, boundaries, and abstractions; a thinking that thinks (creates) novelty itself. For such new-thinking, the world is new.

Q4: *What is "thinking" for this thinking?*

A4: This is not a "thinking" that only philosophers do. All actual forms of mindfulness or consciousness are comprised under the catchall term *thinking*: thinking, seeing, imagining, perceiving, smelling, tasting, reminiscing, dreaming, daydreaming, ratiocinating, being absentminded. The thinking now occurring could just as well be called the *perceiving* now occurring or the *creating of the world* now occurring.

Q5: *Why the obsession with "beginning" in this thinking?*

A5: Only beginning anew permits creativity to function as an *absolute* (re)sourcefulness. Absolute creativity cannot work freely if it begins with something fixed or predetermined. To be absolute, creativity must always begin at the beginning. The beginning is now: now we begin. Even what we call the past—past beginnings memorialized—begin in the present and have sway only *now*. This is a philosophy of *absolute creativity* that is fully and only *actual*. "Past" and "future" are figurative features of actuality, of a thinking *now*.

Q6: *Why is the word "absolute" ubiquitous in this thinking?*

A6: Only *absolute*, and no other word, captures the understanding that nothing is left untouched by the sea-change of universal metanoia, the shift to thinking absolute creativity. Just as in Spinoza everything is understood *sub specie aeternitatis* because of the way everything springs directly from the nature of God, so in the thinking now occurring everything is understood as absolute beginning, a creative emergence *ex abysso*. Figuratively speaking, to touch any point of this absolutely new order is to touch the whole. It is a *unicity*: an absolute whole that is absolutely "digitized." The categories of thought are burst by this unicity. There are no a priori categories, no preordained species: there is only a singular absolute existence itself absolutely particular.

Q7: *Why is the word "essential" ubiquitous in this thinking?*

A7: There is no such thing as precreated, canned essence. Thinking *now* creates essence ex nihilo. Thinking is the universe abiding. The abiding of the universe is thinking. The world subsists qua existence ready to be created essentially (free to be created qua essence, essentially free). When we *think*, we create essence—like it or not. This is not to say that we create material existence by fiat; rather, we create the *essential* content of an existing substrate (substance). Substance is a given—the Body exists absolutely—but its identity emerges through our acts of productive receptivity. Everything that thinking does is *essential*. There is no inessential thinking. Therefore, think well; you are responsible for the universe. Bad thinking, botched universe.

Q8: *Why is the word "objectivity" ubiquitous in this thinking?*

A8: Imagine a thinking that thinks absolutely beyond (without, apart from, excluding) subjectivity, beyond every last vestige of every conceivable notion of "self." What would that thinking look like? Heuristically, it might call itself absolute objectivity. Absolute objectivity is beyond every trace of *intentionality* or *purpose*, prescinding from every origin or source (for an exemplary specification of this, see *beyond beyond x* in the glossary of key terms). When "I" think, this is not the work of a self. It is simply thinking that is occurring, specific and specifying, located in the now. It is the "apocalyptic I" that thinks, not myself—my presumed and presumptive "self." Who am *I* to grab and claim possession of this thinking as though it were *mine*? As though it *belonged* to me? As the actuality of the universe (identically universal consciousness) is received as gift, "manna from heaven," appropriation is inappropriate. This absolute gift is actually given in the receiving; this means that *how* it is received decides its essential nature.

Q9: *Why is the word "transcendental" ubiquitous in this thinking?*

A9: The term *transcendental* is absolutely essential, at the heart of the difficulty. The Incarnation means that God transcends into absolute pleromatic existence. The term *transcendental* characterizes an essentially creative order in which the fiat of live creation in the now is the advent of essence or identity: it is *essence-in-the-making*, or the active creating of identity. The primacy of the transcendental in the form of essentially new existence can be contrasted with modernity's formally transcendental mode of thinking, which presupposes essence in the form of metaphysical abstractions. Now an essentially transcendental synthetic "seeing" and "abiding" constitutes a world absolutely new, a *pleroma-now-in-creation*. Cognizant of being plunged in the deep end of the pool, thinking realizes its essential vocation as the active perception of a universal, unscripted actuality of absolute change, with the capacity to intervene in infinite ways.

Q10: *Does this thinking think transcendence or immanence?*

A10: This thinking thinks transcendence beyond the dichotomy immanence/transcendence. Thinking, qua creative reception, is the infinite transcendence of immanence. Creation that is essentially and categorically transcendent eliminates immanence in a transcendental intimacy. In an inversion of Gilles Deleuze, this is not the collapse of transcendence into a plane of immanence but the collapse of immanence into infinite planes of transcendence.[1]

Q11: *If everything is actual, is everything permissible?*

A11: No, an ethical imperative is implied in the absolute asymmetry of existence and nothing (F 265, 383), and the absolute asymmetry of truth and falsehood, once the truth of falsehood is identified (F 287). This ethical imperative is worked out in *Beyond Sovereignty: A New Global Ethics and Morality* (2010) as the unconditional imperative to create the world, which precludes destructive activity (BS 6).

Q12: *Does this thinking require me to be religious, Christian, or Catholic?*

A12: No. If it did it would not be genuinely catholic, nor would it be free. Everything capable to be thought in the domains of science, politics, religion and irreligion, art, comedy, nonsense, and so on has a place qua thinking. The phenomenality of logic is everywhere at work including in the deepest darkness. Yet certain forms of thinking are more fully consistent with beauty, truth, goodness—in short—the creative freedom that is on offer. Other forms of thinking deserve to be outmoded, superseded—judged, but not condemned—as they manifest their limitations. Let them receive their due. A default of creation is resolved with more creation.

Q13: *Does this thinking require me not to be religious, Christian, Catholic, or atheist?*

A13: Yes, if your existing religiosity or atheism blocks receptivity to this new form of thinking. Outdated forms of thinking act as constraints upon this essentially free new form of thinking.

Q14: *Is this just another totalizing thinking, like Hegel's, with the associated dangers?*

A14: No, because existence qua absolute polyontological in-finitude is miraculous birth. The limit of miracle is no limit. Hegel's Godhead is itself a limit: a container. The thinking now occurring is an absolute exteriority that cannot be limited or contained. It is that than which nothing greater or more unlimited can exist, which is to say: an absolute freedom. Leahy's preferred term for this freedom is *created omnipotence*.

Q15: *What do I need to understand about the trinary logic?*

A15: The trinary logic is a formal thinking that supplants and eliminates the uncreative binarity of one (1) and nothing (0). There is no nothing; nothing is unthinkable. Because nothing *is not* for this thinking, a logic is needed in which zero is not nothing. Creating begins from zero, but that zero is not nothing. All binaries, dichotomies, and oppositional dialectics (Being/nothing, good/evil, truth/falsehood, and so on) are eliminated by trinary thinking. The only dialectic that remains is an essential dialectic: *"in the essential dialectic of matter itself, nothing is thought for the first time in history but existence itself . . . matter itself is the integral perception of change itself existing in essence: motion itself: matter itself essentially dialectical"* (F 52–53). For more, see "trinary logic" in the glossary.

Q16: *Why is there so much mathematics in this thinking (i.e., in* Foundation)?

A16: The claim is that this new universal consciousness/actuality can be demonstrated ad infinitum. The trinary logic and the mathematics are instantiations offered by Leahy to exemplify this claim to infinite demonstrability. The gematria employed extensively in *Foundation* is also a domain of this exemplary demonstration. For further exemplification, see chapter 11 in the present volume: Sarah Lilly Eaton, "To Think the Beginning: The Apocalyptic 'I.'"

Q17: *Which of Leahy's texts are most approachable?*

A17: Although clearly there is value in tracing the course of a thinker's ideas in their sequential development from the earliest works to the latest, this is perhaps not the best way to begin reading Leahy—except for the truly undaunted. The movement from first annunciation to further elaboration in Leahy is assuredly not a progression from simple to complex (they are all complex) or from "juvenile" to mature (they are all mature). The first two books in particular, *Novitas Mundi* and *Foundation*, can be an ordeal to attempt to read without critical assistance. The last two books, *Faith and Philosophy* and *Beyond Sovereignty*, are his most accessible and least intractable. But this is not to say they are easy. Many may find helpful the series of video interviews of Leahy conducted in March 2014, several months before his death, by his student and friend Todd Carter, links to which are available on Leahy's website and on the "D. G. Leahy" Wikipedia entry.

Capsule Synopses of the Four Major Works

Novitas Mundi (1980) first announces the thinking now occurring. Densely written and oracular, it declares that ontological thinking has arrived at an absolute historic watershed, and it proceeds to work through the history of thought that grounds this claim, engaging figures from Aristotle, Augustine, and Thomas Aquinas to Descartes, Leibniz, Kant, Hegel, Kierkegaard, Husserl, and Heidegger. The three appendixes are particularly important for understanding the thinking now occurring in its first appearance, and above all the third appendix (*gamma*): "*Missa Jubilaea*: The Celebration of the Infinite Passover."

Foundation (1996) is Leahy's most difficult book. It is also the most polythematic, comprising a congeries of topics and tempos. As his readership grows, it will be established as Leahy's magnum opus in view of the fact that all the core arguments are here: those addressing the death of God, the new world order, the body as foundation, the trinary logic, the geometry, the gematria, and the absolute edge on which creation occurs. In addition to the major modern continental philosophers who reappear (with Derrida a new addition), a focused engagement with American thought, including pragmatism, is special to this work: Peirce, James, Dewey, Altizer, McDermott.

Faith and Philosophy (2003) is Leahy's most accessible book for those who are trained in Western philosophy. It traces out the advent of Incarnation in the history of Western philosophical thought from Aristotle through Descartes, Kant, Hegel, Kierkegaard, Jefferson, Emerson, Nietzsche, and Levinas to an arrival "beyond modernity." The appendix, "Thinking in the Third Millennium: Looking Without the Looking Glass," is especially important for grasping the thinking now occurring, and may prove a fairly accessible and helpful entryway for many readers.

Beyond Sovereignty (2010) offers an ethics of the thinking now occurring. Beyond modernity, a new ethics is needful that does not refer to self or have any qualifications related to the binaries and dualities that typify modern thought. Leahy specifies this as a *physical ethics* because it is an ethics of the existing body, not an ideality or projection of the mind. This is also the text in which he engages contemporary continental philosophers Alain Badiou and Giorgio Agamben.

A Heuristic Entryway

Leahy's work is exceptionally original and maximally coherent in laying out a philosophical and religious thinking that goes beyond the "radical" in a rather literal sense; that is, rather than looking for roots (from the Latin *radix*) to reclaim, retrieve, renew, this thinking conceives an absolutely new departure: an essentially new form of thinking. It is beyond radical, an apocalyptic thinking in which absolute beginning and absolute ending coincide in a current actuality that is absolutely new. Everywhere we turn we face the unprecedentedly new. Whither the new beginning for *thinking* that would be adequate to the emerging global reality on which we are already actually embarked and in which we are profoundly engaged? What thinking is equal to this new reality? How does thinking come to terms with this infinitely multiplicitous yet singular world in which thinking witnesses itself to be existing? Recognizing the new reality brought on by the full logical implications of the death of God in modernity, Leahy's epochal works call for a categorically or essentially new thinking that would be congruent with the "new world order" that is actually taking shape globally. Here it must be carefully understood that Leahy employs the term "new world order" in an entirely original sense, referring to a philosophical order enacted by a new consciousness of the present historical state of affairs. To quote Leahy:

> It is the writer's understanding that the new beginning [of the new world order, which is the end of modernity] is categorical, and that the categories and, indeed, the very structures of modern philosophical, theological, and scientific self-consciousness are essentially inadequate to the new beginning, and, further, that the most fundamental structure, the very notion of *self*—in any but a purely formal sense—is completely and essentially dysfunctional in the light of the beginning of this new world. . . . For the first time the new reality of the world—world unity—is not a mere ideal. . . . The consciousness adequate to the beginning of real world consciousness is a universally new consciousness, in fact, a perfect other-consciousness, a consciousness categorically and essentially beyond the other–self relation. . . . It is possible to understand the beginning of absolute other-consciousness now actually occurring as finally the Incarnation assaulting thinking. . . . The mind-assaulting novelty of existence is of the essence of the thinking. (F, ix, xiii)

As indicated here, a signature feature of this new departure is that thinking is weaned of all attachment to modern subjectivity—an attachment that begins decisively with Descartes, passes to Kant, Hegel, Kierkegaard, begins to perish with Nietzsche, and is brought to an apocalyptic end in Thomas J. J. Altizer. In the context of this trajectory, Leahy demonstrates not only what is ending (as Altizer does), but what is beginning (as Altizer does not). What is beginning for thought is an apocalyptic newness corresponding to that ending, an absolute novelty that is at once the newness of the world (*novitas mundi*) and the newness of mind (*novitas mentis*). Indeed, the full coincidence of these—new world, new mind—is imperative to be cognized. Leahy's work evinces a new thinking that embodies "absolute objectivity," categorically eliminating subjectivity and self along with all its derivatives (Descartes's ego sum, Hegel's self-consciousness,

Nietzsche's cosmic ego-body, Levinas's self in the accusative, Altizer's death of self-consciousness, and so on). The author's core claim concerns the "absolutely revelatory structure of existence itself" (BS, 49). Revelation occurs not in this or that selective event or moment; rather, the history of thinking reveals in due time that existence itself is universally and essentially revelatory. Matter, the Body itself—this absolutely particular, absolutely differentiated, infinitely finite polyontological existence—is holiness itself.

As this new thinking constitutes "a perfect other-consciousness," eliminating the very notion of self, it is indifferent to who begins thinking this way and where such thinking begins to occur. What matters is that this new thinking, adequate to the new world order, does indeed begin to occur as "the thinking now occurring." The thinking belongs to no one, yet it is the vocation of everyone. It is an objective thinking that occurs, but is not possessed. It thinks existence, an existence that is sheer gift, absolute gift. What gift wants to be possessed? Where it begins occurring, how and when it begins to occur more widely, are a matter of fortuitous circumstance; perhaps we might credit the cunning of the zeitgeist. But it is no accident that Leahy's books consistently speak of "the thinking now occurring," rather than "the thinker" or "the author" or "I." The sole term of self-reference occasionally employed is "the writer" (as exemplified in the quote above), as though the writer were a scribe for a thinking that is the true content, leaving the writer saturated with content yet perfectly empty of self-consciousness. Leahy's thinking is but one manifestation of the thinking now occurring; the thinking now occurring is not by any means limited to Leahy's thinking.

The core breakthrough of the thinking now occurring is that it grasps the essence of existence as transcendental, and existence itself (matter, the Body) as historically revealed fact. We face the enormous difficulty of trying to understand what this means, and in coming to understand this, we understand as well how this breakthrough transforms the task of thinking from the point of view of thinking itself. It means that all thinking is the beginning of essence, and essence begins in all thinking; hence all thinking is *essentially* creating the world, though *essential* creation does not imply material creation. Historically, thinking has discovered *matter* to be a matter of fact, whereas thinking has discovered *essence* to be a matter of continually new active creation. *Materially* there is one Body, infinitely polyontological, but *essentially* that Body is created ex nihilo, and we in our thinking are the creators. Because thinking is infinitely pluriform, the thinking now occurring inaugurates the "incipient existence of the absolute upbuilding of infinite totalities" (FP, 122). Where is God in this picture? God is the logical foundation of this essential imperative to create. God is dead, we are all co-creators now.

The Death of God: Segue to Absolute Newness

In Thomas J. J. Altizer's theology the divine self-sacrifice is the foundational primordial sacrifice that makes possible the actual enactment in time of the self-embodiment or incarnation of God. The Good Friday of kenotic dissolution of God at the end of modernity ushers in an apocalyptic midnight in which no daylight or "noon" of Zarathustra is envisionable: this absolute apocalypse is the final revelation of God in the form of our universal chaos or chaosmos. Altizer witnesses to the "dead Body of God" that remains with us as a consequence of the self-negation or self-annihilation of God, an event that has erupted in the universal apotheosis of Nothingness in our historical world. Being has progressively passed into Nothingness or absolute Abyss, its dialectical opposite.[2] While this passing is recognized by Altizer as the absolute passion or self-sacrifice of God, it entails as well the passing or passion of subjective consciousness, modern self-consciousness, the perspectival cogito of the successive Cartesian-Kantian-Hegelian-Nietzschean subject—which has progressively subsumed and deconstructed "God" as its object. Here "I" am, the voided shadow of my former cogitative self, pervaded by the Nothing, engulfed in the infinite abyss of ratio—to the glory of the self-emptying God. As Leahy characterizes this moment, "Life perishes in the contradiction of its own subjectivity. Indeed, absolutely so, in the event of the Nothing" (NM, 299).

Leahy's fundamental critique of Altizer is comprised within a much broader critique of what he calls the "dialectic of the exhausted self" in modernity; indeed, the thinking now occurring prosecutes "a radical critique of modern thought's essence" (NM, 1). Examining the trajectory of modern thinking from Descartes and Kant through Hegel and Kierkegaard, culminating in Levinas and Altizer, Leahy ventures that "in no event is consciousness anywhere in modernity near being beyond subjectivity and the nothing" (F, xi); rather, modern consciousness reconstitutes itself in endless variation, novel repetitions of the same old song, bound within the essentially uncreative binary oppositions of Being/Nothing, subject/object, transcendent/immanent, noumena/phenomena, sameness/difference.

Pressing for liberation from the entombing solipsism of modern subjectivity, Altizer extends subjectivity to an extreme limit in a quest for its reduction beyond zero, where subjectivity would finally burst out of subjective solipsism into otherness. While Altizer's thought celebrates the death of God as the absolute opportunity for redemptive freedom and grace to abound, per Leahy's analysis his witness remains engulfed in the abyssal solitude and darkness of absolute Nothingness, unrelievedly, even stubbornly, like the proverbial Jewish grandmother who prefers to sit in the dark.[3] Here, Leahy sees in Altizer a *"refusal* to put meaning into things . . . a final *refusal* to re-establish essence in the wake of the disappearance of the divine substantiality of the world" (FP, 120). The apotheosis of Nothing in Altizer "is the perfect barrier of absolute inaction, the perfect elimination of every obstacle to the creation of a new world without in fact creating that order" (F, 577). Altizer heralds the *possibility* of a new faith (F, 603), which, by persisting as unrealized possibility, staves off the actuality of a new faith. It is as though Altizer's obsessive focus on bringing Nietzsche's death-of-God annunciation home to roost with utter finality, and his pure and relentless witness to the apocalyptic *end* (of God, of subjectivity, of modernity, of an ordered cosmos), forestalls the actual enactment of apocalyptic *beginning*, or the undertaking of the present task of incarnation, which is the task of new creation, a refusal that Leahy considers contra-Nietzschean (FP, 120, 102).[4]

In Altizer's witness to "the solitude of the end" we observe the pure ipseity of the self-annihilating subject, persisting ironically as the spit and image of the self-annihilated God, now expanding to fill the infinite expanse of God's own godless universal chaosmos or dead Body. Thus Altizer articulates "the beginning of the loss of God's own subjectivity in the very form of the self-consciousness of the Godhead of God in man" (F, 603). The dark night of the death of God provides passage to a new beginning beyond modernity. As Altizer's thinking brings us to the extremity of that ending (death of God realized as final apocalypse), Leahy's thinking brings us to the ending of that ending in beginning, the beginning of a new world (*novitas mundi*) in and for a new consciousness (*novitas mentis*). The apocalyptic imperative issuing from the midnight madness of the death of God is the imperative to create, to articulate novel essence in freedom. The question, "How can I create the world?" becomes, rather, "How can I not create the world?" inasmuch as "I" am no subject but *in medias res* a world objectively and pragmatically creating itself. Not "I," then, but a particular world creating itself; the creating body, matter, forming itself specifically in thinking; body itself bodying itself, thinking itself essentially. By virtue of existing, we cannot *not* create the world, effectively, pragmatically, whether in a mentality of denial, disinclination, fear and trembling, or faith. The world is absolute objectivity, gift, matter itself existing, impeding on us as such, and all acts of consciousness (thinking) supply the formal logic of its creation.

Beyond Beyond Modernity

For decades, modes of thinking have been purveyed as "postmodern" that concur in their recognition that modern envisionments of God, self, humanity, and world have grown moribund and unproductive. The postmodern imperative has been to get beyond the limiting and inhibiting constrictions of modern categories and problems, their abiding thrall. But to strive to overcome is not to overcome. On the contrary, as long as one is striving to overcome, one has not overcome. There is need not merely to get beyond modernity but, as Leahy puts it in *Beyond Sovereignty*, to get *beyond* beyond modernity. But how does one actually get beyond without falling into the vicious circle of striving to get beyond? How would one recognize when the moribund limitations and constrictions of modern categories and modes of thought have in actuality been overcome? One would necessarily see the world changed by a logical *metanoia*, a new spirit of beginning, a launching of creative act rather than a remaining beleaguered, entrapped, exhausted. Yet this is what has largely evaded postmodern thinking—the ability to open up a categorically new world. Every residual hint of striving to "get beyond" is the rub of not getting beyond in which postmodern reflection languishes, therein demonstrating that it is a late-late modern thinking in inherent relationship with the modern rather than a genuinely *post*-modern thinking.

Late modern thinkers—including Levinas, Badiou, Altizer, Agamben—have recognized the perspectival trap of post-Cartesian subjectivity and have sought a thinking that is emancipated from its limits. The thinking proposed by Leahy makes a clean break with this "curse" of modernity and eliminates wholesale the constrictions of the

Cartesian legacy of the cogito. This thinking does so by grasping the modern legacy in its essential history and identifying its fatal error as viewed from a genuinely post-Cartesian, post-modern point of view. It does not just aspire to think otherwise than the modern, it actively commences to think otherwise than the modern, which makes this thinking difficult to come to terms with not only intellectually but morally and existentially. One must reorder one's mind, one's epochal habits of thinking, one's ethical orientation, and in effect become a visionary to understand it. Pervasive categories of mind and language are overthrown and a new (perception of) reality emerges. This thinking provides a new paradigmless paradigm (see the "non-paradigmatic," BS, 254) that eliminates paradigm-thinking in principle.

Thinking Is Creating: The Logic of Newness

In the new beginning, *newness* itself is a qualitative transformation in how consciousness understands what it is doing when it thinks, and the impact or import of doing it. This is clear in Leahy's answer to the question: What would be a categorically new logic? Hearing the question, we must understand that the term *categorically new* means *originating discretely novel and unique categories* in a way that eliminates paradigm-thinking in principle. "The category of a categorically new logic would be *being for the first time*. The logical category would be *being beginning*. Nothing other than being for the first time would be thought. Thought would be nothing other than being beginning. To think essentially would be to create" (F, 115).

How can we take stock of Leahy's claim that *to think essentially would be to create*? What does it mean to assert this? Heretofore, in pre-Enlightenment Western philosophical thinking—before the advent of Voltairean deism ceded to full-blown Nietzschean deicide—the world was created by God. If we now accept that "God is dead" and that traditional understandings of creation by God are defunct, who is creating the world? Or better expressed: How is *world-creating* happening? When God dies, essence evaporates. Is the world now uncreated? If so, is it now eternal à la Aristotle? Is it uncreated as one of the infinite aspects of God à la Spinoza? Is it essentially illusion à la Hindu cosmology? Or is it chaos? Is it created by the big bang? All these prima facie answers have in common that an existing other-consciousness, a phenomenological content, is actual even if qua illusion or chaos. Wherefrom does it exist in the form that it constitutes? Rather than asking who is creating the world, more neutrally we may ask by what power or agency is *world-creating* happening, that is, letting being or the appearance of being be? The answer is: thinking. In the phenomenological functioning of existing consciousness, things appear in this form and that. How? Wherefrom?

An approach may be made through the essential failure of phenomenology. Merleau-Ponty, in the wake of Husserl's heroic struggles, characterizes the aims of Husserlian phenomenology. He writes that "the real is to be described, and neither constructed nor constituted."[5] Twentieth-century phenomenological practice wants to abstain from abstraction, analysis, and interpretation to capture unmediated experience of lived environment, "the world as directly experienced," as the wellsprings of phenomenological analysis. What is not recognized here, what is glossed over without stringent examination, is the presupposition that to *describe* is not to construct or constitute. The thinking now occurring eliminates the distinction between conception and perception because it maintains that perception is, per se, patently a constructing and a forming; just as in geometry we "describe" a circle or a line, so thinking creates the world—not materially but formally, or rather *essentially*.

However deliberately or stubbornly phenomenological thinking may strive to pull back into a subtending experience that is "pure perception," prevenient to abstracting conception, that quixotic quest is no less a work of construction, or better, of constitution, of creation. Perception per se is a forming and a constituting. There is no possibility for thought to recuse itself to an experience of existing that is prelogical, if here logic is understood in its broadest sense as consciousness at work. It is just as valid to insist that thinking is perceiving and describing as it is to assert that perceiving and describing are thinking. Merleau-Ponty proceeds to write in the same passage: "The world is not an object whose law of constitution I have in my possession; it is the natural milieu and the field of all my thoughts and of all my explicit perceptions."[6] But why this distance, this untenable distinction between world-constitution and world-perception? This persistent problem of the thing-in-itself must be—fully and finally—thought through to arrive at the thinking now occurring.

Jean-Paul Sartre's thought offers a correlative segue: if after the death of God existence precedes essence, then the decisive gift of the death of God is the apostolic responsibility of all actual thinking to create the world. Although, to be more accurate than Sartre, it is not possible for existence to "precede" essence; existence is an absolute content *in medias res* of creating its essence. With respect to worlding, it's *logic* all the way down. The eclipse of God as creator entails the eclipse of all notions of precreated, intrinsic, or "canned" essence. These are eclipsed precisely by the infinite particularity of existence itself, what Leahy calls the Body itself, the thoroughgoing materiality of the world, a body unified by its absolute differentiation (down to its sub-nanoparticles), now *in essence* available for new creation. In this sense, the death of God confers an absolute freedom in which the world is *essentially* uncreated until it is actually created de novo by existence (matter) thinking. Thinking this implication of the death of God, *Novitas Mundi* reads: "Now God himself suffers change itself in essence . . . begins in essence to exist absolutely in the form of *exsistere ipsum*, the body itself" (NM, 383).

This new beginning can only be effected through a new logic, one that is essentially a *logic of newness*. The category of a categorically new logic would be *being for the first time*. But how are we to understand the category of *being for the first time*? A close parallel to this language is the ecstatic speech of Zarathustra's animals to the convalescent Zarathustra: "In every Now, being begins."[7] But to explicate this logic of beginning Leahy turns not to Nietzsche but to Kierkegaard, who articulated the essential notion of Christianity that the eternal has come into time. "For Kierkegaard the beginning of existence essentially excludes thought, excludes sense perception & immediate cognition. [Whereas] in the form of the thinking now occurring for the first time, this Kierkegaardian *beginning* is thought categorically. . . . Thought is now thinking the beginning of being otherwise than thinking the beginning of thought" (FP, 115–16). Thought is never empty when it thinks; it thinks matter, an infinitely particular and universal matter, the Body. Does matter matter? Yes, absolutely. But matter is real and consequential *as matter* for thinking, for logic. There is no prelogical matter. It is *for thinking* that matter matters—as it absolutely does. We can shorten this logical path and cross this divide by saying: matter (qua existing) thinks itself materially mattering.

A deeply synthetic-syncretic co-engagement of philosophy and theology declares itself in this thinking. Since Kant, most philosophical/ethical thinking is sundered into two basic methodological camps: on the one hand, the "secular" makes its claims on the basis of naturalistic and/or cultural grounds (in the image of natural science argumentation), appealing to rational, empirical, or cultural factors rather than to faith, sacred scripture, or supernatural revelation for validity; on the other hand, the "religious" makes claims on overtly religious, often sectarian grounds. An essential claim of Leahy's thinking is that the postcritical distinction between philosophy and faith is outmoded and no longer pertains. Readers will likely have qualms with this stance until or unless they commence this new thinking themselves, but it bears noting that in order to begin essentially anew, thinking has to break absolutely with the categorial logic of the modern and *begin* beyond it, and this includes the faith-versus-reason diremption of modern thought. Thinking from this new locus (which is not a place but a logic, a newness of mind), the past is rendered past. It abides and informs as past but it has no hold on the task of thinking *now*. The essentially new thinking that Leahy articulates is an authentically *post*-modern thinking in that it actually *ends modernity*, leaves it in the past, declaring a categorical RIP and opening a *novitas mentis* beyond the modern.

Leahy's Works Read as a Trajectory

The major works of Leahy trace out a progressively unfolding development of ideas, explicating a new synthesis after modernity, a modernity that in itself was created by the disintegration of the synthesis attempted by Thomas Aquinas between Aristotelian philosophy and *sacra doctrina* (revealed truth). *Novitas Mundi* (1980) traces the development of "the perception of the history of being" in the essential history of thought from Aristotle and Aquinas through Descartes, Kant, Hegel, Kierkegaard, Husserl, and Heidegger. It diagnoses the essential passivity of modern self-consciousness, which began with Descartes's mistake (NM, 188–98). Modern consciousness is a paranoia (= madness, to think amiss, to misconceive, to misunderstand): a progressive displacement of reality itself (noumena) by appearances (phenomena), so that reason perceives itself beside itself, perceives beside things intelligible in themselves of which it knows nothing (noumena) appearances (phenomena) of which alone it has (purely subjective) knowledge. Pure reason is beside itself in a structural schism by which it is objectively divided from itself by that infinite indifference to particularity, qua particularity, that constitutes its transcendental unity (for more, see "paranoia" in the glossary).

Pure reason's passive root is its inability to maintain itself face to face with its object's otherness, the mistake of madness being everywhere a substitution of appearance for reality. Modern science, accordingly, dissociates knowledge from reality itself. So then, within pure reason itself is reflected that external distinction between noumena and phenomena by which, through its particular "mistake," modern science dissociates knowledge from reality itself. *Novitas Mundi* recounts the story of what modern reason hath wrought, and where this history delivers us and our understanding of the task of reason now. The "backstage" but really "frontline" story is the Incarnation's historical occurrence having made its way *surreptitiously* into thought. The Incarnation's absolute objectivity ends the paranoia: "Absolutely nothing is thought except it be the existence of the absolute itself—the existence of existence" (F, 9).

Foundation: Matter the Body Itself (1996) is Leahy's magnum opus and also his most difficult book. It presents Leahy's most decisive expression of the thinking now occurring: the actuality of the Incarnation assaulting thinking (F, xiii). Making an important new innovation, it introduces the trinary logic that is the conceptual foundation of the thinking now occurring breaking absolutely with all modern dialectics, dualisms, and binaries. (See "trinary logic" in the glossary, and "The Law of Absolute Unity," F, 255–98.) *Foundation* celebrates matter, the Body itself, creating itself essentially in an absolutely free and objective thinking grounded in this trinary structure. This new consciousness embodies the pragmatic identity of conception and perception, of acting and thinking, of imagining and accomplishing (FP, 153). The advent of this absolutely objective consciousness obliterates the modern notion of subjectivity or self-consciousness, for "there is no subject–object distinction actually relevant to understanding the I now speaking and there is properly speaking no I now as subject" (FP, 144; see "apocalyptic I" in the glossary). Matter, qua absolute particularity, embodies an absolute pluralism of essence. Everything is body bodying itself at once materially, formally, and essentially, one absolutely complex-and-simple pluralistic body "existing" itself, articulating itself, specifying itself: "an absolute identification of the substance of thought and extension" (F, 521n94).

Faith and Philosophy (2003) provides a point of access to the more forbidding works of Leahy. Chapter 7 and the Appendix are the most original and constructive contributions. Leahy's own express agendum in this book is to examine, at the level of fundamental thinking, "the particular question as to just how Christian faith has impacted the notion of *nous* or divine mind in Western thought up to and including the present" (PF, ix) and this historical inquiry leads Leahy to undertake close textual analyses of the pertinent loci in Aristotle, Plotinus, Augustine, Descartes, Kant, Hegel, Kierkegaard, Jefferson, Emerson, Nietzsche, Peirce, Levinas, Altizer, and Leahy's own published work. These careful technical researches compose the bulk of the book (chapters 1–6), standing forth on their own critical-hermeneutical merit, quite independent of Leahy's constructive position. The essential clarifications wrought in these analyses alone make the book deeply valuable for anyone interested in fundamental philosophy in the West and its historical development.

Beyond Sovereignty (2010) might be compared with Spinoza's *Ethics* or Kant's *Groundwork for a Metaphysics of Morals*; it stands alone as they stand alone, not continuous with or depending on any ethical thinking that came before. The utter elimination of subjectivity in the thinking now occurring is an innovation of such immense consequence that an entirely new approach to ethics becomes imperative: there is need for an ethics absolutely without self, entirely beyond the notion of self-consciousness, entirely beyond the "logic of Same & Other" (BS, 76). Manifesting this ethic is the purpose of *Beyond Sovereignty*. The "sovereignty" to be transcended is the sovereignty of modern selfhood/self-identity, the realm of political/ethical autonomy presupposed by identity (Same/Other) politics, which has been formulated in the history of Western thought in the image of the sovereignty and autonomy of God, and justified thereby. All notions of this kind, grounded in the reign of a divine plan/natural law/autonomy theory, are ended in the new thinking proposed: "For the first time the 'natural law' is to create nature" (BS, 19); "beginning is the *absolute* undoing of the eternal support of the actual" (BS, 34); "the universe itself is essentially the beginning of the universe" (BS, 40). This means that every now of existence is a new creation ex nihilo, absolutely ungrounded in eternal Being, yet existing absolutely (imperishably) qua now beginning created omnipotence.

What the text does is articulate an absolutely new beginning for ethics, what might be characterized as a realized eschatology (see, for example, "the imperative to be in heaven," BS, 293). The ethical commission of this beginning is traced out in the "ethic of simplicity" (BS, 108ff.), which is detailed more specifically in the "morality of the new beginning" (BS, 279–99). The ethic of simplicity is formally parallel to Kierkegaard's idea that "purity of heart is to will one thing," but might be articulated essentially as "purity of mind is to create one (infinitely differentiated and absolutely particular) thing: the Body" (my paraphrase of Leahy). Now that existing is understood to be an essentially creative mode of being, creating indistinguishably in tandem a new world and newness of mind, ethics is now concerned with *love that actually creates the other*. This is perhaps not an entirely novel idea given that the French poet and essayist Paul Valéry wrote: "At its highest point, love is a determination to create the being which it has taken for its object"—but this deep intuition of Valéry is worked out seriously as a philosophical-ethical imperative in Leahy.[8] For this new mode of existing there is only "alio-affection," nothing but attention to the other that is per se productive of the other (BS, xxiv, xviii). That is to say, I exist you, you exist me. Beneficence (*doing* the good), not benevolence (willing the good), is what love is (see "Index of the Ethic of Simplicity," BS, 88).

While the first part draws forth the new ethical imperative in light of the newness of the world (*novitas mundi*), the second and third parts undertake critical engagement with other philosophical-ethical thinkers (most intensively Badiou and Agamben) as a way of elaborating the new ethics more specifically. The author demonstrates the new thinking (*novitas mentis*) by showing how it differs from recent philosophical positions that are its strongest contenders. This strategy proves an effective method for enacting what is here the principal challenge for thought: to break with existing thinking and commence a new mentality that *as such* is a creative ethical act.

Reading Strategies that Work

Because Leahy's foundational thinking remains for the time being relatively unknown and undiscovered, few complaints have arisen concerning the inherent difficulty of reading his writing. But as this new thinking becomes more widely known and studied, its difficulty will undoubtedly become as notorious as are the philosophical languages of Hegel and Heidegger—inviting satire from the good-humored and provoking offense among those of Cartesian taste, who prefer a language that is analytically plain, with sentences setting out clear and distinct bits of sense. To be sure, difficult language should not be put up with for its own sake; the effort has to prove worthwhile. But we do persist in reading Hegel and Heidegger because of the new modes of experiencing they induce us to discover. Leahy himself was well aware of this language problem, calling this categorically new manner of writing a "radical inconvenience" as a consequence of thinking categorically differently, essentially differently, beginning a *new way of thinking* for the first time: "the discomfiture is foundational" (F, xii). "The reader who will enter into this work will discover not only the discomfiture of beginning a new *way* of thinking, but that this initial discomfiture of thought never completely abates, since the mind-assaulting novelty of existence is of the essence of the thinking" (F, xiii).

How to read these writings, in terms of reading strategies? Think of it as a process that will progress with patient trust in the powers of mind. To begin the process, enter in and focus on achieving acclimation at first. It is the case that gradual acclimation to Leahy's language and reiterated themes is an essential avenue to gaining footholds and building up understanding. In this case—to ply an immersion metaphor—not being able to swim won't kill you, so just fearlessly bob around, feel the waters, tread a little, doggy paddle. The creative-synthetic powers of mind effect progress in mysterious ways. Trying and trying again eventually pays off, as does patiently cultivating one's ability to parse unwieldy and complex sentences. Although Leahy's expositions can seem prima facie impenetrable, the language is unfailingly attentive and considered, grammatically parseable, worked through with utmost exactitude to be semantically careful and technically precise. While the writing is highly demanding in its difficulty, any effort on the reader's part to understand is richly rewarded with intelligent, brilliant, mature, lucid thinking. Leahy offers the reader an apologia as follows:

> The language of the new thinking possesses in its sparseness and precision a likeness to complex mathematical formulation. No doubt already the reader has encountered some difficulty. Perhaps one or more of the above sentences was not immediately understood. It has perhaps been necessary to reread a sentence several times to get the exact sense of the relationships described. This style-less style of language is wholly necessary in the attempt to precisely formulate in a rigorously consistent manner certain most fundamental ontological-historical relations. The writer therefore offers his apology to the reader for the inevitable inconvenience of having to read again in order to read. He apologizes

to the reader for the inevitable embarrassment which the reader will feel in having to read slowly, and only wishes to add that he himself shares in this very embarrassment both as writer and reader. (F, xiii–xiv)

In my own experience as a Leahy reader, rereading—coming back to read again another day—repays far more than beating one's head against what seems (for the nonce) a semantic wall. It is productive to listen attentively, absorb all implications as fully as possible, get familiarized with what one is encountering—and yet *keep moving and don't get bogged down*. Push forward patiently, resolving to understand more fully the next reading.

Specificity and concreteness are of the essence in a thinking of absolute particularity. Abstractions and generalizations disregard this to their own peril. Engage specific issues with technical care. Build carefully, step by step. When you reflect on the thinking, in solitude or in conversation with another, be on the alert for red-flag words or intuitions that inadvertently reintroduce modern categories: subjectivity, meaning or meaningfulness, perspectivalism and interpretation, the notion of necessitation or "must." This thinking is not concerned with what is "meaningful"—as though some things have "meaning" and other things don't. It is occupied with bona fide "live" creation of essence, not with meaning—a recursive and derivative bystander-notion—set apart from the primacy of existence. As *light* is the new black, *essence* is the new meaning. The thinking now occurring doesn't "struggle against" anything or take any stances "con" or "anti." Such opposition has no place in a polyontological creative pleroma. On the contrary, there is a logical-ethical imperative to recognize how this thinking in principle eliminates oppositionality. Every thinking is a (re)source, no thinking is "the enemy." To cite but one example of this, the thinking now occurring is not anti-technology but pro-technology. It claims, in fact, to be "absolute technology" (F, 461–62). The limitation it perceives with Heidegger, then, is that he has not arrived at an adequately free technological thinking; it is a deficit of freedom in the *how*, not the *what* of technologies per se, that calls for fundamentally new thinking.

Where to Begin?

Begin at the beginning. The beginning is now, and there is no possibility to defer or deter it: there is no putting it off. How to begin? By beginning now, for the show (the showing of Being, the Phenomenon) now begins absolutely. To understand this, or even try to understand this, is to begin.

Notes

1. My gratitude goes to Michael James Dise for helping to formulate the answer to Question 9, a vast improvement on my first draft; the outlines of Question 10 and its answer were also his suggestion, and his critical review of this introduction was indispensable to me, though I take sole responsibility for any flaws that remain.

2. Thomas J. J. Altizer, *Godhead and the Nothing* (Albany: State University of New York Press, 2003).

3. The lightbulb joke goes: How many Jewish grandmothers does it take to screw in a lightbulb? The answer: "Never mind, don't bother about me, I'll just sit in the dark."

4. The critique of the "dialectic of the exhausted self" in Altizer and Emmanuel Levinas is developed in D. G. Leahy, "The Diachrony of the Infinite in Altizer and Levinas: Vanishing Without a Trace and the Trace Without Vanishing," in *Thinking Through the Death of God: A Critical Companion to Thomas J. J. Altizer*, ed. Lissa McCullough and Brian Schroeder (Albany: State University of New York Press, 2004), 105–24.

5. Maurice Merleau-Ponty, *Phenomenology of Perception*, trans. Donald A. Landes (New York: Routledge, 2012), lxxiv.

6. Ibid., lxxiii.

7. Friedrich Nietzsche, *Thus Spoke Zarathustra*, trans. and with a preface by Walter Kaufmann (New York: Penguin, 1954), 217–18.

8. Paul Valéry is quoted by Simone Weil in *The Notebooks of Simone Weil*, 2 vols., trans. Arthur Wills (New York: Routledge, 1956), 1:85. To date I have not been able to trace the original quotation in Valéry's work.

PART I
HISTORY AND TIME

1

History and the Thinking Now Occurring

CHARLES STEIN

D. G. Leahy referred to his work as "the thinking now occurring," which his students came to refer to as the TNO. This appellation is perhaps as provocative as the work itself. The first time I met the author in person in 1996, he disarmed his interlocutors by never using the locution "I think" to introduce his spontaneous discourse. "In the thinking now occurring . . . ," he would utter, then deliver himself of what he had to say. In his writings, the phrase functions as a complex name for thinking that is no longer quite denominable as theology or philosophy, that occupies the considerable change in the very being of intellectual activity—not to say the transformation of Being itself—that the work proclaims to be occurring in the present epoch "for the first time in history," and which the texts from Leahy's pen and the words from his mouth declaim. The phrase expresses the essentially historical nature of Leahy's thought and the radically particular accent of its articulation of history. The present chapter attempts to work through some aspects of thinking now occurring's historical thinking, but this requires an exposition of the major doctrines of the thinking now occurring more broadly. I present this in two parts: "Faith and Philosophy—The Promise Fulfilled," which contains this exposition, and "Demurrers, Animadversions, Caveats,

Cavils," which expounds difficulties that I have experienced with the work as an all-encompassing historical vision.

Faith and Philosophy—The Promise Fulfilled

There have been many attempts to reconcile religion with modern philosophy and contemporary science. These attempts often seek surreptitiously to court the approval of thought and/or science by proffering more or less arbitrary analogies between present-day scientific results and religious tenets; or else they attempt to dictate to science the grounds for its own research. Leahy's thought, rather, takes the world that science finds as it is and discovers in the history of thought itself a course of development whose outcome is the fulfillment of an ancient spiritual promise: that faith shall find its own legs, as it were, and be reconciled with an exalted form of intelligence that faith itself had fostered; that intelligence—that is to say philosophy and its product, natural science—will open to the faith that in fact had brought it into being.

If Christian revelation included the teaching that in Christ is to be found not only the *Way* but the *Truth,* it is clear that for several centuries now this spiritual Truth has been diverse with respect to the kind of truth with which the modern scientific enterprise has concerned itself. If both forms of truth can be said to be rooted in the matter of the essence of existence, there would seem to be the possibility, the hope, and on the part of revelation, the promise, that in the end the two truths will be seen as one. Leahy's *Novitas Mundi* traces the history from the time of Thomas Aquinas to the recent past of a progressive occluding of the "transcendental essence of existence"—the essence of existence as proclaimed in what Aquinas calls sacred doctrine (*sacra doctrina*)—but it also announces and celebrates the occurrence of a change in the very substance of that history, through which this occlusion clears and the promise is fulfilled.

Novitas Mundi commences with an account of the absence of the notion of *existence* in the ancient world. The ancients—including as an essential example Aristotle—had no explicit knowledge of existence as a completed totality. Aristotle's highest deity, the unmoved mover, keeps the universe revolving but does not bring it into being for the first time. With Christianity, the principle of *creatio ex nihilo* situates the idea of existence itself within a transcendental horizon and equips it with a transcendental essence. Existence as a whole is comprehended as God's Creation. Existence itself is now prepared to become an object of study, and human intelligence can now understand itself as being capable of studying it.

Thomas Aquinas, in the high Middle Ages, through his formulation of the Christian faith as sacred doctrine finds in *natural reason* an adequate instrument for pursuing such investigations, and at the same time gives to it a place within Creation. Natural reason possesses the dignity of being the finite analog of an infinite divine intelligence. There is a limit to human capacity, and where that limit is reached sacred doctrine itself rounds out the picture of the totality of Being. Science is established as pertaining to nature—that is, to Creation—and the instrument for carrying it out, natural reason, is provided to man. But with the clarification of existence and human reason as such, possibilities appear that were not available to thinking prior to the Christian revelation and its establishment of the "transcendental essence of existence." With the *certainty* of sacred doctrine, the *possibility* of doubt emerges. With the appearance of existence itself, the possibility that it might lack its transcendental essence becomes capable of articulation. Thus, beginning with Descartes, a twofold transformation takes place that, while blocking off sacred doctrine from science and reason, removes the limits placed upon them. Provided that thinking not consider existence as Creation, and provided that thinking find some other analysis of its own activity than that afforded to it in sacred doctrine, thinking can and must now expand its researches to include fundamental questions that had belonged exclusively to sacred doctrine previously. Sacred doctrine now falls under a kind of interdict, and serious thought from Descartes through Heidegger and beyond must situate both human reason and existence without recourse to it. For modern thinking, faith is perhaps allowed, but not allowed to penetrate its scientific preoccupations; or, if so allowed, it must secure a grounding in the authority of reason alone.

Leahy's task in the main chapters of *Novitas Mundi* is to trace the history of the interdiction of sacred doctrine and to show how, for each of the thinkers to which the work attends, while the very possibility of the thinking in each case is ultimately provided by articulations first made available by sacred doctrine, still, faith and deity are held under the interdict. A place for faith and deity is put back in, as it were, by hand and for purposes specified by the requirements of thinking in each case (by Descartes, Leibniz, Kant, Hegel, and so on); but any intellectual transparency of Being to God is completely obscured. At the end of modernity, however, during the course of the twentieth century, a series of inversions and reversals in thinking occurs such that the very rationale for the interdiction of faith unravels. Today, and for some time now, owing to developments within philosophic thinking and advances within the natural sciences, the question of the *essence of existence* has become an inescapable *preoccupation* for serious thought. This preoccupation does not command a return to any previous way of thinking or an acceptance of sacred doctrine in any of its prior forms.

The thinking now occurring accepts, rather, the extreme objectification of existence that is science's preoccupation. It embraces the enormous wealth of detail, for instance, with which science has been able to specify the nature of material reality; it finds no difficulty in situating human sentience within the provenance of the material world; it allows experience, perception, conceptual activity, logic, mathematics, language, all to appear on the same footing as matter, and it allows all to appear within the unfolding of a completely external historicity. But in the midst of all this, faith finds itself no longer on the other side of a barrier, excluded from serious participation in the preoccupations of thinking. The very inclusive character of existence itself forces the questioning of the essence of existence, and in this questioning, the matter of faith can no longer be seriously left aside. Suddenly it appears that the very direction of thinking that led to this inclusive character of existence was there, not "all along," but precisely since the advent of the doctrine of *creatio ex nihilo* and the appearance of the transcendental essence of existence in revelation and sacred doctrine. Now, "for the first time in history," the sense of that revelation can be truly seen by the eyes of faith and, at the same time, the pertinence of faith as providing the missing element for the comprehension of existence as a whole comes to appearance. The two truths of faith and reason are no longer held apart from one another, and the ancient promise is fulfilled.

Existence Itself

It is a commonplace of the cultural historiography of the West to see a massive reorientation of spiritual attention occurring at about the time of the European Renaissance of the fifteenth and sixteenth centuries. Whereas the Middle Ages valorized the eternal, the otherworldly, the incorporeal, with the Renaissance conscientious thought and cultural production begins increasingly to lavish attention on the this-worldly, the historical, the radically particular and concrete character of experience, objects, and events. Leahy's incarnationist ontology attributes the very possibility of an orientation toward the historical, the material, the radically particular to a transformation of and within Being that is the extension, elongation, and progressive fulfillment of the Incarnation event. The work of the Incarnation does not occur all at once. It develops historically through a series of phases that can be traced in the thinking of major Western figures—in particular Aristotle, Plotinus, Augustine, Aquinas, Descartes, Leibnitz, Kant, Hegel, Kierkegaard, Marx, Nietzsche, Peirce, James, Dewey, Husserl, Heidegger, Sartre, Derrida, McDermott, Altizer, and finally Leahy. The thinking now occurring is the current installment in this series. Its content involves an assertion that the resistance to sacred doctrine that seems to infect the substance of philosophy since Descartes has been once and for all overcome by the Christ's so fully entering into existence that whatever in fact exists is now his Body, and that this is so with such thoroughness that the oppositions that animate all previous thinking—matter/spirit, thought/reality, mathematics/physics, perception/thought, imagination/matter, and so forth—are one and all dissolved into the single overwhelming fact of the Incarnation qua existence.

Again, so thorough is this leveling of all categorical distinctions that faith need no longer concern itself with the particular form of the Christian narrative that has been handed down in the tradition. Faith is constituted by the single recognition of the overwhelmingly sacred character of existence itself without reference to that which transcends or stands outside it. Each individual person becomes the Creator of existence itself, while existence is sustained in and by our experience. The Creator has transferred his own creative capacity to each of us, and we ourselves wield this power in every moment, and this is so willy-nilly—whether or not we are cognizant of it. It is asserted that this power has been transferred to us on the level of fact in such a manner that it is not particularly relevant whether we *believe* this has occurred or not: faith is utterly distinct from what in the old dispensation would be understood as belief. We are not asked to assent to a set of propositions that are claimed to be adequate to a reality exterior to our thinking them, since reality itself has become intrinsic to our own act of taking thought, our own perception, our own imagination. Rather, we are asked to respond to the power that has been transferred to us—by wielding it! Further, since there is no separate reality to which our cognitions might be adequate, no set of beliefs any longer qualify as acts of faith, but each of us is the initiator of whatever ontology we might have, in an earlier view, professed, and our thinking and our acting (each understood as aspects of the other) are thoroughly responsible to and for the world that we severally and in the aggregate create.

This constitutes not merely a new ontology—a new view of how things are—but a *poly*ontology: there are as many ontologies as there are not only individuals, but as there are acts of thought and even of acts in general.[1] The entirety of existence is constituted anew in every moment through, by, and as each of us. This creation of existence is not an internal affair of private souls, isolated by an interior depth from each other and from the world that they create: creation is, rather, utterly external, and the old interiority is understood in retrospect as the habitat of a self that is the correlate of a self-consciousness that has now been entirely released, overcome, abandoned. There is no longer a self to be conscious of itself, though there is indeed awareness, which, even when it attends to its own somatic condition does so in a manner of attention not different from that paid to the external world.

The Thinking Now Occurring and Its Enemies

The Incarnation announces the radical particularity of each individual and the radical particularity of the things in the world, and that the metaphysical cause of that condition of things is the birth, death, and resurrection of Christ who, while being the universal God, took it upon himself to become a radical particular. This fact instigates progressively our transformation from being mere copies of eternal paradigms to being fully existent identities. Absolute particularity applies universally: it delivers to *all* particulars their status as particulars; it imparts to each thing the condition of its identity, granting to it what in the past it only had as it were on loan from its eternal original. And yet the Incarnation is able to become a universal cause by becoming a particular fact. What for Platonic thought, for instance, belonged to a realm of atemporal forms or ideas has entered history. The forms are in the world as the schemata for the things of the world, fully existing only *as* those things.

As existence itself is sustained in each moment by the creative act of each individual, individual existence is radically transitory. It is not simply that each objectively present moment and its contents vanish as they arise (as in traditional occasionalist thought), but that the acts of thought that create the vanishing moments are themselves vanishing. And yet the course of this evanescence is not reduced to a featureless flux: the identity of the individual "Creator" is sustained, but only through the changing events of her creation. Identity exists, but identity is change itself—the changing character of existence that includes both Creation and Creator.

The thinking now occurring thus finds itself vigilant to denounce any appeal to Platonic forms or atemporal archetypes as sustaining the identity of persons or things in existence. It views the influence of Platonism on early Christian thought through Plotinus and other Neoplatonic thinkers (particularly upon Augustine) with some aggression as impenitent resistance to the Incarnation event. Insofar as this influence persists through the Middle Ages and into modernity (insofar, that is, as all philosophy seems to be but a "footnote to Plato," as Alfred North Whitehead once quipped), that persistence too is viewed as resistance and as entirely deleterious. The thinking now occurring is resolutely in opposition to any contemplative reference to an inner world of eternal forms, or any access to timeless intuition, or any sense of interior depth that seeks to find the historical world resonant with crepuscular, enigmatic, intriguing structures or entities. The thinking now occurring expounds and celebrates the richness and brilliance of a complex surface, where the utterly transitory shimmers with an utterly present creative power.

Similarly, the thinking now occurring finds itself distant from, if not utterly inimical to, any form of contemplative practice that aims to merge the individual with, dissolve her into, or subsume her by a supervenient or subliminal spiritual continuum. It would in this manner distinguish itself from various moments of both Christian mysticism and the enlightenment traditions of the East, at least insofar as these traditions proffer such an image of the individual's merger with a godhead or some other transcendent substance. But how then can a multiplicity of ontological centers combine to create anything like a world we hold in common? Existence in the thinking now occurring is neither a multiplicity of internally separate, privately held universes, nor a merged totality to which each unit simply contributes a separate part, but rather a hyperdimensional multiplicity whose nature is a "discontinuous continuum," each point of which—each individual—is distinct from each other, each one creating a particular version of the whole. But the whole does not exist in isolation somehow from the multiple acts of its creation. Leahy's image for this is a circle formed by distinct, separated points.

The thinking now occurring also experiences the subtle recuperation of Platonic thought in Derrida and the poststructuralists as unacceptable as Platonism proper. The former is neither to be valorized in its inscrutability nor decoded by the application of semiotic analyses. The rational promises that the poststructuralists find shot through with unconscious obscurities are abrogated at the root: no such promises are any longer in effect. The rationality that now pervades existence is utterly transparent and unexceptionable. The entire congeries of quasi-metaphysical entities called into appearance by the self-referential structures in previous representational and finally self-representational discourse are, to borrow a phrase from Zen, abolished with a single blow. There is no re-presentation anywhere, no gap between thought and its object, no ontological difference between signifier and signified, between code and codified. The last barrier between the phenomenology of existence and existence itself, the last impediments to sacred doctrine, have fallen away; and with the unexceptionable nature of the sacred reappearing as a new possibility for thought, the sacred character of immediate existence and our own act as the production of it are given with the self-evidence that a Descartes once required of sense and thought to render the world and thought perspicuous. Again, the Promise fulfilled.

Demurrers, Animadversions, Caveats, Cavils

Leahy presents the edifice of the thinking now occurring in several texts that constitute a formidable and intricately worked out ongoing project. It is, I would imagine, quite impossible to study this work in a thoroughly detached and academic matter. These texts do not readily yield their contents without a certain participation on the part of the very being of the reader. Their discourse is as dense and both as welcoming and as forbidding as any in the history of Western thought, Hegel or the most difficult texts of Heidegger not excepted. One must give oneself to the text in order to pass materially through its page-long sentences, its complex recapitulations, its reworking of its own developing idiolect and its elaborately wrought formulations. Faith, in accordance with a text from Augustine that Leahy comments on in *Faith and Philosophy*, can be understood as a positive response to the Word; faith, in this sense, animates the reading of any text whatsoever in that one must trust the concourse of an utterance to follow it to its end. Faith would thus seem to be more a category of momentary understanding than settled belief, for whether or not each of us creates the entire of existence in every moment, as we do according to thinking now occurring, it is undeniable that we create our understanding of the text we read moment by moment as we read it. But as one's understanding accumulates, difficult texts and their tortuous readings will yield, parallel to one's assent to them and understanding of them, demurrers, animadversions, caveats, and cavils.

The exposition of thinking now occurring in the previous sections of this essay does, in one sense, little justice to Leahy's thought, attempting to render it perspicuous without requiring that the reader undergo it. Still, my own engagement with these texts, on and off for more than ten years now, has excited and tested my own faith in the above sense continuously, and I would be doing an injustice to my experience of them, and in a sense to the work of the thinking now occurring itself, if I withheld a report on the philosophical and spiritual difficulties I have encountered in this process. The rest of this essay spells out some of those difficulties.

Heidegger, Ontology, Historicity

Leahy's tour through the history of Western thought taken as a history of Being itself has its precedents in Hegel and Heidegger, and Leahy is careful to separate his own procedure from his two predecessors. His readings in *Novitas Mundi* of Kierkegaard, Husserl, and Heidegger, and in *Foundation* of Marx and Peirce, focus on their being only partly successful antithetical responses to Hegel; and Leahy himself devoted a course under the auspices of his New York Philosophy Corporation to Heidegger. Since I take it that it is Heidegger who opens and attempts to keep open the question of Being and Being qua existence for thinking in our time, and Heidegger who also sees the history of ontology as tracing the history of Being itself, I wish to make certain remarks regarding Leahy's reading of Heidegger and its pertinence to the matter of polyontology.[2]

The turn toward the radically particular that is supposed to achieve a certain denouement in the thinking now occurring is also a determination of the nature of history. In fact "history" functions in the thinking now occurring as a general term for the turn to the radically particular, and the possibility of history in precisely this sense is the event of the Incarnation. But the commitment to the Incarnation amounts to an ontological decision at a particular level of the inquiry into the nature of Being that Heidegger opened, and therefore, there is an inevitable tussle between Leahy and Heidegger: Does History, fixed ontologically as Incarnation, determine the history of Being—a history that in turn allows Heidegger's questioning to emerge? Or is Incarnationism to be understood within a more general history of Being, itself but one of the ways Being is given a specific form and content? Heidegger views Christian revelation as a fully determined ontology that closes out the kind of inquiry into the nature of Being that his work's own form of piety professes.[3] Leahy in turn views Heidegger's philosophy of Being, though a step on the path to the thinking now occurring, finally as the pretense of "Being for its own purposes" and as the work of "the last impenitent."

Leahy in fact is somewhat careless with Heideggerian terminology in a way that he would not tolerate in regard to his own. He renders, for instance, *Sein und Seiendes* as *Being and Existence* rather than "Being and beings"; and he collapses, for his own purposes, the notions of existence, the universe, and the world. But Heidegger's "existence" (his *Existenz*) is that to which Dasein relates "in one way or another" and is specifically not to be conceived as "the universe." Again, the "world"—in Heidegger a highly specific term developed in *Being and Time*—does not render any sense of "the universe" that today would be legible. Also, Heidegger means by "the oblivion of Being" the oblivion into which the question of the meaning of Being is cast by its various determinations in the philosophic tradition. Though *What Is Metaphysics?* does power up around a reflection on "Nothing," *Being and Time*, the earlier and certainly more fundamental work, begins with a conceptual circle in which the question of the meaning of Being emerges from a going back and forth between an understanding of Dasein as that being for whom Being is of concern in his Being, and the question of Being itself. "Nothing" is not the absence of beings but the ontological morass into which we are thrown when our "world" disintegrates.

The Heideggerian enterprise, as I see it, is a performative action undertaken to hold open a space of ontological inquiry, not the determination of one last ontology. This performativity remains effective even where Heidegger himself stalls or closes out or closes down. If it appears, as it occasionally does, that Heidegger is declaring, indeed, a final ontology, the possibility of holding the question of Being open in spite of Heidegger's own views remains an important concern. To me anyway. That is to say, the historical effect of Heidegger, or one of these effects, has been to open the question of Being—and incidentally to open it in such a way that thinkers outside the Western tradition have been able to join in the questioning. So the question for me is this: Does the thinking now occurring, in its characterization of Heidegger as "the last impenitent," intend to hold open the question of Being against even Heidegger's occasional lapses and apparent tendency to close it down, or does the thinking now occurring itself claim to register the closing down of that question once and for all? I think that Leahy's answer would be that the kind of ontological questioning with which Heidegger was concerned *has* indeed been closed down by the advance that is the thinking now occurring. According to the thinking now occurring we are no longer at a time in history at which such questioning is any longer pertinent. Heidegger's opening of the ontological path was one of the final steps toward the thinking now occurring, but it has been overtaken by a decision that makes each individual the agent of an ontological originarity. This might include Heideggerian openness but without the dark and uncanny quality that Heidegger's engagement with *the Nothing* tinctures such inquiry. In any case, "inquiry" would no longer seem to be the appropriate mode for engagement with Being. One must, to use a favorite image of Leahy's, "step through the door" and Create! But this means—I must observe—that a particular form of history, a particular ontological determination of the Being of history, is being asserted. At the same time, the possibility of an inquiring openness as to whether such a determination of the Being of history is possible at all is completely foreclosed—precisely by faith in "the thinking now occurring." For me, a thinking that forecloses questioning is hardly recognizable as a "thinking" at all.

Some detail regarding what I mean by levels of ontological inquiry:

The question of Being in Heidegger's later formulations is articulated on three levels: questions about *beings*, questions about the *Being of beings*, and the question of the *Being of Being*. At the first level, we would have lists of beings and being types; analytical philosophy calls such lists "ontologies." No covering concept establishes their nature in general, and the question of the nature of Being itself is not on the horizon. At the second level, the Being of beings, tells us not so much *what* entities there are but *how* they are. It gives a covering notion that determines their range and character. Traditional Christianity determines Being as Creation. Each thing that exists is given its positive determination by the prior fact that all of existence is created by God. In the early years of Christianity, the determination of Being as Creation invited the interpolation of Platonic ontology, where the Being of beings is given by the forms, and the forms themselves could be assimilated to a region outside of the material world, but a region also understood by Christian theology as God's Creation. Each early Greek thinker, by contrast, determined the Being of beings metonymically: each thinker, respectively, thought everything as water, or fire, or earth, or flux, or numerical ratio, or the unbounded, and so on until Parmenides arrived at the non-metonymical vision of Being itself. With Parmenides, ontological inquiry potentially shifts to a level where one is no longer asking about the general character of the things that are but rather entering into an inquiring relation to Being itself; though, as has rarely been observed, subsequent metaphysics rarely sustains Parmenides's level of inquiry. Heidegger repeatedly attempts to orient us to the unthought matter in Parmenidean thinking.

The Being of Being is the subtlest and most recondite level, most worthy of continuing inquiry; it concerns the nature (*sic*) of Being itself, and it would be at this level that the possibility of polyontology might open, because surely the possibility of a multiplicity of ontologies would derive from Being's Being being such that the Being of beings would not be unique. There could be a multiplicity of ways that beings as a totality might be disclosed. How each of these ontologies proceeds to dispose of the question of the Being of beings would have to be open.

Now I ask, at what level are ontological issues in general disposed by the thinking now occurring? At what level are the ontologies opened by Leahy's polyontology? Does each individual in each moment create a fresh sense of the Being of beings, or rather does each produce the existent entities materially, and can these be distinguished in the thinking now occurring? Finally, does the very nature of Being itself depend on moment-to-moment determinations by humans? But if each of us were free to enter into the disposition of the question of the Being of Being, that would mean that certainly the question of the Being of History would remain suspended and would have to be determined by each of us as an aspect of our own ontological orginarity. So we would be involved in a logical conundrum, a kind of truth-teller's paradox! For the very term under which our ontological freedom were given to us would be in fact open to the exercise of that freedom! I am not sure if that is quite what Leahy envisions. For the various positions mentioned above which are anathema to the thinking now occurring, including not-yet-imagined uses for Platonic thought, for contemplation, for depth, for enigmas and inscrutabilities—would surely remain within the horizon of inquiry requisite for determining the Being of History, let alone the Being of Being.

But in the thinking now occurring there is no distinction between the act of thought and the fact of existence, so the distinction between these levels collapses. If there is no difference between the thought of the Being of beings and the beings themselves, there certainly can be no inquiry into the Being of Being. *That* question does seem utterly closed off by the historical character of the "thinking now occurring for the first time in history." Being itself is collapsed into existence, and its nature—quite as it is in traditional Christianity—is disposed utterly by the master narrative of Incarnation. Any vital inquiry into the ultimate nature of Being is not part of the thinking now occurring. But then either the thinking now occurring is itself only one possible reading of the history of Being, in which case it is not uniquely "the thinking now occurring," or it really does claim to express the closing down of ontological inquiry and its polyontology is greatly circumscribed.

Mircea Eliade

A view of human experience as it is supposed to have been prior to the Incarnation of Christ as Jesus of Nazareth and as it exists in non-Incarnationist thinking in general is articulated by an aspect of Leahy's thought that is essentially derived, it would appear, through Thomas J. J. Altizer, from the historian of religion Mircea Eliade as expressed most thoroughly in the latter's *The Myth of the Eternal Return*.[4] Leaning on anthropological erudition, Eliade views what he calls archaic humanity as dwelling in the shadow of eternal forms—not articulated conceptually, as in Plato, but expressed in myth and ritual process. The origins of the great patterns of nature and the determinants of human action lie in an ontological yonder that provides the very terms by which archaic humanity understands existence. The realm of myth occurs *in illo tempore*—"in that time"—a time discontinuous with the time of actual existence. The mythical narratives enacted "there" constitute a superior and more fully actual reality, providing the paradigms for quotidian occurrences. What happens *here* is rendered intelligible by having its exemplar *there*. Nothing new can happen in what for us is the real world. Concrete, particular, unmediated existence is barely existence at all. Only when matched with its archetype *in illo tempore* is reality bestowed upon it.

Through the new sense of history that the Old Testament brings to bear and which the Incarnation brings to fruition (this is Altizer now, reading Eliade into his death-of-God theology), humanity experiences an enormous ontological transition in the direction of concrete, actual, empirical, material reality: what is real is now the particular, the directly experienced, the situationally laden process of history, and not the paradigms that render them intelligible. Whereas archaic or contemporary tribal man sees daily events as instantiations of archetypes whose being holds sway in another ontic zone, modern post-incarnationally-motivated Western humanity experiences history as the site of the real. What actually occurs is reality, not the types and archetypes of myth or intellect which they exemplify.

Leahy in effect extends this picture. He reads the history of philosophy as a progressive transformation of archaic habits of thought into a thoroughly modern historicism. Even where concept replaces myth in philosophy proper, concepts themselves repeat the structure of archetypal myth: concepts *represent* events and objects in accordance with categories and types, eventually applying representational consciousness to the individual person himself in the form of self-consciousness. Thus, the philosophical tradition retains a sense of reality that it inherits from myth, for in conceptual thinking too the individual thing and particular event are subsumed under the greater reality of the general idea or the universal notion—until thinkers such as Marx, Peirce, Dewey, and others reinstate the primacy of the concrete against the concept. In all this Leahy sees the further work of the Incarnation, culminating in a radical break with the "elsewhere" of myth, representational thought, and self-consciousness. Thought itself now occurs as concrete event, and concrete event is replete with its own conceptual identity, its essence.

I do not quarrel with the desirability of this concretism, but with the Eliade–Altizer–Leahy account of the history that determines it. A critique, or at least a thoroughgoing questioning of Eliade's dichotomy between archaic and modern humanity and the generalizations pertaining to them are in order. I only suggest here the directions such a critique might take. Any reader familiar with Claude

Lévi-Strauss's structural anthropology (and the poststructuralist critique of Lévi-Strauss does not change this) will not recognize the "savage mind" in Eliade's forlorn, archaic victim of William Blake's "same dull round."[5] Lévi-Strauss understands the application of structural constants as something quite distinct from this inevitable repetitiveness. Tribal humanity's "bricoleur" is ever-responsive to the incursion of contingencies with a spirit of improvisation and delight that is rarely encountered among the highly civilized. His mythic categories, far from determining a limiting ontology, or sacrificing the immediate to a more potent reality off somewhere, render vital and available the present moment in all its richness and spontaneous variety. The "savage mind" has recourse, in fact, to what Lévi-Strauss refers to as a "science of the concrete."[6]

Marshall Sahlins, in another vein, challenges the myth that preagricultural humanity (which constitutes ninety-nine percent of human history, if we abandon the convenient fiction that "history" began with literacy) lived lives that were, in Hobbes's much-quoted phrase, "nasty, brutish, and short," but on the contrary, in the words of Peter Lamborn Wilson, involved "a process of maximizing autonomy and pleasure for the whole group. . . . The hunter-gatherer economy—even in ecologically disadvantaged areas like deserts, rain forests and the Arctic—is based on abundance and leisure."[7]

It is by now no longer unexceptionable to see the progressive rise of modern man as culminating grandly in a humanity deriving from the events of early Christianity and the aftermath of Greek philosophy. We are beginning to know far too much about our so-called prehistory to countenance such wildly foreshortened pictures of our past without embarrassment. We can read the genetic code back to an Africa of more than one hundred thousand years ago; our sense of the specificity of Neolithic and even earlier man grows constantly with archaeological exploration, and though of course we cannot provide ourselves with narrative detail regarding significant events in early humanity's history, the idea that humanity rises from its primate ancestry in two phases—one archaic, one civilized—is no longer credible. But with the fall of this picture, the two-beat rhythm leading to the thinking now occurring seems an inadequate picture of history as well.

Again, in Greek myth and theophanic narrative—as registered in a rich literature that the Western tradition has routinely mined for evidences of the "archaic" mind and, therefore, in which one might expect to find Eliade's paradigms most clearly articulated—the advent of the Divine typically takes the form of an *incursion* into natural and social order. Though on one level mythological narrative and ritual practice derive clearly from seasonal and cosmic patterns and recurrences, still, when a Greek god acts in human affairs it does so precisely by *disrupting* human expectations. Even without being conceptualized as linear history, human event and its commerce with the Divine are already most vivid and intense where they are most particular. Gods erupt on the human scene to bestow being or to disrupt being—and they do indeed erupt—in oracles, dreams, prodigies, trances, visions, the lives of heroes, the migrations of peoples, the songs of poets. They do not simply stay aloof *in illo tempore* to provide the ideal patterns of quotidian existence. But if for the Greeks, many centuries before Christ, myths depict the breaking of repetitive patterns as much as the articulation of patterns themselves, though Plato sought to elevate form to a higher site in the real than singular events, the divine character of the particular was already envisioned long before the Incarnation began the process of correcting the "same dull round" of eternal recurrence.

Radical Particularity outside the West

Humanity did not have to wait for the Christian epoch to attend and appreciate particular existence, however the course of Western thought appears—at least in one major stream of its history—to have been determined by the need to shake off the Platonic hypostatization of a realm of ideal forms supervenient upon concrete experience. Zen Buddhism, the Taoist tradition deriving from Chuang Tzu, the Dzogchen tradition in Tibetan Buddhism, and countless examples from animist peoples all give ample evidence of an anchoring of Being in the radically particular that, in terms of precise practice, far exceeds anything propounded in this regard in the West. From the perspective of these practices as spiritual perspectives, the radical particularism of the thinking now occurring appears a bit like too little too late.

These traditions offer many and varied forms of practice geared to explore what there is every reason to view as ontological possibilities unknown in the West. Much of Buddhist thought, of course, abrogates ontological speculation as such; in general, it does not seek to deny or affirm the existence of objects or the truth of concepts but seeks rather to transform our relation to that ground in our sentience from which ontological concern arises. But that does not imply the irrelevance of Buddhist experience and practice to our present ontological concerns. The cartoon version of Buddhist, Taoist, and Hindu traditions as involving the subsumption of the individual by a supra- or sub-venient continuum begs the question of the value and nature of the ontological territory these practices open. One does not know what the Buddhist means by nirvana without undergoing the initiation that reveals it. Gautama Buddha, for instance, refused to answer questions that to us would be essentially ontological ones, including whether there exists an individual entity that survives from birth to birth and that undergoes enlightenment—presumably because he understood that the nature of existence as experienced once the enlightenment process has been undergone is no longer what it was experienced to be prior to this. We need to be as wise as Buddha in this respect and not exclude from our polyontology the ontological perspectives that these practices quite plausibly might open. Many essential practices of the master Buddhist-practitioner involve a radical attention to the minute particulars of sensory and mental experience, so that experiential regions that for the Western thinker are matters of speculation, for the Buddhist are open in depth to empirical exploration. In this regard, the attention to the concrete, and in that sense the historical, is far more advanced in the East than it is in the West, in spite of the fact that Buddhism does not take a full-blown interest in what we call history. What we think of as history in the sense of a running narrative of the concrete appears to the Buddhist as the runaway elaboration of mental construction.

Mathematics

The thinking now occurring discovers an entirely new system of numeration oriented by a symbolic understanding of certain numerical proportions and relations. But it is not clear how the thinking now occurring stands in relation to the mathematics that the West has so elaborately developed (or discovered) and continues to elaborate (and discover). The thinking now occurring calls to witness the probable technological future as evidence for its own vision, but technology is thoroughly dependent on the continued expansion of mathematical theory and the continued search for new practical applications of mathematical thought. The great foundational questions regarding the ontological status of mathematics that dominated mathematical thinking at the end of the nineteenth century and continued to do so through the first decades of the twentieth—questions that affected philosophy substantially outside of mathematics proper—are simply ignored in the thinking now occurring. Foundational mathematical thinking asked and continues to ask: What *is* mathematics? Is it the realm of Platonic forms? Are mathematical structures historically mediated constructions or socially determined conventions? Are they projections of the structure of the human mind or brain? Foundational studies remain unresolved around these issues, yet the application of mathematics to technology and scientific theory remains standard practice. There is a profound ontological hesitancy at the heart of postmodern thought that can be attributed in part to the unresolvedness of these questions. The thinking now occurring declares that postmodern hesitation has been surpassed decisively by its own gestures. But it seems, in regard to mathematics, we need to know just how it has accomplished this. I doubt that in fact it has. The picture of what the thinking now occurring calls *logic* opens a gap so vast between its own inventions and the still-living questions within modern philosophy of mathematics that I, in any case, have thus far not been able to bridge it.

As an example of a topic within mainstream mathematics that it would seem the thinking now occurring would be challenged to address is the realm of Georg Cantor's transfinite numbers and their development in the century or so since their advent. Much in modern mathematics follows from the experience of Cantor, so much so that in order to fully rationalize the arithmetical continuum a science of the infinite had to be invented. Cantor himself was not insensitive to the theological pertinence of his discoveries and sought to calm the turbulence he thought he was stirring up by declaring a distinction between the transfinite numbers he had succeeded in investigating and the Absolute Infinite—an infinite that involved contradictory properties, and that remained comprehensible to God alone.[8] Few mathematicians were interested in his theological anxieties or his attempts to quell them, and several of them have proceeded to investigate the "inconsistent multiplicity" that Cantor thought was exclusively God's prerogative. But in a theological context such as the thinking now occurring, one would expect that a serious encounter with Cantor would be inescapable.

Creatio ex nihilo

It is not clear at all from contemporary philosophy how the question of the origin of "existence," taken as our material cosmos, is to be understood, nor is it any longer possible to say that the concept of existence is rendered perspicuous by a doctrine that says that this universe came into being out of nothing either at the edge of time or at a particular point in time. The coming into its own of scientific cosmology with the articulation of the theory of the big bang, which seemed at first to confirm *creatio ex nihilo*, today confirms nothing of the kind. Various interpretations of the big bang construction exist, and the very rigor and seriousness with which these variations are entertained portends ill for any clarification of the notion of existence in the near future. For with the specification of the physical laws this universe obeys, many metaphysical questions arise regarding how "existence" is to be understood. Surely these laws "exist," but is their existence on the same ontological footing as the material universe they specify? In the thinking now occurring, no doubt, this distinction is moot. The laws that specify Creation are interior to Creation, now understood to be the prerogative of each of us. But cosmologists today speculate quite conscientiously on a range of problems: on the possible existence of other universes, whether with the same or different laws; on whether other universes exist in some way parallel to our own, or anterior in some transcending time; on whether time itself, and in what sense, came into existence with the big bang; on whether a hyperdimensional manifold wraps this universe within itself so that time, as one of its dimensions, does not "pass" at all.

That "existence" might include the mathematical and logical laws that determine how universes emerge and endure renders the question of "existence" quite unclear and susceptible of only arbitrary arbitration. If, per the thinking now occurring, existence itself is the body of Christ, does that mean that the Christ includes the range of all possible sets of laws for specifying the existent cosmologies? Does it include the mathematics that allows the specification of those laws? And what of the ontological status of mathematics? For mathematics goes far beyond the specification of any particular model of any universe. Do these possibilities define the polyontology of the thinking now occurring, or are they themselves together but one possibility within the thinking now occurring? Does the uniqueness of the historicity of the Incarnation tell us whether physical laws or mathematical systems themselves are historically generated or historically unique? Does polyontology mean that each of us is free to establish these laws, create our own mathematics? Does the "whole of existence" that each of us is in each moment responsible for include the existence of other universes in principle out of communicative range with ours? No doubt, the thinking now occurring can provide determinations for some of these questions; but it is clear that the question of existence as a whole that the advent of *creatio ex nihilo* launched no longer pertains in the way it once did, but only in a wholly transformed way.

No Shadows Anywhere

The thinking now occurring's understanding of absolute particularity and the valorization of the universally concrete as the sloughing off of self-consciousness is of a piece with its disclosure of the sacred character of existence itself as created *now* and yet possessing a transcendental essence. There is no eternal reference that authorizes or guarantees the sacrality of concrete existence in detail, no Platonic scaffolding consisting of sacred types of which the concrete things are instances or examples. The things themselves, we ourselves, in our immediacy and materiality are the sacred. The mantle of divinity has been passed all the way over to us, and to that which is here and that which is coming into being precisely now through our creative auspices. The transcendental essence of existence as the Christ has entered the world. Existence itself is its own "schema." No timeless paradigm outrides as residue in some atemporal acosmic station. The thinking now occurring asserts this much, and the consequence of accepting or even entertaining it can be experienced. But one might demur as to whether it can be *thought*. The thinking now occurring's answer: the nature of thought itself has been radically changed, so that this question loses its sense. If the transcendental essence of existence has entered the world, thought no longer distinguishes itself from that of which it is the thought. The impossibility of maintaining a distinction between thought and world—which modern philosophy gradually discovered and postmodern philosophy roundly proclaims—is exploded by the thinking now occurring as a cause for agonizing and is demonstrated to be the new condition for faith. Faith thinks the transcendental essence of existence as inseparable from existence itself: Christ as the world. But in face of this claim our response may be "an and yet and yet and yet."[9] Why, except by virtue of personal history, would one find this transcendental essence in and as the Christ? Why not the Dharmakaya, Unqualified Brahma, or the Tao—terms from the East which for several thousand years had already found the transcendental essence of existence inseparable from existence itself, in the form, for instance, of such formulas as "nirvana and samsara are one"? Differences in detail between these systems and the thinking now occurring need to be weighed reflectively as appropriate for any thinking responsive to present-day intellectual conditions, and this reflection cannot be dismissed by remarking that the nature of thought has been altered by the thinking now occurring. Maybe. But those worlds of thought, as much as thinking now occurring, require participation to be understood authentically. If participation in the thinking now occurring is a matter of "walking through the door," and if we are to have polyontology, we must have many doors!

It is surely possible to ask whether the rejected Platonic alternative to the concrete character of sacred existence characterizes uniquely the mystery of atemporality as experienced, say, in Eastern religions, where there is clearly an atemporal experience, but not one based on a set of timeless paradigms to which concrete things and experiences are subordinate and in relation to which they gain their sacred character by conforming. To the contrary, just as in the thinking now occurring the displacing of immediacy by any form of representational thought is precisely what leads to the impasse of modern self-consciousness, so in Eastern contexts, particularly in Madhyamika Buddhism, assignation of identity to external and internal objects and finally to one's self are what constitute the obscurations that prevent the immediate realization of precisely the atemporal character of one's actual being. Constructions of determinate atemporal realties are obscurations, but that which shines forth when these obscurations are removed is not something ensconced in time. In fact it is the *now* stripped of representational content that radiates in its immediacy an atemporal archetype: that *now* itself is an eternal Now, and if this nowness is the correlate of our being the Creators of existence, then it seems that that creativity is *also* happening in a Now that is not in time.

This indeed was something like the view inherited by Augustine from Plotinus and passed on through Christian tradition to Kierkegaard and beyond. It embraces an essential paradox that interrupts any fully rational ontology, and it is not at all clear how the consistent rejection of this paradox (as articulated in Kierkegaard, for instance) in favor of the univocally concrete character of the present world—at the expense of any atemporal element—achieves anything but the refusal to expose oneself to an essential ontological mystery. If the concrete present is sacred in its particular content and this is so in every case and at every moment, it is hard to see how or why the Now itself loses its creative and novational quality by being in each instant the instantiation not of some archetypal or paradigmatic *content,* but of that eternal Now itself—a now-character that stands outside of time and imparts itself to each transitory moment precisely insofar as it is occurring in and as its Now. To deny this seems to be to throw the sacred baby out with the Platonic bath water, whereas to embrace the eternal present as archetype of the historical Now seems to be to embrace the uniqueness of the historical itself. It does not require accepting any sort of paradigmatic other-where or other-when or other-form determining the character of the present; to the contrary, it requires only engaging a self-evident paradox: that though the content of every moment is radically new, the now-qua-now does not alter with its content. Further, each moment occurs in such a manner that its own "schema" is coincident with its own event, its identity identical with its own changing occurrence, as in the thinking now occurring. But of course such an engagement would come at too great a cost for the thinking now occurring, for it would mean that the novational character of the radically particular and the anchoring of ethical life in the present would be a possibility for any time whatsoever and not the consequence of the radical incursion of the Incarnation event, whereas the thinking now occurring traces the emergence of this possibility as occurring through the unique—Christian—history of the West. The thinking now occurring must shunt aside any suggestion that human experience outside of the West and without the contribution of what the thinking now occurring takes to be not only the history of Western thought but of Being itself might have come upon the wealth of the radically particular and the sacred character of creative being in the now.

The abrogation of the mystery of time/eternity is coherent in the thinking now occurring with a certain noonday quality to its vision of renovated existence. To quote Wallace Stevens again, in the thinking now occurring "there are no shadows anywhere."[10] All ambiguity, all resonant depth, all layered and textured play of presence and absence has been, in its opinion, "transcended." The entire sphere of depth-spirituality—not only the dark caverns and moody grimnesses of the Romantic and the modern West, not only the spirituality subsequent to the interdiction of sacred doctrine—is excluded from the sensibility tolerated by the thinking now occurring. No place in polyontology for the spirituality of the Kabbalah and its intricate and resonant theosophy of layers, coverings, veilings and unveilings that Leahy's sometime colleague Elliot R. Wolfson details in his many works, nor for the intricate and sophisticated theosophy of time that Wolfson magisterially teases out of kabbalistic texts.[11]

Thinking as Poetics

Finally, there seems little room for what George Quasha and I have been writing of as a *poetics of thinking*—a view of thought itself as a truly open, configurative making.[12] Precisely because what philosophical thought has been since its inception in ancient Greece seems to have reached an epochal denouement, it need no longer manifest exclusively as an ever-renewed stage for a competitive drama, ever-postponing but ever-longing for the last word. We suggest a practice of a general poetics (obviously by no means limited to prosody) which would in fact find the thinking now occurring and Leahy's texts a salient and exemplary witness. All the difficulties treated in this essay notwithstanding, the greatest difficulty for me is that the thinking now occurring itself, with its powerful capacity to draw one into an intellectual terrain in which all of existence scintillates with the radiance of its own transcendental essence, seems very much to have a place among the great visionary and indeed poetic works of human history. The thinking now occurring's truest term is the Creative, and it is among the great acts of the imagination of Being (subjective and objective genitive intended) that this uncategorizable *poetic* work belongs.

It would be an essential task to develop in detail the notion of poetics that would welcome the thinking now occurring as an act under its provenance. Let me here briefly sketch some of the features of Leahy's textual practice and suggest how these features might render a treatment of the thinking now occurring as a poetic practice likely and appropriate, even in the more limited sense of transformative language. The thinking now occurring is "projective" in a sense that can be developed from the American poet Charles Olson's concept of *projective verse*; that is, the form of the language both projects and is a projection of the dynamic and formal characteristics of that of *which* it speaks—to the point of effecting a sensation that no distinction exists between form and content. In the phrase borrowed from Robert Creeley in Olson's seminal essay "Projective Verse": "Form is never more than an extension of content."[13] That which is to be said projects a form appropriate to what is to be said and, as a form, extends it.

The language of the thinking now occurring is fashioned in such a way as to create in the reader's experience the precise sense of ever-beginning existence that is at the heart of its doctrine. Passage after passage in each of Leahy's major texts proceeds by articulating a series of declarative sentences in the present indicative, most commonly constructed around the copula "is." The distinctive style or "sound" of Leahy's texts is dominated by cascades of passages of such sentences. The overwhelming sense is that the thought in a given sentence is indeed amplified by its successor sentence; nevertheless, the successor sentence begins from the beginning anew. There is no supervenient textuality that accumulates or assembles meaning into a cognitive space constructed above or parallel to the actual sentences of which a given swatch of text is composed. But there is a rhythm created by the iteration of similar sentence forms and by the linked repetition of other rhetorical features. And yet it is as if the entire force of the thinking now occurring in its most essential aspect is projected in this manner—that the coming into existence of existence itself is occurring in each moment—as if the entire force of the thinking now occurring were concentrated in each sentential utterance. As the new thinking steps forth from the husk of self-referential intellectual and textual practice that constitutes an essence of modernity—a self-referentiality born of self-consciousness and functioning as its now-to-be-recognized-as-hellish means—there is no room in the new textual practice for self-reference or self-reflection. Sentence follows sentence with such intimate density of utterance that there is no room for speech to step back or step away. It is not that there are no summative gestures within the text; it is just that each such gesture records itself as replete with the gift of existence that it carries. It does not, as I say, supervene upon the rest of the text or establish a hierarchy of topoi such that one aspect of the text reflects upon the text itself, positioning it from a metalevel.

Here, in closing, is a swatch of quotations from *Beyond Sovereignty* almost arbitrarily chosen. I have broken up the typography to show the serial character of the sequence of declarative utterances:

> The distance between creature and Creator is transcended in essence:
>
> for the first time relation is the absolute actuality of the world itself:
>
> as never before the relation creature and Creator is an absolutely unconditioned intimacy in existence.

As never before the Creator shares itself with the creature.

For the first time history is existence *with the other* absolute.

For the first time the transcendental is essentially transcendence: beginning in time the foundation of the reality of time: time founding itself in beginning. (BS, 3)

The iterations of the declarative sentences are counterpointed by a rhythm of repetitive introductory phrases. The rhetorical form is powerful, not to say hypnotic. The passage, I repeat, is not exceptional; such passages abound in Leahy's work. Its movement is an energetic forward thrust of thought. In my view, its rhetorical means and its relation to the matter being articulated fall entirely under the provenance of poetics.

Notes

1. See, for instance, BS, x, xix, xx. Although there is no focused treatment of polyontology in Leahy's writings, he discussed and used the term extensively in a course offered under the auspices of the New York Philosophy Corporation that I attended.

2. A full-scale examination of the relation between the thinking now occurring and Heidegger's thinking is beyond the scope of this essay. It would require a prolonged reading of Leahy's published remarks on Heidegger as well as working through the transcripts of his course on Heidegger for the New York Philosophy Corporation, together with a study of Heidegger's writings and recorded remarks on the relationship between his thinking and theology. But a starting point must be the fact that Heidegger emphasized that the distance between Christian theology generally and his thought must be heightened in order for a fruitful dialogue between the two to be possible, whereas in the thinking now occurring the very distinction between philosophy and theology has disappeared. In the thinking now occurring it seems to be the case that this collapse of difference is neither a subsumption of philosophical thought under theological systematics, nor the recovery of theology within a philosophical frame, but a genuine overcoming of the very distance that Heidegger insists must be maintained between faith and philosophy. Precisely this "overcoming" deserves a careful and prolonged examination along several fronts, some of the terms of which I try to suggest in this section.

3. See Heidegger, *The Piety of Thinking: Essays by Martin Heidegger*, ed. James G. Hart and John C. Maraldo (Bloomington: Indiana University Press,

1976), in particular "Appendix: Conversation with Martin Heidegger, recorded by Hermann Noack."

4. Mircea Eliade, *The Myth of the Eternal Return, or Cosmos and History*, trans. Willard R. Trask (Princeton: Bollingen, 1974).

5. William Blake, "There Is No Natural Religion," in *The Collected Prose and Poetry of William Blake*, ed. David V. Erdmann (New York: Doubleday, 1965), 2.

6. Claude Lévi-Strauss, "The Science of the Concrete," ch. 1 of *The Savage Mind* (Chicago: University of Chicago Press, 1966).

7. Marshall Sahlins, *Stone Age Economics* (New York: de Gruyter, 1972); Peter Lamborn Wilson, "The Shamanic Trace," in *Escape from the Nineteenth Century and Other Essays* (Brooklyn: Autonomedia, 1998), 73.

8. See, for example, Joseph W. Dauben, "Georg Cantor and Pope Leo XIII: Mathematics, Theology, and the Infinite," *Journal of the History of Ideas* 38, no. 1 (1977): 85–108.

9. From Wallace Stevens's poem, "An Ordinary Evening in New Haven," in *The Collected Poems of Wallace Stevens* (New York: Vintage, 1982), sec. 1, 465.

10. From Stevens, "The Man with The Blue Guitar," in *The Collected Poems*, sec. 5, 167.

11. See particularly Elliot R. Wolfson, *Language, Eros, Being: Kabbalistic Hermeneutics and Poetic Imagination* (New York: Fordham, 2005) and *Alef, Mem, Tau: Kabbalistic Musings on Time, Truth, and Death* (Berkeley: University of California Press, 2006).

12. George Quasha and Charles Stein, *An Art of Limina: Gary Hill's Works and Writings*, foreword by Lynne Cooke (Barcelona: Ediciones Poligrafa, 2009). Although this book engages the work of Gary Hill, it is in fact an extended meditation on the nature of poeisis. On thought as configurative making, see Charles Stein, *Persephone Unveiled* (Berkeley: North Atlantic, 2006), particularly "Afterword: Configuring History," 189–90.

13. Robert Creeley in Charles Olson's seminal essay, "Projective Verse," in *Collected Prose: Charles Olson*, ed. Donald Allen and Benjamin Friedlander (Berkeley: University of California Press, 1997), 239–50.

2

Temporal Diremption and the Novelty of Genuine Repetition

ELLIOT R. WOLFSON

> A thinker is not beholden to a thinker—rather, when he is thinking, he holds on to what is to be thought, to Being. Only insofar as he holds on to Being can he be open to the influx of thoughts which thinkers before him have thought.
>
> —Heidegger, *What Is Called Thinking?*

In this essay, I focus on the temporal underpinnings of D. G. Leahy's signature notion of the *thinking now occurring for the first time*. Let me state unequivocally at the outset that I subscribe to Leahy's conviction that the new path of thinking is one in which there is "an absolutely transcendent coincidence of thought itself with existence itself" without the one being reducible to or derived from the other (F, 112). It is plausible, as Heidegger observed in *Sein und Zeit*, to mark the launch of Western philosophy by the Parmenidean aphorism that being and thinking are one and the same[1]—a metaphysical precept that implies, as Hegel astutely observed in the first book of the *Wissenschaft der Logik*, published in 1812, that "thinking and the determination of thinking are not something alien to the subject matters, but are rather their essence, or that the *things* and the *thinking* of them agree in and for themselves (also our language expresses a kinship between them); that thinking in its immanent determinations, and the true nature of things, are one and the same content."² In the thinking now occurring, "for the first time in history, the appearance of the transcendental essence of existence itself is understood to be the *transcendent essence of the conversion of thought itself* from being something essentially conceived to exist as an absolute form (self-conception in essence) to being essentially existence itself in the form of thought identifying itself wholly with its object" (NM, 323–24). The identity of thought and being is considered from a post-Derridean vantage point:

> To hear the word sounding being itself the absolute, this absolute discrimination of the species of perception, as being newly articulate, this absolutely historically existent liberation of the essence of thought from the *necessity of itself to be distinguished from its own necessity* is personality transcendent. From this necessity thought in essence before now is liberated by the absolutely unconditioned violation of articulation which is *la différance*, which essentially renders the dictum of Parmenides ("one should both say and think that being is") *one should neither say nor think that differance is, one must write differance,* a torturing of the truth out of the saying of Parmenides, dictated by the fact that before now it became essentially necessary to say and to think *that being was not being,* that the limit of thought was reached but not crossed (out/over)—*la différance,* the crossing out of the logic of identity. (F, 162)

The epistemological and ontological change championed by Leahy in the thinking now occurring rests on the assumption that time is construed as the absolute now of creation, the "inalienable body itself transcending the form itself of past and future" (F, 47). Consider the christological and apocalyptic formulation in the following passage from the third appendix of *Novitas Mundi*:

> *What now occurs is not the elemental reconstruction of the world in the image of a mere man (as was the case with modern thought from its very inception), not the perception of the world as a mere appearance. What now occurs for the first time in history is the elemental reconstruction of the world essentially in the*

image of God. It is the perception of the world itself of its being the intelligible appearance itself of the essence of existence. What is celebrated in the *missa jubilaea* is not simply the human resurrection of the dead one (Jesus the Nazarene), but the divine resurrection of the dead messiah (Christ Jesus). The essential element in the reconstruction of the world now occurring is the Christ-element, the essential element of history. This thinking now occurring is the unreservedly pathetic form of an absolutely passionate essence. (NM, 350–51)

It lies beyond the scope of this analysis to unpack all the threads woven together in this text, but suffice it to note that Leahy has applied the scholastic understanding of God—in the Avicennian language that impacted Maimonides and Aquinas[3]—as the necessary of existence, that is, the being whose essence it is to exist, to the material body that is the world at large. This is the intent of the statement that what has occurred for the first time is the reconstruction of the world in the image of God and hence the world is perceived as the intelligible appearance of the essence of existence. As Leahy put it elsewhere, "The thinking now occurring is *ex nihilo*, is nothing but the known necessity of itself, where existence is the necessity of itself absolutely and essentially, the perpetual existence of itself in the midst of itself, itself separating itself in essence for the first time" (F, 176). In the new thinking, the essence of the world, which is the created Godhead, enters existence continually but always in the now *ex abysso*; that is, the historically existent essence of thought is without any fixed essence beyond its own necessity, which is to be distinguished from the necessity of itself (F, 162). Moreover, corporeity is understood as substantially identical to thought, the *transcendental essence of existence in existence itself*. For Leahy, this is the philosophical import of the historical event of the resurrection and its consummation in the eucharistic rite of the *missa jubilaea*, the sacrament wherein the "intelligibility of appearance" is conceived "as the unleavened bread of existence itself in the form of man. . . . In the celebration of the infinite passover the appearance of the eucharist, *qua* appearance, is now seen for the first time in history to be itself the eucharist in essence: to transcend appearance, to be appearance itself. . . . In this thinking now occurring there is nothing beside the unleavened bread of existence itself, nothing beside the wine new in essence" (NM, 344–45).[4] The transcendental essence of existence, which is the God who enters the world, is not some otherworldly reality but the appearance of existence itself.

The apocalypse bespeaks the transition from the exclusivity of the *missa solemnis* to the inclusivity of the *missa jubilaea,* that is, a shift from the substantial appearance of the transcendent passion of faith in essence to the essential appearance of the transcendental essence of existence in the form of thought construed corporeally (NM, 347). The consciousness apposite to the apocalyptic unveiling, consequently, is the discernment that there is nothing but the unleavened bread of existence. The longstanding schism between reality and appearance is overcome through the recognition that *to transcend appearance is to exist as appearance itself*. In a slightly varied terminological register, Leahy writes: "What now occurs in thought for the first time in history (transcending in fact the end of the world in essence) is *the perception itself of the body*—God in God in essence—the Temple of the New Jerusalem—effected now in essence inclusively in the *missa jubilaea,* the center of an essentially new consciousness in the conversion of the universe into an entirely new stuff" (NM, 348).[5]

Hyperbolically, in my judgment, Leahy insists that the reconstruction of the world in the image of God transpires *for the first time in history,* a rhetorical trope frequently deployed in his writings. What this means concretely is that in the thinking now occurring the disparity between spirit and matter is reconciled, albeit without having to resolve the dyadic difference between them dialectically by positing a synthetic unity. Positively expressed, the binary is foreclosed by the identification of the universe as the Godhead ex nihilo, an identification articulated as well as the unicity of the trinitarian God made flesh.

> Now the end of the world created in essence is confirmed with the appearance of the substantial form of the body itself. Now nothing remains to be effected but the absolute conception of the Spirit of Christ. The restriction on that thinking now occurring, while essentially not the self-restriction of that thinking belonging in essence to the past, is, nevertheless, the restriction of *the other* remaining in the form of matter, that is, in the form of the transcendental difference. The transformation of transcendental to essentially absolute difference is to be the appearance itself of the transcendental essence of existence *in existence itself*. Then there is to be no distinction whatsoever of matter from

form, not simply in essence . . . but in essence identically substance. In this thinking now occurring there exists in essence an identity of substance and function in the form of transcendence, in the utter finality of the fact itself the substantial identity of the transcendental essence. . . . This is what reflection is to be in the substantial identity of the transcendental essence: the resurrection of the dead. That universe now coming into existence for the first time in history in the form of thought itself is to be in its perfection essentially the conception of creation itself wherein nothing is to be known of an essence distinguished substantially from that of existence itself. (NM, 352–53)

The new creation of the essence that occurs in every now propagates the absolute novelty of matter in the form of the absolute transcendence of the absolute identity of thought (F, 140). Matter, rendered new by the absolutely novel essence, is cast notionally as "the meta-identical transcendence of a meta-identity," and hence "for the first time the *meta* meta-identically exists in essence. Existence for the first time is conceived essentially as itself absolute novelty. This existence is the matter of thought itself" (F, 177).

For the first time, in the thinking now occurring, "logic coincides with existence in the known necessity of the absolute identity of matter itself with the essence of thought, in the knowledge/essential experience of the identity of the essence of matter with the actual existence of thought, with the knowledge that knowledge is the knowledge of existence itself" (F, 177). The matter of the law of identity apposite to this beginning is "motion itself, absolute temporality, the very Being of magnitude. In this beginning the transcendence of time itself, now itself, is thought in essence in the form of thought itself absolute" (F, 141). I take issue with the understanding of the temporal interval that bolsters Leahy's categorical conviction that *existence is for first time conceived essentially as absolute novelty* or his equally far-reaching assertion that in the center of the new consciousness there is the *conversion of the universe into an entirely new stuff*. Juxtaposing these two statements allows us to interpret the latter in terms of the former, and hence we surmise that, despite the effort of the new thinking to get beyond both the dualism of mind and matter and the idealistic monism that would reduce the latter to the former, the conversion of which Leahy speaks is a transformation in consciousness; that is, the new stuff is not an alteration in the molecular structure or the quantum field of being but a shift in the manner that matter is configured in mind.[6] Listen carefully to Leahy's language:

> In this conversion of thought itself to being formally transcendent, now, for the first time, the universe is transformed essentially from being *something new* to being *what is now new*, its *appearance itself*. The universe, in essence, *its very appearance* (it being of the essence of that thinking now occurring that *everything is now itself*, that is, *its appearance*, nothing is hidden in essence, the merely apparent essence of things is reduced to nothing whatsoever, or to the recollection of Being upon itself). . . . That is, thought is identified with *its appearance itself*. . . .
>
> In this thinking now occurring *it is the same as an essentially new identity: to be conceived in essence, to appear in existence*. The form of thought's comprehension of its identity with the transcendent energy if the universe is *time itself*, through which thought comprehends the appearance itself of what has occurred, a complete change in essence now appearing" (NM, 324–25).

Admittedly, Leahy labored to find the words to communicate the aspect of the thinking now occurring that seeks to transcend the age-old polarity of reality and appearance, but it does seem that the transfiguration of the cosmos that he envisions in the form of thought's comprehension of its identity with the transcendent energy of the universe, which is time, entails an altered state of mindfulness rather than a quantifiable physical modification:

> This is the transcendent identity of an essentially transcendental thinking in which transcendence itself is essentially transitive, that is, thought's new object. This object is the essential unity of indivisibles, the form of an essentially new universe now existing for the first time in thought. The realization of this form is now but a matter of time itself in thought. This realization, in turn, is but the preparation in essence for the termination of history itself. In this thinking now occurring there are no elements in essence apart from the elements of Christ. The appearance itself of the

eucharist is transformed in essence into the form of man, into Yahweh's flesh and blood, into his essential property, thereby obviating in essence the thought itself of appropriation, rendering it essentially unnecessary (appropriation itself) in every one of its forms, holy or unholy. . . . *What is essentially new about the form of thought now occurring is that it is form in essence not thought in essence: there is no essence beyond the formality of thought itself now seen to be transitive in essence, that is, the form itself of transcendence.* (NM, 345–46)

Insofar as the universe is conceived absolutely differently in the form of thought in essence not thought in essence for the first time, it is witnessed as essentially new. Leahy adds that this newness itself produces a crucial change in the nature of temporality: the realization of a new universe, a new world consciousness, and a new humanity (F, 232) heralds the termination of history, which is to say, the thinking of time is thought for the first time as a matter that is thought in the time of thinking. The reciprocal temporalization of the noetic and the noetization of the temporal are embodied fully in the incarnation of Christ, the event that renders appropriation itself inappropriate, insofar as the distinction between holy and unholy becomes inoperative in the face of *the absolute nullification of the possible* wherein e*verything now comes to exist actually in the form of the body itself* (NM, 360). Contrasting his perspective on the new thinking with Kierkegaard's idea of the embodiment of omnipotence in the interiority of *den Enkelte*, the single/particular, Leahy argues that the thinking occurring now turns *den Enkelte* absolutely outside, for the first time the absolute exteriority is conceived as the embodiment of the singular/particular. To grasp this dimension of the new thinking, let us consider Leahy's account of the identification of the interior and the exterior in Altizer:

> This is the self-circling actuality of that which wills its own oblivion in the form of the body, in the form of the forgiveness of sin, in the form of an absolute inner outer/absolute outer inner: the self-embodiment of sin: the sin of self in the form of the forgiveness of sin, sin in the form of the self-forgiveness of sin: that circle of which the total self-embodiment of God is the oblivion, the circle of its own willing not-willing its own other, the circle of its own body not its own: the actual and real transformation

> of what before now was old into something actually new: *the divine metamorphosis of self into other: the circling from its own beginning into the body of the other* . . . the absolute self circling itself in the form of another within, in the form of the new form of the absolute self/the absolutely new form of self, in the form of the absolute self-extension of the point within itself to another. This is the exterior actuality of the body the interior identity of the exterior: the interior the exterior of another form of self-consciousness: the new form of interior self-consciousness, the exterior: historical self-consciousness now visible ending in the exterior of consciousness, in the anonymous, objective form, circling, but not returning to its own beginning: the single, solitary turn infinitely multiplied in the form of the other, in the form of objectivity/anonymity: the divine metamorphosis of self into other multiplied in the form of the anonymity of an absolute identity, in the form of an absolute anonymity: the metamorphosis of self itself in the form of the infinite multiplication/division of the other, in the pure form of the body, in the form of the addition-subtraction identity, in the pure form of the exterior identity of the interior, in the form of an absolute purity, the purity of form itself (the pure form of the forgiveness of sin). (F, 222–23)

The absolute metamorphosis of the inwardness of self into the outwardness of the other, the dissipation of absolute identity into the form of absolute anonymity, logically necessitates that the pure form of the exterior identity of the interior coalesces with the interior identity of the exterior, the self-circling of the willing not-willing, that is, the kenotic potency of the will to not will. The thinking now occurring purports to move beyond the lingering dichotomies of the exterior and interior even in their dialectical overcoming as proposed by Altizer. Not to appreciate this, of course, is to miss the crucial turn initiated by Leahy. But the latter is still indebted to a circularity, albeit an absolute circularity that undermines the notion of cyclical repetition insofar as the permanency of the circle bespeaks the radical differentiation of *the absolute novelty of the world (novitas mundi) in the world as the novitas mentis* (NM, 14). Thus, as Leahy puts it, "What is known for the first time is that the circle itself is nothing but the confirmation of the fact that there is no generic circle, but that the absolute circle is perpetuity itself, that the absolute identity of terms is the absolutely integral relation to measure, that the 'itself' (the identity of the existing thing) is absolutely unconditioned transcendent identity, the actual/negative of the contra-actual, the proof/position of existence *itself*, there being nothing but the transcendental difference of the thing from the *thing itself*, the existence of the thing itself, the existence of existence itself. There is nothing but the absolute existence of existence for the first time, the absolutely complex absolute existence of very simplicity" (F, 158). We can discern in this depiction of the contra-actual negativity, the absolute lack of the absolute itself (F, 159), a foreshadowing of what Leahy eventually called the "absolutely polyontological reality" in conjunction with his positing of the "absolute discontinuity of the continuum."[7] What is noteworthy for our purposes is that the immanent form of the transcendence of the circle is transformed through the intermediation of the absolute measure into the circle itself, which is differentiated from the circle as time itself, insofar as the perpetuity of existence as existence is always to be ascertained from the potency of the essential difference that is time, *the now for the first time that is the time absolutely* (F, 355). The now is the *nihil* that transcends the bifurcation of eternity and time and, as such, in the thinking now occurring, there is "no alternative to existence itself absolutely unconditioned" (F, 101). Seemingly, it would follow that this thinking should dispense with the language of willing as not willing, as we encountered in the aforecited exposition of Altizer, but even Leahy avers a sense of omnipotence envisaged as "absolutely nonexisting in its existing" (BS, 44). Extrapolating the dialetheic logic[8] of the paradox further—something is both A and not-A and therefore neither A nor not-A—the form of the essentially transcendental objectivity is labeled a state "without being God & without being without God I am God's new beginning" (BS, 13). The I assumes the role as God's new beginning but it is a beginning that is both without being God and without being without God. Alternatively expressed, the beginning of the transcendental unity of transcendence is absolutely manifest as *nihil ex nihilo* (F, 353), the nothing of the absolute actuality that comes from nothing, that is, the absolute that does not belong to some otherworldly realm but which is fully present in the here and now, the *ruaḥ elohim* hovering over the abyss of the abyss that is the beginning of existence:

> The being atoning in every now: the Name Itself of God. This name is the identity of nothing *ex nihilo*. This is the absolute *epoché* of the mystical without reference to an other world: the One for the first time absolutely itself here & now: everything essentially existing, absolutely nothing extant: the thought of the extant reduced to Nothing: the transcendence-to-Nothing of the being of the *Dasein* reduced to Nothing: Nothing absolutely extant: the abyss of the extant/the extant Abyss/existence *ex abysso*. This *epoché* of mystical existence, this *epoché* of the mystical name, is the Spirit of God hovering over the absolutely-nothing-at-hand. . . . This is the thought of existence for the first time the *epoché* of extant thought, the abyss of the thought of existence *ex abysso* . . . the abyss not itself the matter of a beginning not the abyss of the abyss at once not not the abyss of the abyss itself, not the abyss of the abyss not not the abyss of the abyss, not the (metanoetic) abyss of the abyss of the abyss, but the beginning of existence the revolutionary metanoēsis of the abyss of the abyss. (F, 353–54)

Translated christologically, the beginning of actual existence is Jesus, "which is I AM NOT, where I AM NOT is not I AM denominated NOT/NOT denominated I AM/denominational I AM NOT, but I AM immediately NOT/NOT immediately I AM/immediate I AM NOT" (F, 412).

The supersessionist bias is conspicuous in Leahy's avowal that in the thinking now occurring *there are no elements in essence apart from the elements of Christ*. Needless to say, this approach has deep roots in Christian dogma, epitomized scripturally by the baptismal formula, "For in Christ Jesus you are sons of God, through faith. For as many of you as were baptized into Christ have put on Christ. There is neither Jew nor Greek, there is neither slave nor free, there is neither male nor female; for you are all one in Christ Jesus" (Gal. 3:26–28). What is conveniently ignored by many interpreters of this seminal passage is that the pledge that we are one in Christ is an inclusivity that excludes its own exclusivity; that is, the capacity for alterity attested in this text, and the ritual of baptism implied thereby, disregards those who might not desire to be incorporated into the body of Christ. For those baptized in Christ it may be reassuring to know there is an eradication of ethnic, socioeconomic, and gender difference, but what is the fate of those who resist assimilation?

We would do well to recall the verse that immediately succeeds the liturgical pronouncement, "And if you are of Christ, then you are Abraham's offspring, heirs according to the promise" (Gal. 3:29). The universal—to be of Christ—is presented here as the fulfillment of the particular—the covenantal promise to Abraham's seed. Contrary to Badiou, who surmised that Paul's reasoning exemplified the syllogism, "if it is true that every truth erupts as singular, its singularity is immediately universalizable," and thus universalizable singularity necessarily breaks with identitarian singularity,[9] I would contend that Paul does not escape the dilemma that lies at the heart of Jewish messianism: by including the excluded in the claim to exclusivity, the exclusivity is rendered even more inclusive. The aforementioned language of Badiou presents a false dichotomy and, as a consequence, he fails to ascertain that the Pauline universalism—already at the scriptural level—is expressed through the prism of the singular that is embroiled in the friction between the identity of difference and the difference of identity. On this measure, Leahy's philosophical translation of the Christian soteriology is wanting. The *missa jubilaea* may announce the now wherein "*the appearance itself of faith itself in essence is effected in a transcendentally differentiated substance, that is, without being other than itself in essence,*" but, in the end, it is not clear that this mass is as all-encompassing as Leahy supposes it to be. At the very least, the claim concerning the new apocalyptic actuality exhibits an unresolved tension between the universal and the particular.

What is even more troubling is that the temporal disjointedness of a dramatically new commencement cannot be justified epistemically, ontically, or ontologically; both philosophically and scientifically the operative notion of newness endorsed by Leahy is not tenable or defensible. Restating Leahy's conjecture does not constitute proof; like any philosophical worldview, the thinking now occurring is subject to critical examination. I readily admit that one must be mindful of imposing a modernist logic on a mode of speculation purportedly transpiring for the first time in history, but this should not serve as an excuse to deflect all disagreement. Indeed, it is precisely the temporal basis of the assertion regarding unparalleled novelty that must be interrogated. The radically diremptive nature of the absolute time as the absolute now transcending past and future may be questioned on grounds that discontinuity of the present—which follows ipso facto from the postulation of an absolutely novel moment—can be discerned only to the extent that we grasp that the present is not only continuous with but, in its deepest valence, the reverberation of the past that remains open as the future that is to come.[10] In contradistinction to Leahy, I would hypothesize that the absolute actuality of the now is neither past nor future because within it the past is always future and the future is already past. Consider Leahy's description of the *missa jubilaea*:

> What is in fact happening in essence is the transcendental repetition of the creation itself. This is the appearance itself in the world in essence of the repetition of existence itself in the form of man, of what, before now, even in its appearance in essence remained itself absolutely, or remained essentially intelligible, but which only now, in this thinking occurring for the first time in history in material consequence of the truth occurring in the Mass (*solemnis et jubilaea*), is actually intelligible, that is, absolutely nothing but itself in its appearance in essence without remainder. (NM, 350)[11]

That the mass celebrating the infinite passover is the *transcendental repetition of creation* (NM, 365, 374) implies to my ear that the end is a return to the beginning even though I concede that the thinking now occurring precludes the possibility of envisioning the beginning whither one returns as being the same as the beginning whence one departed. There is, technically speaking, no return in time if we understand by return a retrieval to where one has been since the only temporal mode that is accorded actuality is marked as *for the first time time absolutely now* (FP, 123). I grant, moreover, that creation is not an evocation of a primordial or a historical origin but the perception of the body of the world as the foundation of matter as difference conceived ex nihilo (F, 49–50). This is what is intended by *the transcendental repetition of the creation*. "There is neither nothing nor something prior to foundation itself to serve as the foundation: there is foundation itself for the first time *ex nihilo*, for the first time *exsistere ipsum ex nihilo*" (F, 139). Minimally, this sense of ex nihilo entails reiteration of what is novel inasmuch as each incomparable now is a recurrence of the "first integral repetition of being itself" (F, 50), the "absolute repetition" of "the new itself, of the body itself existing, of the quantum absolute" (F, 112). Implied in this quantum absolute—the *absolute becoming itself absolute objectivity itself*—is the presumption regarding the "identity itself for the first time the memory of the absolute repetition of the absolute, the catholicity itself of existence, absolute perpetuity. There is no non-identity arising out of the repetition of perpetuity (while the original absolute non-identity was a perpetual non-existence): there is the absolute repetition of absolute existence, the perpetuity of existence itself" (F, 145). Existence, on this score, is the "unnecessary repetition of creation itself: creation itself absolutely unconditioned" (F, 388). Creation is absolutely unconditioned but nonetheless recurring, albeit unnecessarily so.

Leahy avers that the now in which the end is experienced occurs in the thinking now occurring for the first time in history. How can something be both retrievable and unprecedented? To make sense of this we must presume that the property of newness concretizes sameness in the replication of difference—the absolute repetition of the new, the perpetual return to where one never was; the timeline is thus open at both ends of the circle. Lest one object that the image of the circle is inapplicable to the thinking now occurring, it would be useful to recall the densely mathematical account of creation, the beginning, and the abyss offered by Leahy in his reflections on how thought has moved beyond Galileo's conclusion that an infinite circle cannot exist because the circumference of such a circle would be a straight line:

> But now for the first time in history just such a line, just such a center exists, indeed, is existence. Existence is the line/the center/the time/the text the elements of which form a rational unity: the unconditionally absolute expansion of absolute unity: the absolute opening time itself for the first time the circle itself the fourfold proportionality identically the indivisible point: the absolute existence of dead center measuring the circumference of the circle. Insofar as the truth of THE PLACE identical with creation is the measure of an infinite order of squares . . . or cubes . . . each one of which, in the absolute exteriority of the within now actually existing for the first time, here in the form of the foundational segments of the exploded central square (cube) of any square (cube), measures the diameter of a circle (sphere), there exists for the first time in thought, not "a single sphere which expands in size without limit," but an infinite number of infinitely transparent absolute actualities: the sphere of absolute objectivity now existing: the sphere of spheres infinitely newly beginning, the sphere

> of infinitely new, infinitely separate spheres: the sphere the surface of which is the beginning of an absolutely transparent depth. . . . This is the beginning of the circumference of the infinite circle. This is the line for the first time. This is the time of beginning. This is creation displacing the abyss itself: the body of the Living God in the form of the beginning, depth absolutely surface, the infinite identical with the finite: the absolute incompatibility of the infinitely numbered points of the circumference of the circle: the absolutely transparent circle. (F, 533–34)

By the metric of the center of the circle that is the line of the beginning of the circumference, the depth that is absolute surface, time is the continually discontinuous reappearance of what is yet to become apparent, the congruence of the incongruent.

In *Foundation: Matter the Body Itself*, Leahy elaborates on the paradox of the essentially new in language that pushes to the edge of intelligibility:

> But now for the first time the new itself transcends the necessity of itself. Now the beginning of the circle itself itself exists. For the first time order itself the beginning even the end. *Novus ordo seclorum exsistit*. This is the absolute repetition of time itself: the circle itself (the itself-transcendence of time itself/being itself) circles itself within itself: without division, within identity, the absolute clarity of thought itself (remembering that there is no without within which division might be, that there is no outside of the text where thought itself might be nothing with a name, where thought itself with a name might be nothing, where nothing might be itself, remembering that there is no outside of the absolute plaintext, that there is not itself outside of itself: the itself-transcendence of itself is nothing but the circle of existence, nothing but time/being itself existing). The existence for the first time of foundation itself: the absolutely substantial existence of time. Not the *eternal* recurrence of all things, not being beginning in every now, but the *temporal* occurrence of all things, the absolute itself now existing beginning and end (the itself-transcendence of time not "eternity" but being itself absolute temporal-

ity), not freedom itself outside of itself-transendence, but freedom itself existing now for the first time in the form of personality which is itself new, to wit, *one is free to say and think identically that being is*, which is to say *that one is free to exist in time*, that the Incarnation itself absolutely exists in the form of thought itself absolute. (F, 164–65)

The circle, which signifies the absolute repetition of time—the itself-transcendence of time/being—is unremittingly interrupted by time as absolutely now. The characteristic of perpetuity replaces the reflexivity of the circle circling itself inasmuch as what is constant is inconstancy, what is enduring is the evanescence of the now that is at all times the same in virtue of being different. The absolute repetition of the new world order is identified as well as the absolute clarity of thought, which is compared figuratively to the plaintext in which there is no exteriority that is not interior and no interiority that is not exterior, the experience of the singularity of the "abyss of infinite non-existence, the Body Abysmal" (F, 191). The apocalypse is thus depicted as the moment when the "absolute exteriority of time-consciousness is the resurrection itself of the Body of the Finite God absolutely at the disposal of another. . . . Time itself for the first time is המקום, The Place, in which we live and move and exist, in which we have not 'our being,' but the being of the other being at the disposal of another" (F, 593). In the essentially new world, the temporality of time has become place—the use of the Hebrew term *ha-maqom*, one of the traditional rabbinic epithets for God, suggests that what Leahy has in mind is the divinization of time in the breakdown of the distinction between spatial and temporal dimensions. The divine status is also expressed by the image of the perpetuity and repetition of the circle. However, instead of Nietzsche's eternal recurrence, Leahy—in what strikes me as acquiescent with his interpretation of Kierkegaard (FP, 70–74)—speaks of the temporal occurrence, the absolute now that is concurrently beginning and end, not an eternity beyond time but an eternity instantiated in time, indeed the absolute temporality, immediately manifest as the freedom to exist in time, an ethical freedom secured theologically by the incarnation of the word that exists absolutely in the form of absolute thought.[12]

Within the parameters of the *linear circularity* of time, a locution that I have employed in my own thinking, the advance to the future is naught but a reversion to the past that is, paradoxically, a return to where one has never been. In this respect, there is affinity with Leahy's insistence that the repetition of creation—the word being spoken in essence in the time of the beginning that is the constantly renewed beginning of time—is creation thought for the first time in history (NM, 341). The duplication of the novel—the return of the same that is different—undergirds the movement of the circle of existence and renders ineffectual the distinction between actuality and possibility insofar as the moment at hand can be considered actual only in virtue of being possible and possible only in virtue of being actual; in the thinking now occurring, time is thought materializing as the obfuscation of thought: "*But it is precisely this possibility itself that is annulled in the absolute clarification of the absolute now occurring in reality in the form of the transcendental repetition of creation itself* (the essential repetition of history in thought), *in substance the absolute nullification of everything including thought itself* (in which, therefore, the history of thought is for the first time actually thought in essence), *transcendentally distinguished as now occurring in essence*" (NM, 360). Reiterating the point in slightly different terminology, Leahy writes: "The change of essence from potentiality, not to actuality, but to existence/existence itself, to actual/absolutely unconditioned actuality, the change of the law of identity itself from non-existence, not to existence, but to identity itself/the transcendence of the law of identity itself, to absolute existence/the absolutely unconditioned identity, the change of the circle to time/the absolutely unconditioned explosion of the circle, the specific transcendence of the circle/the explosion of the circle perpetuity, the time-transcendent change of time, measures the essence of existence, measures the essence of absolute balance, which essence, the species of the absolute measure, is, as such, itself the absolute balance: *the absolute balance, having no essence of its own, nevertheless absolutely exists*" (F, 160).

For our purposes what is most significant in this typically intricate passage is the thematic nexus between temporality and circularity. In particular, it is worth noting Leahy's remark that the circle changes into time, a variation he designates as *the time-transcendent change of time*, once more anchoring the thinking now occurring in the language of paradox—the change in time is transcendent of time. Time in its circuitousness is the measure of the essence of existence of the absolutely unconditioned explosion of the circle, the measure of the absolute balance. Diverging from the more traditional metaphysical idea of the absolute balance of the absolute form, Leahy introduces the counterconcept of the imbalance of the breach as a critical factor in understanding the absolute balance point and the time of the beginning (F, 521). Leahy's intent can be gleaned from the following passage:

> But the absolute complexity of the breach (at once the absolute transcendence of the merely essential complexity of the simple, of the absolute breach in its simplicity), the absolute repetition of the absolute breach absolutely without the division-within, is itself *the absolute breaching of balance itself with absolute identity,* such that the absolute transcendence of absolute imbalance is not in fact the restoration of absolute balance, indeed, it is in essence precisely not the absolute balance, rather the transcendence of the balance itself that is the absolute breach in its simplicity, the transcendence, even, of that balance itself an absolute balance only in the precise form of identifying the breach itself as the unsettling prop of philosophy in the form of the contra-actual conditional, viz., there is no absolute transcendence of the philosophical essence. (F, 157)

In a postmodern revision of the classical metaphysical understanding of identity as self-identity—that is, the determination of the identity of self from the standpoint of the coincidence of the self with itself—and its relation to the ideal of harmonization conjured by the image of the balance, Leahy proffers that, in the thinking now occurring, absolute identity is understood for the first time as the absolute explosion of balance, the "absolute complexity of the breach in the circle, such that where the circle was, indeed, even where the point of the circle was included in the midst of the logic of supplementarity so as to bend the circle beyond the point of recognition . . . there is now perpetuity itself. Where the circle was, indeed, where the noncircular violator of the circle was, there is now the transcendental imagination of change itself transcending in essence the absolute balance, itself an absolute balance only in the precise form of the absolute measure, only in the form of absolute coincidence itself, only in the precise form of that identity which is the absolute transcendence itself of the point of departure, only in the form of that absolute measure of the magnitude of being which is the form of the *absolute* separation of absolute difference from the point itself" (F, 157). Leahy's insistence that time emerges out of, and therefore is distinct from, the circle is consonant with his assumption that the perpetuity of identity is constituted by the explosion of identity; perpetuity ensues from the breach in the circle, that is, the permanence of the now consists of its impermanence and its impermanence of its permanence. Time is the other-than-self that engenders the absolute identity of the nonidentity of the other vis-à-vis the nonidentity of the identity of the self (F, 155).[13]

The depiction of the temporal interval as that which persists in passing and passes in persisting yields the proposition that genuine innovation consists of the repetition of the same that in each occurrence is altogether otherwise.[14] We can further presume that the nature of the beginning must always be *in medias res*; this paradox, argues Leahy, is fully ascertained in the thinking occurring now from the fact that the absolutely existent beginning is manifest as the center that is absolutely existent for the first time (F, 406).[15] As Leahy deduced from Augustine's discussion of the truth of faith and the relationship between things temporal and things eternal, "And, indeed, 'our beginning' is the middle of the middle, the very middle of the Incarnation by which [*per ortum nostrum*] we are united eternally to the eternity of the divine" (FP, 59).[16] The absolutely existent beginning thus assumes the nature of the middle; this middle is always existent for the first time, but it still occupies the position of the middle and therefore cannot be first unconditionally. Elaborating his belief in the beginning of a completely new existence, troped in the apocalyptic terms of the end of the old world and the beginning of the new world (FP, 158), Leahy avails himself once more of the image of the circle:

> The midpoint of fully apocalyptic consciousness is not the midnight of self-consciousness but midday, high noon, not the midnight opposite the beginning & end of the circle, but the midday after the end and before the beginning of the circle: the absolute point of arrival & departure: the I the beginning immediately end. The midpoint of fully apocalyptic consciousness absolutely explodes the circle: the apocalyptic circle is the perfect discontinuity or independence of its constituent points. Indeed the perfect independence in being of each constituent point of this circle is the reciprocal of the apocalyptic I which is Alpha & Omega, the beginning & end of the beginning & end of the circle. (FP, 162–63n43)

On balance, Leahy is far more emphatic about the unconditional nature of the beginning and the attendant novelty and uniqueness of his conception of the now, repeatedly contrasting the past with what is being thought in the present allegedly for the first time. In a tone that is almost kabbalistic in nature, Leahy writes about the experience of the absolute silence of the beginning, which is the experience of the actual quiescence of nothing:

> This Nothing is the pure beginning of a new world: the absolute first nothing, God the Creator nothing. Beyond the abyss of beginning which is the essence of modernity, this post-modern consciousness is the abyss of the first: not the beginning of the abyss, but the first abyss: the realization of the beginning of the abyss: not merely the beginning not the beginning, but the first not the first: *the beginning not the beginning absolutely*, the beginning of the beginning of existence, the beginning of Nothing. . . . This beginning is the end of Nothing in the form of the infinitely minute opening . . . in the form of the absolutely unconditioned pure possibility of imagination. (F, 600)

The new beginning that he envisions is the being beyond beyond being, that is, the being beyond the antinomy of being and nothing in which there is no thought of the triple negation of nothing: not nothing, not not nothing, not not not nothing (FP, 116–17).[17] As Leahy puts it in "Note to Faith and Philosophy Further to the Ontology of Real Trinary Logic" included as a backnote in *Beyond Sovereignty*: "In the thinking now occurring for the first time the beginning otherwise than the beginning of being not otherwise than being is the beginning of being and nothing otherwise than otherwise than x, or beyond beyond x. . . . Then the real trinary logic conception of existence absolutely differentiated for the first time is the beginning of absolute thisness, the beginning of the absolute here (and) now . . . THE NOT YET = BEYOND BEYOND X" (BS, 293–94).[18] Explicating this passage, Leahy comments: "The thinking now occurring for the first time—beyond hither and thither the beginning of consciousness—is beyond beyond x, beyond hither x and thither x, beyond the hither the beginning of consciousness of Levinas' absolute past and the thither the beginning of consciousness of Altizer's absolute future" (BS, 133). The thinking now occurring is the beginning of consciousness that is the absolute actuality thought essentially for the first time in the now that is beyond the historically specific forms of hither and thither attributed respectively to the absolute past of Levinas and the absolute future of Altizer. But the now, which is delineated as the beyond beyond x, is characterized as well as the not yet, a characterization that circumvents the law of noncontradiction insofar as the depiction of the now by the polar opposites of no more and not yet defies the principle that contradictory statements cannot both be true in the same sense and at the same time. Be that as it may, from Leahy's evaluation of the nature of the now we can infer that the beginning is the actuality of the inception of the temporal minimum in the absolute wholeness of the being of the finite, the infinitesimal that is, at once, the maximal minimum and the minimal maximum. The existence of the minimum assumes the form of the beginning that is the fractal wholeness of the absolute relative being, the new beginning that betokens the infinitivity of finitude, the imperishable perishability (BS, 13).

Each moment is steadfastly in the state of both "not having happened as of now" and "having ceased as of now," or in the symbolic notation used by Leahy, $\tilde{p}(/)\,\tilde{q}$, "not yet (/) not still" (BS, backnote 4, 311). The philosophical import of the present so construed bears affinity to Aristotle's conception of the now as the indivisible monad by which the mind measures the motion of bodies in time.[19] Particularly germane is Heidegger's account of the "double visage" (*eigentümliches Doppelgesicht*) of Aristotle's understanding of the now:

> Time is held together within itself by the now; time's specific continuity is rooted in the now. But conjointly, with respect to the now, time is divided, articulated into the no-longer-now, the earlier, and the not-yet-now, the later. It is only with respect to the now that we can conceive of the then and at-the-time, the later and the earlier. The now that we count in following a motion is *in each instance a different now*. To de nun dia to kineisthai to pheromenon aiei heteron, on account of the transition of the moving thing the now is always another, an advance from one place to the other. In each now the now is a different one, but still each different now is, as now, always now. The ever different nows are, *as different*, nevertheless always exactly *the same*, namely, now. Aristotle summarizes the peculiar nature of the now and thus of time—when he interprets time purely by way of the now . . . that is, in each now it is now; its *essentia*, its what, is always *the same* (*tauto*)—and

nevertheless every now is, by its nature, different in each now . . . nowness, being-now [*Jetztsein*], is always *otherness, being-other* [Anderssein] . . . the now is in a certain way always the same and in a certain way never the same. The now articulates and bounds time with respect to its earlier and later. On the one hand it is indeed always the same, but then it is never the same. . . . This constitutes its always being-now, its otherhood [*Andersheit*]. But what it always already was as that which it is, namely, now—that is the same.[20]

The subversion of the mathematical understanding of a chronological series, and the implied interpretation of time as an objective being or an existing actuality, and the positing of an alternate chronology is elicited by Heidegger from Aristotle's own attentiveness to the quality of *Jetztsein*, the time of the now that personifies otherness in virtue of its being *in a certain way always the same and in a certain way never the same*. This resonates with Leahy's assessment that the Aristotelian now, which is the measure of time, is depleted of temporal coordinates:

> The Now, for Aristotle, is to time as the moving object is to motion: that by which consciousness counts the time of motion (or rest); nothing moves through, or rests in, this Now. The coincidence of two times in one Now is actually no time at all; in actuality there is no coincidence in time. If two things, or two times, exist together, this is in virtue of their being between two Nows; this is to say that their coincidence in time is not an actuality, but a potentiality, since the identity of the period of time between the two Nows exists only in consciousness.[21]

Intriguingly, the meaning of the *now* in the thinking now occurring is similar to what Leahy attributes to Aristotle. For the former, as for the latter, the only dimension of time that is real is the present, but the present exists only between two nows, since it is no more and not yet, indeed no more because not yet and not yet because no more.

One might counter that my suggestion fails to heed Leahy's insight regarding the transtemporal status of the "now" in the thinking now occurring. The matter is articulated with characteristic density in the following passage:

> The absolute explosion of the complex absolute itself, in the form of the absolute perpetuity of an actually existing person, in the form of the essentially historical meta-matter of the *metanoēsis* which is *thought existing for the first time in the form of man*, which is man-thought/God-thought, species-thought/meta-thought, mid-thought/quantum thought (which *metanoēsis* is to *metanoia* as the transcendence of the *quantum* absolute is to the transcendence of the *unum* absolute, the proof of which proportion is: *the identity of the quantum absolute the meta-identity of the unum/the meta-identity of the unum the absolute minimum*: the *unum* absolute existing *ex nihilo, unity ex abysso, qua* product of history, freely existing in time without the necessity even for the capacity of dividing itself in two, *an absolutely unconditioned unicity*, the meta-material existence of the meta-conception of identity, which proof itself is thought itself transcending the analogy of being: for the first time the absolute analogy of being), is the absolute transcendence of time itself. . . . The absolute perpetuity of an actually existing person/the *metanoēsis* of an essentially historical meta-matter is the form of *the unum absolutely transcending—unity ex abysso*—the death of philosophy, the death of metaphor, the metaphor of death, the (now for the first time seen to be) absolutely pure nothing. (F, 179–81)

The christological underpinning of Leahy's language should be clearly discernible to the attentive ear from his remark concerning the complex absolute that assumes the form of the absolute perpetuity of an actually existing person, the essentially historical meta-matter of the *metanoēsis,* an event that both materializes historically and is historically beyond the material, indeed, beyond thinking, the *thought existing for the first time in the form of man,* the Word become flesh in the person of Jesus, the "abyss of the Godhead conceived in the form of the God-man" (F, 598).

It should come as no surprise that Leahy purports that reason conforms to faith for the first time in the thinking now occurring. Relating this shift in consciousness to the Aristotelian legacy that played such a dominant role in medieval theology and its aftermath, Leahy asserts confidently that "now for the first time occurs the *essential* clarification of the Aristotelian essence, the clarification of the essence of the Aristotelian essence. What now occurs for the first time in history is *the clarification of the created godhead*. This clarification is the perfect perception of the absolute quality of metanomous being, such that being *is* person, being *is* itself, person *is* itself, *itself* is person (nor is being anything but person)" (F, 161). The full repercussion of the Incarnation—the appearance in time of the transcendental essence of existence—is the breakdown of the distinction between object and subject, being and person, quality and quantity. The final binary affords Leahy the opportunity to expand—again, I would add, in language so pristinely logical that it lurches toward the periphery of the illogical—on the convergence of the scientific and theological implications of the thinking now occurring:

> The quantum identity of being *is* quality, *is* the freedom of personal identity, is the person's actual *itself*, the person's absolute existence. Just here in the midst of the absolute articulation itself of thought itself, in the absolute harmony itself of the absolute itself, in the midst itself of the perception of the absolute itself, in the absolute balance of personality itself, in the perception which is the discrimination of the midst of discrimination itself as voice itself itself articulating the absolute word, as the absolute in the midst of saying itself/the absolute saying itself in the midst of saying itself/the absolute absolutely interrupting itself, here in the midst absolutely without spatiality itself, in the identification of the interminable interruption itself, personality manifests itself, personality itself is manifest as the perception in essence of the voice of God saying itself "I am Christ," *itself* (the absolutely unconditioned balance itself) *the absolute quality of quantum: the voice of number itself singing the song of the absolute word*. The absolute quality of quantum itself is personality. Quality identical with quantum is metanomy. The absolute quality of quantum itself is being-bound-existence, existence itself, objectivity itself. Quality identical with quantum is existing thought, thought itself now very existence. (F, 161–62)

The now of the thinking now occurring is this metanoetic and meta-material *unum* that incarnates the identity of the meta-identity, the absolutely unconditioned unicity, the *unum* that absolutely exists ex nihilo, the abysmal unity, the maximum of the absolute minimum that is simultaneously the actuality of thought and the actuality of being.[22] This is a convergence that signals the death of philosophy as the death of the metaphor of death, a death that opens the possibility of the re-embodiment of the absolutely disembodied death, that is, the death of the disembodied Christ (F, 194), the absolute passion of existence understood as *Christ without Christ,* the "I Am speaking for the first time without existing in time, the first absolute silence" (F, 197),[23] a creation *ex abysso* that is the form of the immanence of the passion, a creation that transcends the opposition of transcendence and immanence, the absolute integration of the absolute disintegration that portends the existence of nonexistence (F, 195). Articulating the paradox in another passage, Leahy writes: "Occurring in time for the first time now, it is essentially historical, at once itself the transcendence of history. . . . The transcendental dichotomy is at once the transcendental dichotomy of time itself, the transcendental dichotomy of expectancy: the creation of an essentially practical existence, at once the beginning of an absolutely practical existence, in the form of the absolute now: an absolutely revolutionary consciousness transcending the difference between past & future in the form of the transcendence of expectancy, in the form of *time itself actually opening and expanding into a world,* in the form of time transcending temporality, in the form of time transcending the measure of time, in the form of time categorically the other, in the form of the end of time itself, in the form of the absolute objectivity of time, of the world itself—in the form of the appearance meta-identically the window" (F, 426).

The now of the thinking now occurring alludes to the timespace wherein the difference between potential and actual is dispelled, the absolutely new beginning of time expanding constrictively and opening up the window that is the world, the time of commencement that is the end of time, the time that transcends the measure of time, the time transcending temporality that is the absolute objectivity of time. But to the extent that the event to which Leahy refers is historical—a matter that is necessitated by his argument that his thinking for the first time discloses the phenomenological essence of the actually existing world (F, 87)—then it is difficult to accept the idea of an absolute novum. This seems contradictory to Leahy's own acceptance of the "essentially historical form of the death of God" as the "foundation of Christianity" (F, 603). To be sure, this foundation is "the necessity to create the elimination of history, that is, the essentially new foundation of

Christianity itself is the necessity to create the elimination of the actual death of the Godhead of God. The new Christianity is essentially the conception of the necessity to create the absolute elimination of nothingness. For the first time in history the very form of Christianity is the necessity of the elimination of nothing" (F, 603–604). The thinking now occurring is grounded in this radically diremptive understanding of the present severed from any organic connection to past or future, a new actuality that is the elimination of the beginning of nothing, a beginning that is the nothingness of beginning, that is, the resurrection of God as the beginning in which nothing begins, a beginning that is "beginning and ending at once" (F, 605). Leahy audaciously declares: *"What now occurs for the first time in history is the absolute penetration which is the absolute suspension of the process of beginning and ending/the absolute suspension of the beginning and ending of the process: the absolute unity of the absolute penetration is the midst itself absolutely existent for the first time, the absolutely existent beginning"* (F, 406).

It is credible to posit a sense of nowness that transcends the other two temporal modalities, but can we presume that the present has no link to what was or what will be? What meaning can we ascribe to Leahy's repeated oratorical appeal to *the first time*? Can there be a time demarcated as first that is not outside of time? Is not *for the first time* veritably a signpost of the beginning of time that is not in time at all and therefore not a beginning? Prima facie, it would seem that Leahy himself struggled with this very question in the following comment that both upholds and subverts the possibility of a first time that is the beginning of the being that is itself not being for the first time:

> The absolute species of being is for the first time *unum esse*. In the language of language itself *esse* is identical with *exsistere*. *Ipsum esse unum* identifies the absolute existence of being itself. For the first time very existence is the absolutely unconditioned transcendental identity. It is not as if existence itself were but a form, as if after the first there were no second itself, as if itself were not itself transcending itself for the first time, as if time itself were not the *existence* of the beginning, as if there were a being itself not being for the first time (in the absolute rupture from *metaphysics* of which contrary-to-fact condition consists *la différance*) but being in some mode (the generic essence of modernity being itself the not-being of something), being itself not

being but being something: the merely formal predicament of existence: the non-categorical existence either absolute idea or absolute matter. (F, 186–87)

Describing the intent of *Novitas Mundi*, Leahy writes that the "book sets out for the first time the transcendental limits of the essentially new form of thought which is what the new world's new thinking really is if it be really new" (NM, xi). In somewhat more pedantic language, Leahy elaborates:

> The appearance of the transcendental essence of existence itself is, in its being identically what has occurred to it during the course of its worldly being or being in time, that which makes that time *to be* what it is, identifying it through its transcendental essence with existence itself. . . . What we now see is truly seen for the first time. What we now see occurs through no necessity whatsoever. It is the manifest freedom of the fact of creation in history at this time. This critical occurrence of the transcendental essence of existence itself in thought is the essence of its history, manifested in the historical essence it is the *templative authority* of the history in essence of thought. In the essential history of thought, this world's *existence* is contemplated for the first time (a fact made possible by history's *essential indifference* to time); for the first time, what has occurred presents itself in absolute evidence. (NM, 6)

Moving beyond the more conventional options of an apotheosis of the particular into the universal or the corporealization of the universal within the particular, the thinking that is now occurring is the thinking of the transcendental essence of existence itself, a thinking keenly attuned to the contingency of the factual in the present liberated from the constraints of being determined by the past:

> In its faithful attention to the essence of what occurred to being in time, this thinking now existing brings each object into existence on its own terms without making those terms in themselves its object but only the appearance in them of the transcendental essence of existence itself. It is in the historical essence, through which each object in perpetuity is

> at once made wholly itself within that existence accounting for this world's existence, that everything comes into existence on its own terms. . . . This is the absolute evidence of purely *factual* contingency. This absolute evidence is in the thinking now occurring radically discontinuous in essence with every point of view that encumbers existence with its own perspective, imposing upon it a *logos* of its own, that is, a purely *logical* contingency, essentially unhistorical, by which the past is bound to its thinking, the essence of which is termination in itself, or *world-determination*. . . . But the termination of the transcendental essence of existence itself is the termination of essence in existence; its *appearance*, or *the essence of history*, terminates in existence itself, not in its *de*termination. (NM, 7–8)

I assent to Leahy's call for the need to uphold a new logic—*the logic of faith that is beyond modernity*—that will demonstrate the paradox of being "without meaning but not meaningless," transmitting the sense of *"being for the first time*. The logical category would be *being beginning*. Nothing other than being for the first time would be thought. . . . The essence beyond essence—the exception to essence that *is* essence—of a categorically new logic would be the essence of the new. For the first time the essence of logic would be novelty" (FP, 115). Moreover, this new logic will reclaim the beginning as the middle excluded by the logic of the excluded middle; that is, a beginning that is not the beginning of the end and therefore not a foreshadowing of the end of the beginning, but the beginning of the beginning that is always also the end of the end, albeit in a distinctly nontautological way.

> The mean proportionally this thing & that thing would be the excluded middle, the beginning. If this beginning is the excluded middle then this mean proportional is not the end of the beginning and the beginning of the end, but is the beginning of this thing, the beginning of the first term and the end of that thing, the end of the last term, the beginning of the beginning and the end of the end. . . . But then the thinking now occurring for the first time *is* the actual transcendence of the beginning of the thinking of modernity, the transcendence of the thought of the beginning as essentially the included middle, the transcendence of the

beginning of modern consciousness. . . . The thinking now occurring is otherwise than being not at the expense of beginning: the excluded middle is essentially & categorically the beginning of being. . . . The excluded middle is not able to be thought without being without beginning. But what is now thought for the first time is the transcendence of Kierkegaard's notion of the thoughtlessness of faith, thinking on the *far* side of thinking the included middle: thinking the excluded middle otherwise than thinking the included middle: thinking the excluded middle without thinking without the included middle (without thinking the thoughtlessness of faith) & without thinking together with the included middle (without thinking the transcendence of being before the beginning): thinking the excluded middle categorically the beginning of the beginning and the end of the end. Thought is now thinking the beginning of being otherwise than thinking the beginning of thought: thinking coming into existence without thoughtless faith & without beginningless transcendence of life. (FP, 115–16)

Two critical questions beg to be asked. First, has Leahy articulated the most felicitous understanding of newness, and second, is it possible to speak of a beginning that exists for the first time in history without presuming that there is a concatenation of successive nows, each coexisting in the absolute relativity of its own spatial-temporal dimensionality? Can there be an absolute now that breaks absolutely with the continuum of time, an absolute newness of an absolute creation,[24] the transcendence of being before the beginning that is the absolute transcendence of time? The presumption regarding such a possibility is what leads Leahy to relate the thinking now occurring in the third millennium—the *looking without a looking glass* (FP, 143)—to speculation about the apocalypse. Against the commonplace understanding, Leahy maintains that just as creation is not the demarcation of the beginning of the world as an event in the past but rather the beginning of the beginning, that is, the beginning that always begins anew, so the apocalypse is not just about the end of the old world or the beginning of a new world, but rather about the end of the end and the beginning of the beginning. "We are dealing not with the beginning now of the world, not with the creation of the world, but with the beginning of the beginning now of the world, not merely with the beginning, but with the beginning of the beginning. We are dealing not with the final now of the world, not with the end of the world, but with the end of the final now of the world, not merely with the end, but with the end of the end" (FP, 146). The now of the apocalypse is deemed "the first now of the world. Then the beginning of the new heaven and the new earth is the beginning of the universe now beginning. . . . For the first time the I now speaking is apocalyptic" (FP, 146–47). Implicit in this turn is the collapse of the temporal divide for the "not-yet is absolutely now" (BS, 232). To heed the imperative of the urgency of the apocalypse, consequently, is to discern that *tomorrow is now because now is tomorrow*. An absolutely new beginning logically necessitates an absolute ending of the beginning that is now ending. Leahy is attentive to this possibility and thus he theorizes that the "beginning of fully apocalyptic thinking is anticipated in previous conceptions of mind in the history of thought. But precisely because previous thought *anticipated* this beginning of an essentially new form of mind its actuality before now is precluded" (FP, 147).

With all due deference to Leahy, I would suggest that the pure immediacy of now occasions the reiteration of the new that renders the supposition of an absolute novum untenable. This plainspoken wisdom is deftly and succinctly expressed by Emmanuel Falque: "The new, in philosophy as in theology, cannot be formulated except insofar as it arises from what was there before."[25] Expressing the point more technically, Charles S. Peirce wrote:

> It does not, therefore, follow, because a new constituent of thought gets the uppermost that the train of thought which it displaces is broken off altogether. On the contrary, from our second principle, that there is no intuition or cognition not determined by previous cognitions, it follows that the striking in of a new experience is never an instantaneous affair, but is an *event* occupying time, and coming to pass by a continuous process. Its prominence in consciousness, therefore, must probably be the consummation of a growing process; and if so, there is no sufficient cause for the thought which has been the leading one just before, to cease abruptly and instantaneously. . . . There is no exception, therefore, to the law that every thought-sign is translated or interpreted in a subsequent one, unless it be that all thought comes to an abrupt and final end in death.[26]

One might demur that my criticism is too dependent on the modern logic that the thought now occurring for the first time seeks to depose. I would counter, however, that this overly historicized view of thinking has the capacity to obscure difficulties in the new logic of faith. Nuancing and further complicating the dispute with Leahy, I would submit that what was before can never be retrieved except as what has not yet taken place. Hence, rather than speaking of the thinking now occurring as existing for the first time historically, it is more accurate to speak of the present in which that thinking transpires as the reprise of what has always been what is to become. Utilizing a distinction made by Edward Said, we can say that the point of departure is inaccessible because it is not a transitive property determined by an anticipated end or an expected continuity; it is rather a radical and intransitive starting point that has no object other than its own relentless clarification. The beginning is thus "*making* or *producing difference*; but—and here is the great fascination in the subject—difference which is the result of combining the already-familiar with the fertile novelty of human work in language."[27] By his own admission, Said's conception is indebted to the Husserlian phenomenological reduction whereby the search for the absolute beginning leads to its own undermining inasmuch as the beginning shows itself sensuously only as the beginning constructed intentionally in the constitution of the intuitive object that "attains original givenness in and with the *form of a temporal duration*, rendering an encompassing and objective unity possible."[28] Even in its immanent essence as an absolute givenness, the beginning is always noetically at a distance from being the beginning of the beginning of being.[29]

The logic of this argument can be adduced further from Husserl's remark in the lectures on the internal time consciousness of 1905: "But this *question of origin* is directed towards the *primitive* formations of time-consciousness, in which the primitive differences of the temporal become constituted intuitively and properly as the original sources of all the evidences relating to time."[30] Phenomenological apperception is not concerned with the empirical genesis whence the intuitions of objective space and objective time evolve, but only in the immanent sense and descriptive content of the experiences (*Erlebnisse*) bracketed from the natural standpoint and the ensuing epistemological inquiry into the presumed existence or nonexistence transcendent to consciousness. As Husserl boldly states, "We do not fit experiences into any reality. We are concerned with reality only insofar as it is reality meant, objectivated, intuited, or conceptually thought. With respect to the problem of time, this means that we are interested in the *experiences* of time.... We seek to bring *the a priori of time* to *clarity* by exploring the *consciousness of time,* by bringing its essential constitution to light, and by exhibiting the apprehension-contents and act-characters that pertain—perhaps specifically—to time and to which the *a priori* temporal laws essentially belong."[31]

The origin, then, is not an objective time that can be calculated instrumentally by the ego in the world of physical things and psychic subjects, but it is rather the interior time of the eidetic experiences accessible phenomenologically and not psychologically.[32] When gauged from this vantage point, the origin of time can never be something that originates in time, and thus the essence of the *arche* inessentially is *an-archic*. Husserl himself, it is worth recalling, defined philosophy more generally—although obviously phenomenology is privileged—as "a science of true beginnings, or origins, of *rizōmata pantōn*."[33] But the true beginning is the beginning that cannot begin. The constant quest for origin, which is the watchword of phenomenology as the science of pure phenomena, to go back to the things themselves (*zur Sache selbst*), is perforce a recoiling to the domain where the very question of origin is interrogated as the origin of the question. At the beginning stands the impasse of the beginning. In lieu of a unitary point whence all things originate, we find a fold, duplicity, contravention, the doubling of infringement that marks the way of the beginning in the beginning of the way.

A similar account, albeit betraying the influence of both Husserl and Merleau-Ponty, is offered by John Sallis: "Radical philosophy is a peculiar *return to beginnings,* a turning towards what already determines it. It is a circling which sets out from the beginnings so as to return to them, which it can do only if in its circling it never really leaves them.... Radical philosophy, as return to beginnings, is thus simultaneously a turning towards its own beginnings, towards those beginnings with which the return to beginnings is initiated."[34] I would add, by way of amplification and not dissension, that the return to the beginning is a return to where one has never been because the very notion of beginning, as Sallis himself wrote elsewhere, is always a "redoubling—which is to say no beginning at all."[35] The beginning bears the paradox of existing only "after the fact," that is, it "has always already been the beginning," but if this is so, then there is no beginning that has not begun prior to beginning and therefore destabilizing the very possibility of beginning.³⁶ In Derridean parlance, the onset can never be anything but second, an echo, a trace, the "originary iterability."³⁷ Only that which is distinct can be duplicated, since what recurs is invariably the same difference that is indifferently the same.

No one can deny the pioneering and far-reaching ramifications of the thinking now occurring. The contributions of Leahy, if they will be properly considered by future generations, are enormous and consequential. Nevertheless, the entire edifice, in my opinion, rests on an unstable foundation. The conception of time that buttresses his philosophical project, the assumption that something utterly new can appear in history for the first time, is problematic, as is his hypothesis regarding an absolute now that summons "the beginning of the end of the world in essence, the beginning of the end of time itself" (F, 423). I concur with Leahy that the beginning of existence is the beginning of consciousness, which comprises the consciousness of the beginning, and hence every now begins the transcendence of consciousness that is the body (F, 422). This is a major evolution of thinking that has the capacity to promote a new universal consciousness as Leahy sincerely believed. However, the question is what semiotic valence do we accord to the notion of newness, and this, in turn, very much depends on how we assess continuity and discontinuity across the temporal divide. Leahy is committed to the notion of the embodiment of the body/consciousness in an omnipotence that is *an infinitely open infinite particularity beginning* (BS, 121). But can the possibility of a beginning that is infinitely open and therefore infinitely indeterminate, on the one hand, and infinitely particular and therefore infinitely determinate, on the other hand, be sustained ontologically, ontically, or phenomenologically? Let us consider Leahy's fuller elucidation of this possibility, which enters into more detail regarding the nature of identity and nonidentity, perception and memory, repetition and becoming:

> In the delicate factuality of transparent identity complementarity itself is absolutely transcended: memory itself absolutely coincides with perception, absolutely exists in the delicate transparency of perception, the simulacrum which is no simulacrum, the product of an absolute repetition, identity itself. The repetition of absolute self-identity, the absolutely impossible repetition, actually now occurs as the existence of absolute difference, the absolute difference of existence. . . . Indeed, memory itself for the first time is

the absolute transcendence of the negation within actuality by actuality itself. In memory itself for the first time there is absolutely no trace, no repetition of the becoming itself of absolute subjectivity, no repetition of repetition itself, no actual trace of trace itself. The absolute indifference of memory itself to becoming itself is identity itself absolute. Identity is the absolutely unconditioned indifference of memory itself to becoming. Memory absolutely unconditioned indifference is identity to becoming: the actual repetition of repetition the absolutely unconditioned trace of the trace is identity itself, the transcendent identity of the simulacrum of the simulacrum (of the simulacrum which is no simulacrum) is the transcendence of non-becoming itself absolute: the absolute becoming itself of identity is identity itself. . . . There is no non-identity arising out of the repetition of perpetuity . . . there is the absolute repetition of absolute existence, the perpetuity of existence itself. There is absolutely no alternative to actual identity. The absolute other of identity itself is not other-than it, because absolute identity itself is not other-than. (F, 144–45)[38]

Self-identity, as we might expect, is correlated with repetition, which is dependent on memory that itself coincides with perception, but Leahy qualifies this ostensibly innocuous premise as absolutely impossible. He states nonetheless that this impossibility is actually now occurring as the existence of absolute difference, which is the absolute difference of existence. Again, we confront the dialectical drift of the thinking now occurring: repetition is what fosters difference.

Presumably, the possibility of the absolutely impossible repetition alters the nature of memory as it assumes the quality of the absolute transcendence of the negation within actuality by actuality itself, which I further suppose is the import of the reference to the absolute indifference of memory to becoming itself, an unconditional indifference that is the ground for absolute identity. Even more astonishingly, Leahy proclaims that for the first time there is absolutely no trace in memory, no repetition of the becoming of absolute subjectivity, no repetition of repetition, no actual trace of the trace. The absolute becoming of identity is still linked to the absolute repetition of absolute existence, the perpetuity of existence in relation to which there is no other-than, but in the absence of any trace or repetition, then we must presume the nonidentity of subjective identity is constituted by a monadic sense of time. In the flow of the divine stream of existence consequent to the "absolute elimination of the death of God," imagined as the apocalyptic vision of the new beginning at the end, "every notion of self is completely dissolved. . . . There remains neither the 'almost nothing' enveloped in the pure 'nothing,' nor the pure 'nothing' enveloped in the 'almost nothing.' . . . What now actually occurs is the perfect envelopment of the beginning of which the Torah speaks essentially. The *totality* of being *after* nothing, the totality *not* after (either) being (or) nothing (the totality of being *not* after 'either nothing or . . .'), i.e., no *from/out of* nothing, is the absolutely existing edge, the edge every part of which is identical with the edge itself. . . . To create the absolute edge is to begin to operate *essentially* without reference to self: time *after* nothing is neither not 'our' now, nor 'our' place" (F, 592–93). In somewhat less technical terms, Leahy explicates the interface between the experience of the absolute manifestation of God's presence vis-à-vis the alterity of the cosmos and the augmentation of self through its diminution that is characteristic of the new conception of essence that is integral to the essentially new world proffered by the thinking now occurring:

> Being & nothing, whose truth I am not & whose truth is not the truth of the I that I now am, being & nothing, neither left to nothingness by God, now, as such, for the first time constitute the complete matter of the body's unmirrored consciousness. The object of a completely objective consciousness beyond presence is the core of the created world. The something wasted by God is the objective I whose entire content is the created world whose truth is absolute otherness & whose form is absolute gift. . . . Everything I am is not mine; yet I am it completely. Everything I have is not mine; yet I have it completely. Everything I make is not mine; yet I make it completely. The infinitely transparent I is the surface identifying body and world absolutely. . . . Every I that I meet objectively is not me; yet I meet it completely in differentiating it. (FP, 159)

One can reasonably protest this dissolution of self on the grounds that it is based on the conception of a now that can be atomistically severed from other points of the timeline—indeed, the very notion of the timeline disappears—such that we can speak cogently of the event at the terminus of history emerging disjunctively *ab initio*. It is not, however, clear that this is a feasible or justifiable position. I would argue to the contrary that there can be no first time that is not a repetition of the past, no last time that is not an anticipation of the future, no novelty that is not a genuine iteration of the present. Hermeneutically, what is brought forth each moment is a renewal of what has been, albeit always from a different vantage point. To speak of redemption as the act of creation now beginning, therefore, is to discern that what is new is new precisely because it is old, that what is disclosed in the guise of the unprecedented is a concealment of what was formerly revealed. Closer to the mark are Leahy's own statements to the effect that the beginning is the opening that is the nucleus of the circle, expanding into a world by bending back on itself, the dead center measured *ex abysso,* the void absolutely eliminating nothing/eliminating absolutely nothing (F, 429–30), the measure of the substantial nothingness, the not nothing, lacking measure (F, 434), the middle of the middle through which eternity is temporalized and temporality eternalized.

Notes

1. Martin Heidegger, *Being and Time*, trans. Joan Stambaugh, rev. and with a foreword by Dennis J. Schmidt (Albany: State University of New York Press, 2010), §36, 165 (*Sein und Zeit* [Tübingen: Max Niemeyer, 1993], 171): "This Greek interpretation of the existential genesis of science is not a matter of chance. It brings to explicit understanding what was prefigured in the statement of Parmenides: τὸ γὰρ αὐτὸ νοεῖν ἐστίν τε καὶ εἶναι. Being is what shows itself in pure, intuitive perception, and only this seeing discovers being. Primordial and genuine truth lies in pure intuition. This thesis henceforth remains the foundation of Western philosophy. The Hegelian dialectic has its motivation in it, and only on its basis is that dialectic possible" (§36, 165).

2. Georg Wilhelm Friedrich Hegel, *The Science of Logic*, trans. and ed. George di Giovanni (Cambridge: Cambridge University Press, 2010), 25; *Wissenschaft der Logik. Erster Band: Die objective Logik. Erstes Buch: Die Lehre vom Sein (1832). Zweites Buch: Die Lehre vom Wesen (1813)* [Hauptwerke 3] (Hamburg: Felix Meiner, 2015), 29.

3. Elliot R. Wolfson, "*Via Negativa* in Maimonides and Its Impact on Thirteenth-Century Kabbalah," *Maimonidean Studies* 5 (2008): 404–5nn32–34; Rollen E. Houser, "Avicenna and Aquinas: Essence, Existence, and the *Esse* of Christ," *The Saint Anselm Journal* 9 (2013): 1–21; John F. Wippel, "The Latin

Avicenna as a Source for Thomas Aquinas's Metaphysics," *Freiburger Zeitschrift für Philosophie und Theologie* 37 (1990): 51–90, esp. 57–59, 67–72 (reprinted in John F. Wippel, *Metaphysical Themes on Thomas Aquinas II* [Washington, DC: Catholic University of America Press, 2007], 31–64). See also John F. Wippel, *The Metaphysical Thought of Thomas Aquinas: From Finite Being to Uncreated Being* (Washington, DC: Catholic University of America, 2000), 134–37, 405–406, and references to other studies on the influence of the Latin translation of Avicenna's *Metaphysics* on Aquinas, 230n114.

4. For discussion of Leahy's exposition of the *missa jubilaea*, see Thomas J. J. Altizer, *History as Apocalypse* (Albany: State University of New York Press, 1985), 244–48. Altizer's own rumination on the eucharistic festival of the *missa jubilaea*, the "all-inclusive Mass that encompasses the entire cosmos," is discussed by Mark C. Taylor, *Tears* (Albany: State University of New York Press, 1990), 64–65.

5. From a scientific perspective, how can we intelligibly construe the idea of the conversion of the universe into an entirely new stuff? It is more viable to assume that the transformation is a matter of how one perceives the nature of matter vis-à-vis the mind. Thus, commenting on Leahy's passage, Altizer, *History as Apocalypse*, 245, writes: "The universe is converted into an entirely new stuff when the universal body of humanity finally appears and is real as the Lamb of God, and therefore in and as that Eucharistic table wherein and whereby the matter of the universe becomes the apocalyptic and sacrificial body of God. Nothing is more fundamental to this cosmic and apocalyptic metamorphosis than a radically new integration of mind and matter, of body and soul, as body or matter finally becomes indistinguishable from both the center and the depths of mind and consciousness. Accordingly, a real presence that once was real in the moment of consecration and thereafter now becomes real in a cosmic and universal epiphany."

6. See previous note. And compare the description of the apocalyptic vision in *Foundation* that the world will be revealed "to be such a novelty that man cannot stand even so much apart as to be a participant, so as to (merely) *take* part in the creation of the world, avoiding thereby the absolute responsibility of creating a new world" (F, 592).

7. D. G. Leahy, "The Epidermal Surface"; http://dgleahy.net/p40.html. See Lissa McCullough, "D. G. Leahy," in *The Palgrave Handbook of Radical Theology*, ed. Christopher D. Rodkey and Jordan E. Miller (New York: Palgrave Macmillan, 2018), 271: "Revelation occurs not in this or that selective event or moment; rather, the history of thinking reveals in due time that existence itself is universally and essentially revelatory. Matter, the Body itself—this absolutely particular, absolutely differentiated, infinitely finite poly-ontological existence—is holiness itself." On polyontology, see also Alina N. Feld, "Teilhard de Chardin and D. G. Leahy: Philosophical Foundations for Sustainable Living," *Knowledge and Enchantment: A World without Mystery? The Twenty-fourth Ecumenical Theological and Interdisciplinary Symposium, December*

3, 2016 (New York: The Romanian Institute of Orthodox Theology and Spirituality, 2017), 40–41.

8. In contrast to the Hegelian dialectic, which entails a sublation of the difference between antinomies and their resolution in a higher synthesis, the neologism *dialetheia*, in defiance of the logical principle of noncontradiction and the law of the excluded middle, signifies that there are true contradictions and thus a statement can be both true and false at the same time and in the same relation, the contradictory nature of which is syllogistically diagrammed in the form of "α and it is not the case that α." See Graham Priest, *Beyond the Limits of Thought* (Oxford: Oxford University Press, 2002), 3; idem, *In Contradiction: A Study of the Transconsistent*, 2nd ed. (Oxford: Oxford University Press, 2006), 3–6. For an extended discussion of dialetheism and the problem of truth and falsity, see ibid., 53–72. Leahy repeatedly makes use of this logic. To mention one example, instead of saying that the absolutely now is a beginning that transcends the dyad of beginning and end, he will speak of the beginning and end of the beginning and end, which implies that we posit and negate the beginning and the end. Another useful path of inquiry would be to compare the symbolic logic of the thinking now occurring and the tetralemic logic of the path of the middle way (*madhyamaka*) of the Mahāyāna Buddhist tradition, which can be diagrammed as S is P; S is ~P; S is both P and ~P; S is neither P nor ~P. Both of these possibilities would force one to reconsider the accuracy of Leahy's constant insistence that the consciousness of the thinking now occurring is occurring for the first time in history.

9. Alain Badiou, *Saint Paul: The Foundation of Universalism*, trans. Ray Brassier (Stanford: Stanford University Press, 2003), 11. For an analysis of this passage and Badiou's portrayal of Pauline universalism, see BS, 50–51, and compare the comments of Leahy, BS, 70, on the relation of sameness and equality in the universal promulgated by Paul as discussed in Badiou, *Saint Paul*, 109. See also Audronė Žukauskaitė, "Ethics between Particularity and Universality," in *Deleuze and Ethics*, ed. Nathan Jun and Daniel W. Smith (Edinburgh: Edinburgh University Press, 2011), 188–206.

10. For a related critique of Leahy, see Thomas J. J. Altizer, *The Apocalyptic Trinity* (New York: Palgrave Macmillan, 2012), 164. After noting that the total realization of the *novitas mundi* only occurs in Leahy's "thinking now occurring for the first time," Altizer qualifies his statement: "Nevertheless, this radically new thinking is in deep continuity with a purely Catholic thinking, and is even in continuity with the radically Protestant thinking of Kierkegaard, for Leahy's is unquestionably a Christian thinking, and the first Christian thinking since Hegel's which is a universal thinking" (164). This is not to say that Altizer does not acknowledge the novelty of the new thinking promulgated by Leahy; he extols that newness by emphasizing that Leahy is "a truly postmodern thinker even as Hegel is a truly modern thinker." I agree with Altizer's observation, however, that the radically new thinking is in continuity with older Christian sources. My own attenuation of Leahy's

recurrent claim to innovation—most often marked by the expression *for the first time*—is based on a varied approach to the nature and cadence of temporality.

11. See also Altizer, *History as Apocalypse*, 245–46.

12. A less christological presentation may be elicited from the comparison of Nietzsche and Levinas in *Faith and Philosophy*: "Caught up in the inversion of the entire framework of consciousness, the conversion of the eternal recurrence of all things to the immemorial temporality of the recurrence of oneself to the other on the hither side of self is the conversion beyond being alike of the evil & the good, of the one willing & the one not willing to sacrifice oneself for the future, the conversion indifferently of each to the futuration of the future, both the 'last man' & *le surhomme* indifferently converted to the self, despite itself, immemorially sacrificed for the other. The inversion of consciousness in Levinas is the recurrence of oneself to an irrecuperable past which is at once the *imperative* signification of the future (beyond being & nothing), in which the future (beyond present & future) & the truth (beyond falsehood & truth) prevail (beyond good & evil) at the expense of the will, in which irrecuperable past the self, despite itself, is devoted to the Other" (FP, 108).

13. In Heideggerian terms, time gives itself and refuses itself simultaneously; in the giving that gives time, the bestowal is commensurate to the withholding; indeed, the givenness can be given only as ungiven in the same manner that what is unthought is the most crucial dimension of a thinker's thought. See Martin Heidegger, *What Is Called Thinking?* trans. Fred W. Wieck and J. Glenn Gray (New York: Harper and Row, 1968), 77; *Was Heißt Denken?* [GA 8] (Frankfurt: Vittorio Klostermann, 2002), 83; Martin Heidegger, *On Time and Being*, trans. Joan Stambaugh (New York: Harper and Row, 1972), 15–16; *Zur Sache des Denkens* [GA 14] (Frankfurt am Main: Vittorio Klostermann, 2007), 20. Leahy contrasts his conception of time as it relates to the beginning and the end with Heidegger's view of the authentic classification of the three modalities of time as expectancy (*Gewärtigen*), retention (*Behalten*), and making-present (*Gegenwärtigen*), as opposed to the vulgar understanding of time as a sequence of nows—now (*jetzt*), not yet now (*jetzt noch nicht*), and now no longer (*jetzt nicht mehr*) (F, 423–24). The text that Leahy cites is Martin Heidegger, *The Metaphysical Foundations of Logic*, trans. Michael Heim (Bloomington: Indiana University Press, 1984), 202–203; *Metaphysische Anfangsgründe der Logik im Ausgang von Leibniz* [GA 26] (Frankfurt am Main: Vittorio Klostermann, 1978), 261–62. In my assessment, Leahy's position is closer to Heidegger than he acknowledges, but this is a matter that needs to be pursued separately.

14. My formulation is indebted to Martin Heidegger, *Contributions to Philosophy (Of the Event)*, trans. Richard Rojcewicz and Daniela Vallega-Neu (Bloomington: Indiana University Press, 2012), §33, 58; *Beiträge zur Philosophie (Vom Ereignis)* [GA 65] (Frankfurt am Main: Vittorio Klostermann, 1989), 73. Heidegger writes that the wish to navigate the course of the question of being, in the hope of recuperating the lineage of antiquity, can be fulfilled

if one comprehends that the matter of repetition means "to *let* the *same*, the uniqueness of being, become a plight *again* and *thereby out of a more original truth*. 'Again' means here precisely 'altogether otherwise' [»*Wieder*« besagt hier gerade: ganz anders]" (§33, 58). Regarding this aphorism, see Elliot R. Wolfson, *Giving Beyond the Gift: Apophasis and Overcoming Theomania* (New York: Fordham University Press, 2014), 243–44, and "Retroactive Not Yet: Linear Circularity and Kabbalistic Temporality," in *Time and Eternity in Jewish Mysticism: That Which Is Before and That Which Is After*, ed. Brian Ogren (Leiden: Brill, 2015), 33–34.

15. See also F, 160–61: "The intelligible absolute exists in the form of existence itself, neither its own form nor that of another, but in the form of absolute existence, in the form of the essentially new reality, in the form of the absolute transcendence, of the absolute existence, of the middle term which *is* reality, of the reality which *is* the middle term."

16. On the importance of Augustine to Leahy, see FP 116: "The new thinking now beginning is the return to Augustine after Levinas."

17. Concerning *being beyond beyond being*, see BS, 298: "It is precisely here that the thinking now occurring for the time qua beyond beyond x is clearly able to be seen to be not only beyond origin, beyond the God, beyond cause, but to be consequently the nonbeing of Heidegger's originary sovereignty, the nonbeing of own-dom, the nonbeing of avoidance of the Good: thinking for the first time actuality absolutely now. Beyond beyond being (beyond the Good, not the Good and not not the Good, beyond the God, beyond the One) thought essentially the act of world-creating, the absolute simplicity of act of existence for the first time."

18. See BS, 71: "For Badiou what there is is nothing else than differences, what there is is infinite alterity. Infinite alterity *is*, the situation *is*, the world *is*. In the thinking now occurring this infinite alterity that is the essence of the world is otherwise than being—neither being nor not being: infinite alterity/ what there is the essence of the world begins absolutely now . . . infinite alterity otherwise than being—essence the exception to essence beginning absolutely now." Leahy attempts to contrast his affirmation of the radical particularity of being implied in the universality of divine omnipotence from Badiou's view that "the world remains as the nonsublatable substrate of infinite differences: differences are subsumed by sameness but not thereby sublated: differences are not contradicted but supplanted by the universal, but therefore supplanted in the form of an infinite procedure, the conception of whose completion is the creative fiction that forces the transformation of the situation." It seems that, in his mind, Leahy proffered an even more radical sense of the infinite alterity for which is the no sameness that would level out the differences of each particular embodied manifestation of the eventfulness being. See BS, 85, where Leahy explains that the claim "same for all" implies a "circulation of sense" that is "infinitely interrupted" and hence "infinitely open to the newness of existence," the "existence of truth as *singularity absolutely particularized*— singularity actually embodied in existing omnipotence." And compare BS, 89:

"It follows from the omnipotent unconditioned embodiment of every-thing for the first time that nothing is not contained in nothing. Every-thing except nothing contained in nothing is embodied in omnipotence—every-thing embodied in omnipotence is the actual annulment of the void. There is then nothing but infinite alterity. There is no Same to which the infinity of differences might be compared. There is nothing but the infinitely evental being of existence itself—being-here infinitely that identifies the readiness of consciousness whose readiness for being is the form of faith." I find Leahy's depiction of the omnipotent embodiment of polyontological difference as the annulment of the void to be compatible with Heidegger's reflections on the nothingness of beyng, bracketing the obvious disparity generated by Leahy's commitment to his Christian heritage. I detect a similarity to Heidegger as well in the rejection of an idealist resolution to the problem of sameness and difference in BS, 104: "The disorganization that *is* organization, the disorder that *is* order, is a not a breaking in two of a One. Nor is unity, unbroken by the infinite alterity of existence itself, a Same. The unity beyond the One—the unity beginning absolutely now—is the absolute otherness of omnipotence itself now embodying that which embodied omnipotence when hitherto omnipotence compared itself to the creature. As such the unity beyond the One, unity *ex abysso*, is the simplicity that is existence itself: the simplicity of omnipotence the embodiment of infinite & unconditional difference(s)."

19. See the extensive discussion of the Aristotelian perspective in NM, 157–161.

20. Martin Heidegger, *The Basic Problems of Phenomenology*, trans., intro., and lexicon by Albert Hofstadter (Bloomington: Indiana University Press, 1982), 247–48; *Die Grundprobleme der Phänomenologie* [GA 24] (Frankfurt am Main: Vittorio Klostermann, 1997), 349–51.

21. NM, 160.

22. See F, 88: "The absolute minimum is actuality itself for the first time. This minimum absolute itself is knowledge, the actuality of thought itself, being itself, to which in the new state of the world there corresponds no essentially unrealized potentiality, but which, itself, is an actually new saying."

23. Compare what Leahy writes in *Beyond Sovereignty*: "God without Christ for the first time is God beyond the God—not the God and not not the God: the very existence of God without the very existence of God: not passionless God without Christ but Christ without Christ, very existence the passion of Christ, the very Christ embodied in very Omnipotence. In the thinking now occurring what is essentially conceived for the first time is not the essentially unhistorical God who does not take place but is the taking place of whatever takes place, but, rather, God the taking place of all things the very essence of history the perfect simplicity of being who takes place not taking place. This is precisely the absolute exteriority of everything the very passion of Christ" (BS, 184). Leahy's paradoxical depiction of God as the simplicity of being that *takes place not taking place* can be fruitfully compared

to Heidegger's idea of the fullness of the bestowal of beyng in the refusal of beyng to bestow, that is, the nihilating ground of the nothingness that withdraws from all beings in the giving of the gift of beyng. This, too, is a matter that requires a separate treatment.

24. See BS, 243n70, where the author adduces a mathematical proof to support his idea concerning the ninefold nature of the beginning by utilizing the Hebrew expression *ḥiddush gamur*, "Absolute Newness"/"Absolute Creation." See also BS, 296n11. I will not reproduce the details of the argument, but those familiar with Leahy's thinking are well aware that he developed his own form of an alphanumeric code to reinforce many of his abstract ideas by calculating the mathematical value of Hebrew expressions. See, for example, the impressive list of Hebrew terms in *Foundation*, 692–96. In the preface to *Foundation*, Leahy contrasts the meta-identity of language and number conceptualized in his approach in Section III.5 of his treatise and the traditional *gemaṭriya*: "The methodology for the mathematical reading of language there employed is essentially distinguished from the *gematria* of the ancients and the kabbalah by virtue of the fact that letters are treated in an essentially mathematical way, viz., as elements in a proportion or members of a series of ratios, and no substitutions are allowed" (F, xv). The contrast is then repeated: "The reader is, by the way, cautioned to bear in mind that the methodology for the mathematical reading of language employed here and below in the text is essentially distinguished from the *gematria* of the ancients and the kabbalah by virtue of the fact that the number-values of letters in the ancient languages are for the first time in history treated in an *essentially* mathematical way, viz., *as elements in a proportion or members of a series of ratios*, and no substitutions are allowed, and that these and other related significant technical differences distinguish this methodology from earlier and, in *some* respects, similar practice, thereby reflecting the essential novelty of the new world consciousness set forth in this work as a whole" (F, 357n13). There is no question that the complexity of Leahy's mathematical reading of language is to be distinguished from the traditional numerology, but it seems to me that here, too, he exaggerated the sense of novelty with regard to the claim that this is the first time in history that letters are treated in an essentially mathematical way. Moreover, there seems to be some confusion on his part with regard to the matter of substitution. I assume what he means is that the traditional practice of *gemaṭriya* assigns a numerical value to a word or a phrase, and at times that word or phrase is linked to another word or phrase that has the same numerical value. This does not detract from the fact that the assumption underlying this technique is that there is an intrinsic relation between the word or phrase and the number itself, and that the purpose is to anchor an independent idea to that word or phrase through the numeric association. To my mind, this is precisely what underlies Leahy's practice as well even though his mathematics is far more intricate. Bear in mind that Leahy described the thinking now occurring for the first time as the cracking of a

code; see F, 428n147. The quasi-kabbalistic method of Leahy merits a separate treatment. To return to the aforementioned note from *Beyond Sovereignty*, Leahy refers to Moses Cordovero's use of the expression *ḥiddush gamur* based on the discussion in Elliot R. Wolfson, *Alef, Mem, Tau: Kabbalistic Musings on Time, Truth, and Death* (Berkeley: University of California Press, 2006), 75. A close scrutiny of my analysis, however, actually proves the very opposite of the conclusion Leahy attempted to elicit in support of his notion of the absolute novelty of an absolute beginning. Cordovero does refer to creation as *ḥiddush gamur*, since there was nothing prior to it; but he also speaks of the time-that-was-no-time (*zeman she-eino zeman*) and the moment-that-was-no-moment (*et she-eino et*) in which the infinite brings forth everything into being. From this we may deduce that an absolute creation does not mean there is an absolute newness in the manner that Leahy construes it, that is, an absolute beginning that begins absolutely. For Cordovero, as for other kabbalists, the beginning is not absolute in this manner; on the contrary, the beginning—conveyed by the word *bere'shit*, the opening of the Torah—is the first that is second. The newness of creation, therefore, is a renewal, an iteration of the origin that is always veiled in the disclosure of the beginning. See Wolfson, *Alef*, 119–26. Compare the Christological reading of the first verse in Genesis, *bere'shit bara elohim et ha-shamayim we-et ha-areṣ*, to elicit the idea of the beginning of the absolutely unconditioned body, the dead center or the point zero of energy, the absolute transparency of consciousness, in Leahy, *Foundations*, 505. In that context as well, Leahy combines the exegetical method of *gemaṭriyah* and the mathematical method of integral calculus (see F, 522, 528, 584).

25. Emmanuel Falque, *The Metamorphosis of Finitude: An Essay on Birth and Resurrection*, trans. George Hughes (New York: Fordham University Press, 2012), ix.

26. Charles S. Peirce, "Some Consequences of Four Incapacities," in *Collected Papers of Charles Sanders Peirce*, ed. Charles Hartshorne and Paul Weiss, vol. 5 (Cambridge: Harvard University Press, 1934), sec. 284, 170.

27. Edward W. Said, *Beginnings: Intention and Method* (New York: Basic, 1975), 72–73, xvii.

28. Edmund Husserl, *Experience and Judgment: Investigations in a Genealogy of Logic*, rev. and ed. Ludwig Landgrebe, trans. James S. Churchill and Karl Ameriks, introduction by James S. Churchill, afterword by Lothar Eley (London: Routledge and Kegan Paul, 1973), 157.

29. Said, *Beginnings*, 48–49.

30. Edmund Husserl, *On the Phenomenology of the Consciousness of Internal Time (1893–1917)*, trans. John Barnett Brough (Dordrecht: Kluwer Academic, 1990), 9. For an alternative version, see Edmund Husserl, *The Phenomenology of Internal Time-Consciousness*, ed. Martin Heidegger, trans. James S. Churchill, introduction by Calvin O. Schrag (Bloomington: Indiana University Press, 1964), 28.

31. Husserl, *On the Phenomenology*, 9–10; compare the alternative translation in Husserl, *Phenomenology of Internal Time-Consciousness*, 28–29.

32. Edmund Husserl, *The Idea of Phenomenology*, trans. Lee Hardy (Dordrecht: Kluwer Academic, 1999), 33, 35.

33. Edmund Husserl, *Phenomenology and the Crisis of Philosophy*, trans. with an introduction by Quentin Lauer (New York: Harper and Row, 1965), 146.

34. John Sallis, *Phenomenology and the Return to Beginnings* (Pittsburgh: Duquesne University Press, 2003), 17.

35. John Sallis, "Doublings," in *Derrida: A Critical Reader*, ed. David Wood (Oxford: Blackwell, 1992), 120. The position I have articulated regarding the circle opened at both termini is to be contrasted with the "closed temporal lines" implied in the scientific assumption (traceable to Kurt Gödel) that the structure of the light cones—the oblique lines that delimit the discrete phenomena that fill the gravitational field of spacetime—displays a continuous trajectory in the present toward the future that returns to the originating event of the past. See Carlo Rovelli, *The Order of Time*, trans. Erica Segre and Simon Carnell (New York: Riverhead, 2018), 52–53. On the illusory nature of the present and, by extension, of time more generally, see Carlo Rovelli, *Seven Brief Lessons on Physics*, trans. Simon Carnell and Erica Segre (New York: Riverhead, 2016), 59–60; idem, *Reality Is Not What It Seems: The Journey to Quantum Gravity*, trans. Simon Carnell and Erica Segre (New York: Riverhead, 2017), 175–83. Consider the summation offered by Rovelli in *Reality*: "We must learn to think of the world not as something that changes in time. . . . Things change only in relation to one another. At a fundamental level, there is no time. Our sense of the common passage of time is only an approximation that is valid for our macroscopic scale. It derives from the fact that we perceive the world in a coarse-grained fashion. Thus, the word described by the theory is far from the one we are familiar with. There is no longer space that 'contains' the world, and no longer time 'during the course of which' events occur. There are elementary processes in which the quanta of space and matter continuously interact with one another. Just as a calm and clear Alpine lake is made up of a rapid dance of a myriad of minuscule water molecules, the illusion of being surrounded by continuous space and time is a product of a farsighted vision of a dense swarming of elementary processes" (182–83). And see the stark evaluation later in the book, which underscores the gap separating our ordinary perception and the scientific perspective: "We are too used to thinking of reality as existing in time. We are beings who live in time: we dwell in time, and are nourished by it. We are an effect of this temporality, produced by average values of microscopic variables. But the limitations of our intuitions should not mislead us. . . . Time is an effect of our overlooking the physical microstates of things. Time is information we don't have. Time is our ignorance" (252).

36. Hans-Jost Frey, *Interruptions*, trans. with an introduction by Georgia Albert (Albany: State University of New York Press, 1996), 23. For a similar formulation of the paradox of the temporality of the beginning, see Wolfson, *Alef*, xiii, 131–32.

37. Jacques Derrida, *Specters of Marx: The State of Debt, the Work of Mourning, and the New International*, trans. Peggy Kamuf, introduction by

Bernd Magnus and Stephen Cullenberg (New York: Routledge, 1994), 163. See citation and discussion of some other Derridean sources on the nature of the beginning in Wolfson, *Giving*, 184–85, and the analysis of the circle and the trace in John Protevi, *Time and Exteriority: Aristotle, Heidegger, Derrida* (Lewisburg: Bucknell University Press, 1994), 76–110.

38. Leahy cites and analyzes part of this passage in BS, 121–22.

3

A Metaphysics of Enchantment or a Case of Immanentizing the Eschaton?

GRAHAM JAMES McALEER

We Christians have erased the whole sphere of the gods.

—Jacques Lacan

To talk about the bottom of the universe
The way it truly is, is no child's play,
No task for tongues that gurgle baby-talk

—Dante, *Inferno*, Canto 32

Is the world alive? Is there a cosmos? Does God or do gods reign? Do furies and demons stalk us? If so, the modern dream of human sovereignty—humanitarianism—is punctured and constraints on our self-creation exist. The metaphysical precondition for humanitarianism is disenchantment. Leahy is a critic of modernity, but is his a metaphysics of enchantment?

Descartes inaugurates the age of disenchantment. Prior to Descartes the stars were visible gods and the cosmos ornamental, Aphrodite's spell adorning the work of Zeus.[1] In Homer, arrows had will and might disobey the bowman.[2] Plato thought all reality shot through with *Eros*,[3] and in Aquinas's metaphysics matter desires.[4] The world was enchanted with magic and alchemy. Rémi Brague points out that Aquinas does not even raise a skeptical eyebrow when talking about magic, never mind demand the stake for magicians.[5] These gods and powers withered quickly with Descartes's division of reality into *res cogitans* and *res extensa*. There are thinking things, *res cogitans* like you and me, and all the rest—including our dogs and cats—is just matter in motion (*res extensa*). Enchantment now consisted in consciousness and otherwise the world was mechanical, dead matter moving in predictable arcs described in laws that held fast throughout space.

Descartes also gave a graphic example. Looking out of his window he observed hats and cloaks moving about down in the street below. He chastised himself for thinking people were in the street when, for all he knew, beneath the hats and capes might be automatons. Descartes was enchanted but could he be sure anyone else was? It did not take long for other thinkers to take the hint and collapse Descartes's division. La Mettrie proposed "the material unity of man": you and I are just like Descartes's cats and dogs, mere matter in deterministic motion.[6] Today, disenchantment is the ruling orthodoxy and the reason our universities and cultural publications reject the idea of a living cosmos.

Descartes has proven resilient, for heterodoxy abounds. By this I do not mean that eighty-five percent of the world's population still proclaims the Spirit or spirits in formal religion—and legions more consult psychics, mediums, and are "spiritual but not religious"—but rather that thinkers of the first rank recoil from disenchantment. Sixty years after Descartes, Leibniz gave us the monads: a hundred years after the monads, Kierkegaard was brooding about the utter peculiarity and unpredictability of God's will, and today's undergraduates thrill to the arguments of Schopenhauer and Nietzsche that fundamental reality is surging will. What about Leahy?

A Catholic thinker of astonishing range and subtlety, Leahy's metaphysics invokes God and the Church, "the blood witness to the love of God" (NM, 356). His *Novitas Mundi* is a brilliant work of philosophical theology. I will argue, nonetheless, that Leahy's metaphysics reaffirms disenchantment. Elsewhere, drawing on each of Leahy's books, I have argued that Leahy's metaphysics is univocal.[7] Let me press that case again: Leahy is right to ponder the soteriological character of metaphysics, only his univocity can get no further than humanitarianism.

In his *Analogia Entis* (1932), Jesuit theologian Erich Przywara distinguishes three types of metaphysics: the univocal, equivocal, and analogical. The univocal fuses God and nature, the equivocal isolates them, and the analogical links them, despite significant abiding distinction. Historically, Catholic theology began to judge metaphysical systems by this rubric in 1215. The Fourth Lateran Council affirmed analogical metaphysics as orthodox and the Council's talented enforcer was Thomas Aquinas.

The rubric was polemical, a way to steer Catholic theology away from the influence of Joachim of Fiore. In my opinion, Leahy is a Joachimite. Eric Voegelin argues that Joachim is the inspiration behind modernity: "Joachim created the aggregate of symbols which govern the self-interpretation of modern political society to this day."[8] His univocal metaphysics fused man and God with the consequence that human powers are valorized. Przywara puts it this way: Joachim construes "the trinity of God as a human society of three persons" (AE, 373). He posited an identity between the communion of the divine persons and the Church understood as a collective, "just as many persons are called one people, and many believers one church" (AE, 353). The model for God is an idealized human gathering, "spiritual monks," a perfect blending of insight and love (AE, 358). Deep in the Middle Ages, Joachim sowed the seed of humanitarianism and the Lateran Council jumped into action purifying schemas "of all dreams of identity" (AE, 423).

Joachim crafted the transcendental form of modernity—his "spiritual monks" becoming an expert technological administrative state obedient to humanitarian sympathy managing perfectly our needs. Divine logos fused with the providential state, Voegelin famously identifies as Gnosticism and dubs "the immanentizing of the eschaton." The salvific modern state offers itself as an enchantment: people experience nature purified, made into a benevolent cosmos by a cadre of experts. In *Post-Modern Natural Law*, I argue this is a false promise for a metaphysics of morals that affirms personal dignity requires a "posture of distance" (Przywara). Leahy's metaphysics runs the risk of immanentizing as he repeatedly affirms the soteriological as clarity, a motif both epistemological and ethical. The role of clarity in Leahy's personalism is the particular focus of my essay.

Christ sits at the heart of Leahy's metaphysics: being, knowledge, and history entwined; the "story which is identically what has occurred to the storyteller" (NM, 193). The life of Christ is a "rift in time,"[9] "perfect clarification of essence,"[10] an offer made to every human being to enter into clarity: "The clarification of the luminous opacity of the essence of the human person is the historical occurrence *par excellence*" (NM, 194). In Leahy, metaphysics is an icon onto this narrative. In becoming coincident with Truth, we share in Christ's "perfect ease of access," at the ready for service (NM, 194, 233).

Clarity is the suspension of self. This is Leahy's signature thesis: "the form of a new world absolutely without self to begin with. . . . In this light it is seen that appropriation itself is the final form of impenitence" (NM, 346). Univocity—the metaphysical term for the human inherence in the story of Christ: "In the thinking now occurring there are no elements in essence apart from the elements of Christ" (NM, 345)—secures clarity, releases us from the grip of the Notion of the Self (NM, 357) and frees us into generous service.[11] The cosmos, and human reality itself, has the form of a "gentle friend" (NM, 345).

The hint that something might not be quite right in this metaphysics of morals is found in Przywara: he casts the soteriological as the "babbling of the babe" (AE, 500). Lacan's Schema L—a challenge to the idea that story and storyteller coincide—gives psychoanalytic confirmation of Przywara. The Schema L shows that language puts us at a distance from ourselves. There is (perhaps)[12] a difference: in Lacan, distance is alienation, but in the *analogia entis* solemn veneration. And yet further confirmation: it is an astonishing vision, but Leibniz conceives of his monads as babbling babes shimmering in gardens.

Leibniz, a principal figure in *Novitas Mundi*, is judged critically to have built a bridge across the "rift in time," to have hidden clarity behind the cloak of reason (NM, 214). At the start of *Fear and Trembling*, Kierkegaard argues that Descartes is wrongly accused of being the source of disenchantment. For Leahy, Leibniz is a strident rationalist (NM, 199) but I think he is more theological than Leahy allows. He is a panpsychist—the position that every piece of matter is conscious. Leahy does not address Leibniz's panpsychism[13] but it culminates in an image of monads as gardens, a potent way to think about enchantment.

In Leibniz, the ultimate constituents of reality are monads and each is alive, having perceptions to highly varying degrees. He offers an arresting image: "Every portion of matter may be conceived as like a garden full of plants and like a pond full of fish. But every branch of a plant, every member of an animal, and every drop of the fluids within it, is also such a garden or such a pond. . . . There is, therefore, nothing uncultivated, or sterile or dead in the universe (*The Monadology*, pars. 67, 69)"[14]

How to grasp this image of a monad as like a garden full of plants? It surely recalls the ancient motif of God as gardener but what does it mean for a metaphysics of morals?

Modernity sits uneasily with the Leibnizian vision of the garden. Leahy argues that modernity denies history and the limit it puts on the future: for an essential dream of modernity is independence from constraint, whether natural or historical (NM, 193): "not history, but a blueprint for engineering" (NM, 194). Fascinated by machines and computational logic he may have been, but Leibniz's conception of a garden teeming with life suggests a restraint on engineering.

Leahy focuses on Leibniz's claim (NM, 197) that each monad asserts a natural right that God weigh its worth when pondering which possible essences to make actual (M, 55, par. 51): "each possible thing having the right to claim existence in proportion to the perfection which it involves" (M, 56, par. 54). In Augustine, creation is prompted by mercy. In Lacan, wit—the play of language—creates us (E, 712 [840]). In Leibniz, creation is a requirement of justice. Leahy draws a contrast with Thomas. In Thomas, possible essences stem from participated existence with God prior to which they existed "not at all," whereas in Leibniz "their claim to exist is recognized by God" (NM, 198). Leahy cleverly dubs the monads' claim of justice the "Republic of Being" (NM, 198). In this telling, it strongly suggests that Leibniz thinks the possibles are not truly created ex nihilo. In that case, God's act of creation is curtailed by an order to which God must, in some measure, defer. Instead of the asymmetry of divine decision there is a symmetry imposed by obligation. Such a metaphysical conception Leahy calls a "bridge built over the rift in time" (NM, 200), a disenchantment.

Are Thomas and Leibniz as far apart as Leahy believes? In the fourteenth and fifteenth centuries, metaphysicians traded blows over whether God could create contradictory natures: Was God's power able to strip a nature bare and craft it anew with utterly different properties? Thomists argued not.[15] Leibniz follows the Thomists: "For God, in comparing two simple substances, finds in each one reasons obliging him to adapt the other to it" (M, 55, par. 52). Natures expressing necessary truths are the "inner objects" of God's consciousness (part of the logic of understanding itself) while natures expressing contingent truths are products of will, God's "choice of the greatest good" (M,

54, par. 46). These natures or *rationes* are brakes on engineering and Leahy's gloss clearly overstates Leibniz's position: possibility contains "within itself the reason for its own existence. This is a claim upon God to exist" (NM, 204, 208).[16] In the Thomistic tradition these *rationes* are the source of the natural law: "A doubt arises whether it would not be enough for all human law to derive from positive law? What need is there for it to derive from natural law? The reply to this is that even positive divine law itself is to a certain degree dependent on natural law, because God 'ordereth all things graciously' (Wisdom 8:1). Hence there has never been a divine law which did not have some reason in natural law."[17]

Gardening is an endeavor to arrange things graciously—a point well understood by Tolkien.[18] It depends on harmonics, a guided fitting together of value tones or *rationes*. Leibniz is famous for his theory of preestablished harmony—the idea that the soul and body are coordinated not by their own actions but by the operation of God. The moral and aesthetic implications of this idea—the monads shimmering as mirrors—are missed if Leibniz's panpsychism is skipped over.

Leibniz seems so rational and computational because he speaks of the body as a "divine machine or natural automaton" (M, 58, par. 64) but it is crucial to appreciate that the body *is* the intentional object of the perceptual acts of the monads. Matter is consciousness. In Leibniz, the presentational objects of consciousness are machines because organized by God according to predictive laws. Monads are never without perceptions and so monads are always linked to space and time: intentional objects appear *as* in space and time. The perceptions of the monads are automata but not the desires of the monad. These desires seek fulfillment in presentational objects and always attain them to a degree (M, 49, par. 15). This is the distinction between appetite and manifold (M, 48, par. 11 and 12).

All monads have bodies—gardens! By preestablished harmony, the value tones of these gardens and landscapes are organized by God and gifted to monads as their bodies.[19] God does not have a body and is outside the cosmos being its inventor, prince, and father (M, 61, par. 84). The possible essences are, says Leibniz in another image, like parts in a play, though "there are only a few chosen ones which come out upon a greater stage" (M, 60, par. 75). Monads look upon their bodies, landscapes not of their own making: it follows from the distance implied by harmony—hence the conceit of the mirror (M, 56, par. 56)[20]—that monads are not examples of the "story which is identically what has occurred to the storyteller." Indeed, the life of the garden goes on beyond the ken of the monad:

> There are at every moment numberless perceptions in us, but without apperception and without reflection; that is to say, changes in the soul itself of which we are not conscious. . . . These *minute perceptions* are then of greater influence because of their consequences than is thought. It is they which form I know not what, these tastes, these images of the sensible qualities, clear in the mass but confused in the parts. . . . These insensible perceptions indicate also and constitute the identity of the individual, who is characterized by the traces or expressions which they preserve.[21]

Leahy's gloss on this passage: "Thus the radical passivity of modern thought, displayed in its inability to maintain itself transparently face to face with the transcendental essence of existence [Christ]" (NM, 212). Here, once more, clarity conveys univocity. But is it true that God in Christ is utterly and unreservedly available? The distance implicit in preestablished harmony suggests not: there is no suspension of the *missa solemnis* in favor of a *missa jubilaea* (per Leahy). *Novitas Mundi* closes with a meditation on the Mass but the phenomenology of the Mass shows it to have the character of a game, to be role-play, exhibiting a posture of distance.[22] No matter the intimacy with God, analogy puts us at a distance, and it is for this reason Dante's God dumbfounds: a point of light. Solemnity is the only adequate response to such wonder.

In Przywara, the "babbling of a babe" is the symbol of "the babbling of the *Mysterium Mysteriorum*" because to see God face to face is to know God personally, but not God personally through and through. The *analogia entis* cannot be suspended: "the in-and-beyond of the 'symbol' is immediately transparent to the in-and-beyond of the Divine *Mysterium Mysteriorum* that resides in-and-beyond all divine manifestations and revelations, however great" (AE, 500).[23] The "babbling of a babe" is not a bad accounting for the personalism emerging from Lacan's psychoanalysis. His thinking blocks any hope for the ideal of "spiritual monks," as persons have little in the way of insight or kindness. The possibility of humanitarianism is foreclosed because the furies are back.

For Lacan, the basic problem psychoanalysis addresses is identity. Identity is fraught—"donned armor of an alienating identity" (E,

78 [97])—inescapably mixed up with affirmation and aggression, the desire for recognition. This tussle begins in our own psyches—Lacan's famous "mirror stage":[24] a tussle compounded and exacerbated because inextricably linked to establishment, public structures of recognition (E, 708 [835], 715 [843]).

Persons understand themselves through words and symbols. There is no self-definition that does not rely on these means of communication: "the radical defile of speech" (E, 40 [53]). This fact necessarily puts each of us at a distance from ourselves.[25] I am "precipitated" (E, 76 [94]) and cannot know precisely what causes me. Parts of language—words, clothes, institutions—are sustained through the intricate constellation of signs that gives relative meaning to each part: one part is comprehensible only through connection with another (E, 416 [499]). Indeed, multiples are generated, and not multiples of "me," but multiple semblables: what Lacan calls "staging" (E, 425–26 [511–12]). Thus, the primary experience of each person is "the drama of primordial jealousy" (E, 79 [98]), the semblables contesting within "me" (E, 717 [845–46], 436 [524]). This is what Lacan calls the barred subject.[26]

I am a barred subject because only able to approach my being through the ever-shifting meaning of others about me[27]—my adornment for good or ill: "spangling the space of spectacular communion" (E, 92 [113])—and the law shaping those meanings (castration). This being is therefore always and forever closed off from me (E, 433 [520]): because castrated, being itself is barred to me, yet I forlornly seek it out again and again (*jouissance*), unity and cohesion sought rather than partibility (E, 692–93 [817–818]). Though the language is different, there is clear continuity between Lacan's personalism and Leibniz's idea of a life of the garden beyond the ken of the monad: the signifying chain that generates me cascades bewilderingly (E, 709 [835–36]; and see *The Monadology*, 58, par. 65).[28] If Leibniz gives us gardens based on harmony and symmetry, Lacan's gardens are Gothic. This personalism has more theological resonance than might at first be thought. Przywara directs us to Augustine's idea that the core of each of us is *secretarium tuum* (AE, 262). *Secretarium* is derived from *secernere* and can mean secret or inner room and has links to ideas of put asunder and private papers. The linguistic sundered self—*secretarium tuum*—matches nicely Lacan's idea of the barred subject. I am not in identity with myself in the secret room. It is not the impregnable me but me barred, for the *secretarium* is a "mirror in an enigma," says Augustine: I grasp my definition but only as a reflection of "an infinity of incomprehensibility," God enacting the analogy of being (AE, 264).

What does this mean phenomenologically? What is it like for an enigma to offer me a reflection of myself? Przywara turns to Augustine again: "Before they might be they are not, and when they are they are fleeting away, and when they have fled they no longer are." Thus, best to think of persons "just as a spoken work of art depends upon each verse, each syllable, each letter 'passing away'" (AE, 245). Who am I? A plaited self:

> And it is precisely the contrariety of things contending with one another (to the point of mutual extinction) that plaits them into a unity: "Beauty is composed from the opposition of the world's contraries" (Augustine). The only appropriate posture, then, is that of "flowing with what flows" ("I confess that I endeavour to be ranked among those who, having made some progress, write and who, through writing, continue to progress" [St. Paul]). (AE, 265)

A posture of obedience, a humble bow to myriad value tones, links the barred subject with being, shifts each of us from not to Is. Adorned by values—refinements of gardens, machines, fashion, commerce, institutions, festivals, and liturgy—we are plaited through veneration. Ultimately, this adornment is the beauty of God. As Augustine writes: "God through whom all things, which of themselves would not exist, tend towards being. God who does not allow to perish even that which mutually destroys itself."[29]

Our universities and other institutions of the "commanding heights" live in a disenchanted world: for them, there are no gods or furies. These same "commanding heights" are a product of Joachim's humanitarianism, however, for his univocal metaphysics gave us the transcendental form of modernity. By placing Leahy's work alongside Leibniz, Lacan, and Przywara, I wanted to show that his treatment of clarity relies on univocity and thus his metaphysics of morals inevitably repeats Joachim's "immanentizing of the eschaton" (Voegelin).

The barred subject is the psychological reality of the analogy of being. Neither sufficient (univocal) nor abandoned (equivocal) we are adorned by a love that draws us from possibility into being (analogy). I do agree with Leahy about "the eucharistic essence of existence itself" (see chapter 5 of my *Ecstatic Morality and Sexual Politics*), but to move beyond modernity a cosmological soteriology must needs be analogical. Leibniz rejects the idea that the universe is "uncultivated, or sterile or dead" and puts a constraint on humanitarian engineering by enchantingly thinking of reality as cascading gardens and landscapes. Adorned by values—refinements of gardens, machines, fashion, commerce, institutions, festivals, and liturgy—we are plaited through language (Lacan) and veneration (Przywara). Obedience to distance suspends the grip of the transcendental form of modernity. The dark night of the barred subject is the psychological reality of the cosmic response (*missa solemnis*) to the mystery of love, the inner reality of which is the "night of God's marriage on the Cross," the "night of God's going out into the night of the most real night of the creature" (AE, 612).

Notes

1. Max Scheler, *The Nature of Sympathy*, with an introduction by Graham McAleer, trans. Peter Heath (New York: Routledge, 2017), 85; Erich Przywara, *Analogia Entis: Metaphysics; Original Structure and Universal Rhythm* (Grand Rapids: Eerdmans, 2014), 489; hereafter cited as AE.

2. Henry Home, Lord Kames, *Essays on the Principles of Morality and Natural Religion* [1779], ed. Mary Catherine Moran (Indianapolis: Liberty Fund, 2005), 28.

3. Scheler, *The Nature of Sympathy*, 82–84.

4. Graham James McAleer, *Ecstatic Morality and Sexual Politics: A Catholic and Antitotalitarian Theory of the Body* (New York: Fordham University Press, 2005), ch. 1.

5. Rémi Brague, *The Kingdom of Man* (Notre Dame: University of Notre Dame Press, 2018), 53–54.

6. For a skeptical examination of the assumptions of physicalism, see the work of Philippe Goff, which I discuss here; https://www.lawliberty.org/book-review/materialist-oh-and-about-modern-sciences-disenchantment-of-the-world-not-so-fast/.

7. See Graham James McAleer, *Erich Przywara and Postmodern Natural Law: A History of the Metaphysics of Morals* (Notre Dame: University of Notre Dame Press, 2019), ch. 5.

8. Eric Voegelin, *The New Science of Politics* (Chicago: University of Chicago Press, 1952), 111.

9. "The clarification of human essence is metaphysically a change of being itself" (NM, 195).

10. "To that clarification of his own essence in which he exists transparently in the knowledge itself of existence, or as himself a manifestation of the glory of God" (NM, 194).

11. "The world itself in essence is the body itself, is the living flesh of Jesus the Nazarene transformed into being here at the disposal of another in essence" (NM, 348).

12. It is not clear that Lacan is right to observe alienation rather than veneration as the final human reality since his account of language—which is constitutive of being—repeats the in-and-beyond logic of analogy: "between this shy of [*en-deçà*] the Subject and this beyond [*au-delà*] of the Other" (Jacques Lacan, *Écrits*, trans. B. Fink [New York: Norton, 2006], 40 [54]); hereafter cited as E.

13. The following is not right: "Leibniz' perpetuation of the separation of spirit from matter effected by Descartes" (NM, 196).

14. G. W. Leibniz, *Discourse on Metaphysics and The Monadology*, ed. Albert R. Chandler, trans. George R. Montgomery (Mineola, NY: Dover, 2005), 58–59.

15. For example, could God make fire naturally cold? For a summary of the debate and why it matters, see Francisco de Vitoria, *On Homicide* (Milwaukee: Marquette University Press, 1997), 71–73. Przywara and John Paul the Great follow de Vitoria and contemporary Thomists who think of the divine ideas along the lines of Gottlob Frege's objective object are, I think, right; http://vivianboland.blogspot.com/2012/06/freges-third-realm-and-aquinas-on.html. Like a Thomist, Leibniz makes the content being of possibles dependent upon divine being (M, 54, par. 43).

16. Leibniz is surely in line with tradition, pondering: "It is certainly doubtful among theologians and philosophers: Whether God can change the nature of things or could have from the beginning made them other than they are now" (Vitoria, *On Homicide*, 71).

17. Francisco de Vitoria, *Political Writings* (Cambridge: Cambridge University Press, 1991), 173.

18. Graham McAleer, "Gardening and Nobility in Tolkien," September 16, 2018; https://voegelinview.com/gardening-and-nobility-in-tolkien/.

19. Interestingly, Andy Warhol thought of the body as a landscape.

20. For a remarkably similar idea in Dante, see the first nine lines of *Paradiso*, Canto 28.

21. A passage from Leibniz's preface to *New Essays on the Human Understanding*, quoted by Leahy (NM, 211).

22. See the concluding chapter of McAleer, *Post-Modern Natural Law*.

23. "The *Mysterium Mysteriorum* is even more rooted in the reality of God as the *ens realissimum*, whereat and wherein it appears as unapparent" (AE, 500).

24. Jacques Lacan, The *Seminar of Jacques Lacan: The Ethics of Psychoanalysis, 1959–1960*, vol. 7, ed. Jacques Alain-Miller, trans. Dennis Porter (New York: Norton, 1997), 261; henceforth cited as S7.

25. "In the irreducible margin as well as at the limit of his own good, the subject reveals himself to the never entirely resolved mystery of the nature of his desire" (S7, 237).

26. This barred subject that I am—and you, too—begins in language even before we are born. Who I am as a baby is always already shaped by the food my mother ate, the managerial and commercial conditions that made food available, what the baby books said about child development, the smoking, drinking, or yoga that was fashionable at the time, and thus also the medical and juridical environment in which early life is fostered, cancelled, or postponed. I am always who others have wanted me to be, or not to be.

27. "Thus, if man comes to think about the symbolic order, it is because he is first caught in it in his being" (E, 40 [53]).

28. "What we must say is: I am not, where I am the plaything of my thought; I think about what I am where I do not think I am thinking" (E, 430 [517]).

29. Augustine, *Soliloquies* 1.1.2, as quoted in AE, 265n222.

PART II
APOCALYPTIC ACTUALITY

4

Apocalypticism in Modern Thinking

Descartes, Hegel, Leahy

THOMAS J. J. ALTIZER

While the power of apocalypticism in Western history is now acknowledged, we have little sense of its power or even meaning in thinking itself, and this despite the fact that so many of our primal modern thinkers, such as Hegel, Marx, and Nietzsche, have manifestly been apocalyptic thinkers. Indeed, the very advent of modernity can be understood to be an apocalyptic event, an advent ushering in a wholly new world as the consequence of the ending of an old world. Nowhere was such a new world more fully present than in thinking itself, a truly new thinking not only embodied in a new science and a new philosophy, but in a new reflexivity or introspection in the interiority of self-consciousness. This is the new interiority that is so fully embodied in the uniquely Shakespearean soliloquy, but it is likewise embodied in that uniquely Cartesian internal and radical doubt that inaugurates modern philosophy. Cartesian philosophy could establish itself only by ending scholastic philosophy, and with that ending a new philosophy was truly born, and one implicitly if not explicitly claiming for itself a radically new world. That world can be understood as a new apocalyptic world, one that becomes manifestly apocalyptic in the French Revolution and German Idealism, and then one realizing truly universal expressions in Marxism and in that uniquely modern or postmodern nihilism that was so decisively inaugurated by Nietzsche's proclamation of the death of God.

Yet a truly modern subject or "I" is a doubled or self-alienated center of consciousness, and is so in a uniquely Cartesian internal and radical doubt, one never decisively present in previous cognitive or philosophical thinking, although its ground had been established by Augustine's philosophical discovery of the subject of consciousness. Even as Augustinian thinking had been deeply reborn in the late Middle Ages, thence becoming a deep ground not only of the Reformation but also of Cartesian thinking, this new modern subject that is now established and real is an interiorly divided subject, and so much so that its internal ground is a truly dichotomous ground. Nothing else is so deeply Augustinian in modern thinking and in modern consciousness itself, and if Augustine discovered the subject of consciousness by way of his renewal of Paul, it was Paul who discovered the profoundly internal divisions and dichotomies of consciousness and self-consciousness. This is the Paul who is so deeply renewed in the dawning of modernity, but also the Paul who was the creator of Christian theology, a theology that, if only in Paul, is a purely and consistently apocalyptic theology, and Paul's realization of the ultimate polarity or dichotomy of consciousness is an apocalyptic realization, one reflecting an apocalyptic dichotomy between old aeon and new aeon, or flesh (*sarx*) and Spirit (*pneuma*).

Descartes himself acknowledged that his *cogito ergo sum* is already fundamental in Augustine's philosophy (letter to Andreas Colvius, November 14, 1640), and he believed that his philosophy was the first to demonstrate the philosophical truth of the doctrine of transubstantiation, and could go so far as to claim that scholastic philosophy would have been rejected as clashing with faith if his philosophy had been known first (letter to Marin Mersenne, March 31, 1641).[1] Indeed, nothing is more revolutionary in modern philosophy than its dissolution of the scholastic distinction between natural theology and revealed theology. This initially occurs in Descartes and Spinoza, but it becomes far more comprehensive in Schelling and Hegel, and so much so that the whole body of dogmatic theology undergoes a metamorphosis into pure philosophical thinking in Hegel's system. So it is that in the preface to the *Phenomenology of Spirit* (§11), Hegel can declare that ours is a birth-time and a period of transition to a new era, for Spirit has broken with the world it has previously imagined and inhabited, and is now submerging it in the past, and doing so in the very labor of its own transformation.[2] While the new Spirit has thus far historically arrived only in its immediacy, it is destined soon to transform everything whatsoever, a transformation that is clearly an apocalyptic transfiguration. Just as we can now know that Jesus was an apocalyptic prophet who proclaimed and enacted the actual dawning of the Kingdom of God, a comparable dawning occurs in the advent of a uniquely modern thinking, each promises a finally total transformation, and each calls for a total break from an old aeon or old world.

Such an ultimate break is already manifest in the birth of modern science, a revolutionary event issuing in the realization of an infinite universe, a universe in which the *physica coelestis* and the *physica terrestris* are unified if not identified, and also a universe in which every formal and final cause has disappeared. Descartes's was the first philosophy to incorporate this revolutionary transformation, but Descartes believed that God is the universal cause of everything in such a way as to be the total cause of everything (letter to Elizabeth, October 6, 1645), and such a totality of God is profoundly deepened not only in Spinoza but throughout German Idealism.[3] Thus we discover the paradox, most purely in Spinoza but most comprehensively in Hegel, of a deeply pantheistic philosophy that is nevertheless a deeply atheistic philosophy, atheistic in its dissolution of the absolutely transcendent God, but pantheistic in knowing the absolute totality of God, and a totality of God that is inseparable from a negation of the pure transcendence of God. Twentieth-century Protestant theology will discover such an atheism in every philosophical theology, but this is clearly a reaction to a uniquely modern philosophy, and a modern philosophy that is implicitly if not explicitly an apocalyptic philosophy, and is so in its very calling forth of a new totality.

Nothing is so unique in apocalypticism as is its enactment of a new totality, an absolute novum that is the polar opposite of a primordial totality, but a novum in full apocalypticism that is already dawning or near at hand, just as it is in Jesus's initial eschatological proclamation that the time is fulfilled and the Kingdom of God is immediately at hand (Mark 1:15). Nowhere in modernity is apocalypticism more open and manifest than it is in our great political revolutions, and if these begin with the English Revolution, this was our most apocalyptic revolution until the French Revolution, a revolution that innumerable thinkers at that time—and above all Hegel himself—could know as the ending of an old world and the inauguration of a truly new and universal world. This is an apocalyptic ending that here, too, is known as the end or the consummation of history, an ending that is comprehensively embodied in Hegel's philosophy. Nothing so clearly unveils Hegel's system as an apocalyptic system as does this ending, but such an ultimate ending is unique to apocalypticism, for even if it parallels archaic visions of eternal return, it wholly differs from all primordial vision in knowing an absolute and final ending, an ending that is apocalypse itself. This is that unique ending which is not only a repetition or renewal of genesis, but far rather an absolutely new beginning, a new creation or new aeon, and absolutely new because it wholly transcends not only an original creation but an original eternity as well. All of the major German philosophers of the time responded to the French Revolution as just such a beginning, and the French Revolution is the deepest historical ground of German Idealism, thereby giving it a historical actuality found nowhere else in the world of philosophy. Here, apocalypticism is profoundly historical, just as it was in the time of Jesus, but now incarnate historically as it never was in the ancient world.

It is well known that Hegel could conclude his lectures on the philosophy of history by speaking of the last stage of history as our own world and our own time, but it is not well known that this apocalyptic ground is absolutely fundamental to his two most ultimate works, the *Phenomenology of Spirit* and the *Science of Logic*. Hegel's *Phenomenology* is often judged to be the most revolutionary of all philosophical works, and it is clearly revolutionary in understanding consciousness itself as a consistently and comprehensively evolving consciousness, evolving from the pure immediacy of sense-certainty to absolute knowing, and this evolution is internal and historical at once. Here, the primal events of our history are reenacted philosophically, and now we can understand them as being absolutely necessary to and in the evolution of absolute Spirit, which is modern idealism's philosophical renaming of the most primal of all New Testament categories, the Kingdom of God. The *Phenomenology of Spirit* is the work in which Hegel first fully realized his most fundamental and original thinking, one centered in a radically new philosophical method of pure dialectical negation (*Aufhebung*), a negation that is negation, preservation, and transcendence simultaneously, and which is the deepest driving power not only of consciousness and history but of absolute Spirit itself. There can be little doubt that this revolutionary work culminates in apocalypse, an apocalypse unveiling an absolute knowing, and an absolute knowing that is the inwardizing and the Calvary of absolute Spirit, a Calvary that is the actuality, truth, and certainty of the kingdom of Spirit, without which Spirit would be lifeless and alone.

Unfortunately this conclusion is extraordinarily brief and abbreviated, probably being little more than notes for a full conclusion, but it does reveal the deep ground of the *Phenomenology* in the Crucifixion, and not insignificantly this work is the first full philosophical realization of the death of God. Indeed, if only here, we can understand the Crucifixion as a full and pure apocalyptic event, one shattering all ancient horizons and worlds, and ushering in an absolutely new world. It is to be remembered that at this time New Testament scholarship had little if any awareness of the apocalyptic ground of the New Testament, the transformation of New Testament scholarship entailed by this realization did not occur until the end of the nineteenth century, but already the original apocalyptic ground of Jesus and of primitive Christianity was profoundly recovered and renewed in the radically new imaginative vision of Blake, just as it was in the radically new philosophical thinking of Hegel. One word is deeply revealing here, and that is the Pauline word *kenosis* (Phil. 2:5–8), a word that Hegel explicitly employs in many of the most crucial and difficult passages of the *Phenomenology*, and that calls forth the theological meaning of *Aufhebung* as a divine and ultimate self-emptying or self-negation. This is the kenosis that fully and openly occurs in the Crucifixion, but which Christian orthodoxy from its very beginning had affirmed to occur only in the humanity and not in the divinity of Christ, an orthodoxy reversed by Luther, and if only here, Hegel was a deeply Lutheran Christian.

A philosophical reenactment of the Crucifixion could well be said to be the very center of the *Phenomenology of Spirit*, and not only its center but its deepest ground, or its deepest theological ground, and here far more than previously in modern philosophical thinking theological and philosophical thinking fully coincide. Surely nothing else gives this work a deeper ground in the actual consciousness of Hegel's time, one that was profoundly even if largely unconsciously shaped by a uniquely modern realization of the death of God, which both Blake and Hegel could understand as occurring in the French Revolution, and not only in the dechristianization of that revolution, but in each of its deepest breakthroughs and transformations. The

French Revolution, for Hegel, is a world-historical event, and it issues in a truly new world in which secular life and history is the positive and definite embodiment of the Kingdom of God. Accordingly, this is a glorious mental dawn, all thinking beings shared in the jubilation of this epoch, for a new spiritual enthusiasm thrilled the whole world, as if the final reconciliation between God and the world was first accomplished. Now Spirit historically realizes itself as absolute freedom, for now self-consciousness realizes that its certainty of itself is the very essence of the real world, and the world for it is simply its own will, and this is a "general will" (*Phenomenology of Spirit*, §584). This will is the will of all individuals as such, so that now the self-conscious essence of each and every individual is undivided from the whole. What appears to be done by the whole is at bottom the direct and conscious deed of each individual, and every truly individual consciousness is universal consciousness and will.

But the greatest antithesis to this universal freedom released by the French Revolution is the freedom and individuality of all actual self-consciousness, for here universal freedom is a cold and abstract universality, a universality bringing with it a new "self-willed atomism" of actual self-consciousness. And this new and modern atomism of the existing individual is the consequence of this new universal freedom, for an abstract universality gives itself to the destruction of all human and historical traditions, thereby reducing the individual to a bare integer of existence. For Hegel, the French Revolution is precisely that time and world in which Spirit is first fully manifest and real in its full and final opposition to and alienation and estrangement from itself. Now there occurs the advent of a fully abstract and objective consciousness that is inseparable from the birth of a radically new subjective and interior consciousness, a new "I" or pure self-consciousness that is only and purely itself, and is so by virtue of its antithetical relationship to a new objective and universal consciousness that is the intrinsic and necessary otherness of itself. Moreover, the interior depths of this new subjective consciousness are inseparable from their ground in the universality and totality of a new objective consciousness, for a universal consciousness can fully realize itself objectively and actually only by negating its own subjective ground or center. Now, and for the first time, and above all so in the terror of the French Revolution, death is objectively meaningless and insignificant, a new death with no inner significance whatsoever. For what now perishes is the empty point of the absolutely free self, and this is the coldest and cruelest of all deaths, with no more significance than cutting off a head of cabbage or swallowing a mouthful of water (*Phenomenology of Spirit*, §590). Such universal freedom is wholly an abstract freedom, and its ground and object a wholly abstract existence, so there is left for it only negative action, and one realizing the fury of destruction. Absolute freedom becomes explicitly objective to itself in this fury, for in itself absolute freedom is a purely abstract self-consciousness, and it is objective to itself in a new terror of death, a terror that is an actual vision of its own negativity.

Therefore this absolutely free self-consciousness is an absolutely empty self-consciousness, and absolute freedom as the pure self-identity of the universal will can realize itself only in a pure negativity, a negativity that is the ultimate abstraction of the universal will, but a pure negativity that here and now becomes all in all. Here lies the modern historical origin of a pure and total negativity, one actually and historically realized only in the modern world, that very world that is the final stage of world history. Ours is truly the final age of the Spirit, but it is actually so only in the universal realization of pure negativity, one released by the advent of a pure and total abstract universality, which is itself the very opposite of Spirit. Yet it is vitally important to realize that the advent of a full abstract universality is itself an apocalyptic event. Only now does God become manifest and real as a vacuous Supreme Being, and only now does an absolute contradiction become fully real and realized in history and consciousness, a final contradiction that by an ultimate dialectical necessity must explode into apocalypse. This is the apocalypse that initially appears and is real in a purely negative actuality, an actuality that is the consequence of the real and historical advent of a final and total abstract universality.

So it is that the French Revolution is precisely that time and world in which Spirit is first fully and wholly manifest and real in its full and final opposition to and alienation and estrangement from itself. And the very advent of a fully abstract and objective consciousness is inseparable from the birth of a new subjective and interior consciousness, an "I" or self-consciousness that is only and purely itself, and is so by virtue of its antithetical relationship to an objective and universal consciousness that is the intrinsic and necessary otherness of itself. Moreover, the interior depths of this new subjective consciousness are inseparable from their ground in the universality and totality of a new objective consciousness, for a universal consciousness can realize itself objectively and actually only by negating its own subjective ground or center. If death is for the first time objectively meaningless and insignificant, it is subjectively more real than ever before, and thus death itself becomes the one and only portal to a full and final subjective and interior resolution and fulfillment. Hegel's term for this form of consciousness that realizes itself by losing all the essence and substance of itself is the *Unhappy Consciousness,* a consciousness that realizes itself by interiorly realizing that God Himself is dead (*Phenomenology of Spirit*, §785).

Spirit alone, for Hegel, is finally actual and real, yet this is only because world or substance finally and fully becomes and realizes itself as "Subject." Historically, this does not actually occur until the full birth of the modern world, and then it subjectively or interiorly occurs in the realization that God is dead, a realization inaugurating a new universal self-consciousness, which is the very center and ground of an apocalyptic explosion and transformation of the world. Thus Hegel, even as Blake, correlates and integrates the death of God and apocalypse, for the French Revolution is the historical advent and embodiment of the death of God, yet this is the death of a wholly abstract and alien form or manifestation of God, an epiphany or realization of God that does not occur or become real until the full and final birth of the modern world. Consequently, the death of God becomes possible and actually real only when Spirit has realized itself in its most negative mode and epiphany. Only when Spirit exists wholly and fully in self-alienation and self-estrangement from itself can it undergo an ultimate movement of self-negation or kenosis, a movement in which a real end or death occurs of a wholly alienated and estranged form and mode of Spirit (Blake's Urizen or Satan). Thus, it is dialectically and apocalyptically necessary that Spirit become wholly estranged and alienated from itself before it can realize and effect its own death or self-negation. Yet this is the ultimate apocalyptic event, one finally releasing an absolutely new world, but only insofar as it is the actual death of God.

That crucified God who is absent from all premodern Christian thinking now undergoes its ultimate conceptual realization, and it is precisely that realization which makes possible what Hegel knows as pure negation, an absolute negation that is an absolute affirmation, and is so precisely because it is the absolute negation of absolute Spirit. Now even if there is no direct exposition of the "death of God" in the *Science of Logic,* every movement of this purely forward moving logic is an abstract realization of this "death," for not only is a metaphysical transcendence here dissolved, but every trace of a truly and finally transcendent God has vanished, and this vanishing is the realization of a pure and total immanence. Nowhere else is such a total immanence so purely and so comprehensively enacted, but nowhere else is the totality of God so purely conceived, and even conceived as the pure subject of pure thinking itself.

Nothing is more important in Hegel's logic than its purely and totally forward movement, this is its greatest innovation in the perspective of all other logics, just as at no other point is the modern consciousness itself more clearly distinct from virtually every other mode or form of consciousness. Until the advent of modernity, all pure thinking as such was closed to the possibility of the truly and the actually new, then the future could only finally be the realization of the past, for history itself is ultimately a movement of eternal return, and even revelation or a divine or ultimate order is a movement of eternal return. Only one tradition challenged the universality of eternal return, and that is Israel's, and above all the prophetic tradition of Israel, and even more specifically the apocalyptic tradition of Israel, which already in Second Isaiah envisions not only a radically new future but a truly comprehensive and universal future. This is the tradition that is reborn and renewed in primitive Christianity and the New Testament, but unlike Buddhism, Christianity never realized a pure thinking or pure logic incorporating its deepest ground, or did not do so until the full advent of the modern world. Even if only implicitly, this is the deepest theological claim of a uniquely modern idealism, and for the first time, the deepest ground of the Bible and of Christianity itself is apprehended as becoming incarnate in a purely conceptual expression.

Only in modern idealism is there a full and pure conceptual realization of the total immanence of God, a conceptual realization that in Hegelian logic culminates in an enactment of an absolute mediation that here and now is all in all. This is that absolute mediation that Hegel declares is the final liberation of all and everything, a mediation that is apocalypse itself, and yet a totally immanent apocalypse. And only here is apocalypse realized in pure thinking itself, for even if this seemingly occurs in ancient Eastern Christian thinking, the apocalypse that Orthodox Christianity knows is an apocalypse of eternal return, or an apocalypse of an original or primordial eternity, whereas a uniquely modern apocalypse is an absolutely immanent apocalypse, and precisely thereby an absolutely new apocalypse. If only through this perspective, we can know that the deepest movement of orthodox Christian thinking is a backward movement of return, a return to an absolutely primordial Godhead, a movement that is inevitably the reversal of an absolutely forward apocalyptic movement, so that the very victory of ancient Christian orthodoxy was inevitably the reversal of an original Christian apocalypticism.

The twentieth century has embodied a violent rebirth of nineteenth-century apocalypticism, one most clearly occurring in the totalitarian political movements of the twentieth century, but no less so in our deepest imaginative vision, and even in the very advent of a seemingly total electronic and technological revolution, one apparently issuing in the birth of postmodernity. And if the pure subject of consciousness is the deepest center of nineteenth-century thinking and vision, now that subject is violently disrupted, as most deeply understood by Nietzsche himself, and in the wake of that disruption there has occurred the advent of a truly anonymous consciousness and society. America is clearly a primal site of this advent, and perhaps thereby an original America is now being reborn, for the American Puritans believed that they were inaugurating a new apocalyptic world, and it is not insignificant that the first imaginative vision of the death of God occurs in Blake's *America* (1793), a vision that inaugurated Blake's full apocalyptic vision. America may well be the primal site of contemporary apocalyptic thinking, and it is America that has given us our purest and deepest contemporary apocalyptic thinker, D. G. Leahy.

Leahy is a deeply contemporary and a deeply Catholic thinker, and his first book, *Novitas Mundi* (1980), intends to be a revolutionary breakthrough to an absolutely new thinking, and while conceptually enacting the history of Being from Aristotle through Heidegger, at bottom this book is an apocalyptic calling forth and celebration of the absolute beginning now occurring of transcendent existence in pure thinking itself. For the dawn of the Day of Yahweh is now occurring, and it essentially occurs in pure thinking as the "glorification of existence itself" (NM, 395), a glorification that Leahy names as the *missa jubilaea*. *Novitas Mundi* is radically Catholic precisely by being apocalyptically Catholic, celebrating an absolutely new thinking that is the unleavened bread of existence itself, as over against the essential finitude of past thought: "What happened before now in the Mass exclusively (*missa solemnis*) now happens in the Mass inclusively (*missa jubilaea*)" (NM, 347). At the end, in extremis, and even by a Hegelian irony of history, it becomes the destiny of the Eucharist to be the substantial experience of the world at large: "What now occurs in thought for the first time in history (transcending in fact the end of the world in essence) is the perception itself of the body—God in God in essence—the Temple of the New Jerusalem—effected now in essence inclusively in the *missa jubilaea*, the center of an essentially new consciousness in the conversion of the universe into an entirely new stuff" (NM, 348). The *missa jubilaea* is the infinite Passover of God, and precisely thereby the death of God in Christ, and therefore: "God is in fact (being there) in the absolute nullification of God" (NM, 364). This apocalyptic nullification of God is the blood of the Lamb, or the blood of the God who is absolutely Christ, and thus it is the resurrection or glorification of existence itself, a glorification that is the resurrection of the body.

Novitas Mundi is our most intrinsically difficult book since the *Phenomenology of Spirit*, but Leahy's next book, *Foundation: Matter the Body Itself* (1996) is even more difficult and complex, even if it is in full continuity with *Novitas Mundi*. Once again, there is a purely conceptual embodiment of the end of modernity and the absolute beginning of a new world order, an order that is an actually universal new world consciousness, and an absolutely new consciousness in which the body itself is nothing but existence itself. Now, and for the first time, an explosion of reason has occurred in the form of faith, so that in the thinking now occurring for the first time faith has raised reason itself to the level of faith. Of course, this is a claim fully embedded in German Idealism, and above all so in Hegel, but now what is at hand is a Catholic universal reason and a Catholic universal faith. And if German Idealism was inaugurated by the French Revolution of 1789, and culminated in its reversal in Marxism, this new world order only becomes "a clearly visible fact" in 1989, the "Year of the Beginning," which is not only the year of the public ending of Marxism but the year of the final ending of modernity itself.

Moreover, America is a deep site of this ending, for America is the furthest extension of modernity, and whereas the historical limitations of European self-consciousness preclude in fact the realization of its own demand that God actually die, the complete actualization of the death of God occurs for the first time in the American consciousness (F, 596). Once again this is a death of God releasing apocalypse itself, and an absolute apocalypse that is the identity of the new world now beginning. As opposed to *Novitas Mundi*, now American pragmatism is the true prelude to the thinking now occurring for the first time, and most immediately so the uniquely American theology of the death of God, a theology that while voiding pragmatism is the last gasp of modernity, and it is in these death throes that a final apocalyptic thinking is born. And this is a truly new apocalyptic thinking if only because of the primacy here of the body itself, a new body that is an apocalyptic body, the apocalyptic Body of Christ, and a body calling forth an absolutely new thinking in which "the body itself is the totality of life itself now for the first time" (F, 104).

Matter, the body itself, is the apocalyptic beginning of an absolutely new universe, a matter precluding the present possibility of that abyss which is the ultimate ground of modernity, for the body itself is nothing but an absolutely apocalyptic thinking. This is that thinking now giving birth to the new creation, and history is transcended for the first time by the death of death itself, in the absolute inconceivability of either a potential or an actual nothingness. If now there is no existence that is not "foundation" itself, no grounding of Being that is not the proclamation of the body itself, this body is Christ, or the apocalyptic body of God, revealing itself in the absolute freedom of personality saying itself, hearing the voice of the absolute freely speaking of itself: "I am Christ absolute existing for the first time—I am the absolute temporality of existence" (F, 165).

Indeed, there never was a nothing, because in every now is the beginning absolutely. Christ is that beginning, an absolute beginning that is an absolute ending or apocalypse, for in every now begins the transcendence of consciousness, in every now begins the body itself, and this is the beginning of the end of the world in essence, the beginning of the end of time itself (F, 423). Consequently, Leahy can identify the absolutely new essence of thought as the passion of Christ or Christ absolute. His is a transcendence that is the transcendence of transcendence itself, an absolute passion repeating itself for the first time in history in the essence of thought, existence itself for the first time the passion of Christ (F, 197). But this passion of existence is the absolute creation of the world: the creation *ex abysso*. And this absolutely passionate creation of the world is the "foundation," and the foundation of an absolute world society now beginning to exist for the first time. This world is constructed *ex futuro*, after the future, and *ex nihilo*, after nonexistence, after the pure Nothing that modernity knows as total presence. For modernity can only know apocalypse in its most abysmal form, its absolute idealism is the idealism of the Nothing, and here and here alone God becomes the Nothing in an absolutely reverse and inverted thinking. Nor is the death of God that it knows the actual death of the Living God, but only the actual death of the God of Death, or that Satan who is only fully born in the fullness of modernity. So it is that modernity culminates in a historically inevitable and eschatologically ultimate nihilism, that nihilism which Nietzsche enacts most profoundly, but this very nihilism necessarily calls forth its reversal and transcendence in an absolute apocalypse.

Both *Novitas Mundi* and *Foundation* pose an ultimate challenge to Catholicism, and not only to Catholicism but to Christianity itself, and nothing is newer here than a purely philosophical thinking and a purely theological thinking that wholly coincide, one that is manifestly the calling forth of a truly new world. At no point is this challenge more overwhelming than in that radically new understanding of matter and the body itself that is incorporated here, just as nothing is more ultimately new than an enactment of the body itself in pure thinking. This is the very point at which Leahy is most manifestly a truly new thinker, just as it is precisely here that Leahy can be understood to be an authentically Catholic thinker, and perhaps the first purely Catholic thinker in history. Surely, this is the first time that the Incarnation has been absolutely central in Catholic thinking, the first time that matter and Spirit have been so deeply and so purely united, and so much so that now Spirit is the body itself (F, 96), and even as this thinking intends to be an apocalyptic consummation of the totality of history, never before has such a Catholic consummation actually been conceived, although there are those who would see it as having been imaginatively enacted in Dante's *Paradiso* and Joyce's *Finnegans Wake*.

A deep question to be asked of modern apocalyptic thought is its relationship to ancient apocalypticism, and more particularly its relation to the apocalypticism of primitive Christianity and the New Testament. Here, Paul is extraordinarily important, for he is our first purely apocalyptic thinker, and so far as we now know the first ancient thinker fully to draw forth the subject of consciousness, an "I" or subject that he could know as a dichotomous subject, a subject wholly divided or doubled between an old "I" of "flesh" (*sarx*) and a new "I" of Spirit (*pneuma*). Paul could know this dichotomous subject as a consequence of the ultimacy of the Crucifixion and the Resurrection, or even of the Crucifixion alone, a transformation that even could be understood as the full and final advent of self-consciousness. This is a subject or self-consciousness that becomes deeply reborn in early modernity, thence being renewed in a uniquely modern apocalyptic thinking, only to be absolutely negated in Nietzsche's apocalyptic dissolution of the "I," an "I" that he could know as the creation of *ressentiment*. Leahy's absolutely apocalyptic thinking is also a pure negation of interiority and selfhood, a negation issuing from the advent of an absolute exteriority, or absolute body itself. But all these thinkers are reborn or renewed Pauline thinkers, and are so precisely in their apocalypticism, an apocalypticism inseparable from an enactment of absolute ending, but that ending is absolute beginning itself.

Now even as ancient Jewish apocalypticism profoundly challenged the orthodox guardians of the Torah, a challenge that is profoundly renewed in Paul, modern apocalypticism profoundly challenges Christian orthodoxy. Indeed, this is the greatest challenge that Christianity has ever faced, as witness modern apocalypticism's ultimate enactment of the death of God, and one also occurring in the radically Catholic thinking of Leahy, even if it knows the death of God as the apocalyptic resurrection of God. So, if a pure enactment of the death of God occurs throughout all the full expressions of a uniquely modern apocalyptic thinking, does this movement fully and finally distinguish ancient and modern apocalypticism? Or is modern apocalypticism a genuine recovery and renewal of an original Christian apocalypticism, one that had perished or become wholly transformed in the victory of an ancient Christian orthodoxy, then only to be renewed in profoundly subversive and heretical expressions? Surely apocalyptic thinking and apocalyptic vision have been ultimately subversive and heretical throughout their history, and if modern apocalyptic thinking is totally subversive and heretical, it may well be an authentic renewal of a seemingly invisible or hidden apocalyptic tradition. But if a uniquely modern apocalypticism is inseparable from the death of God, a death of God that it can know as apocalypse itself, might this be the first purely conceptual realization of the Kingdom of God? Or is it the first purely conceptual expression of an absolute atheism or an absolute desacralization? Or could it be both at once? And might this be said of the whole world of modern apocalyptic thinking?

There are guardians of orthodoxy in Judaism, Christianity, and Islam who know all forms of apocalypticism as assaults both upon revelation and upon the majesty and sovereignty of the absoluteness of God. And there is good reason for this, apocalypticism is inevitably subversive, and perhaps the most purely subversive force in history, all of the great political revolutions in modernity have been apocalyptic revolutions, and even the advent of both Christianity and Islam can be understood as the consequence of apocalypticism. So, too, all full forms of apocalypticism have assaulted both social and religious orthodoxies, and Jewish, Christian, and Islamic orthodoxies have arisen only by way of dissolving the apocalypticism upon their horizons. We can also understand modern political conservatism as having arisen to assault and reverse the apocalypticism ushered in by the French and Russian revolutions, and if modern theology in virtually all its expressions is deeply anti-apocalyptic, this too could be understood as a uniquely modern conservatism. But if a uniquely modern thinking is at bottom an apocalyptic thinking, or is so in its deepest and purest expressions, it is finally a theological thinking, and a theological thinking that therein could be understood as a rebirth of an original Christianity, an original Christianity that from this perspective was most deeply negated and reversed by the very advent of an orthodox theological thinking and faith.

Nothing is more essential in a full and genuine apocalypticism than the *coincidentia oppositorum* that it realizes between an absolute No-saying and an absolute Yes-saying, one inseparable from the final advent of an absolute darkness and an absolute light. This is luminously clear in Nietzsche's proclamation of the death of God, already the madman's proclamation of the death of God (*The Gay Science*, §125) reveals that we are now straying as through an infinite nothing, night and more night is coming on all the while, a night of the world that is an apocalyptic night, and one that is the deepest ending in history.[4] Here, the death of God is not only an ultimate historical event, it is the most ultimate event that has ever occurred, one wiping away our entire horizon. But even if this is the darkest of all nights, it is nevertheless the most glorious of all possible dawns, for it releases an absolute and final Yes-saying, a Yes-saying that is the very opposite of *ressentiment*, and a Yes-saying whose revelation is Nietzsche's ultimate calling. Now and only now a history inaugurated by *ressentiment* is ending, an ending that is the ending of the actuality of every possible subject, and is that ending precisely because it is the death of God. Yet this is the very death releasing a final and ultimate nihilism, a nihilism that is the tomb of God, and a nihilism that is the very arena of the ecstatic affirmation of a uniquely modern or postmodern Eternal Recurrence. So, too, Paul could celebrate an apocalyptic grace that is the consequence of the ending of an old creation, an old creation that ends in the Crucifixion itself, and just as Paul declares to the Corinthian Christians that he had decided to know nothing among you except Jesus Christ and him crucified (1 Cor. 2:2), this is what makes possible his celebration of the absolute love of Christ, a love that is fully and finally actual in the Crucifixion alone.

Despite the centrality of the Crucifixion in the New Testament, a centrality inseparable from its enactment of the final triumph of the Kingdom of God, Christian theology throughout virtually all its history has most resisted the theology of the cross, and done so most clearly in its continual affirmation of the absolute sovereignty and the absolute transcendence of God, thereby refusing the Crucifixion as a divine event, or as an enactment or embodiment of Godhead itself. This is a refusal that is continually and comprehensively reversed throughout a uniquely modern apocalypticism, and at no other point is there such a clear unity between all the radically divergent expressions of modern apocalyptic thinking and vision, and if that is a unity deriving from a uniquely modern realization of the death of God, nothing is more fundamental in modern apocalypticism, just as nothing is more fundamental in the New Testament than is the Crucifixion itself. So that if an original Christian apocalypticism is truly reborn in the modern world, that rebirth is inseparable from the death of God, even as a uniquely Christian apocalypse is inseparable from the Crucifixion.

Notes

1. René Descartes, *Descartes: Philosophical Letters*, trans. Anthony Kenny (Oxford: Clarendon, 1970), 83–84, 98.

2. G. W. F. Hegel, *Phenomenology of Spirit*, trans. A. V. Miller (New York: Oxford University Press, 1977).

3. Descartes, *Philosophical Letters*, 174–81.

4. Friedrich Nietzsche, *The Gay Science*, trans. W. Kaufmann (New York: Random House, 1974).

5

The Shape of Catholic Apocalypse

CYRIL O'REGAN

Leahy's thinking lays out how modern thought in its egological mainline from Descartes to Hegel both promised and foreclosed on being responsive to radical novelty and how, on the other hand, thinkers such as Kierkegaard, Nietzsche, and Heidegger were not sufficiently novel to overcome modernity's totalizing egological regime, however right they were with regard to this line's foreclosure and their attempt to think novelty. My analysis focuses on three features: First, the content of this apocalyptic discourse as an absolute novelty whose schema is the dynamic inseparability of creation–death/resurrection–community, with emphasis falling on the latter. Second, Leahy's shocking elevation of Aquinas's *sacra doctrina* as providing the basic grammar for a postmodern apocalyptic thought that is set against Hegelian totalization and postmodern reneging on thinking. And third, the ways in which Aquinas gets discursively recalibrated in order to function as the base for an apocalyptic thinking that can never truly be anticipated.

In Descartes's methodological turn, from which the *ego cogito* emerges as foundational principle, thought can be said to constitute a new science (NM, 93), and thus in a sense constitute a revolution. At the same time it represents a wrong turn in that the foundational principle of the cogito absorbs both nature and God into humanity (NM, 108). In addition, the Cartesian turn effectuates a rationalistic naturalism that eclipses grace (NM, 105, 117). The accent falls, on the one hand, on the emergence of the autonomy of reason as an ineluctable that will not tolerate a rival (NM, 105, 118) even if this rival is a familiar such as Christian faith and, on the other hand, cleaning up inconsistencies in Descartes in which the French thinker feels obliged to appeal to God to move beyond certainty to truth (NM, 93–94).

In Hegel, Kant's transcendental ideal becomes real (NM, 127) as Hegel completes the modern project inaugurated by Descartes in identifying human self-consciousness and divine reason (NM, 128). Thereby, contingency and grace are eclipsed (NM, 131, 217, 223), and with it any genuine understanding of creation and the value of particulars (NM, 130, 223). Most importantly, Hegel's claim that the modern subject has risen in principle to the divine point of view abolishes the finitude of knowledge whose mark in faith lies in telling the story of creation, redemption, and sanctification. Leahy rises to eloquence in pointing to the self-involving character of commitment to the Christian narrative: "It is clear that if history is to be understood to be the identity of the storyteller with the story of what has occurred to him in the course of his worldly being, essential history is not possible in Hegel, since to the essence of man, indistinguishable from the Spirit of the world, nothing is able to occur" (NM, 227). Leahy fully understands that charting the increasing subjectification of reality from Descartes to Hegel falls far short of a full and adequate account of modernity and serves merely as a synecdoche of a much more complex and differentiated story of which he can at best provide the outline. Encouraged in particular by Heidegger's reflection on the history of Being as the history of forgetfulness (*Seinsvergessenheit*), from time to time (NM, 202) Leahy also implicates Leibniz in this derogation. Leibniz may well carry forward the doctrine of *creatio ex nihilo* into the modern period (NM, 280), but the prominence of the language of possibility in his thought marks him as an essentialist (NM, 207–208).[1]

Nor does Leahy fail to note that significant figures in modern philosophy aim at a correction. Heidegger, who famously presents the narrative of decline from Descartes to Hegel, is one such figure (ch. 12, 270–93). Leahy neither doubts that Heidegger intends to overcome modern subjectivity (NM, 275–77), nor that in *Being and Time* and in other texts that he achieves a measure of success. Among other things, Heidegger is a superior critic of Hegel's essentialism and models openness to the primacy of existence and its insistence (NM, 286). The measure of success in Heidegger's thought, however, is limited: Heidegger does not so much escape the gravitational pull of modernity as represent an "extenuation" of it (NM, 275–78). In a critical evaluation that recalls early-twentieth-century Catholic criticisms of Heidegger by the likes of Erich Przywara and Edith Stein,[2] but also in line with a student of Heidegger such as Karl Löwith,[3] Leahy accuses Heidegger of nihilism (NM, 272, 287). Heidegger's is not the only voice that attempts a major correction of modernity in general and in Hegel. Kierkegaard's is another. As the supreme critic of Hegel's Idealism, throughout his oeuvre, but especially in *Philosophical Fragments*, Kierkegaard attempts to overcome Hegel's self-dissolving skepticism (NM, 135) and its inordinately essentialistic view of history (NM, 223) that vaporizes the contingent and particular (NM, 225–26), which essentially makes of it a theodicy (NM, 138). More than anything else, Kierkegaard exposes Hegel's instrumentalization of Christianity (NM, 141), and resolutely opposes his covering over the revelatory event that is constitutive of it (NM, 146, 151). Of course, the two are intrinsically related: the universal predilection of Hegelian discourse is calculated to deny the unanticipatable and unrepeatable appearance of the essence of existence. Still, no more than Heidegger does Kierkegaard escape the gravitational pull of modernity in general and Hegel's final statement of it in particular. While his philosophical struggle with Hegel is admirable (NM, 233–36), in the end Kierkegaard's thought is a reaction formation caught in the matrix of the Idealism it would overcome (NM, 236). It is thus fated to continue rather than revoke a contraction of revelation into reason (NM, 244) and the derogation of time that is the hallmark of the Hegelian concept (NM, 243–44).

For modern and postmodern religious thinkers of apocalyptic persuasion who underwrite novelty, the thought of Thomas Aquinas is usually adduced as the static form of metaphysics that is anachronistic at best and fallacious at worse. At its very best the thought of Aquinas lends itself to apocalyptic update. Leahy very much proves to be the exception to this rule in *Novitas Mundi*, both in the obvious devotion to the thought of Aquinas expressed in chapter 2 (NM, 54–72) and in his deployment of Aquinas's thought—or thinking—as a critical measure vis-à-vis both the clarification/emendations of modernity enacted in thinkers such as Heidegger and Kierkegaard as well as the philosophical highroad of increasing subjectification from Descartes to Hegel. If the chapter solely devoted to Aquinas starts out pretty conventionally as a contrast between Aquinas's existentialism and Aristotle's essentialism, and repeats without attribution the kind of proposal one finds in the likes of Étienne Gilson and Cornelio Fabro (NM, 54–56), the special quality of Leahy's interpretation quickly becomes evident. In contrast to neo-Thomism and Vatican I, Leahy does not underscore natural reason and its power to achieve knowledge of God. Rather, Leahy underscores the singular importance of *sacra doctrina* in Aquinas (NM, 58) and underwrites the primacy of faith, which, because it deals with revelation, is more nearly disjunctive than conjunctive with natural reason (NM, 56–57).[4] Even as Leahy underscores the absolute novelty of sacred doctrine and insists both that it produces a genuinely "new science" (NM, 58) and has its own principles distinct from those of natural reason (NM, 61), it would be a mistake to think of him being Pascalian. He still is operating within the Thomistic ordinance that faith completes rather than destroys reason. The purpose of emphasizing disjunction is to underscore what faith adds to reason: this is nothing less than a vision of God and God's relation to the world; a vision of God's self-emptying without limit or without why; a God at once of erotic as well as agapic love who begets love in return (NM, 62–63). It is hardly accidental that in figuring this God as a truly ecstatic God who exceeds reason (NM, 63, 72) Leahy makes the link between Aquinas and Pseudo-Dionysius, whose entire mystical theology is a form of doxology.[5]

There is much in Leahy's account of Aquinas that is of general interest, but what is most important about his reflection on Aquinas is that in this chapter Leahy sets down criteria whereby he can judge modern philosophy from Descartes to Hegel as a deformation, and the histrionic philosophical attempts to overcome the deformation in Heidegger and Kierkegaard as inadequate. The criteriological effect is in evidence in Leahy's criticisms of all three major links in the rationalist chain, with Leibniz's principle of sufficient reason a possible fourth (NM, 189, 198–99). The "new science" of Aquinas's sacred doctrine is opposed to the "new science" of Descartes in that it is the science of love and mercy in contrast to the science of subjectivity and immanence (NM, 117). The new science is also opposed to the explication of immanence in Kant that sidelines faith (NM, 118) and Hegelian thought that sublates it (NM, 128, 130–31). Whatever Hegel's talk of Love as foundational of reality, unlike Aquinas, he asserts the primacy of essence over existence (NM, 202) and refuses to honor either contingency or individuality (NM, 223). Although Leahy recognizes that sacred doctrine in Aquinas includes the entire gamut of Christian topoi and especially the encompassing topic of the Trinity (NM, 56), the nodal point in terms of criteria is the doctrine of creation, which does not fully fall within the coordinates of natural reason. What Leahy seems to want to underscore in Aquinas is what we might call the ontology of gift. At the time of the writing of *Novitas Mundi*, arguably, Thomists such as Joseph de Finance and Cornelio Fabro were already implicitly underscoring this point. It would do a disservice to Leahy to argue actual dependence, even if one can find traces of Fabro in a genealogy of decline that essentially follows Heidegger, but makes the fall from genuine thinking not a fall from the Presocratics but rather a fall from Aquinas's thinking of ontological freshness in and through his thinking of *esse*. In any event, Leahy's and Fabro's insight have become common coin and have been articulated in a variety of forms of phenomenological (Jean-Luc Marion) and nonphenomenological thought, variously sympathetic to Catholicism (John Milbank) and actually Catholic (David C. Schindler, Antonio Lopez).[6] Leahy uses Aquinas's thought—or better his *thinking* (verb rather than noun)—as a measure to critique the attempted correction of modern thought, and in the process thereby asserts the superiority of Aquinas's thought to that of both Kierkegaard and Heidegger. Heidegger, whose critique of subjectivity as foundational, as the *hypokeimenon* underlying all modern thought and action, is obviously so influential for Leahy in the text that it comes in for particular opprobrium. Heidegger does not give Aquinas's articulation of *creatio ex nihilo*—which is basically his ontology of gift—its due. Indeed, he fundamentally distorts it (NM, 287). In doing so, he gives way to a cheap nihilism that does not do justice to the *to be* of individual things that so wondrously appear (NM, 252). Nor does the philosophical purism, which bears a close relation to the philosophical imperialism of Kant, allow Heidegger to acknowledge and be led by that sacred doctrine which specifies the transcendental essence of existence itself (NM, 254). Here, Leahy echoes a point made in different ways by Catholic thinkers of Thomist persuasion such as Cornelio Fabro and Gustav Siewerth, but perhaps also by Erich Przywara and Hans Urs von Balthasar.

In *Novitas Mundi* a real Aquinas provides the critical measure for modern thought as well as its corrections. Given the visionary nature of the text it would not make sense to assimilate this preference to a commitment to neo-Scholasticism's urge for certainty and demand for a closed philosophical system. But neither is Aquinas a mere trope for a Catholic tradition not otherwise specified. The figuring of sacred doctrine suggests that (1) in Aquinas the essential perception of reality is that of gift, and (2) the original gift of being undergoes recreation and a process of perfection. The second of the two points concerning repetition is truly clarified only in the appendixes, though it is implied in Leahy's genealogical remarks in the main body of the text. Even if Aquinas is not a trope, Leahy shows some interest in supplementing him, and Augustine explicitly serves this function in the text. While never displacing the primacy of Aquinas, Augustine's close connection to both experience and scripture allow features of Leahy's constructive proposal to come out that would not otherwise. Importantly, with regard to Augustine Leahy disputes two influential stereotypes: first, the view that Augustine does no more than essentially baptize Neoplatonism (NM, 174–76) and, second, the view that Augustine's journey toward self-recognition before God in the *Confessions* anticipates the modern subject of Descartes (NM, 177). Leahy calls Augustine a "prophetic" thinker (NM, 171). Now, the meaning of that label is not clear in the text. Leahy might mean, for example, evidences to the contrary, that Augustine is a truly biblical thinker with interest in the neighbor as well as God. Certainly, this interpretation cannot be ruled out. The apparent association with the term *watcher* suggests, however, that Augustine's thought might be apocalyptically coded. Now, more than in his chapter on Augustine (ch. 7, 157–78) is Leahy anxious to adduce all the supporting evidence. One does not find, for example, any discussion of books 21–22 of *The City of God*, where Augustine is at his most apocalyptic. What does come through clearly, however, is Leahy's acknowledgment of Augustine's powerful recognition of existence in general and his own existence in particular (NM, 173). To acknowledge the existence of world and self is not simply to acknowledge brute facts; it is to acknowledge existence as gift. This seems to be intimated in Leahy's association of mercy with creation. Unlike Hegel, who cannot acknowledge contingency, and Heidegger, who acknowledges it but wraps it in nihilistic indifference, for Augustine, created beings not only are stunningly held out beyond nothing, they intimate divine benevolence, solicitude, and grace. Consequently, the true purpose of the *Confessions* is to give an account of how a human being becomes a deep-down form of gratitude to the God who creates, saves, and perfects and manages to shape a life as a thank you. If we join this to the apocalyptic reference, I think we can take Leahy to be saying that while there are some aspects of Augustine's thought that should be left behind, and others again that might be left behind, the declarative doxological component of

Augustine's theology is a permanent contribution to Catholic thought as well as proving a necessary supplement to the thought of Aquinas, which overshadows and outbids modern thought and even that of its correctors who, if they search for the right thing, that is, ontological novelty, do not have the means to find it and even less to explicate it.

Adducing Augustine as a supplement does nothing to displace Aquinas from holding pride of place when it comes to providing a criteriology for the critique of modernity. While stopping short of suggesting dependence, I have already pointed to Cornelio Fabro as a fellow traveler here. But what kind of Aquinas? In part, this question probes whether the Aquinas retrieved by Leahy is focused in creation or broadens out to incarnation/redemption and eschaton. The question is fairly pointed, since operationally in the genealogical section, the "sacred doctrine," which Leahy invokes in his chapter on Aquinas and evokes elsewhere, tends to be restricted to creation and its abiding and un-erasable mysteriousness. In contrast, in the constructive apocalyptic theology Leahy provides with regard to sacred doctrine the emphases fall decidedly on redemption and eschaton. I take this to be a tension rather than a contradiction. Given Aquinas's own view of the content of sacred doctrine, it seems best to think of Leahy wishing to include incarnation/cross and eschatological perfection as well as the trinitarian foundation of creation, which the great scholar of Aquinas, Gilles Emery, has recently brought to our critical attention. To follow Aquinas is, then, to favor Leahy's constructive articulation in the appendixes rather than the genealogy presented in the main body of the text. In addition, it is not surprising that when Aquinas is deployed critically throughout the text, the focus will tend to be on that part of sacred doctrine that has the largest overlap with metaphysics in its modern subjectivist mode, that is, the doctrine of creation.

What then does the fully comprehensive and adequate profile of Aquinas look like in the apocalyptic and eschatological environment of the radically "new" and "now" and "for the first time"? As in sacred doctrine, creation is intrinsically connected to redemption, and redemption in turn to eschaton. Thus, existence is doubly repeated in redeemed and sanctified being constituted at once as holy and whole. In the historical Aquinas, the relations between original created being and the two repetitions is highly complex in that, on the one hand, redeemed and sanctified being represent a return to original existence that has been marred and, on the other, a measure of excess is allowed. If we take Leahy's constructive apocalyptic as our guiding thread, however, we can see not only that the narrative pattern has the eschaton as its term, but that the full meaning of sacred doctrine is to be found in its eschatological exclamation. Put differently, the novelty that is the object and subject of Leahy's doxological postmetaphysical thought is only given eschatologically and in a significant sense therefore "for the first time." This means that the doubly repeated individual and social existence—that is, existence as *communion*—is only anticipated in the modalities of creation and redemption.

Even if it were not dismissed as fanciful that Leahy's Aquinas has been marinated in an interesting form of apocalyptic that presented itself as something of an alternative to Hegelian apocalypse, still, would not Leahy's apocalyptic be speculative at best, and entirely lacking explanatory function at worst? My suggestion is that Aquinas has been subjected to such eschatological and apocalyptic torque that essentially Leahy has dissolved real differences between the historical Aquinas and Joachim de Fiore. Joachim is the great apocalypticist of the medieval period, the great decipherer of the symbols of the book of Revelation, and the grafter of the concordances between the New and the Old Testament.[7] He laid a bold path for the Spiritual Franciscans and Italian poetry, while making medieval masters such as Aquinas and Bonaventure nervous. We know that Aquinas objected to Joachim's emphasis on the economic Trinity, and furthermore his temporalization of the Trinity into the ages of Father, Son, and Spirit respectively, and more specifically his thinking of the age of the Spirit as the age of de-institutionalization and full realization of freedom and knowledge. If Christ was a condition for the coming to be of the spiritual plenitude (*plenitudo spiritualis*), Christ's existence is intrinsically preparatory and anticipative, although in Joachim's case Christ is always more than the "vanishing mediator" (to borrow Žižek's term) that he comes to be in Hegel and before him in Lessing.

These and other significant changes seem to be rung on Aquinas's articulation of *sacra doctrina* in the appendixes to *Novitas Mundi* (NM, 367). In the appendixes the insistence is on the "new" as it appears in the *Endzeit*, that is, in its exclamatory or hyperbolic form. In addition, to the extent that Leahy authorizes language of the Trinity, the sole referent is the economic Trinity (NM, 363). Similarly, although, as Aquinas thought, Christ is the condition of the Church, at the same time, for Leahy, the raison d'être of Christ is the Church as his body (NM, 361), which eschatologically is the body of all and not simply the elect. Furthermore, if the Eucharist is the "transcendental repetition" of creation (NM, 350), the disseminated Eucharist, the Eucharist generalized beyond the institutional church, is what Ernst Bloch,[8] a Joachim aficionado, would call the *ultimum optimum*. Needless to say, it would be too much to expect the resurrection of a pure species of Joachimism that exerts torque on Aquinas's sacred doctrine. This is a lesson repeated in different forms and with very different attitudes in Hans Urs von Balthasar and Jacob Taubes, Henri de Lubac, and Gianni Vattimo. Undoubtedly, despite the inexorable critique, Hegel the German Idealist still makes his way into Leahy's consideration of the new or the inceptual, most nearly in that it crosses out from consideration the God who would be without the world: a Godless world and a worldless God are equally impossibilities in Leahy's grand scheme. This is to repeat the axiom of reciprocal implication of God and world that is central to German Idealism in general.[9]

As with *Novitas Mundi*, it is in the appendix to *Faith and Philosophy* (PF, 143–63) that Leahy presents his constructive apocalyptic proposal. This formal continuity bears on the substantive continuity in terms of apocalyptic both as an existential ontological horizon and as the discourse responsive to it. In this text, Leahy seems to retain the essential features of his genealogy of modernity, as well as his commitment to Aquinas as providing the outline of an adequate theology after the crisis of modernity. Leahy's constructive proposal is laid out in "Thinking in the Third Millennium" (PF, 143–63), which has a decidedly apocalyptic cast (see especially PF, 147, 153). Leahy's assertion that modern subjectivity has come to an end presents one of the clearest synoptic statements of Leahy's thought (PF, 143). As in *Novitas Mundi*, apocalypse is about the "nearness" of the divine (PF, 144) in the dynamic sense of advent or nearing of a reality which, if other than human being, is also unrepealably no-other (*non-aliud*) and the elevator of human knowing and freedom (PF, 147). Apocalypse is not about an end but concerns a radical transformation: "what now occurs for the first time in history" (PF, 153).[10] Apocalypse is the step beyond the beginning and the end, or as Leahy writes in *Novitas Mundi*, the end of the beginning and the beginning of the end. That Hegelian thought is, for Leahy, the adversary none greater than which can be thought is just as evident in this constructive essay as it is in the main hermeneutical section in which Hegel once again is the term of the movement of subjectification that begins in Descartes (PF, 148). Hegel's form of thought is the acme of totalization in which nothing is wasted, including waste itself (PF, 158).[11] This diagnosis reminds of the constitutive complaint made by Derrida in *Glas*,[12] which bears on the constitution of Hegelian thought as a theodicy. Nothing remains beyond the comprehension of Spirit: "The absolute self-consciousness is absolute self-knowledge when the divine subject is in truth the whole of reality and there can be nothing unknown" (PF, 149). Hegel provides a spurious form of apocalyptic at odds with Christian apocalyptic properly understood (PF, 149).[13]

Leahy's account of Descartes in *Faith and Philosophy* finesses somewhat the reading of Descartes prosecuted in *Novitas Mundi* by offering a bifocal view of Descartes as having not one foundation but two: God as well as the cogito. The focus on Descartes's ontological argument and especially on Descartes's idea of the infinite suggests Leahy's accord with Levinas's reflection on Descartes in *Totality and Infinity* (PF, 120). The critique of Hegel continues as well: Hegel sublates faith (PF, 59, 65), distorts revelation (PF, 62), eclipses transcendence (PF, 57; also 54), and is destructive regarding the finite (PF, 37). Leahy once again constructs Kierkegaard as the most important critic of Hegel, and in particular applauds Kierkegaard for bringing out the disproportionality between the infinite and finite that was compromised in Hegel's absolute Idealism (PF, 67). What is unusual about the chapter is how Aquinas is entwined throughout with Kierkegaard. That the thought of Aquinas functions criteriologically vis-à-vis the philosophical economy of modernity should not surprise given what we have seen in *Novitas Mundi*. Leahy very much signals that this is his intention when he devotes the first chapter to a treatment of the novelty of Aquinas's articulation of creation with respect to Aristotle from whom Aquinas takes so much. Leahy wants to show that Kierkegaard's negation of the entire complex of Hegelian dialectical negation (PF, 63) is determined by the system it would overcome and that it is a repetition of the realism exhibited in every aspect of Aquinas's thought (PF, 63). Equally, however, Leahy suggests that it is a repetition otherwise, or a nonidentical repetition, of Aquinas's grasp of the incommensurability between the Creator and the created. Although Kierkegaard reverses Hegel's inversion of Aquinas's disproportionality between Creator and the created (PF, 66, 70), no pure return to Aquinas is possible (PF, 64).

Faith and Philosophy seems preoccupied with Hegel's logic, judged to be an opening and a shutting at once. As Leahy elaborates this in a truly important essay "The Logic of Faith, or, Beyond Modernity" (ch. 7, 115–42), in its questioning of the law of excluded middle, Hegel's logical articulation represents a promise to think through and beyond modernity (PF, 115). Of course, this promise is betrayed: Hegel's logic of becoming from being and nothing (PF, 117) is calculated to set up a teleological matrix of beginning and end that denies genuine novelty. What is demanded, then, is a new logic of the coming into existence on the "far side" of Hegel's logic (PF, 116–17). It is just here that we see the first of Leahy's two main innovations, that is, his appeal to the logic of the pragmatist Charles Sanders Peirce, on the one hand, and his use of mathematics as a discourse equivalent to the argument of novelty that he tries heroically to put into words, on the other. One of the important points that Leahy makes about Peirce's "ternary" logic of Firstness, Secondness, and Thirdness is that while similar to Hegel's logic of the "included middle" (PF, 115), it represents a step beyond it. Peirce's prioritization of Firstness, that is, the sheer givenness of reality, is declared right over Hegel's giving functional priority to conceptuality or Secondness (PF, 132). This priority makes possible—although not necessary—a more adequate account of the synthetic aspect of logic, in Hegel's case the concrete universal, in Peirce's case Thirdness, which involves the relations between elements (PF, 132).

In *Foundation*, Marx's revolutionary thought has a new prominence. While Leahy's apocalyptic remains consciously Catholic, its catholicity is more formal, with a mystic such as Eckhart now playing at least an equal role with canonical thinkers such as Aquinas and Augustine; there is a shift of register from being to nothing, with Meister Eckhart and Jacob Boehme (1575–1624) being the two major figures, but with Leahy also indebted to Altizer and Ray L. Hart.[14] Two useful questions can be asked to broach the text. First, is there a contemporary analogue for the form of apocalyptic that Leahy is articulating in *Foundation*? Second, and especially in light of the complex relation between Leahy's consciously Catholic form of apocalyptic and Altizer's death of God theology, is there any way in which Leahy's shift in apocalyptic protocol allows him to remain broadly within the range of Catholic apocalyptic? I want to respond in the affirmative to both questions. With regard to the first, I suggest the Lacanian Marxist Alain Badiou as the appropriate analogue. And with regard to the second, I want to suggest that the form of apocalyptic constructed by Leahy in *Foundation* is greatly illuminated by recurring to the Renaissance Catholic traditions of Hermeticism and Kabbalah with their sense of secret, neo-Pythagorean sensibility, and commitment to revelation that troubles the distinction between faith and knowledge.

If *Foundation* invokes a new way of thinking, it also involves a new way of speaking, one that breaks with the conventions of modern philosophy and theology. It does so by a kind of fiat, in a defiant act of freedom to speak another language, to construct a demanding idiolect, rather than (as with the case of postmodern thought) by destabilizing conventional philosophical, religious, and theological language from within. In contrast to Derrida, who is satisfied in revealing discourse's tendency to prevent and to amortize, in *Foundation* Leahy attempts to bring language through the crucible of ecstasy and suffering in order for it to be new and strange enough to have the capacity to name the new. And, again in contradistinction to Derrida, Leahy no more believes in the end of conceptual language than in the indifference of philosophical and literary discourse. Although its history has run aground, for Leahy this simply means that conceptual language undergoes a fundamental transformation.

The first page of *Foundation* speaks to the beginning (ix), and the text is replete with *new* used adjectivally, "new universal" (F, 45) and "new law" being but two examples. *Foundation* repeats one of the most frequently used locutions in *Novitas Mundi*, the epochal marker "for the first time" (F, 14, 26, 58, 85, 113, 143, 161).[15] *Now* as a more or less freestanding term also makes a reappearance (F, 108) and continues to be distinguished from the punctual, disappearing *now* in being kairotic, a *now* semantically and ontologically of utmost significance. To the extent that the *now* carries a significance none greater than which can be thought, the *now* is pleromatic as well as kairotic: it is nothing less than the fulfillment of time. The new or beginning is structurally underscored in the first chapter by the attention Leahy devotes to Marx's articulation of a revolutionary new order of existence that, if not identical to the revolutionary state of being articulated by Leahy, is at least an analogue of it. As the phenomenon disclosive of the real, the new is a gift: no *why* can be supplied to account for or explain its sheer givenness. In this sense, formally speaking, the new can be described as "absolutely unconditioned" (F, 96) and as ex nihilo (F, ix, 19, 383, 410). These two notions, one philosophical, the other theological, in turn seem to regulate and be further specified by two clusters of substantive signifiers.

Considering the philosophical signifiers for the moment, the "unconditioned" of Kantian and post-Kantian thought is behind Leahy's insistence that while there is obviously a "before" of the phenomenon of the new, nonetheless, nothing prior to the phenomenon of the new conditions it to the point of explaining it. In a manner not dissimilar to Hegel, who speaks of the absolute dissolving or absolving its presuppositions,[16] Leahy suggests that the unconditioned in a sense deconditions anything that occurred in the past that might be thought to be conditions of its emergence. At the same time, *Foundation* makes clear that Hegel is more target than precedent in that the new cannot be locked into an anticipative/teleological view of history and thought, since this would have the deleterious effect of making the new more or less logically necessary (F, 116–17). In *Foundation*, however, the opposition to necessity both on the plane of logic and the historically real by no means implies that the new is contingent. For Leahy, associating the new with contingency is no less a category mistake than associating it with necessity: necessity and contingency are just two aspects of the same Hegelian logic that *Foundation* aims to transcend. Qua fully actual—indeed, actuality itself—the new is not tied to potentiality as its fulfillment, nor can it be identified with chance, nor absolutely separated from it. A further specification of the "unconditioned" is the category *a posteriori* (F, 114, 154). The new is emergence that cannot be captured in any apriorist philosophical system. The "unconditioned" is "pure becoming" (F, 26) of which time itself is a functional equivalent (F, 17, 118, 142).

The theological signifiers, on the other hand, specify the categories of "gift" in general and "from nothing" in particular. As one might expect having read *Novitas Mundi*, one finds "incarnation" (F, 127, 142; also 368–69), "love" (F, 9; also 356), and the hugely important "word" or logos intrinsically connected to both (F, 15–16, 98, 163–64; also 368–69, 472), and "saying" as the present participle of "to say." In *Foundation* we also come across "miracle" (F, 94), "grace" (F, 105), "truth" (F, 384),"peace" (F, 364, 366), "joy" (F, 105), and the very Johannine categories of "light" (F, 142) and "life" (F, 103, 142, 359). The new represents a decisive and inalienable caesura making possible the absolute now of ontological fecundity. The eschatological now is the unconditioned made manifest. One can hear the New Testament note of making all things new, and the specifically Kierkegaardian contextualization of repetition as the plenary mode of conversion, which involves things shedding their past and moving from a state of death into life.

Leahy details the subjective correlative of the phenomenon or *Ur*-phenomenon of novelty. The sole proper gnoseological response to the phenomenon is perception, although such a response, precisely because of the immediacy of seeing, can also be identified as "absolute consciousness" (F, xi). Perception is precisely the contrary of conception, structured by the subject–object difference and grounded in the legislating transcendental ego: "The perception of the real is not a matter of thought's *own* construction" (F, 143). The perception of novelty participates in the phenomenon of the new that is received. Since the really real is the new as such, it is apt that Leahy refers to perception or immediate knowledge as the *novitas mentis* (F, 15), a new thinking or new mind that is not capable of being anticipated. As with the new, ontologically considered, the new gnoseologically considered is "for the first time" and is kairotic all the way down. In a graphic locution, which seems to recall Blake's famous poetic reflection on "cleansing the doors of perception," Leahy speaks of the new form of thinking shelling "the eyes of thought" (F, 143).

Although the recall of biblical topoi may be less explicit in *Foundation* than in *Novitas Mundi*, one comes across "manna" with reference to *novitas mentis* (F, 94, 107), the "new law" that is the new imperative for adequate response to the new, and even more pertinently "the wedding feast," which intimates the New Jerusalem (F, 92). Closely related to the recalling of the eschatological epithalamium is the "body of God" (F, 127) that,[17] if it in significant respects corresponds to the "kingdom of God" (F, 388, 408, 410),[18] also suggests a reality that is protological precisely because eschatological, and thus opens on other speculative discourses in the Jewish and Christian traditions.

Although the symbol of the Trinity is not as conspicuously present in *Foundation* as it was in *Novitas Mundi*, it does make a number of explicit appearances (F, x, xv, 161, 365–66, 595). The figure of Christ remains pivotal throughout *Foundation* as it was in the earlier text. The discussion of Christ is especially concentrated in Leahy's dialogue with Altizer.[19] Throughout, "Christ" functions both determinately and something like a free radical, determinately insofar as Christ is identified with the Word, which in turn is identified with Saying (F, 15–16) and in particular saying or manifesting the new.[20] Of course, Saying the new is the New as saying. At the same time there is an intrinsically close relation between Christ and the body of God, without as much explicit invocation of the Holy Spirit,[21] as was the case in *Novitas Mundi*. Leahy writes of Christ as the necessary personalization of the "created Godhead." Given the traditional way of talking about "Godhead" (*thearchia*, *Gottheit*) in the Christian mystical tradition as being so real as to be beyond the Creator with whom the creature already finds herself incommensurate,[22] this locution is odd at best, possibly oxymoronic at worst. I hope to make sense of this when I come to discuss Leahy's important meontological turn in *Foundation*, which, if not entirely indebted to the heterodox Dominican figure, is in some respect dependent on this remarkable thinker of isness, divine birth, and suspension of the relation between Creator and creature in favor of the nearness of what is truly fundamental in human being and divine source.

Foundation characterizes the new thinking as having a "catholic" form or logic. Thus, his references to "catholicity" (F, 113–14) to capture what he takes to be a fundamental quality of his thinking that corresponds to the upsurge and unveiling of the absolutely new. Thus also Leahy's use of the adjective "catholicological" (F, 38–39, 421) and his even more arcane but extraordinarily interesting use of the adverbial "catholicologically" (F, 6, 98, 154).[23] The fact that the adverbial form dominates suggests that "catholic" is connected intrinsically to the energy and dynamism of the new: this phenomenon makes all new, including the wording that would be adequate to its emergence, while also signifying the corporate reality of the novum that is the integrator of hither-to-fore wounded reality.

In *Foundation*, Leahy increases the punctiliarity of the apocalyptic style of thinking inaugurated in *Novitas Mundi*. It gives greater epochal determinacy with regard to the apocalyptic moment than Leahy supplied in the earlier text. Leahy writes in the preface: "1989 was the Year of the Beginning. It marked the beginning of the new world order as a clearly visible fact. . . . The beginning of the new world order is the end of modernity. For the first time in history the *perpetual newness* is universal."[24] Not all modern and contemporary apocalyptic thinkers are as determinate in chronologically marking the moment, though some are, for example, Alain Badiou, who gives 1968 as his preferred date.[25] Nonetheless, the giving of a date is more important than the actual date given for it foregrounds a momentous shift in time of time itself. The new, Leahy insists, can be characterized as "absolute interruption" (F, 45)—which is to echo the famous formula of Walter Benjamin. The new that discloses itself in "essentially new" thinking is not the kind of new that will become old, the kind of present that will become a past.

Leahy's "saving" of Karl Marx in the first part of *Foundation* refuses the interpretive convention of a Marx overcoming Hegel by replacing theory with praxis. In line with poststructuralists such as

Louis Althusser, Alain Badiou, and Slavoj Žižek, Leahy underscores the contribution of Marx in soldering theory and praxis together: praxis does not merely follow through on theory but expands it insofar it achieves contact with the real world (F, 14ff.). Marx, the theorist of revolution, is an authentic apocalyptic thinker because he recognizes "the absolute existence of reason itself absolute, the transcendental passion of an absolutely new order now actually occurring in the form of the transcendence of the practical absolute—the perception itself of the transcendental absolutely existing now" (F, 114). While the linking of Marxism and Catholicism has a history in French Marxism, in England with Catholics such as Herbert McCabe, and in the multiverse forms of liberation theology, Leahy's conjugation differs from all in melding apocalyptic Marxism with a catholicism focused on the actuality of the new community.

Pragmatism figures in *Foundation* as an instrument to restrain totalizing apriorist thinking in general. Peirce especially is a useful ally in constructing an alternative logic to classical logic and especially Hegelian logic (F, 259ff.). American Pragmatism is a precursor of the new thinking, which is necessarily for the first time and thus cannot be said to anticipate it, if by this one means participation in this new thinking in advance (F, 560, 570).[26] Pragmatism can be celebrated because it represents a step beyond modernity (F, 581–93). It remains something of a halfway house that can and should be taken seriously, provided one acknowledges that the seeing of the *new* relativizes all thought that has preceded it, including thinking that has attempted to break with modernity.

Foundation introduces a meontological inflection, an apocalyptic thinking of appearance in a full-blown ontological register. For Leahy, the new is no longer best captured as the plenitude of reality or *esse*, as it was in *Novitas Mundi*. Nothing, rather than being, is now primitive in *Foundation* (F, 359, 303, 352, 359, 467, inter alia) because it has come to be regarded as primordial source and ontological and doxological exclamation. This meontological horizon has in turn two major loci, the one anthropological, the other what might be called "theo-ontological," even if these two foci in the end represent two aspects of the one horizon of realty and thinking. Leahy commends Nietzsche for at least grasping something of the anthropological locus in his "abyssal thought" (F, 94; also 353). This is a necessary condition for the German philosopher's being in any sense a seer. Formally, this is also to accept nihilism. Importantly, for Leahy, nihilism of this sort, rightly understood, is speculatively productive: an apocalyptic breakthrough. Leahy's embrace of Nietzsche is at once cautious and restricted, presupposing a distinction between positive and negative forms of nihilism.

The second meontological focus is theo-ontological rather than anthropological. Here, Leahy engages Altizer's later texts that focus on the apocalyptic "self-embodiment" of God (F, pt. 1, ch. 4). Leahy wants to take his distance from Altizer's thanatology, indeed, from any suggestion of dialectic of death and life, pain and joy, in which the former serves as the real condition of the latter. In *Foundation*, the *new* as meontologically characterized is unanticipatable *jouissance*. Near the close of Leahy's massive tome, one comes across a hugely important discussion of the relation between nothing and the immanent Trinity and the consequent relation between the immanent Trinity and the world (F, 575–77). The Trinity is not the primordial reality; the primordial reality, which is also the eschatological reality, is the emergent creation from nothing. The relation between Leahy's audacious speculation and that of Aquinas is no longer merely tenuous; it is entirely broken. The Trinity is not the absolutely real. Moreover, as Leahy makes clear earlier in the text, especially as the ground of reality is associated with love, love is no longer tri-personal, but personal (F, 84–86). Nothing and personality seem to define each other. As the manifestation of the nothing that is absolute, the Trinity empties into world and time. This represents considerably more than the correction of the view of the Trinity as connected with aseity and an argument for something like reciprocal dependence; rather, it suggests that the Trinity is simply a placeholder and that time is the proper medium of nothing. With this connection now fully argued we can make sense of Leahy's very strange locution of "created Godhead" earlier in the text. What that locution means is that the primordial nothing dynamically traverses the imaginary space of an independent trinitarian dimension, which it turns out is but a sketch or schema of time and/or the order of existence.

Foundation not only provides extensive treatment of Fibonacci series, Fermat's theorem, and analytic geometry, but submits them to revision in order for them to disclose the radically new (F, 279). Leahy's new mathematics (F, 255), which is also a new logic (F, 259), presents a new standard of truth: this new logic is constructed on the basic insight that zero is not nothing and not not nothing (F, 255, 265). The most conspicuous example of revision, guided by this perception, is provided in his fundamental revision of Fibonacci's sequence. Instead of following Fibonacci's sequence of integers that commences with 1, Leahy commences with zero [0], and generates surprising theorems on the basis of this, which we need not go into here. In addition, we have his extraordinary appendix in which he attempts to interpret Augustine's *De Trinitate* according to his revised model of Fibonacci's sequence (F, 629–34). Correlative to the focus on zero-not-nothing is the focus on infinity. Leahy revises this mathematical concept essentially along the same philosophical lines as his revision of zero, and does so not in the area of number theory but in the area of analytic geometry. The mathematics of *Foundation* bewilders the theologian and philosopher because the basic mathematics on which Leahy enacts his revisions is essentially beyond their grasp. Meanwhile the mathematics of *Foundation* baffles the mathematician because Leahy completely subverts mathematical conventions.

The apocalyptic shape of *Foundation* is visionary, epochal, adventist, postmodern or post postmodern, definitely Christian, and—albeit in an idiosyncratic way—"Catholic." Its linguistic mode of operation is ecstatic, its vocabulary at once philosophical, theological, and mathematical, its overall grammar synthetic and constructive, while also genealogical in significant part. While similar to *Novitas Mundi*, the apocalyptic content is focused on emergent novelty with an eschatological twist; there is now a much more compact rendering of creation/incarnation/resurrection/communion-of-saints. *Foundation* signals that the shape of Leahy's apocalyptic thought is regulated by meontology, but also by an insight, filtered through American philosophy, of the eschatological privilege of American democracy (America the living instantiation of *pluribus in unum*).

Of contemporary thinkers, Alain Badiou provides the most self-consciously apocalyptic rendition of Marxism. If the condition of the possibility lies in the centrality in Badiou's oeuvre of the category of *event*, the conversation is in turn facilitated by Badiou's constitutive epochalism with its tendency to provide privileged temporal markers, his critique of the egology of modern thought, his refusal to endorse a doctrinaire distinction between Marxism and Christianity, and his commitment to the view that Christianity represents the beginning of the beginning, the annunciation of the event with universalistic consequences that belatedly breaks forth in time precisely as time and its recognition.[27] A few brief words about some of these characteristics. For Badiou, as articulated in *Being and Event*, the category of event is used to describe a truly radical break or rupture in the tissue of reality and thought: reality is temporal and thus chancy all the way down, and if thought has the aspiration to be adequate with regard to reality, given rupture, thought too is constituted as fundamentally different than the thought that preceded it. As a category, event both displaces and replaces being, which, on Badiou's view, continues to suggest the stability of an underlying substance that fails to break from a kind of constitutive Parmenideanism.[28]

In Badiou, as in Leahy, specific historical moments are marked as cuts or interruptions, rather than interruption functioning (as in Benjamin or a Catholic follower such as Johann Baptist Metz) as a formal apocalyptic ascriptor without temporal instantiation.[29] Whereas Leahy has 1989 and the millennium as the privileged points, Badiou has 1968 and the Maoist revolution.[30] Coming from the Marxist rather than Christian side, Badiou links Christianity, as universal promise and promise of universalism, to Marxism as fulfillment both in the order of reality and thought, even as he insists that promise and fulfillment cannot be inserted into the teleological matrix.[31] From the point of view of a specifically Christian apocalyptic, it is interesting that the emphasis in Badiou falls more on Paul than the figure of Christ.[32] While this might well be explained as a reversal of Nietzschean preferences, very likely the positive underscoring of the importance of Paul has everything to do with Agamben's New Testament exegesis, which applies Benjamin's apocalypse of interruption to Paul, to his letter to the Romans in particular.[33] Badiou's vision, like Leahy's, is one of the impossible community that is the other both in thought and reality to the history of the West with its egological and monadic predilections.

Badiou's privileging of mathematics is consistent across a wide variety of texts, both in focal and penumbral ways.[34] Badiou is not a mathematical intuitionist. Infinity is not mystically apperceived, but concerns, as Cantor in particular insisted, transfinite numbers laid out in quantities and ratios that can be calculated.[35] It should be said that Badiou's mathematical range, while impressive, is narrower and more conventional than Leahy's; its main focus is on the paradoxes of set theory common to *Principia Mathematica* and the consistency-completeness paradox of Gödel's theorem. Nonetheless, no more than in the case of Leahy does mathematics in Badiou simply provide matter which philosophical thought has to ponder, develop, and translate. Rather, it provides a language in and through which the real is disclosed as event and as a unity that cannot be reduced to identity.

The unveiling function of mathematics is a unique marker of both of these forms of apocalyptic and, together with the above, features as a kind of pedestal that invites—even demands—further investigation into relations and also differences between these apocalyptic forms without necessarily prejudicing the priority of Altizer.

Again, in its deployment of higher order mathematics in general and number in particular, *Foundation* opens another line of relation in the space of apocalyptic seeing that is broadly speaking more traditional and Catholic than anything we find in Badiou, who at best drinks in some of the philosophical Joachimism that makes its way through Hegel and Schelling into a postmodern apocalypticist such as Gianni Vattimo.[36] As is the case regarding Badiou, there are intimations in *Foundation* as to where one might look. The first is supplied in the recurring use in *Foundation* of the language of "minimum." This is a well-known motif in the thought of the Renaissance Catholic thinker Nicholas of Cusa, who famously used mathematics to adjust minds to handle paradox and see anew.[37] In particular, mathematical paradoxes such as the intimate relation between the minimum and maximum throw light on the meaning of both Christ and the Trinity, and vice versa. In addition, while Cusa is not as promiscuous as Eckhart when it comes to the ascription of "nothing" to the divine, he does permit it as part of a large apophatic register. Again, not only do we find echoes in *Foundation* of Cusa's locution of "non-other" (*non-aliud*), but it functions similarly—although not identically—to dismantle highly contrastive ways of conjugating the relation of the divine to the world and to human being.[38] Now, if Cusa is not in the strict sense an apocalyptic thinker, and given his hierarchical and Neoplatonic credentials, Leahy could plausibly find his apocalyptic credentials, somewhat suspect,[39] his thought serves as the presupposition of the far more audacious Giordano Bruno, who is fed by the new science of Copernicus. Even more than Cusa, Bruno saw philosophy and theology as two intimately related forms of wisdom, to which one could add mathematics as a third. Like the first two, mathematics is a universal discourse capable of unveiling what has been hidden since the foundation of the world, that is, an infinite universe that is essentially coextensive with the divine.[40] Bruno's revolutionary insight is that of one world, named in a triad of discourses: in philosophy a plural complex unity, in theology a divinely inspired cosmos, and in mathematics an actual numerical infinite. For a number of important commentators on Bruno, his lack of demonstration when it came to mathematical proof and his providing mathematics with a universalistic rather than regional disclosive function suggest that effectively we have transcended the order of mathematics entirely and that Bruno, as is the case with neo-Pythagoreans in general, opens up a kind of hermetic field of para-mathematics.[41] This is a discussion that would likely prove fruitful in the case of Leahy, who also treats mathematics as an unveiling discourse not only of number but through number of the complex unity of the whole.

Throughout *Foundation*, Leahy energetically engages the Kabbalah's articulation of divine names or *sephirot*, not excepting the name of origin or beginning, that is, the Ein Sof, which is determined as a productive nothing that defines the Godhead.[42] This engagement, however, does not increase the Jewish ratio of *Foundation*. It is evident that throughout the text Jewish Kabbalah is made to speak not only to a general philosophical truth, but also to a specifically Christian truth. In this sense, Leahy recapitulates a move made by the Renaissance Florentine polymath Pico della Mirandola and his student Johann Reuchlin.[43] In a repetition of what we find in Pico and Reuchlin, in *Foundation* the Tetragrammaton is Jesus Christ (F, 360–61). Again, "the absolute Holy One Blessed Be He" is Jesus of Nazareth (F, 419–20). Similarly, under analysis, numerical and otherwise, the Tetragrammaton is revealed to be the divine Trinity (F, 417). Moreover, since the general auspices of all interpretation and translation, according to Leahy, is catholic in form ("catholicological"), this enables translations of divine names such as *shalom* (F, 364, 366) and *malkuth* (foundation) to be associated with Eucharist (F, 368–69) and the body of God or Catholic communion of saints (F, 388, 408), respectively.

My claim here, in closing, is the modest one that even if Altizer's apocalyptic provides something of a template for the apocalyptic shape articulated by *Foundation*, we do honor to the irreducible singularity of the apocalyptic shape articulated by *Foundation* by broadening the horizon of prospective relation. Cusanus and Bruno, Pico and Reuchlin are broadly "Catholic" thinkers at the beginning of the modern period who, if they troubled and complicated Catholic orthodoxy in a manner not dissimilar to Meister Eckhart, also provided critical leverage in advance against the egological turn that identifies modernity. Both nonkabbalistic and kabbalistic forms of Renaissance thought were focused on unveiling the complex divine whole, presumed to have been hidden, by any and all discourse that had such a power. Mathematics joined philosophy and experimental theology in such *apocalypsis*.

With respect to Leahy's apocalyptic thinking, it is more accurate to speak of apocalyptic in the plural—more specifically, to speak of a shift in apocalyptic register from the more or less Joachimite shape of Catholic apocalyptic articulated in *Novitas Mundi* to a more Hermetic and Kabbalist shape of Catholic apocalyptic rendered in *Foundation*. I want to end as I began by insisting on the singularity of the opus of Leahy: as applied to a form of thinking that is irreducibly for the first time—what William Desmond would say is fundamentally "idiotic" in the Greek sense of *idiotes*—apocalyptic taxons are gestures that give us a fleeting hold on an emergent reality.

Notes

1. Even before *Being and Time*, Heidegger is an unrelenting critic of Leibniz's search for rational and logical grounds of appearances. Heidegger does not exempt Aquinas from the constitutive rationalism of the West, whereas Cornelio Fabro does in his great tome *God in Exile*—even as he follows Heidegger in fundamentally questioning Leibniz's essentialism. See Fabro, *God in Exile: Modern Atheism* (Chicago: Paulist, 1968).

2. I have treated of the early Catholic reaction to Heidegger's *Being and Time* in which Erich Przywara and Edith Stein figure prominently in two articles. See Cyril O'Regan, "Heidegger and Christian Wisdom," in *Christian Wisdom Meets Modernity*, ed. Francesca Murphy and Kenneth Oakes (London: Bloomsbury, 2016), 37–57, and also "In the Realm of Apocalypse: Heidegger and the Impossibility of Christian Death," in *Christian Death*, ed. Matthew Levering (Eugene: Cascade, 2017).

3. The nihilism charge was made by Przywara and Stein from the late 1920s; it emerged within Heidegger's circle of students with Karl Löwith in the 1940s. See Löwith, *Martin Heidegger's European Nihilism*, ed. Richard Wolin, trans. Gary Steiner (New York: Columbia University Press, 1995).

4. Among those who promote the primacy of revelation in the work of Aquinas, we can include such very different thinkers as Mark Jordan, John Milbank, and Gilles Emery. See Jordan, *Rewritten Theology: Aquinas and His Readers* (Oxford: Wiley, 2005); Milbank, with Catherine Pickstock, *Truth in Aquinas* (London: Routledge, 2000); Emery, *The Trinitarian Theology of St. Thomas Aquinas*, trans. Francesca Aran Murphy (Oxford: Oxford University Press, 2007).

5. The doxological reading of Pseudo-Dionysius has been made in both the historical and philosophical fields. For a good historical example, see Alexander Golitsin, *Mystagogy: A Monastic Reading of Dionysius the Areopagita* (Collegeville, MN: Cistercian, 2014). For a good philosophical example, see Jean-Luc Marion, *The Idol and Distance: Five Studies*, ed. with introduction by Thomas A. Carlson (New York: Fordham University Press, 2001), 139–95.

6. Arguably, Antonio Lopez is the Catholic philosopher who, in the ontological rather than phenomenological domain, has done most to rethink the Catholic tradition as lifting up gift. In his *Gift and the Unity of Being* (Eugene, OR: Wipf and Stock, 2013), Aquinas's commitment to *creatio ex nihilo* is read as being constitutive of gratuity in a manner very similar to Leahy. In *Spirit's Gift: The Metaphysical Insight of C. Bruaire* (Washington: Catholic University of America Press, 2006), Lopez puts into circulation the work of Claude Bruaire (1932–1986), a gifted Catholic philosopher important to Jean-Luc Marion, who in conversation with modern philosophy and especially Hegel and Schelling argued for the priority of gift.

7. Joachim de Fiore, *Liber de Concordia Novi ac Veteris Testamenti*, ed. Randolph Daniel (Philadelphia: American Philosophy Society, 1983); also *Enchiridion super Apocalypsim*, ed. Edward K. Burger (Toronto: Pontifical Institute of Medieval Studies, 1986). There is some fine secondary literature on Joachim. See, in particular, Marjorie Reeves, *Joachim de Fiore and the Prophetic Future* (New York: Harper and Row, 1977); *The Influence of Prophecy in the Later Middle Ages: A Study in Joachimism* (Oxford: Clarendon Press, 1969); and Bernard McGinn, *The Calabrian Abbot: Joachim de Fiore in the History of Western Thought* (New York: Macmillan, 1985). McGinn gives attention to the ways in which Joachim stretches to the breaking point consensus Catholic views, and also pays heed to Aquinas's and Bonaventure's responses to Joachimism.

8. Ernst Bloch, *The Principle of Hope*, 3 vols., trans. Neville Plaice, Stephen Plaice, and Paul Knight (Cambridge: MIT Press, 1995); the German original *Das Prinzip Hoffnung* was published in 1959.

9. It is Fichte who formulates this axiom in the *Wissenschaftslehre* (1794), and thereafter it is taken up by Schelling and Hegel as they enact their critiques of divine transcendence beyond the world. This is not to say that there are no anticipations of this view in philosophical and religious thought. In philosophy the name of Giordano Bruno comes to mind; in religious thought, Meister Eckhart and Jacob Boehme. Each of these three thinkers is known to Schelling and Hegel.

10. The following is perhaps the clearest statement regarding apocalyptic to be found in Leahy's entire oeuvre: "Now, closely considered, the apocalypse is not about the end of the world. The apocalypse is about the end of the end of the world. . . . The apocalypse is about the *beginning* of a new heaven and earth. The *beginning* of a *new* universe is the beginning of a world *recently or newly begun*. If we take *newly begun* to its limit—we have a now that is the first now of the world" (FP, 146).

11. For the sublation even of waste in the Hegelian tradition, see Cyril O'Regan, "Hegel, Theodicy, and the Invisibility of Waste," in *The Providence of God*, ed. Francesca Aran Murphy and Philip G. Ziegler (London: T and T Clark, 2009), 74–108.

12. Jacques Derrida, *Glas*, trans. John P. Leavey Jr. and Richard Rand (London and Lincoln: University of Nebraska Press, 1986). For an essay of mine that presents a reading of *Glas,* see Cyril O'Regan, "Hegel, Sade, and

Gnostic Infinities," in *Radical Orthodoxy: Theology, Philosophy, and Politics* (Fall 2013): 383–425.

13. This is a major point of emphasis in my book on the critique of Hegel by the Catholic theologian, Hans Urs von Balthasar. See Cyril O'Regan, *The Anatomy of Misremembering: Balthasar's Response to Philosophical Modernity*, vol. 1: *Hegel* (New York: Crossroad, 2014).

14. Ray L. Hart, *God Being Nothing* (Chicago: University of Chicago Press, 2016).

15. See also F 354, 355, 408, 544, 566, 575. Even with these we are only scratching the surface.

16. This is a major point of criticism of Hegel made by Derrida in *Glas*. For another view on this structurally important aspect of Hegel's system, see Cyril O'Regan, "Hegel and the Folds of Discourse," in *International Philosophical Quarterly* 39, no. 154 (June 1999): 173–93.

17. See the following interesting passage: "We, embodying the integral absolute, declare today the Third Day, the day after the sabbath, the first of a new creation" (F, 92). One wonders whether Leahy here really means the Eighth Day.

18. In *Foundation*, as befits its apocalyptic strain, the language of the "kingdom of God" evokes the eschatological *Shalom*. The emphases on doctrine, ritual, and ethics notwithstanding, this connection is longstanding in Catholic thought and is prominent in Augustine's *City of God*.

19. For the dialogue with Altizer, see F, 194–211.

20. At one level, Leahy simply wants to speak to the dynamism of Logos and the intervolvement of language and reality. He might be thinking of the Hebrew *dabar* to interpret logos especially as logos is identified in the Western tradition with reason and logic. At the same time, it is impossible not to notice the Levinasian evocation regarding Saying and its implied contrast with the said.

21. The contrast here is merely approximate. Spirit is a topic of analysis in the chapter in which Leahy engages Altizer (see F, 194–211).

22. The incommensurability clause concerning the Creator–creature distinction is standard in Catholic thought. The language of *thearchia* and *Gottheit* is the language of Pseudo-Dionysius and Eckhart respectively.

23. This is interesting because Leahy can be understood to be bending language to match the emergent quality of the new as the really real.

24. "Perpetual newness" mimes the very particular Catholic locution of "perpetual virginity," which is traditionally ascribed to Mary.

25. See Alain Badiou, *The Communist Hypothesis*, trans. David Macey and Steve Corcoran (London: Verso, 2015).

26. Here the point is that there is no prolepsis in an ontological sense.

27. The clearest articulation of the hinge concept of *event* is to be found in *Being and Event*, trans. Oliver Feltham (London: Continuum, 2005). As a category, event both interprets "being" and replaces it. Badiou's ambition

is very much on the same level as Leahy's, that is, he aims to reinterpret and overcome the entire philosophical tradition and concentrate it on the in-breaking of event.

28. The actual category that Badiou uses is "Platonism." For him, the ascription Platonism is a pejorative to the degree to which it rules out chance and contingency. To the degree to which Platonism can be integrated with contingency and chance, then it can be affirmed.

29. J. Matthew Ashley, in his *Interruptions: Mysticism, Politics, and Theology in the Work of Johann Baptist Metz* (Notre Dame: University of Notre Dame Press, 1998), highlights the extent to which Metz is deeply indebted to Walter Benjamin in general and his category of "interruption" in particular. I also attend to the Metz–Benjamin relation in *Anatomy of Misremembering*, 426–501.

30. While 1968 is a major epochal marker for Badiou, as it is for a host of French intellectuals including Foucault, it is not the only one. There is the Maoist revolution, and also the works of Karl Marx.

31. Nonteleological matrix in terms of promise–fulfillment.

32. See Alain Badiou, *Saint Paul: The Foundation of Universalism*, trans. Ray Brassier (Stanford: Stanford University Press, 2003). This thesis has subsequently been taken up by Slavoj Žižek.

33. Giorgio Agamben, *The Time that Remains: A Commentary on the Letter to Romans*, trans. Patricia Dailey (Stanford: Stanford University Press, 2005). Both Badiou and Agamben presuppose the much earlier articulation of the connection between Paul and universalism in Jacob Taubes, *The Political Theology of Paul*, trans. Dana Hollander (Stanford: Stanford University Press, 2003).

34. Badiou is a prolific writer on mathematics. See among other books *Number and Numbers*, trans. Robin MacKay (London: Polity, 2008); *The Logic of Worlds*, trans. Alberto Toscano (London: Continuum, 2009).

35. Christopher Norris's book on Badiou's classic text is marvelously lucid, especially in charting the relation between Badiou and the Lacanian Marxist atheist Gilles Deleuze who also has a deep interest in mathematics. See Norris, *Badiou's Being and Event: A Reader's Guide* (London: Continuum, 2009).

36. Although, arguably, it was the Swiss Catholic theologian Hans Urs von Balthasar who grasped the connection between German Idealism and Joachimism as early as the publication of *Apokalypse der deutschen Seele: Studien zu einer Lehre letzen Haltungen*, 3 vols. (Salzburg: Anton Pustet, 1937–39), the most trenchant formulation of the relation was provided by Jacob Taubes in *Abendländische Eschatologie* in the 1940s. For a recent translation of what was his dissertation, see *Occidental Eschatology*, trans. and with preface by David Ratmoko (Stanford: Stanford University Press, 2009), 83–194.

37. The great Renaissance thinker Nicholas of Cusa (1401–1464) was not only a philosopher and theologian of distinction, but a polymath who more than dabbled in mathematics, albeit with broadly philosophical and theological aims. Mathematics is both explicitly discussed and used. Explicit discussion of mathematics occurs throughout his career. There are texts on arithmetic and

geometry that date from 1445, with bookends provided by Cusa's reflection on mathematical construction *De conjecturis* (1441–42) and on mathematics in general in 1455. Cusa uses mathematics throughout this philosophical and theological works to square the appearances, that is, the use of mathematics helps us to see the possibilities of incarnation (*De docta ignorantia*) (1440) and Trinity (*De li non-aliud*) (1461). For convenient translations of these texts, see *Nicholas of Cusa on Learned Ignorance*, trans. Jasper Hopkins (Minneapolis: Banning Press, 1985); *Nicholas of Cusa on God as Not-Other*, trans. Jasper Hopkins, 3rd ed. (Minneapolis: Banning Press, 1987). Cusa was particularly drawn to such mathematical constructs as the coincidence in infinity of the circle and triangle, and cord and arc of an infinite circle. Scholars of Cusanus have grasped that his sense that mathematics opens up the arcana of divine and physical reality not only has deep roots in Neoplatonism, but roots in the esotericist Raymond Lull (1232–1315).

38. There is significant scholarship on Cusa's concept of not-other and real arguments about whether it is proto-pantheist in inspiration. While Jasper Hopkins fiercely denies pantheistic tendencies, others have embraced it. Robert P. Scharlemann, a friend of Leahy, spoke to the pantheist side; see his "God as Not-Other: Nicholas of Cusa's *De li non-aliud*," in *Naming God* ed. Robert P. Scharlemann (New York: Paragon House, 1985), 116–32.

39. In *Foundation*, Leahy makes it clear that he is against Neoplatonism to the extent to which it holds to an ontological hierarchy. A case can be made that this hierarchy is troubled in Cusa, especially in *De li non-aliud*, as it was troubled before in the mystical thought of Meister Eckhart. This is also the case in Bruno and is especially to the fore in his two most famous texts, *De l'infinito universe e mundi* (1584) and *De la causa, principio et uno* (1584).

40. Arguably, however, in a way not repeated by Leahy, both Cusa and Bruno continue to distinguish between real and mathematical infinity and demonstrate that they are not fully ready to think of mathematics as constitutive rather than illustrative of reality.

41. Similarly to Cusa, Bruno not only used mathematics with respect to cosmology and ontology or theo-ontology, but also directly reflected on it. *De monade numeo et figura* (1591) and *De innumerabilibus, de immenso et infigurabilii* (1591) are two of the more prominent. Nonetheless, neither of these texts is mathematical in the strict sense, but more nearly a philosophical reflection on how number opens up the world beyond the imagining of the premodern. Mathematics is more nearly a kind of philosophical para-mathematics which is invested with an unveiling function.

42. Of course, the divine nothing is oriented toward *Adam Kadmon*—a corporate reality—that has fascinated not only Jewish mystics but Christian writers from the Renaissance to German philosophical thought. For some general remarks on this, see O'Regan, *Gnostic Return in Modernity* (Albany: State University of New York Press, 2001), 200–205; for Christian ingestion of Kabbalah in Jacob Boehme, see O'Regan, *Gnostic Apocalypse: Jacob Boehme's*

Haunted Narrative (Albany: State University of New York Press, 2002), 193–210; for Hegel, see O'Regan, "Hegel and Anti-Judaism: Narrative and the Inner Circulation of the Kabbalah," in *The Owl of Minerva* 28, no. 2 (Spring 1997): 141–82. See Glenn Alexander Magee, *Hegel and the Hermetic Tradition* (Ithaca: Cornell University Press, 2001), 150–86.

43. For a brief discussion of the trajectory of Kabbalah from Pico to Hegel, see O'Regan, "Hegel and Anti-Judaism," 168–72; Magee, *Hegel and the Hermetic Tradition*, 21–50.

6

The Act of Omnipotence

Abolition of the Mystical Quest

MICHAEL JAMES DISE

For the gifts and calling of God *are* without repentance.

—Romans 11:29 (KJV)

The very ultimacy of the revelation of the divine name [I AM] is a once and for all releasement, a releasement that having occurred can never simply be annulled, and cannot be so annulled because it is an irreversible actuality.

—Thomas J. J. Altizer, *Genesis and Apocalypse*

This personal freedom essentially the new world order is *the Creator* transcending the goal: the means absolutely the goal for the first time. Transcending the goal the Creator exists for the first time in essence: in the realization of the end the Creator *is* the Creator: the Creator exists now for the first time in history in the absolutely unconditioned intimacy of the absolute neighborliness of being itself.

—BS, 21

In the classical theism that reached its philosophical pinnacle in Thomas Aquinas, God's essence was known to be identical to God's existence. This implied that God's inward eternal nature was immediately and infinitely expressed in God's outward being without there being any "fall" or lapse from Platonic Idea to imperfect matter. The pillars of immutability, impassibility, and impassability were essential ingredients to divine omnipotence, reinforcing the perfection of God: God's *immutability* meant that God does not *change*, and indeed that God *cannot* change; God's *impassibility* meant that God cannot be affected by the act of another so as to experience *suffering*, which would immediately be a violation of immutability; God's *impassability* meant that God's being is impenetrable, that God cannot be *crossed* or *passed through*, just as in the Aristotelian universe two objects cannot occupy the same space at the same time. The irony here is that while omnipotence implied the infinite *potency* to create ex nihilo, it also implied an infinite *impotence* in its incapacity to change. The necessity for God to remain within Godself in order to remain safe from the other was thereby the absolute weakness of God, an absolute weakness that reached its modern pinnacle in Hegel's Absolute Spirit, whose absolute self-enclosure required the infinite negation of every other existent in order to maintain its Absolute Self. And even in the case that Hegel posited the necessity of God negating Godself within Godself in order to actualize God's own existence, God only underwent change *in form* but not *in essence*, since the essence of God was the Absolute Idea of God's own Self, and every existing form in the divine body was another constituent form of the divine Idea in its infinite elasticity.[1] Regarding Hegel's God as a simulacrum of omnipotence, D. G. Leahy writes: "The absolute elasticity of the Hegelian Idea has no room for what neither contains nor can be contained, no room for actual omnipotence itself. The absolute Idea was precisely the *simulacrum of omnipotence,* the turning inside out (were it possible) of omnipotence, but then (since that is not possible) merely the turning inside out of the *notion* of omnipotence so that its *definition* was its having nothing outside itself" (BS, 105).

Contrariwise to both classical theism and Hegel's modern panentheism, Leahy describes his trans-theistic[2] conception of omnipotence in the following way: "In fact omnipotence now actually the body of existence for the first time—omnipotence the absolute power body—is the absolute elasticity that is Hegel's absolute Idea turned inside out" (BS, 105). This absolute inversion of the Godhead in the thinking now occurring is at once the absolute outwardization of the Thomistic divine essence; the essence of God that was *ipsum esse,* or the act-of-being itself, self-possessed within the aseitic and ipseitic being of God, is now in existence without self as the absolute exteriority of the spirit of God. This divine essence that is *ipsum esse* ex-isting, absolutely extant from an infinitely finite singularity in the universe's spaceless indeterminacy—the form of this magnitude being the abyss extant, *nihil ex nihilo* (F, 273)—is referred to by Leahy as the "transcendental essence of existence itself" (NM, 2). This transcendental essence that is the essentially creative essence identically *ipsum esse* is, through the Incarnation, now apparent in both time and thought. Its appearance in time as an interruptive rift in time is the appearance of the beginning of time *within* time; the beginning that is the absolute discontinuity of the absolute minimum, the absolute Moment of creation, appears in its essential indifference to time as that essence which historically perpetuates time qua the unconditioned tautology of change. This unconditioned tautology of change that *ipsum esse* is establishes the priority of history to time itself, and the truth of omnipotence as the inexhaustibility of the creative act itself. Here, then, the absolute discontinuity of the absolute minimum singularity of divine spirit is its very existence qua essential change now occurring in the eternal Now of God.

Now that the transcendental essence appears in the thinking now occurring, the beginning of thought appears in its very midst as an interruptive rift in thought, the foundation of thought occurring *within* thought: now the absolute discontinuity that creates thought is thought's very essence, and the unconditioned tautology of thought is identically its own essence, eliminating the necessity of "self" in its conversion of thought into an essentially historical but also essentially creative thinking. Here, thought is both a discontinuous continuity and a continuous discontinuity. Leahy variously refers to this essentially new form of thinking as "transcendental historical thinking" (NM, 13), "the transcendental imagination" (NM, 380; F, 157), and the *novitas mentis* (NM, 14). (Here, the transcendental imagination should be carefully distinguished from Kant's as one that is unified by essentially creative synthesis rather than the a priori transcendental ego.) *Here the "act of omnipotence"* (F, 622) *is conceived in its transcendental character as the incarnation of change*: omnipotence itself moves to new ground (BS, xxvi). As contrasted with the Deleuzian notion of a differential field of existence as a "plane of immanence," in Leahy there is the infinite transcendence of the plane of immanence in multiple planes of transcendence: groundless emergence from a singularity without preformal matter or matterless form, existence itself as groundless transcendence in the creation ex nihilo of an unlimited number of a posteriori grounds.[3] This complexity from simplicity is integral creation, creation without a Plan, and essentially transcendental existence. Hence, omnipotence moving to new ground is the creation of the ground itself/the grounds themselves.

At the height of philosophical modernity Hegel's God posited the conditions of its own existence: now, in the thinking now occurring, God posits the existence of an Other without conditions. This unconditional existence of the Other is "intrinsic" to the trinitarian structure of the Godhead: eternal otherness in the Godhead is its essentially differencing itself from the essential "self" of the Creator. For the Creator in essence implies *both* creative efficacy *and* the lasting efficacy of the created—*the absolute multiplication of the transcendental essence in its effect*—so that Leahy can delineate omnipotence in the following way: "Omnipotence never rests. Omnipotence completely ceasing works absolutely for the first time. The working of omnipotence qua omnipotence is its completely ceasing from its works and from its working to make its works without the latter thereby ceasing to exist" (BS, 277). This creative existing qua divine ceasing, identically the finished work in the omnipotent efficacy of the ontological fact of created subsistence in the form of the absolutely particular body, is the actual beginning of infinite being from the essentially tautologous point of departure that is the infinitely discrete identity of an existing Person (a point of departure absolutely exploding into the body itself, absolutely embodying its own history).

Leahy defines divinity as "absolute metaboly" (BS, 11), an absolutely supervenient change transcendentally relating two absolute others as another absolute Other, an absolute third which is a "relative absolute" (BS, 255): the individuation of an absolute other-omnipotence moving to new ground, the new unity precluding the dictatorial *Self* through the omnicratic *withness* of actual existence itself. The Godhead is absolutely capable of undergoing change, and in effect the oft-repeated question as to whether omnipotence implies that "God cannot make a rock so big/heavy that God cannot lift it" is nullified. A truly omnipotent God, whose inessential form appears in open theism's claim that divine *self*-limitation creates and runs the world, essentially implies creating an absolute Other in the context of *other*-limitation. Or further simplified: God creates an absolute Other so absolute that God cannot negate that Other's existence or bring that Other under God's own sovereign control.[4] Open theism's claim to a God omniscient without being omnipotent—knowing every possible future world while refraining from acting unilaterally (divine self-limitation)—is displaced in the thinking now occurring by a God omnipotent without being omniscient, creating an absolute Other absolutely different (divine other-limitation). Hence, in open theism the Creator's knowledge of the future, that is, God's foreknowledge of infinite possibilities, is itself subordinate to the self-limitation of omnipotence that provides freedom to the creature. By contrast, in the thinking now occurring, the Creator's knowledge of the future is nonplused by the omnipotent capacity to create that which is essentially new and unforeseeable, while the creation of an absolute Other is essentially the other-limitation of omnipotent freedom, indeed, the gift of the unconditional freedom of the creature.

The noncausal efficacy of omnipotence is its lasting fruit:[5] the "immediately mediated immediacy" of the creative act of God is irrevocably incarnate as the transcendental individual. This noncausal efficacy has as its form the Gift of the body itself: the "absolutely productive receptivity" that is an existing person is its absolute relation to and "infinite transaction" with an infinite number of others (BS, 3), prescinding from sovereignty but not from beginning. This infinite transaction that is the trans-action between perfectly distinct Others—the perfectly differentiated congress of the absolute multiplicity of *ipsum esse*—nonpluses the very notion of an a priori Plan or Idea. Leahy writes of the notion of plan in relation to the concept of omnipotence:

> The ultimate offense is that omnipotence itself reveals there is absolutely and essentially no plan, no plane, therefore no "new plane of immanence" alternative to a "new plane of transcendence," no *tabula rasa*—there is nothing but the writing that always and everywhere is for the first time, "*texte hors d'hors-texte*, TEXT BEYOND BEYOND-TEXT, the beginning the very real of existence." There is no planning that is not the plan that is the absolute transcendence of the plane of absolute immanence. Here is the plan: the plan/plane of existence is what I/we am/are now writing for the first time. This being of omnipotence itself without plan

or plane other than what occurs, this being absolutely now, is creating love. Without plan or plane for the first time conceived in essence Omnipotence itself is indeed absolute nimbleness. (BS, 208–209)

This new omnipotence that confronts the former notion of nature as essentially entropic and destructive is now seen to be, essentially, creative love: its transcendental essence is love that creates the Other essentially, as the very nature of nature itself. Here and now the Godhead is the Creator existing without plan or a priori nature in the essential novelty of the universe identically a new beginning. This new beginning occurs concretely in individual persons whose congress is now beginning to build a new world order, and this new world order is the beginning of the absolute exteriority of the Godhead in existence itself. Qua incarnation, this essential conversion of omnipotence to new ground—from uncreated omnipotence to created omnipotence—is the absolute differentiation of the Godhead as the creation of absolutely other existent persons creating each other. Concerning the efficacy of the incarnation now occurring in thought as a radical sea-change of thought, Leahy writes:

The creaturely life of the Godhead—the resurrected Body of Christ the divine Word incarnate wherein "all that God knows" is known—is now for the first time infinitely digital, infinitely parsed, infinitely particular, and, indeed, infinitely deictic. The now occurring infinite parsing of the resurrected Word made flesh is the eucharistic essence of existence at once omnipotence itself now actually embodying the Incarnation for the first time in an absolutely *non-para*digmatic form, in the form of the schema itself the absolutely real. (BS, 209)

This new omnipotence now incarnate as essentially creative love toward the other is a tautologous embodiment of the change itself that divine spirit is, at once a sacrificial act that is the generation of an absolute Other not at the expense of the imperishable creating I: a sacrifice identically at-one-ment. Hereby divine sacrifice and omnipotence are atoned: the "death of God" is revealed to be the omnipotent God immediately ceasing from the divine work without any net loss on either "side": for the infinitely one-sided existence of God is the inexhaustible fruit of the creative act of actual omnipotence, indeed, the irrevocable Gift of the transcendental essence as the transcendent existence of every existing person/thing.

The Augustinian revolution in thought—shattering the Aristotelian world in which the animating spirit of the human creature was an originally imperishable divine mind—posited a chasm between God and creature as a function of the new fact that the creature, whose contingent being was essentially distinguished from the Creator, had been created ex nihilo. Although the category of the mystical in the West had its historical origin in the Greek mystery cults, taken up initially by Christianity in variant forms of Gnosticism that emphasized a realization of inner union with divinity, in the course of time Christian mysticism sought a bridging of its new Creator–creature chasm through an inner path back to God. This path was the mystical quest, and inner union with God was the mystical goal. The realization of this union would then resolve the separation of the finite creature from the absolutely other God.

Where the goal of mysticism is union with God beyond the veil of the natural (created) world, this veil can be construed as ontological *or* epistemological. In Thomas Aquinas, a transitional thinker between the high and late Middles Ages, this union was an ontological achievement culminating in the beatific vision, a final Moment achieved whose ontological reality is the outworking of an intellectual/revelatory journey. But soon after Thomas, the mystical philosopher Meister Eckhart arrived at a more radical and quasi-atheistic apophatic mysticism that posited the goal of the path to God as the realization that one had *already* been one with God all along. For the end of the inner journey was to arrive at the ground of one's own soul and to discover this ground to be identically the Godhead. Indeed, so radical was this discovery that this Godhead in the soul was the very ground of God. Hence, beneath the particular self there was the gnostic realization of the creature's inner being as the divine universal Self, a Self before which all creatures and creation are as nothingness, but also a Self that from the point of view of creation is a divine and actual Nothingness. Not only does the creature realize its true Self through union with the Godhead, but the Godhead realizes its true Self through the creature qua the "birth of the Son in the soul." This was the occurrence of the late medieval delimitation of Gnosticism: the realization of divine union was not conceived to be a fruitless union eliminating particularity or existence, but rather a fruitful union incarnating the divine life in the everyday world of ordinary particular existence. This divine unity was to be the anchor for a creature otherwise tossed and turned by the vicissitudes of worldly being.

This Eckhartian identity of the I with the Godhead in the late medieval imagination was the beginning of a new form of radical mysticism: one could now know God as identically one's innermost ground, the ground of both one's mind and body, and even their primordial union in eternity past, a *coincidentia oppositorum* of being and nothing. This *coincidentia oppositorum* was an essence to be distilled in many modern variants. But Nicolas of Cusa, oriented toward the Incarnation and the legacy of Thomas's *positive* infinity of the Godhead (as opposed to Eckhart's *negative* infinity of the Godhead), arrived at the tail end of the late Middle Ages, on the cusp of the early modern world. In contrast to Eckhart, Cusa posited a radically *cataphatic* mysticism in which the existing universe, expanding out from the Godhead into infinite worlds and infinite creatures, was the very body of God infinitely beginning. This nonseparability of the relational manifold of creation, also nonseparable from God, marks a radical shift in Cusa from Eckhart.

The process theologian Catherine Keller writes, concerning Eckhart: "It would be precisely the radicality of the apophatic deity that ab-solves it from relation. In this it bears resemblance to the orthodox freedom of the transcendent One."[6] Contrasting this with the more heretical Cusa, Keller writes:

> In his exposition of the relation of affirmative and negative theologies, Cusa does not seek a balance of the two or a *via eminentia* beyond both, but rather their mutual enfolding in the *coincidentia oppositorum* he has coined in the same text. And in the context of the docta ignorantia the co-incidence of the negative and affirmative theologies answers precisely to that of the infinity of the all-enfolding *complicatio* and the unfolding, *explication,* of all finitudes. (93)

According to Keller, Cusa's thinking "can be said to open a third way, that of a participatory ontology indebted to Thomas but radicalized, open-ended, and so precisely infinite, a way between relativism and certainty into a modernity that never quite was" (95). Hence, Cusa's radical cataphatic mysticism, maintaining a nonseparable relation to the apophatic dimension through a *coincidentia oppositorum,* anticipates at the brink of modernity that essential thinking now actually occurring for the first time in history.

Where this thinking is most fully occurring, the *coincidentia oppositorum* is left behind and the apophatic dimension is transformed into the transcendental negativity of actually existing otherness, where the relational manifold of existing omnipotence is now seen to be existing other-consciousness, beyond all interiority or self-consciousness. Just here the interiority of the I as self is displaced by the selfless I now-beginning, beginning in every now in absolute relation to "a definite infinite of others, at once a number of infinite others" (BS, 8). Regarding this I existing at the edge of the universe infinitely beginning, Leahy writes: "The absolutely sharp edge of this beginning is absolutely roomless of other than action; the first transcendental reality—which itself is not unnameable—is absolute act. If it is not action entire, the necessity of the new beginning is infinite self-division, the absolute self-severing of self in the rest which is death" (BS, 9). Hence, the I at once "absolute act," *ipsum esse* existing as an "infinitely discrete identity" (BS, 265–67), is not at all anonymous but neither is it a self. Hence, in the thinking now occurring the I is no longer to be found in the interior depths of the divine Self, the latter rendering the identity of a particular person anonymous, but rather the I is to be found in the exteriority of the perfectly sharp edge of the divine Body, rendering it an absolutely discrete individual absolutely intelligible and particularized. This is existence essentially new in the artifactual body of Christ. Leahy writes: "The artifactual body is the perfect conception of the new creation. The artifactual body is the inception of the absolutely selfless interchangeability of absolutely discrete individualities, the initiation of the absolutely unconditioned unicity of plural personalities, the beginning of the complete joy of existence" (BS, 7).

If the goal of the mystical quest was the unity of the Creator and creature, that unity is now absolutely outwardized in the dynamic co-creative activity of the essentially other-related artifactual Body. Indeed, the unity of this artifactual Body now actually existing is "an absolutely unconditioned intimacy in existence" (BS, 3) between Creator and creature. The new consciousness of this co-creative symphony, which is at once a new world consciousness and a new world order, is a new universal beginning, indeed, the very first actually universal beginning. The former beginning of this universe was absolutely particular and from an infinitely finite point of departure (the latter's scientific referent the "big bang") which at the zero-point is an absolute singularity, which in the thinking now occurring is a zero-not-nothing whose "nature" is to-begin. Leahy writes:

> Beginning essentially conceived is existence *ex nihilo*. This is the beginning *identically* the end for the first time, *with* the Creator as never before: the beginning of the infinite wholeness of the world the Creator's actually embodying the universe. "The goal *is* to begin" is the identity of the Creator's first word, the very identity of "I am the Beginning." . . . *Not the absolutely new totality displacing the Creator, but the Creator placing the universe as the other of an absolute intimacy: the beginning of the new itself the Creator's absolute withness.* Not the "totality transcending any possible origin or goal" [as in Altizer], but the totality transcending the actual beginning which is itself the goal. (BS, 15)

Where the goal is no longer the *gnostic* quest to *recover* an original unity, presupposing an inwardized ground that is the a priori infinite Self (the One qua containment, the divine Self-containment that appropriates creation as its own a priori truth), the goal is now an *a-gnostic* act to *create* an apocalyptic unity, inaugurating an outwardized singularity that is the a posteriori infinite Body, or in other words, the One qua embodiment, the divine other-embodiment of the infinite congress of others—coincidentally the fruit born the a posteriori plurality of truth, which Leahy articulates here: "The construction of the category of truth is at once the construction of the plurality of truths whose unity is not a matter of compossibility but rather the absolute actuality of existence. . . . When it comes to the void what is said cannot be truth. Since saying is identical with truth for the first time it is false to say there is a void of truth" (BS, 83). Just here the new conception of omnipotence in the thinking now occurring is revealed to be not that of an all-consuming, self-creating Godhead that *contains* and thereby *appropriates* creatures, but qua incarnation, that of an all-giving, other-creating Godhead that *embodies* and *incarnates* creatures; no longer is God the truth of finite spirit but not the truth of human freedom—as if finite spirit had no truth of its own and perpetually depended on an external ground to exist (having its own freedom left outside of God's truth), but the truth of creaturely freedom *is* God's truth, such that "God is now the truth of human freedom & not the truth of finite spirit" (FP, 162).

The new divine unity qua unconditioned relation between uncreated omnipotence and created omnipotence—the uncreated Foundation integrating the fruit of the created foundation, the latter creatively increasing the former—is the essentially omnicratic constitution of the Godhead qua an Absolute Society (FP, 160; BS, 185f.) beyond civil society and law and beyond individual extraction from the whole, beyond subjectivity and original Plan. Before now, the realization of the mystical goal lifted the veil concealing a past truth as the excavation of an eternal secret: an always already preexistent oneness with God. But now the veil is banished by an ever-new oneness or unicity existing in/as the body of God, gifting the infinite multiplicity of Others. This multiplicity of infinite others qua created (incarnate) omnipotence is embodied in meta-identity with uncreated omnipotence as the Foundation, an unconditioned absolute relation that replaces modern containment with embodiment as the new thought of omnipotence (BS, 43–44). And so the existing apocalyptic I qua absolute act-of-change (created omnipotence) in the Foundation (uncreated omnipotence being-created) is a finite embodiment of its proportional relation to the Body even as the Body is an infinite unicity of all other-bodies in their creaturely freedom and unceasing newness. Hence, every finite spirit qua essential individuality is an absolute instance of absolute beginning, an absolute instance of absolute originality, whose absolute act creatively shares in the entire Foundation, such that every creative act co-creates the Kingdom of God and a furthering of the transcendental history of God (BS, 20–21).

This new I qua essential beginning whose thinking is the beginning of essence, this outwardized *ipsum esse* whose universal particularity is created omnipotence, is a foundation-stone through whom the "transcendental repetition of the creation" (NM, 350) is now taking place in the Foundation as "the Place" (F, 513). The frontier or absolute edge upon which a new creation is taking place is essentially a sea of indeterminacy/the magnitude of indeterminate singularity (zero-not-nothing), but its *form* is the abyss itself, the "abyss extant" whose outwardized indeterminacy is indeterminate otherness, not yet specified anew as *essence*. But the incompletion, the open edge, is not a matter of impotence or failure: it is a matter of the matter itself of the universe anticipating a new beginning that has already begun. Here the finite spirit, an essentially *incarnational* unicity (other-synthetic oneness), enacts the transcendental creation of the Foundation itself within itself, its absolute act an absolute beginning of singular efficacy. Each absolute act is an absolute instance of the discontinuity of the continuum of being and nothing, an apocalyptic I together with being and nothing in their creative discontinuity/transcendental interchangeability. What this surfacing I enacts qua omnipotence is not a matter of causality, neither is it continuous with the past, for its creative receptivity is absolutely differential without subjective referentiality. But what occurs in this pure enactment of change itself *in essence* is creation itself "beyond beyond x" (BS, 293f.), not only beyond the past but *beyond* beyond the past, absolutely without after-reference to the past. Creation occurs without necessity and without goal, indeed, *after* the goal and *after* the future, *ex futuro* (F, 198).

Creation *ex futuro* is a function of the fact that what now occurs is now-occurring—novelty always and everywhere occurring absolutely *now*—differentially recreated memory with no fidelity to the past, essentially immediately mediated immediacy. Its form is the body, existence, as an absolute Gift and, as such, absolutely productive receptivity. This is not a passive reception of the Gift but an active reception that immediately produces ontological fruit, and the Gift received is not a spectral Sabbath in the aether of transcendent mind but the Sabbath of existence itself, indeed, the body itself matter itself *spirit itself*. Having entered once and for all into God's Place, creative existence is burdenless, or its burden is light, indeed, *light itself*, without the necessity of self or depth, without the necessity of yeast, without the necessity of spatial extension; the unleavened bread (NM, 344) is the matter of the Eucharistic Body now occurring whose magnitude is gapless otherness in the form of time itself (essentially, history itself). Hence, it is no longer conceivable that there could be a gap between Creator and creature: the absolute efficacy of their at-one-ment eliminates the necessity of a passage or medium. Indeed, the realization of this oneness is the matter of history itself in its unconditioned transfiguration without any blueprint or timetable. There is no standing room in the Body for anything otherwise than infinite trans-action: the now-occurring universe absolutely trans-versal is the irreducible traffic of verse, of speaking identically acting, the infinite transaction of the Word in which the transcendental identity of power and act is irreducible to causality.

By analogy with the Pauline depiction of Christ as both fulfillment and abolition of the law, the thinking now occurring both fulfills and abolishes the mystical quest. In the Middle Ages, the basic threefold path of the mystical quest in its many variants consisted of a purgative, illuminative, and unitive stage. In the purgative stage the particular self is an illusion to be stripped away as the very source and origin of the "sin" that blinds the I from seeing God. In the illuminative stage the loss of self-particularity gives way to a purified vision of God, the universal Self. In the unitive stage this illumination gives way to the unity of the I with the divine Self of God, and thereby to its union with a universal Self not at all the particular self (which has been incinerated in the Fire of divine Truth). But in the thinking now occurring this threefold itinerary collapses into a singular Moment of absolute glory: the disappearance of the self *as such* is simultaneously the illumination of the particular self-less individual to its ecstatic material communion with the ecstatic Foundation itself, the Godhead itself existing in the form of the universe. Just here an essentially new thought appears beyond all modern passivity as "the pure activity of contemplative judgment (*ho logos katholikos* [the universal word]) essentially liberated from the *logos* of *beginning with* anything apart from its own historical essence, but then *it begins absolutely*" (NM, 50–51). It is difficult to convey the significance of this thought, but this is perhaps the most radical contemplative thought to have occurred in history, for the universal Word is not a universal Principle *except that it be the principle of absolute beginning*. But then, the universal Word is not at all *an absolute Idea of any-beginning-whatsoever*, as it was in Hegel, but *an absolute Beginning to any-idea-whatsoever* (FP, 115). Here, the inward journey to God is nullified as unnecessary because absolutely fulfilled in an exterior ecstatic com-unity with God: there is nothing left to do but to create the world here and now, which is the new absolute imperative (BS, xvii).

In Hegelian modernity the mystical quest was fully intellectualized. In Altizer this quest was converted into an exterior historical realization; the sublation (*Aufhebung*) of every particular selfhood realized a wholly anonymous selfhood, indeed, the very incarnation of the self-emptying of God, the empty form of the Self of God embodying others.[7] But in the thinking now occurring, beyond beyond mysticism, every notion of self is annihilated to reveal the apocalyptic I as a *universal particular/absolute particular* (BS, 249–56). Here, the apocalyptic I absolutely sharing the omnipotence of God—an absolutely subsistent relation within the ecstatic Godhead—thereby an absolute instance of created omnipotence, the metabolic I relating creatively and unconditionally *with* the metabolic Foundation, is absolutely mutable, passable, and passible *withness*. Leahy writes:

> For the first time the do-able is in fact the actual achievement of I conceiving I, I thinking the passibility and passability of I in the face of very omnipotence, and, in the immediately mediated immediacy of the divine, the achievement of omnipotence thinking omnipotence in the face of the I of I think. This beginning is the perfect mutuality of human and divine conceptions of existence, indeed, the perfect grace of perfect mutuality. Now as never before the non-being of the finite is not merely as it was in Hegel the ground of the infinite, indeed, now as never before the non-being of the Finite God is not merely as it is in Altizer the ground of the infinite, at once the actual, final nothingness of the transcendent God. Now as never before omnipotence itself, very love, actually moves to new ground: now for the first time in history the finite is absolutely, i.e., absolutely without reference to the infinite, without reference to non-being, the absolute ground of *ipsum esse,* and in the perfect mutuality of this absolute ground omnipotence itself suffers passibility without ceasing to be omnipotence, as in this mutual change the finite itself suffers passability without ceasing to be the absolute ground. (F, 620–21)

Beyond the quantitatively con-formed monads of Leibniz, appropriating differences as self-contained properties whose egoic unity is windowless to the other except for transcendent mediation (epistemologically a preparation for Husserl's transcendental a priori egoic phenomenological horizon), the infinite finitudes of the differential magnitudes of the thinking now occurring invert the finite infinities of the Leibzinean monadology. Here, what essentially takes place is the in-finite differentiation of the inexhaustible finite: the inexhaustibility of the infinitely finite roomless of other than action, absolute finitude absolutely differentiated ec-statically, the "big bang" the appearance of ontological actuality itself, the act of omnipotence the infinite beginning of an infinite finitude.

The absolute efficacy of the act of creation is, qua noncausal, the immediacy of trinitarian spiration (F, 622) in absolute thirdness: the immediate unity of singularity and difference is novelty itself, the new essence or new fact itself (F, 274), the *"fact of identity"* (F, 460). This absolute efficacy, absolutely noncausal, is the actuality of *ipsum esse* conceived *beyond beyond x,* beyond reference to the past, beyond appropriation—this nonplusing of the past the elimination of the possibility that an absolute Other could possess, contain, or determine the being of another absolute Other (the notion of selfhood). Here there is no property but the unconditioned Foundation qua pure tautology, pure efficacy, perfectly shared freedom and perfectly shared omnipotence. This is the absolutely shared beginning: the absolute discontinuity of the finite the absolute sharing of *ipsum esse*. Here thought itself enters a new crucible beyond mystical apophasis or deconstruction, beyond the postmodern nothingness: eradicated of even the very *notion* of self as a fundamental category, beginning ex nihilo is the very first category of the essential thinking now occurring, the very first category of that thinking now occurring for the first time in history, where absolute emergence qua irreducibility of shared omnipotence creates an essentially transactional otherness actually existing. Thought's individuation—qua the creative acts of a universally particular apocalyptic I—is not its own, for the fiat occurs unconditionally without reference to origin or source. Leahy writes:

> Beyond beyond being the divine essence of existence exists. Existence Absolute exists for the first time. Righteousness is the thanking and the praising of this perfectly specific existence; the divine is the thanking and the praising of this righteousness. The distance between creature and Creator is transcended in essence: for the first time relation is the absolute actuality of the world itself: as never before the relation creature and Creator is an absolutely unconditioned intimacy in existence. As never before the Creator shares itself with the creature. For the first time in history existence is *with the other* absolute. (BS, 3)

Here, the new thinking is beyond the self but not beyond reference to the transcendence of self: thinking undergoes metanoia issuing in an *epoché* of the *cogito,* an *epoché* of the mystical, putting out of play the category of self from fundamental discourse (F, 352–53), beyond beyond self. Now thinking is identically acting, the Word identically existing. Here *exsistere ipsum* is not the zero-sum game of inverse proportionality that is intrinsic to self-other logic; rather, existence itself is a direct proportionality of absolute thirds. Transcending the absolute elasticity of the abyss of the infinitely self-negating God in Altizer's negative Hegelianism, the thinking now occurring announces the infinite absolute Othering of Godhead itself *ex abysso* in novel actualities of difference.

In the aftermath of selfhood, the created I's identity with the uncreated Creator exhibits coinherence within an absolutely actual existence. Qua incarnation, this mutual embodiment of creature and Creator predicates an absolutely creative co-relation between created metaboly and uncreated metaboly. This is what "transcendental" essentially means, conjoining faith and reason as never before in history: to change identically to create identically to begin identically to know. Creating is an absolute act that is acting unconditionally and freely in absolute relation to a history of real relations: creative freedom actually coinciding history. It is inter-activity at once the infinite omnicratic congress of others. Such a measureless (selfless) trans-action with absolute others is the thinking now occurring, a nonplusing of the zero-sum game and an adieu to the void of essentially retrospective thinking. The symphonic co-creativity of the new world order now begins essentially, the new omnicratic ordering now occurring without regard for subjectivity or law or civil society, the triumph of transcendental objectivity in consciousness for the first time in history disclosing the creative power of divine love itself in the absolute priority of beneficently creating the other.

Notes

1. The inverted form of Hegel's God, rendered infinitely self-emptying by kenotic negation, can be found in the work of radical theologian Thomas J. J. Altizer. Altizer's God is the outwardization of the abyss of the Absolute Idea that, qua actuality of the individual person, coincides the empty and anonymous form of the divine Self.

2. Here I am adapting the term *trans-theistic* from Paul Tillich, who first uses the term in 1952 in *The Courage to Be* as an alternative to the theism/atheism binary, a term he uses at the disposal of his conception of God as *das Unbedingte* (the Unconditioned). Where Tillich's own thought can be characterized as trans-theistic, the core of that thinking is a post-Schellingian ontology of *das Unbedingte*. Here in Tillich the finite individuation of unconditioned spirit is the individual self-consciousness of the Infinite. But beyond subjectivity, where the thinking now occurring can be characterized as trans-theistic differently, the finite individuation of unconditioned spirit is

the *making-new-of-the-whole,* or that instantaneous universal change that divine act is, without any trace of appropriation or self. Trans-theism as applied to the thinking now occurring implies no gap/lack between whole and part: the unconditioned intimacy between Creator and creature is an infinite creative transaction that constitutes an irreducible change (*trans*) predicating God (*theos*) as the meta-identity of world. Contrasted with post-theism, which implies that God is irrelevant because the divine Idea is irrelevant, trans-theism places the relevance of God outside of the Idea, instead identifying divinity with change itself. Here the act of omnipotence is *ipsum esse* displacing *causa sui,* or creative efficacy displacing causality.

3. One should take care to note here that Leahy's figurative use of the term *ground* is in essential discontinuity with all modern notions of ground, and indeed the usage is intended for disrupting those modern notions. Here "moving to new ground" refers most precisely to the emergence of new planes of transcendence—new "grounds" in the plural—through the creative act of omnipotence itself. For there is in no way, shape, or form a notion of "grounding" like what one would find in a Descartes, Kant, Hegel, or Heidegger. By contrast, in the thinking now occurring the Foundation does not "ground" things in an indissoluble absolute (which would be a function of self-continuity, distilled in Deleuze as the "plane of immanence"), but qua self-discontinuity/other-continuity the "grounds" are created by the Foundation's other-transcendence within planes of transcendence. Instead of grounding or a universal ground there is pure occurrence identically pure act at once the universal Now of the infinite transaction that is the absolute network (F, 592) of absolutely shared omnipotence (F, 623). It is thereby an always-here-and-now instantaneous universal transaction/change.

4. Open theism is generally understood to be the theological position that God's knowledge of the future is limited by the self-limitation of God's own power in God's refraining from determining future events in order to respect the creature's freedom. One popular proponent of open theism, Greg Boyd, compares God to a master chess player. Although God knows every possible move and situation on the cosmic chessboard, God does not determine what moves another player makes, yet God is never surprised by anything that was not foreknown as a possibility. In the thinking now occurring, by contrast, the omnipotent God is well capable of being surprised, and whereby all actuality is absolutely novel, there are no metaphysically a priori possibilities.

5. Here and following, the terms *fruit* and *fruition* should be regarded poetically with loose reference to the Gospel According to John 15, sans the notion of causality. The Foundation abides in the (plurality of) foundation(s), and each foundation abides in the Foundation: the "fruit" is the transactional intimacy of co-creative co-abiding foundations within the Foundation. This structurally trinary co-abiding is the Trinity existing as the absolutely dynamic Foundation itself, the artifactual Body. Hence, this "fruit" is the absolutely shared "food"/being of essentially Eucharistic existence.

6. Catherine Keller, *Cloud of the Impossible: Negative Theology and Planetary Entanglement* (New York: Columbia University Press, 2015), 31. The quotations of Keller that follow are from this text.

7. See Thomas J. J. Altizer, *The Descent into Hell: A Study of the Radical Reversal of the Christian Consciousness* (Philadelphia: Lippincott, 1970), and D. G. Leahy, "The Diachrony of the Infinite in Altizer and Levinas: Vanishing without a Trace and the Trace without Vanishing," in *Thinking Through the Death of God: A Critical Companion to Thomas J. J. Altizer*, ed. Lissa McCullough and Brian Schroeder (Albany: State University of New York Press, 2004), 105–24.

PART III
A PHYSICAL ETHICS

7

The Ethic of Simplicity

NATHAN TIERNEY

On first hearing of an ethic of simplicity one might imagine that it was an exhortation to the simple life: minimizing material possessions, focusing on primary personal relationships, and eating wholesome and natural foods. Though I am sure Leahy has nothing against such things, this is not what he means by such an ethic at all. Leahy's concept of simplicity stems from what would traditionally be called metaphysics: the general reflection on the nature of reality in terms of the broad concepts of being and nothingness, unity and plurality, existence and essence. Leahy himself disowns this term *metaphysics*, however, for reasons we will discuss, preferring to speak of a physical rather than metaphysical ethic.

The Meaning of Simplicity

What, then, does Leahy mean by simplicity? Simplicity, for Leahy, is embodied identity (BS, 69). It is not the merely logical identity of A = A, but an existential simplicity "transcending the mere potentiality of the law of identity, the mere potentiality of categorical simplicity" (F, 173). Embodied identity has been a philosophical conundrum since Heraclitus, for how can something that exists in space and time, and is constantly changing, be identical with itself? Much of the radical nature of Leahy's thought (which he prefers to call "the thinking now occurring" to indicate both that it is not uniquely his but a new possibility available to all, and that it is in fact now occurring in history) lies in his answer to this question. To exist, for Leahy, is neither to possess nor lack being: "*Existence* is neither some-thing nor no-thing: neither is it to be domiciled in nor taken apart. Existence in essence is the perfectly unnecessary repetition of itself in thought, thereby giving to thought an identity that it lacks to begin with" (NM, 319). Existence in essence (i.e., with identity) is a now-occurring transcendental yet historical discontinuity in time that makes actual temporal existence logically possible for the first time: "For the first time logic coincides with existence" (F, 177). In recovering its identity in thought, existence attains its essence, and thereby its simplicity: "Simplicity itself is temporal existence for the first time" (F, 172). It is not that change has been discovered to be unreal ("Change itself is the fully apparent essence of the construction of existence itself" [NM, 318]), but that it is powerless to disrupt the identity of existing bodies (indeed it is the very condition of that identity).

Several corollaries follow. First, existence in essence is identical with participation in Divine life, for "Omnipotence is absolutely nothing but existence" (BS, 43). For the first time, says Leahy, persons are capable of knowing God objectively—not in a subjective or conceptual sense, but in and through the act of existing in essence. Second, beyond all determinisms, the simplicity of existence in essence makes possible the absolute freedom of human persons: "The existing simplicity of identity is the identity of being with freedom as the categorical itself (together with the absolute complexity thereof). The existing simplicity is for the first time the absolute midst of identity, the midst itself of being itself, such that there is no separation of being from itself that is not the minimum itself . . . the freedom of personality itself existing, simplicity itself existing for the first time in history" (F, 174). The thinking now occurring is "a certain thought *ex nihilo* in which it is absolutely comprehended that being itself is a person" (F, 154).

Third, the simplicity of existence excludes any interiority of the self, indeed any interiority at all: "The disownment of the reality of the self is the absolutely unconditioned exteriority of identity . . . no within, no depth whatsoever to the shining of the light, to the foundation transcending every foundation" (F, 242). Because, however, the simplicity of existence also excludes nothingness (it "puts an end to the Nothing" [BS, vi]), the lack of reality of the self does not negate the reality of the I as the exteriority of the body: "For the first time the nothingness of this I is full of being. For the first time essence is conceived as absolute gift of being. The I acting absolutely is the reception of the gift of being itself. The I that is the infinitely transparent surface of the body is the form absolutely of the absolute gift of being" (FP, 156). We thus have "the perfect reduction of depth to surface" (BS, 69; see also F, 246).

Fourth, the simplicity of existence is to be understood neither as being nor nonbeing but as absolute alterity or otherness: "For the thinking now occurring the infinite alterity that *is* is the essence of the world that *is* otherwise than being—neither being nor not being" (BS, viii). The identity possessed by the body in time is then not sameness but singularity: "There is then nothing but infinite alterity. There is no Same to which the infinity of differences might be compared" (BS, 79–80). Similarly, the unity of existence that holds together the world is not a Plotinian One, a going out and a returning to one and the same, but absolute particularity (BS, 220) related to all other particulars by its very essence as other: "Nor is unity, unbroken by the infinite alterity of existence itself, a Same. The unity beyond the One—the unity beginning absolutely now—is the absolute otherness of Omnipotence itself" (BS, 89).

Fifth, simplicity is to be understood as absolutely new beginning, the actuality of creation. To exist, for Leahy, is to begin to exist. This now existing simplicity of thought/existence, precisely because it arises ex nihilo, is "the absolutely simple complexity, absolutely complex simplicity of the concept of creation. Thought now for the first time identifies absolute dead center as creation in the form of an *absolutely unconditioned Cogito ergo sum (absolutely selfless)*. . . . This is at once itself for the first time the perfect reduction of depth to surface" (F, 439). Its memory, for thought's identity requires memory, is not that of past thoughts but of actual existence: "This memory owes nothing to past thought, which nothing it leaves behind in the fact itself of existing ex nihilo" (F, 176).

The Thinking Now Occurring

I have sketched Leahy's notion of simplicity to provide an indication of the foundation upon which his ethics rest. To be sure, this is an extremely complex simplicity, or a simple complexity. It is a simplicity without depth, without interiority in the Self of God or the self of the thinking subject: "the perfect reduction of depth to surface" (BS, 69) in the absolute act of creation. Before turning to his ethics, however, some remarks should be made about the nature and starting points of Leahy's thought.

Leahy's style is notoriously difficult. His penchant for page-long sentences, his parsimony with the copula, the liberal seasoning of mathematical formulae throughout *Foundation* and other works, his collapsing of philosophical and theological tropes, and the uncompromising density and sheer newness of his ideas—all make for a vertiginous reading experience. The persevering reader, however, eventually begins not only to adapt to the style, but to see the necessity of it as the vehicle for the pioneer of a new kind of thinking. The thinking now occurring, says Leahy, is not striving for knowledge, but beginning from the structure of existence: "Here is knowledge itself . . . knowledge itself the absolute absolute . . . knowledge itself existing" (F,106–107). Its momentum is always to collapse the reader's understanding to a perception of the simplicity of existence. This "man-thought/God-thought" (BS, 70) is not a *thinking about* in the sense of re-presenting an experience for analysis or reflection, indeed not an interpretation of experience at all, for "There is nothing as it were hidden behind sensible existence" (BS, 72), but an event that creates the world. This kind of thinking is "not philosophy, no more than it is theology" (BS, 74). The I which thinks is "neither self nor subject" but a "'simple doing'" absolutely existing—in the perfect mutuality of the act of creation" (BS, 75), "the absolute constructor of truth," "the very form of the body," "the infinitely transparent surface of the body." Hence there are "as many truths as there are bodies," and the actual world is "composed of an infinite number of existing worlds." The *I* "is the reception of the gift of being itself" (BS, 75).

This helps us understand why Leahy sees his ethics as physical rather than metaphysical. Despite the fact that much of Leahy's work deals with traditional questions of metaphysics, the *starting points* (and, for that matter, the ending points) of thought are always physical. Thought begins neither with a reflection on being nor on that from which being might arise: "The thinking now occurring for the first time beyond the beginning of being, thinking absolute thisness, thinks a *physical* ethics" (BS, 115). This thinking generates "not a *metaphysical* ethics, but, indeed, a *physical* ethics, an ethics of the existing body . . . an ethics essentially transformative of the order of reason existing hitherto" (BS, 75).

An Outline of the Ethic of Simplicity

Before exploring the foundations of the ethic of simplicity, it will be helpful to lay out its general structure. There are, for Leahy, four primary ethical dispositions (or dimensions), and nine corresponding imperatives, arranged as three sets of three. The four dispositions are readiness, discretion, beneficence, and gratitude (BS, 78). These dimensions are organic in the sense that the fourth embodies the first three:

Readiness is being at the disposal of another. It is a disposition operating in the domain of art (broadly understood) and is analogous to the theological virtue of faith and the Platonic virtue of temperance. Readiness *is* the complex simplicity of beginning.

Discretion is having the patience to see what's different, attentiveness to what consciousness constructs absolutely now. It is a disposition operating in the domain of science. It is analogous to the theological virtue of hope and the Platonic virtue of courage.

Beneficence is doing the right thing. This is not a matter of forcing preexisting things in a certain direction, but an essentially new shaping for the first time. It operates in the domain of society, and is analogous to the theological virtue of neighbor-love and the Platonic virtue of wisdom.

Gratitude is productive receptivity, flowing from the understanding that omnipotence embodies the universe. It operates in the economic domain and is analogous to the theological virtue of the love of God, and the Platonic virtue of justice. In gratitude, omnipotence itself moves to new ground.

The nine imperatives (BS 197–208) are:

1. You shall be absolutely now: "the creature effected by omnipotence."

    a. You shall be wholly engaged in the world: "being as absolutely unprecedented gift."

    b. You shall love things: "to perceive things as the appearance of the transcendental essence of existence itself."

2. You shall cherish the name: Christ as the form of the creation of the new world, the "beginning that is the *absolute separation* of being and nothing."

   a. You shall create the world: "omnipotence itself moving to new ground." "to create the world is to be merciful" "world-creating mercy *is* morality."

   b. You shall love the truth: the "exaltation of the essential fact of being . . . is love's relation in truth."

3. You shall be holy every day: "that is, to be, always and everywhere for the first time, absolutely whole/wholly in place" (204).

   a. You shall love the body. Absolute placidness is "the imperative to be the resurrected body," for, "the place where something takes place is the cause of its taking place" (206). "So it is that *ethics* is as never before neither meta-crypto-, dia-, nor para-physical, but essentially and absolutely *physical*."

   b. You shall love the person. "Loving the person is readiness for the place where perfect and essentially existent newness takes place" (206), absolutely particular. "The love of the person is absolutely free and unconditioned as is the relation of the Creator and the creature" (208).

Why a New Ethic?

One might begin the approach to Leahy's new ethics of simplicity by asking the question, Why is a new ethic necessary at all? After all, after two and a half thousand years of thought on the subject tracing its beginnings to the ancient Greeks, as well as the sedimented experience and practice of a host of cultures, we have developed a general code that works pretty well and has gained more or less wide acceptance. The essence of this code can be summed up in three core values:

Respect: recognition of the dignity (intrinsic value) of all people,

Responsibility: holding oneself accountable to others, to one's conscience and, for theists, to God for one's life and actions;

Concern: active interest in, and care for, the welfare and happiness of others.

Despite considerable cultural difference in the way these values are embodied and expressed, and varying religious, as well as nonreligious, interpretations of the inner meaning of these terms, most people striving to live an ethical life would endorse these values as central to their sense of meaning, purpose, and self. Also, these values have not been pulled out of intellectual thin air; philosophers and theologians have mined their rational underpinnings for millennia and for most of that period, despite disagreements about what might be the best framework for understanding and founding these values, the primacy of the values themselves have generally not been called into question.

The trouble, of course, is that now these values have been called into serious question. Let me briefly mention three sources of this challenge. First, the rise and current dominance of the scientific outlook has led many to dismiss all ethical norms as groundless to the degree that they are not based on physics, chemistry, and biology. Second, the antimetaphysical temper of empiricist philosophy from the eighteenth century on has pulled away many of the intellectual supports behind these values; even Kant's notion of the intrinsic worth of persons, grounded in a distinction between pure and practical reason and a categorical framework delineating the necessary bases of all rational thought, has arrived at the twenty-first century largely in tatters. Finally, there is that host of intellectual projects, known collectively as postmodernism, which sees its mission as liberating contemporary thought and action from the hidden categories, concepts, and postulates of the past which, it is often argued, serve only to preserve oppressive structures of power. Such despised categories include the autonomous self, sameness, unity, universal moral law, universal truth, universal reason, normativity, the transcendental, being, and essence. Thus, despite the fact that many espouse and affirm traditional ethical values, the intellectual and cultural ground beneath them is quite shaky.

Kant famously declared in the opening sentence of the *Groundwork* that nothing is unconditionally good in itself but the good will. The will, as distinct from desire or inclination, is our capacity to act according to universal moral laws (ultimately only one law) binding for all rational beings. The good will recognizes the authority of those laws as absolutely imperative, and acts upon them for their own sake. Unfortunately, the twin concepts of will and universal moral law have not stood up well to philosophical scrutiny in the late modern period—this for a variety of familiar reasons. Other approaches to ethics, notably a revived virtue ethics and a variety of utilitarianisms, have certainly been explored with varying degrees of success, though they seem to founder on the question of authority: Why are moral laws imperative, and why, in the end, should we obey them? The cost of failing to provide a foundational answer to this question, which is fully transparent to rational thought, remains high: a pervasive and often debilitating relativism, as well as a skepticism about the value of rational thought in moral matters. To be sure, some postmodernists have regarded this state of affairs as healthy and liberating, but their attempts at constructive alternatives have so far been less than convincing.

Leahy's new ethic of simplicity is a radical re-engagement with the foundations of ethics. With Kant, he declares the absolutely imperative nature of the ethical *ought*, but dispenses with the notions of both will and universal law upon which Kant built his system. For Leahy, will, far from being the human location of absolute Good, is precisely its opposite:

> In the ethic of simplicity the fundamental principle of defection is *will*. Not merely the intending of Evil, but the Evil of merely intending—what can only be a departure from attending. The difference between attending and intending—ethical doing and ethical willing is the difference between Good and Evil. (BS, 95)

And again:

> The fundamental principle of an operative ethic of simplicity is attention. (BS, 94).

With regard to the universal law by which the authority of ethics is to be secured for Kant the problem is not, for Leahy, merely that such a universal moral law does not "fit the facts," as many have complained. Rather, it is that universality is always the universalization of a point of view (in Kant's case pure practical reason) conceived as standing apart from the fact of existence. Leahy's ethic of simplicity eliminates the point of view entirely in favor of what he calls "the synthesis of the fact itself of existence in history" (NM, 7).

The prior debates between partisans of the universal or the particular are overcome in the notion of simplicity understood as the embodied identity of omnipotence grasped in thought (BS, 69). In the thinking now occurring there is no question of a choice between Platonic universalism or Nietzschean particularism, and thus no ethical decision to be made about whether to honor the unseen Good or the particular goods of the things of this world. For the world itself is not a totality of beings but an inherently normative structure of "infinite alterity otherwise than being" (BS, 62). Since "being itself is the other itself in essence" (F, 34), there is no question of a relativistic multiplication of individual truths. The I of personal humanity constructs ethical truth as "absolutely particularized productive receptivity of being" (BS, 76). The world itself possesses an absolute sociality, "*concretely existing universality*" (F, 409), which addresses itself to the I as the imperative of existence itself: "The world itself *is* to begin" (BS, 62). Ethical authority, then, is not as a universalized point of view, but the word of existence, "the Absolute Word absolutely embodied in the One World Now" (F, 409).

God and the New Beginning

In "The New Beginning: Beyond the Post-Modern Consciousness" (*Foundation*, ch. 3), Leahy describes how, at the beginning of the modern era, Descartes's invention of himself produced at the same time a new kind of Christian consciousness, which would lead, by the end of the nineteenth century, to the death of God as a knowable object of consciousness. It was man, rather than God that became foundational to thought. God became an idea, the object of Christian belief rather than an experienced and known reality. From the point of view of existing thought, God was the Nothing, while from the point of view of the accompanying theological understanding, God was reified as Divine Otherness. The Incarnation, the Word made flesh, became an idea rather than a reality, and Christianity became "an historically individual and reactionary faith" (F, 596) within the movement of history itself. Christian belief, as long as it could be transposed to a second-order theological level of thinking, could continue, but at the existential and historical level, where the Cartesian absolute self confronted God as Nothing, Christianity was, and could only be, a form of unbelief, a denial of history within history itself. Hegel's and Nietzsche's shocking announcements of the death of God simply brought this new fact to our philosophical attention.

American consciousness, for Leahy, has taken this thought further than any other. It has taken the realization that God, as the Other of the actually thinking self, is Nothing and absolutely dead, to its logical conclusion: "For the first time, God is really and actually dead" (F, 601). Yet far from being a disaster, this abysmal realization is the birth canal through which genuine Christian thought becomes possible for the first time, that is, thought that is at the same time joyfully celebratory of God's reality, philosophically rational to its depths, and able to be thought and known by actually existing historical human beings in the thinking now occurring. God through his death, first in history and now in thought, makes possible a new beginning, indeed makes beginning itself finally possible in actuality—"the first being finally nothing: the first nothing finally being" (F, 602). The essentially ahistorical thinking of modernism, in eliminating history, finally permits the possibility of a new resurrection, in which the death of God is itself eliminated. This is the beginning of the new beginning, the elimination of the beginning of Nothing. It is "the beginning of saying absolutely yes through saying yes absolutely to nothing" (F, 604). This is not a postmodern dwelling in groundlessness, but a foundational thought grounded in a confrontation with being's essence in Nothingness. It marks the end of both medieval Christendom and modern "Christianity" understood as the attempt to actually believe what is precluded by one's starting points.

Now, after the beginning of the beginning, is beginning itself, which is the thinking now occurring. The New Christ of this now occurring universal faith is thought by faith absolutely, without the need to negate or transcend the Christ of past thought. The New Christ is, in fact, beginning itself, absolute novelty now existent. Christ, the new, the Nothingness of God without nay-saying, the elimination of absolute death, is and always shall be the beginning of existence. To exist is to begin to exist. In the thinking now occurring God is now absolutely extruded: "What now actually occurs as never before is the absolute exteriority of the Godhead, the absolute act ending the beyond of the Godhead, Christ Absolutely" (F, 606). He later describes it as "the beginning itself in the very midst of being . . . the Universal Joy in the depths of being surfacing" (F, 611).

In the thinking now occurring, there is no otherness of existence and nothingness. Being and nothingness are not paired, nor do they share a boundary, but they have an identity, which is otherness itself. This identity is the beginning, absolute simplicity, the beginning of God, the beginning of otherness itself, which is now thinkable. Every existing body now partakes of this resurrection of existence as absolute exteriority (F, 615). Existence now is pure creativity: to exist is to begin to exist, to begin to exist is to create the world. Now that otherness as the other-than-being is displaced by otherness itself, there is no nonexperienced other. This is the Mind of Christ which is the universe now beginning. This is at the same time the elimination of that form of self-experience that sets itself against the other. Self-consciousness, which was heretofore incomplete because always postponed by the impossible task of returning to itself from the world, is now complete. This is the "selfless self-consciousness of the Godhead" (F, 615).

Nothingness now is not that which limits the finite. It is the nothingness of the infinite (F, 616), and it is this nothingness that is the actual existence of God, existing for the first time in history. This actual existence of God is not to be understood as the arrival of the "real presence" in any self-personal sense, nor even the presence of God as the totality of history in Altizer's sense. Rather, it is "the immediate elimination of the very notion of the *presence* of divinity: *the form of the divine actually beginning is very existence very divine*" (F, 619). With this, both distance and identity are eliminated as impediments, and transfigured into the simplicity of God Himself (F, 620).

The I can now without egoism selflessly conceive itself as the I, in the "immediately mediated immediacy" of the Christ. There is no more the Augustinian restless heart; the Trinity manifests itself in the very structure of existence (F, 622) for "the common boundary of everything existing is the exclusivity of the beginning" (F, 623). "The human and divine share a common boundary had by both" (F, 623). God is the "beginning of the common boundary which being and nothing have without sharing, and which they share without having" (F, 624). The present of individual consciousness need no longer seek the impossible God in the Kierkegaardian absurdity of a present perpetually dissolving into nothingness (F, 625). For Kierkegaard, a pure present existed as "the very space for objectivity" (F, 626) in which a rational dialectic of an existing self could occur even while denying pure reason a place in Christianity. Now, "the space for objectivity at the center of consciousness is absolutely eliminated" (F, 627). "For the first time the discontinuity of being and nothingness is the very form of thought: in the beginning the absolutely pure continuity of being" (F, 628).

In this new beginning in which distance from the divine is dissolved in the very structure of existence, and in which the self-consciousness of the I is completed not in a Cartesian circle absolutely isolated from the body but in the pure exteriority of the lived body itself, the body itself is absolutely intelligible (BS, 176), both infinitely sharing the contemplation of the Divine Essence, and infinitely sharing the creaturely life of the Godhead. Turning Plato on his head, Leahy treats omnipotence as the opposite of immutability. God qua "absolute nearness/newness/newness" is at the same time historically within time and at once absolutely indifferent to time. It is only thus that the old Heraclitan conundrum of how Being can be and yet be subject to the nonbeing that time's changes produce can be overcome. "God has altogether dissolved the last remnants of the ancient notion of the immutability of the real—of the non-existence of the real" (BS, 40). God, as the power of absolute newness, is precisely "the power to be absolutely surprised" (BS, 40). "Omnipotence precisely is that which is absolutely nonexisting in its existing" (BS, 43).

How is this to be understood ethically, or in terms of what ought we now to do? "In the thinking now occurring omnipotence itself is actuality itself" (BS, 177), so there can be no question of potentiality, an *ought* that has not yet become an actuality. The question, "What am I [are we] to do?" is displaced by the question, "What am I [are we] doing?" Partaking in the absolutely now exposed life of the divine, there can be no question of capacities and plans; we are left with absolute nimbleness at the beginning of an essentially new world. Is this, then, a new voluntarism: do as you will, because whatever you do is right? No. For in the thinking now occurring, in which conception is identical to perception, there is still the possibility of failing to see things rightly, of slipping into a kind of inattention to actuality which, because such inattention occludes the different future lying before our feet in the absolutely now, manifests as boredom. "In terms of the thinking now occurring boredom is the ground phenomenon of *not* 'having the patience to see what's different'" (BS, 183). The first ethical act, then, is to begin to think—that is, to see—the new world.

The fact/value distinction that lay at the heart of modern ethics has absolutely disappeared in Leahy's ethics. The normative, now, "*is* reality . . . *is* the creating/creation that qua absolute quality of existence itself is absolutely without reference to itself or to anything else. The norm that is now for the first time in force *is* the absolute and essential real of existence, where reality is the absolute imperative to create a new world" (BS, 187–88). "As never before *normalcy* is the absolute coincidence of embodiment and membership in omnipotence itself" (BS, 188).

Ethics, for Leahy, is the absolute imperative to create the new world (BS, 188). This is not a political task in the sense of common endeavor to shelter our lives within framing walls of an authoritatively elevated *polis* but beyond all sovereignty: "[I]n the thinking now occurring for the first time the new creature now lives without walls, beyond politics, in the absolute freedom of an actually new creation . . . the dwelling without walls that is omnipotence itself" (BS, 193). Love, now, is no longer a mystery or a secret. "The love of those who dwell with one another without walls in the absolute outside of existence itself is the love of those who penetrate one another absolutely, the love of creatures who dwell for the first time absolutely now" (BS, 194).

The ethic of simplicity, for all the complexity and newness of the thinking that gives rise to it, is readily recognizable as capturing in new form many of the truths of both modern secular ethics and traditional Christian ethics. It does not so much reject them as reframe them. The three core values of respect, responsibility, and concern can be mapped to some degree onto the four ethical dispositions of readiness, discretion, beneficence, and gratitude. Respect and gratitude have many cognates in common. In both, one recognizes the value of a thing as beyond price, honors its existence, and feels called to respond in a manner worthy of it. There are differences, of course. Modern ethics sees gratitude as a species of respect. Leahy would reverse the order. Also, respect is the recognition of dignity (understood by Kant as intrinsic value). Since, for Leahy, human beings have no inner selves, no autonomous being, and do not derive their value from their capacity to act according to the moral law, he would dispense with the notion of intrinsic value altogether as the foundation of dignity, replacing it, I would expect, with the more traditional notion of the *imago Dei*. Readiness and discretion capture much of the notion of accountability built into the concept of responsibility (and of course go further). Beneficence, doing the right thing, covers much of the same ground as active concern for one's neighbor. Similarly, the nine imperatives can with little difficulty be seen to repeat, albeit in new form and with new meaning and emphasis, familiar Christian injunctions. I doubt that Leahy would wish it otherwise.

What is new, then, in the ethic of simplicity is not so much the content, but the ground on which the ethical dispositions and imperatives rest. This is truly, radically, startlingly new. Many of the problem areas of past ethical thought—the relation between fact and value, the concept of intrinsic value, the question of autonomy, the source of moral authority, the relation between self and other—are swept away by this new return of thought to existence. The philosophical theologian Ray L. Hart has remarked in his blurb on the back cover of *Foundation*: "Reading Leahy is like reading Nietzsche: to the degree that one understands, one is shaken in the foundations—and if not so shaken, one does not understand." Just so. The effort to understand Leahy is admittedly not an easy one—I find myself turning to Hegel and Heidegger for comparatively light reading—but it is one that philosophers and theologians will increasingly recognize as essential if we are to comprehend the current state of thought. Even those sympathetic to Leahy will find some of his directions troubling. For me, his rejection of the notions of presence and interior life cause some dismay. Leahy would no doubt call this the residue of old thinking, and he may be right. I look forward to a better understanding.

8

The Vanishment of Evil from the World

TODD CARTER

> The beginning that is the ground of the person is understood to be the perfectly severe trial absolutely roomless of other than action.
>
> —BS, x

Let's say something outrageous: in the beginning, the self is gone and its death throes are upon us in the twenty-first century. We could also say beginning creation is other-consciousness and that the function of selfhood has been surpassed. D. G. Leahy, in his visionary thinking denoted as "the thinking now occurring for the first time," writes: "What now occurs for the first time in history is the invitation to the absolute loss of self from which we dare not withhold ourselves as exceptions in essence to the invitation. We exist in divine opening of the creative act which knows absolutely no hesitation, or not at all" (FP, 123). The beginning is an act actual, not a thought intended. The peculiar descriptor of Leahy's thinking—the thinking now occurring for the first time—ushers one to thinking's edge after postmodernity, a thinking essentially eclipsing self-consciousness, a new (final, complete) apocalypse that settles the dust of the self/past. The darkness of the modern world, a darkness and opacity of an internal self, gives way to other-consciousness. Thinking essentially apocalyptic is the mind and the "I" of the thinking now occurring. Not apocalyptic in Thomas J. J. Altizer's sense of a *coincidentia oppositorum*, where a *no* is a *yes* and a *yes* is a *no*, not a revolution oppositional to the status quo and contrary to the human animal as in Alain Badiou, but a thinking that names evil as the inside of human consciousness, as intentionality itself; a naming of consciousness devoid of void, essentially real, without self, purely receptive, productive, and attentional. The name for evil is simple: a failure to act, a failure to create the new world here and now. Evil is the sin of not acknowledging and receiving the gift of being embodied in omnipotence.[1] In the thinking now occurring the power of omnipotence is not to do whatever one pleases whenever one wants, but a power to receive and enact the guarantee and promise of freedom as created omnipotence, a gift from Creator, the imageless image.

When it comes to endings and the question of evil, the end of self-consciousness is the occasion for a true beginning: a new form of consciousness, absolutely other-consciousness, receptive and productive, the radiant light itself where no sun or moon is needed.[2] We are standing in the light itself of the beginning of the Apocalypse, twenty-first-century-style. This ending of one world is truly the beginning of another; in this case, a beginning so radical that roots are cut, vanishing simultaneously evil and self, as freedom reigns. A rootless and nonoriginary beginning begins, so rootless as to not be radical at all, without tethers to the dichotomy of Being and Nothing. Radical thinking requires a ground from which self can disappear, whereas the shocking thinking of the thinking now occurring strips us bare, leaving nothing to hold on to. Nothing takes hold in absolute beginning; not even Being takes hold. The nothing that has reigned in modern consciousness is no longer. Beginning is not a species of becoming, not attached to Being and Nothing, but is altogether beyond beyond Being. Yes, the end of the world, but the beginning of the end simultaneously, the end of the end, the end of beginning, apocalyptic beginning. The end times, the closing of that which began from nothing, *creatio ex nihilo*, not the substantial matrix of creation made out of the substance "nothing," but a real beginning, a moment of creation wherein the world is brought into being by Omnipotence itself, by that which is Uncreated. This is the beginning of sharing in Omnipotence. Our human inheritance and our share of existence itself made real by the evidence of thinking the Word become flesh, our minds and bodies transformed by thinking the Incarnation of Christ. The "I" that survives when everything and nothing are consumed is the I that is "the truth of everything & nothing, the divine I shares being itself with the human I" (FP, 159), where "the real unity of the first person is the experience of the otherhood of the other, the experience of the 'thinking thing' which in no way whatsoever justifies the attribution of 'self,' but of which the right understanding is that the ego that is the first person unum qua the infinitesimal limit which is 'to begin' exists as other" (BS, 8).

Human existence as created omnipotence is the answer to the question of what prevents evil from having a foothold in the realm of what is created/the created world. The new world—that is, the continual newness of the world—effects a vanishing of self, nothing, and evil in one gesture. As participants in creation ex nihilo, we now come under the imperative to create, to take stock of the fact that "not only is the human organism transcending the human organism but it is now essentially true for the first time that the *human species is the species making species*" (F, 559). No longer *homo sapiens*, but *homo creatio*. As we will see, not to participate in the imperative to create the world is to defect from creating the world; it is in some fundamental sense to remain stuck in the past. As Leahy articulates in *Beyond Sovereignty*, the defections from the Good, de facto, are the real but unnecessary movements away from creating, merely *intending* or *willing* to create (not creating), moving away from otherness, moving in a recessive trajectory toward subjectivity and the self, a consequence of freedom, and our human capacity freely to act and to choose. To create is to be the edge, to be that novelty that has never been before. To be that "text" which has never been written is the ethical imperative of the Apocalyptic God who abandons humans to creation. Otherness creating, not the will of a self that brings a willful order to chaos, as in Nietzsche—where the divine substantiality of the world has been lost—but otherness that speaks productively as children, creating children of Omnipotence.

Infinite alterity is the essence of the world in this *novitas mundi*, the new world ending and beginning in apocalypse. The edge is a creative one, an edge that is less lonely than the world of Nietzsche's *Übermensch* or of Badiou's *Immortal* precisely because its directionality is toward otherness in a world at the beginning of the Resurrection. "The consciousness of man is the creating edge. The essentially narrow part of man, the narrow itself of man—the edge by which man grows is existing ex nihilo" (F, 592). The interstitial world of defections—the place where *willing* is located, those places where one falls from the edge—is the world where evil spells itself out. A fully human place in the case of the thinking now occurring, not an extrahuman place as in Badiou, nor a radical place calling forth the necessity of evil in the theater of opposites, as in Altizer. The ethical imperative in the thinking now occurring is the imperative to create the world here and now. Productive receptivity is the ethical disposition of Gratitude in the thinking now occurring. It is not based in willingness or the human will, but foundationally it is the immediate response to the call of creation, to write what has not been written before. As omnipotence embodies the universe, it formulates ever-new ground, a groundless ground where ethical action (the creation of the world) is the relation of infinite difference as identity itself, an edge-I, neither subsumed or divided. The thinking now occurring produces a fourfold set of ethical dispositions: Gratitude, Readiness, Discretion, and Beneficence. Simply put, as omnipotence embodying the universe, I am at the disposal of another and this readiness is the form of faith. Being at the disposal of another requires attention, patience, and discrimination. These facets of consciousness begin now/new where in turn there is no forcing, but always new creating for the first time. "In the unity of existing truth Omnipotence embodies/accommodates infinitely different truths" (BS, 87).

But where did evil go if it is real but unnecessary? Back in my days in divinity school the term *theodicy* coined by Leibniz was often jocularly referred to as "the idiocy"—a jab in the ribs to those who, simplemindedly enough to be dissuaded from God's sovereignty, wondered how the all-too-human evil that pervades this human realm could be tied to God, the all-powerful Creator. How do we understand Leahy's gloss on the classic subject? His take seems rather Augustinian at first glance, like a nod to the beginnings of Christianity, a version of the privation of the Good seems to present itself. Theodicy in its most common form attempts to answer the question why an all-good, all-powerful, and all-knowing God permits the manifestations of evil. An omnipotent, omniscient God would know in advance all the permutations of evil in the world, so why would He bother to create at all or to offer humans any incentive out of sin and evil—is creation all a cruel joke? The simplest rebuttal to these ideas is that in the work of Leahy the providence of God is given in the absolute freedom that God gives to the creature (created omnipotence). Freedom and omnipotence are not confined to the intelligence of the Divine but are handed over to the creature. In that freedom comes the precise ordering of attentionality over intentionality in the creature. The simplest answer for Leahy to the question "Why evil?" is—*you intend it.*

Conventionally, our human will is our innate capacity to move toward action, but this becomes an impotent machine in the shadow of act and attention, as the dark unformed inner recesses of self-consciousness are erased. "Willing" loses power and stands withered in the face of pure action and creation. Willingness itself becomes the location of evil in the thinking now occurring. Most people would regard the act of willing as an innocent proposal or joyous wish to bring certain things into existence. The power of a new world, its absolute novelty, is not the lonely work of a solitary madman but the work of "a body embodied in omnipotence itself . . . an infinitely open infinite particularity beginning" (BS, 121) creating "the essence of the world—to enact the Good itself" (BS, 117). This gift of omnipotence requires the imperative of attention, and consigns intentionality to the past, as part of the constitution of the self. Evil is a category of the will, a failure to actively attend to the other and thus to fail at what Leahy calls a *physical ethics,* an ethics made real through the body. The fundamental principle of this ethics is *attention,* as opposed to will (BS, xvii). As outlined in *Beyond Sovereignty,* the Good is a set of four ethical dispositions (Gratitude, Readiness, Discretion, Beneficence) and Evil a set of twelve defections (Impotence, Hatred, Malice; Indifference, Avoidance, Denial; Boredom, Dissemblance, Disservice; Inaction, Misfeasance, Malfeasance). Think of the section in Aquinas's *Summa Contra Gentiles* in which evil, described as privation of the Good, is given an inferior ontological status. Initially, this resembles the classical Christian theological gesture: the given-ness of the Good occurs in the holy ordering of the universe as God's creation, whereas disorder is an occurrence disrupting the original organization, a consequence of the Fall. The Good in the thinking now occurring is not a transcendent reality that emanates its light, but a luminous attending simultaneous human/other consciousness.

Evil is never on equal ontological footing with the Good from an orthodox perspective, whereas heterodoxically, à la Altizer, Good and Evil do find equality in the primordial Godhead. In Altizer's thinking, the *yes* comes with the *no,* the radical root of Christianity envisions the identity of Good and Evil, the death and crucifixion of God in Jesus. These opposites are continually outpoured in a universal kenotic movement. Whereas, in the perfectly flat universe of the thinking now occurring, a universe with no depth, no radical roots, the conception of Evil is straightforward: creating the world versus defecting from creating the world. In the postmodern camp, the ordering of Evil in Badiou's thinking is a *diaphysical* ethics; the Good, for Badiou, is the disorganization/disordering of being that arises when a Subject bears a particular truth process. The immortal arises here beyond the physical, beyond the human animal. In Leahy's apocalypse, the world is the freedom that constitutes the particularity of personhood, is the seriousness of moving into a "nonsuppositional place . . . nonsubjective place—the place absolutely *Da* . . . the place beyond beyond place for the first time" (BS, 269–70). We are at the beginning of the Resurrection, where body actual and the infinitely particular and speciated person is beyond the notion of sovereignty, the dynamics of worldly power, and the divisive heart of the political world. Otherwise than Being and Nothing, otherwise than presence and absence, otherwise than beginning being a species of becoming, personhood in the thinking now occurring—the terminus of the actual universe, other-equal and immediate, beyond the internal reservoir of self, is the "roomless of other than action" (BS, x)

One only need look around the world or receive a newsfeed from Twitter to realize that Leahy's utterance, "Evil is real but wholly unnecessary" (BS, 106), can appear trite, foolish, and naive. Common sense will scream, "Humanity is more complex than this, more traumatized, more debased, and stupider than this simplistic non-sense!" What might seem like a point in the direction of innate knowledge of the difference between Good and Evil comes to mind when one hears this. In this world in which we see bad things happening every day, we are alerted that evil is not necessary in the thinking now occurring; it is not prompted out of the Godhead in some predestined and entwined circularity, but simply might be a choice stemming from a defection from the Good—a defection from creating the world. The simplicity at the heart of the thinking now occurring might be too much for one to bear, or better put, it might not offer enough to bear for those attached to modern self-consciousness; the need to be enslaved to a radical ground and the darkness of the occluded self may weigh more for some than the resplendent glory of creation, its imperative, and the absolute otherness of consciousness.

The revolutionary attempts of Badiou and Altizer to ground evil in precise forms has been nothing less than respectively heroic and satanic. One could argue that their responses to the problem of evil have been an inevitable outgrowth of the process and termination/ resolution of modern thinking, a thinking that has had the figures of militant hero and Lucifer at its core. We can see Marx's revolutionary hero and Hegel's "nothing exterior to the Godhead" looming large behind and within the apparati of evil as enunciated by both Badiou and Altizer. On the other hand, and in quite apparent distinction, the thinking of Leahy leaves (post-) modernity and the *coincidentia oppositorum* to the past. Evil exists in the world to the extent that the absolute otherness of persons is not taken seriously. "The unity beyond the One—the unity beginning absolutely now—is the absolute otherness of omnipotence itself" (BS, xvi). The notion of evil as developed in the thinking now occurring focuses on the distinction between creation as doing and non-creation as willing/not-willing, non-creation as willing itself in whatever form. These "wills" are specified and listed as defections from the Good (see above). In short and foundationally, the difference between attending and intending is spelled out from the beginning: actionless intention is the psychological space of the modern self—which the prophetic voice of the thinking now occurring declares to be wholly of the past, dust-binned, as it were.

As Leahy perceives and conceives there is a new injunction in the world: the absolute imperative "*'to write what was never written,' to create, to write essentially and absolutely for the first time*" (BS, 156–57; italics in the original). The imperative to create the world absolutely leaves behind the divisiveness that is the heart of the political world, metabolizes the distinction between philosophy and theology and brings forth the beginning of the Resurrection. Yet this punch line of the thinking now occurring might seem too easy given that, historically, evil has had the infamous place at center stage as that whose origin is difficult to explain because of the question of theodicy (related wholly to humanity's sinfulness) or because the question of evil has been suppressed to protect the identity of God.

A listing of statements concerning evil obtains in the case of the thinking now occurring or what Leahy refers to as revolutionary *metanoesis*:

That Evil is real but not necessary;

that evil may be formally distinguished from the violence of nature not from the violence of the human animal whose nature embodied in existing omnipotence is essentially conceived as a construction of freedom through and through;

that there is no radical Evil, which would only serve to completely obscure the truth;

that Evil cannot be considered as distinct from human predation whose banality is precisely a form of Evil, and is indeed a function of Indifference;

that the possibility of human Evil is precisely the category of the transpersonal subject as an abstraction from the singularity of particular persons;

that there is Evil to the extent that the I that is the form of the body defects from the absolute imperative to create;

that the ethic of simplicity—as the principle of the organic consistently inconsistent patient construction of the infinite particularity that is always the actual structure of existence here and now—is what has always already put out of play the Evil that is actual in "the will to . . ." and "the will not to . . ." (BS, 106).

In the thinking now occurring, the ethic of simplicity leaves no room for a self. The self is the proverbial place inside one's head that has space for thoughts—especially, in this specific instance, thoughts for intending, for willing creation into existence. This subject/self is the actor on modernity's stage that follows us behind the scenes into postmodernity. The whole notion of a girded-inside to a person gets spray-painted black, and human-as-edge replaces sacred interiority. Self-consciousness is a recess of the self that is the access to private worlds, a fortress to be protected and guarded, whether it be a momentary vision, as in Badiou's Platonism of the multiple, or a subject whose ground is the *coincidentia oppositorum,* which is ultimately a misunderstanding about what it means to die. In the thinking now occurring the subject is not merely subtracted or emptied out and de-substantialized, but absolutely banished to the past, vanished from the constitution of personhood. Persons survive in the apocalypse; the self does not. The rending of the veils in the apocalypse happening now is the revelation of the otherness of consciousness. Hear the proclamation of vanishing subjecthood, of vanishing self, of vanishing agency that holds as secret all its intentional reality—all replaced by the absolute otherness of consciousness in the perfectly flat and discontinuous reality of the thinking now occurring.

That which lies at the core of modernity for Leahy is the movement and perturbation of self-consciousness. It is also the preoccupation of Badiou to articulate the place of the self. Our inheritance as created omnipotence is precisely what distinguishes us from nature, but simultaneously the thinking now occurring maintains the integrity of our animality and does not move human identity to an extrahuman realm as does Badiou, who will strike animality from the lexicon of Good and Evil, for animality in his Platonism of the multiple is beneath both of them. In Badiou's thought, evil is not an instantiation of the predator being violent but is an instance of a movement away from the Same, the space for the eventual movement of truth. The universal address of the proclamation of the resurrected Christ is the enunciated space of Paul, rendered Marxist and pragmatic in Badiou, as it relates to the truth of the Event, but not to the truth of the resurrected Christ. Badiou's atheistic stance fable-izes Paul's proclamation. There is an empty space that modernity continuously fills because the history of the Incarnation is not taken seriously; in this case, Badiou takes Paul's enunciation of the resurrected Christ and empties it of history so as to fill it with the Subject. Still held to be a cosmic joke, an apparition that need not be taken seriously, the resurrection is de-substantialized. In Leahy, the form of thinking is readiness itself, is faith itself, a productive receptivity that grasps and engages the task, that creates the world ever anew. It is faith that distinguishes Leahy from Badiou, faith in the reality of the Incarnation and the subsequent effect that this idea has had on the history of thinking/creating: "There is an essentially new form of thought now actually existing for the first time: there is the beginning of a thinking the essence of which is the logic of faith itself" (NM, xiii).

Beyond the empty space in modernity that needs to be filled, beginning begins the new universe. Beginning hides nothing, for the hiding of anything is analogous to the nature of the occluded self. With the power of history making real the form of thinking as faith itself, as a consequence of the Incarnation of Christ, the modern subject appears to be a hole from which evil arises, an evil that is now revealed to be totally unnecessary, and not of the constituent matrix of the immediacy of person-ness.

A Beginning: Attention/Selflessness

An aspect of the *yes!* and the glory of the ethic of simplicity is the naming of thinking's productive receptivity. The fourfold set of dispositions—*Gratitude, Readiness, Discretion,* and *Beneficence*—dethrone the will and unseat the powerlessness of intention. Will versus attention/ love. Attention is the master, created omnipotence the medium. If one is not paying attention when the master comes calling, defections occur. "The road to hell is paved with good intentions," often attributed to Bernard of Clairvaux, has some real weight when it comes to the thinking now occurring. It does not matter what you *meant* to do, in saying to yourself, "I meant to do it!" Action, a physical ethics in the thinking now occurring, shows the light: the pragmatic translation of the end of self-consciousness. "At the very foundations of Western thought, faith in the Incarnation has had the radically surprising effect of perfectly incarnating thought itself—so much so that, in our time, thought itself has become for the first time the very form of the essentially new world in which we live" (FP, xiii). Thinking identically faith. Faith is thinking mattered. Thinking is faith mattered.

When in the course of history—or the history of the Incarnation, as in the case of the thinking now occurring—it has come about that the referential point called the self is lost, consigned to the past in some disappearing act, what are human beings to do? Panic might ensue if we do not have the reflective edifice of self-consciousness upon which to ground ourselves. How can ethics function if there is no self-acting self and no recess in consciousness in which to anchor reflection (good will and intention) and what we are given to as the thinking process? As just mentioned, the proverb "the road to hell is paved with good intentions" can easily be transformed to read "the road to hell is paved with intentionality itself." At least this is the starting point in understanding the notion of Evil in the foundational functioning of the thinking now occurring. The provocation in the present essay's title, "The Vanishment of Evil from the World," calls attention to the vanishing of the Nothing and of the self, and the beginning of a new form of consciousness that is absolutely other-ed. We are dealing with a *novitas mundi* wherein the objectivity of consciousness is grounded beyond the distinction of subject/object, beyond the dualism that keeps intact a revolving self around objects. We are not in a universe like Nietzsche's where we must amalgamate meaning by the will-full ordering of chaos because the order of objective or transcendental meaning has been snuffed out; no, we are in a universe where simplicity reigns and the form of consciousness is, "You, who are not able to say 'I am Christ,' you, nevertheless, are the Jesus Christ who is the beginning . . . this is the beginning of the advent of the totality of history as the advent of completely sensible very omnipotence" (F, 620).

In Leahy, the distinction between attention and intention is paramount to understanding the operation of evil. There is nothing to hold in reserve where attention is concerned, whereas intentionality is forever *beside itself,* forever paradoxical, contrary to faith, and in its etymological root of "contrary to appearance"—meaning that it does not appear, or its appearance is only in and as "willfulness" precisely where defection is situated—there is a wish for an alternative to what is happening now, losing touch with pure perception. To pay attention and observe what is new in actuality is the task of one who is productively receptive, one who is actively creating the world. This is in contradistinction to any thought that is self-consciously the product of itself. Intentionality vows to create its own product. "Own-ness" perishes in the new world; there is no owning and the structure of consciousness itself is without "own-ness." Attention is ready to create productively what is different/novel in actuality. Productive receptivity is productive in that newness appears as the form of difference/actuality itself, and receptive in that it is the result of not the will but of attention, the result of construing all that is actual with newness of mind. The will, in and of itself, ends up the basis of evil because it never ends up in the place of creation; rather, it stays in a space of disconnection from the body and from action. The modern notion of "creating oneself" is anathema to the thinking now occurring. There is no creating of oneself. There is creating productive receptively. There is creating otherness/the world through being at the disposal of another while having the patience to see what's absolutely different, doing the right thing. These are the instantiations of the fourfold ethic of simplicity that ends/begins in creating what is new.

The body of Christ, the incarnational foundation of this thinking, one wherein the body of God is absolutely differentiated in existence, yet the distinction between Creator and creature is maintained. Where the body of God is located immediately as the transubstantiation of the Eucharist, as pure otherness as "a person is I at once other, without loss of identity, not at all self" (BS, 263). One says: "You are Jesus Christ," but not "I am Jesus Christ" (F, 620). Thus, absolute *Da* is the place where this foundation stands. The punch line of Derrida's thought is the beginning point of the thinking now occurring: there is nothing but *hors texte*, nothing but the infinite differencing of actuality as the form of thought itself. "But for the thinking now occurring the infinite alterity that is the essence of the world that is otherwise than being—neither being nor not being: infinite alterity. What there is, the essence of the world, begins absolutely now" (BS, viii). Alterity is foundational; not merely an option or something to tolerate but the very form of thinking itself in the new world. The world absolutely now is difference all the way down, not turtles, but difference, what Leahy calls polyontological difference. The void has been annulled and the notion of sameness has been trounced. "There is nothing but the infinitely evental being of existence itself—being-here infinitely that identifies the readiness of consciousness whose readiness for being is the form of faith" (BS, 89).

Badiou and the Subject

> There is only one question in the Ethic of truths: how will I, as some-one continue to exceed my own being? How will I link the things I know, in a consistent fashion, via the effects of being seized by the not-known?
>
> —Alain Badiou, *Ethics: An Essay on the Understanding Evil*

In the endgame of modernity, it is very tiring always to have to exceed or outdo the already extreme constitution of selfhood, as if some inner critic or attack of the Superego is what keeps in place the ontological ground of the universe. This ever-self-excessive movement is another step on the route to selflessness but never quite finishes the job of putting itself to rest. It never lets the person be the excessive essentiality that is creating the world from the beginning. There is a complex victim in Badiou: his ethical subject. We could call him the eschatological romantic. The complexity is evident in the necessary break of the subject from its underlying human environment. This break delivers the subject into a state of hopefulness that the new (invention) will continue to break in upon the human who is puncturing holes in established knowledge and opinion, thereby transposing him into the immortal that awaits him in the not-known of his being. Badiou's world is a transhuman reality, one that does away with the animal realm. The traumatization of the subject by the event turns him into a potential hero who remains faithful to the event that ruptures his being. Instead of believing in the "actuality of the impossible" (BS, xix), Badiou "settles for the possibility of the impossible: this is the conservatism of the romantic revolutionary. Where Paul speaks of a new foundation in Christ, "Badiou speaks of "scientific re-foundation" (BS, xix). The subject/the Immortal is a mere formality in Badiou's thinking. Forever relegated to a transhuman existence, s/he is emptied of the actual history/story at the site of the Pauline proclamation. Without a body, the specter haunts the environs of the world transcendentally, wishing its appearance to have a body in those few milliseconds of the flash of the event, an ultimately Platonic body, removed from the world anti-incarnationally.

Badiou's Immortal Subject, broken off from humanity, can be given status in the realm of the Real. The ethic of truths causes the unity of the human person to split into two separate continuums: one made of opinion and human bestiality, and the other made of numinosity and immortality—the world of the Real, as Jacques Lacan would designate it. Badiou has no sympathetic feelings for the human animal; on the contrary, in his *Ethics* there is only disdain and contempt, perhaps pity, for the human animal who "has become the absolute master of his environment—which is after all, nothing but a fairly mediocre planet" (60). Even Nietzsche, the grand destroyer of all mediocrity, is relegated to delusional status: Badiou will have nothing to do with his hope for a superhumanity (*Übermensch*) because all human endeavors are beneath Good and Evil. Not beyond, but beneath. The Reality of Good and Evil cannot be based on the stratum of the human animal; it can only be based on what he refers to as a truth-process. Badiou's *Ethics* continues: "Good is, strictly speaking, the internal norm of a prolonged disorganization of life." The principles of self-preservation and self-interest have no bearing in the court of the Immortal Subject. "If Evil exists, we must conceive it from the starting point of the Good. Without consideration of the Good, and thus of truths, there remains only the cruel innocence of life, which is beneath Good and Evil" (60).

The thinking now occurring responds to the evental being of truth with this:

> It is precisely in its resort to the Subject that it can be seen that Badiou's revolutionary *noesis*—dismissing the Pauline proclamation "Christ is resurrected" as a fable, as a "narrative statement that we cannot assume to be

> historical," while appropriating the form of Paul's fidelity to the event of the Resurrection—is completely insensible to the fact that for Paul the "narrative statement" "Christ is resurrected" *is* Christ resurrected, that, in effect, what Badiou "cannot assume to be historical" is for Paul *history itself*." (BS, 108–109)

Poor Christianity! When handled by this French militant, its essential kerygma is hijacked and recommissioned. Left in a twist, serving an Immortal subject, we are pushed into his hands having to toil under the provision of a God who knows in advance all that is and will come to be. Badiou insists on ripping "grace" from the hands of Christianity; he wants to laicize grace in his Mallarméan and hazardous way. This is one way in which Nietzsche's atheism remains on the scene, acting out its play as a kind of *Huis Clos*, although this time the exit is directed toward the Immortal of your being instead of other people. The logical steps that Badiou takes to distance himself from the idea of a Creator-God lead him to same-ify the three notions: omnipotence, omniscience, and transcendent plan. Badiou cannot think omnipotence without disconnecting it from immediate and embodied ontic reality. For Badiou, there will always be a divine calculation or plan involved in the notion of omniscience, hence his always having to link transcendence/omniscience with a knowing in advance. "It does not occur to Badiou that omnipotence is the power to be absolutely surprised—the power—precisely because absolutely unconditioned omnipotence is not being nonplused by absolute unpredictability" (BS, 42).

A certain kind of Calvinism erupts in Badiou's thinking: a reversal of double predestination into an atheism that is his reaction to what he perceives as the triteness of the doctrine of Grace. He is the anti-Calvin, the Calvin who objects to the notion of God on the grounds that any determination of God whatsoever throws the baby out with the bathwater. But the commitment of God to history absolutely and essentially does not mean that this God knows everything in advance. On the contrary, omnipotence, the all-potency of God, is such that knowledge in advance is precisely *not* the definition. The *not* in this case is not a negation of knowing in advance but is, rather, a discrimination that moves omnipotence into the world and into pure freedom. The freedom of God and creation in the thinking now occurring is so thoroughgoing that all notions of advance knowledge of the future of creation are consigned to the thinking of the past.

God makes a clean break with creation, no longer tied to it as if divine transcendence undergirds the materiality of the world; rather, God's transcendence is made matter the body itself as a consequence of the Incarnation: *Verbum caro factum est*. "The essence of the new transcendental involves the conception in essence of everything, the absolute nullification of the possible. Everything now comes to exist actually in the form of the body itself. (It goes without saying that now absolutely nothing is possible but what actually exists in essence. But that what actually exists in essence (in the form of man) now is an other in whom every-thing possesses its transcendental identity). Now nothing is a mere formality; everything is essential" (NM, 360). The "idea of God" is finally mattered, is no longer idea or ideal but is rendered material and actual as a consequence of the Incarnation: "God is in fact (being there) in the absolute nullification of God" (NM, 364).

Altizer: Nothingness and Radical Evil

The Calvinistic underpinnings of Altizer's thinking put us face to face with the Christian notion of predestination of Good and Evil. In the abyss of thinking that is the Altizerean universe, which prioritizes the darkness of the crucifixion, the Christian function of the Nothing is foundational. In Altizer, evil pervades on the horizon and in our midst; dialectically constituted, our innermost being and the being of the world is inextricably woven from the fabric of the coincidence of Good and Evil. Human beings live in a world where evil is inherent in its foundation and origination. Thinking cognizes the absolute thoroughgoingness of the *coincidentia oppositorum*, these opposites entwined. The darkness is the light if we see with dialectical vision:

> Joy is inseparable from absolute judgment, or what Nietzsche could know as an absolute No-saying, a No-saying which he could know as the Christian God, and if that God is the deification of nothingness, that is a "deification" absolutely essential for an absolute joy, or absolutely essential for an ultimate act of Yes-saying. Hence the genesis of an absolute darkness is absolutely necessary for the genesis of an absolute "light," or the genesis of an absolute evil is absolutely necessary for the genesis of an absolute grace. Here an ultimate genesis is necessarily a *coincidentia oppositorum*.[3]

There is no innocence in the thinking of Altizer, unless it is a dialectical innocence of the damned and the saved simultaneously—a kind of Calvinistic innocence in the face of original sin and predestination. The justification of evil is paramount in Altizer—leaving no room for true innocence at all—and evil is justified by way of an original blaming of the Godhead, a naming that divinizes Evil by way of radical inclusivity.

By contrast, the catholicity of Leahy pushes thought to recognize the fundamental notion of omnipotence as the foundation stone by and upon which this world is created and from which the beginning of the new universe, as Christ resurrected, commences. There is an innocence in the thinking of Leahy that allows it to break with modern guilt and blame, simply leaving it behind once and for all. The divided consciousness that has been turned in upon itself since the era of Descartes, as a consequence of his appropriation of the transcendental form of natural reason for the purpose of creating self-consciousness, we have seen this form of consciousness try to christen itself the alpha and omega. This modern project of self-constructing self-consciousness is turned inside out in favor of an actual othering of consciousness in the thinking now occurring—not an othering that remains attached to its own "ownness." The apocalyptic God makes the final break and untethers itself from creation. The postmodern turn to difference is made real, objective even in the thinking now occurring; not merely a proliferation of differences but difference that is essentially polyontological.

The very center of divided consciousness in Altizer is the place of defections in the thought of Leahy. Embodied attention in Leahy is the imperative, no room for the actionlessness of a subject, as referenced at the beginning of this essay, only room for action and attention in the life of the body of Christ, for doing the will of the Father. The subject has *potential*, harbors things that can be willfully expressed or left unexpressed, whereas attention is paid immediately, is paid to the body, in and as the body, the body existing now for the first time, participating in omnipotence through creating, through existing now qua creative omnipotence. In the thinking now occurring there is *no nothing*—no placeholder of that which is not. Nothing does not exist, and the function of negation is not to return us to the beginning or to point us to the existence of what *is* over against what *is not*. The function of negation is to distinguish *that* from *this*, to define the limits of any particular utterance or place. Negation in some specific sense can be said to be strictly positive in that the nothing (empty space, room) that is named is not something nonexistent, but quite to the contrary, that which is "not" is existence itself as it is being created ex nihilo, whatever is new appearing *beyond beyond x*.

Altizer and Leahy concur that apocalypticism is the ushering in of a new world, a *novitas mundi*. This apocalyptic gesture is universal in both thinkers, yet the ultimate meaning of apocalypse diverges in the two. There is an apparent conflation of beginning and origin in Altizer, whereas for Leahy a clear distinction can and must be drawn between beginning and origin. There is no origin in the thinking now occurring, even claiming God as origin is anathema. This life/creation is so absolutely new that no origin can be located; creation emerges from an edge of absolute discontinuity. For Altizer too, absolute *novum* is realized in history, and this realization frees the origin from having to remain back "behind" the newness in order to support its history and existence. Thus, he writes: "Christian resurrection is the resurrection of crucifixion; hence it cannot be a flight to the beyond, or even a transition or voyage to the beyond, for it is beyondness which perishes in crucifixion, and perishes so as finally to end the beyondness of the beyond."[4] But Altizer still hinges his thinking on the correlation of Being and Nothing. That evil cannot be separated from the good is rooted in the origin of Godhead, rooted in that beginning in which the primordial God (Alpha) is shattered by the apocalyptic God (Omega). Good and Evil remain distinct, but their identities are bound together in eternal coincidence. Damnation and salvation are eternally clasped as two solid rings. With this primeval identity, God empties himself into his own otherness, the world he has created. In this kenotic outpouring we witness the incapacity of the Godhead to make a clean break from his creation, an incapacity to enable true freedom to be handed over to creatures. Shackled to his own otherness, God cannot break from himself. Still holding onto the necessity of negating himself into existence (a negative corpse, the dead Body of God), the fabric of reality is pure negation. That presence is absence, that absence is presence, constituted by an unproductive binary dynamism that is deeply bound to God's own negativity. Cut off from omnipotence itself, the unfinished self-negation of God is—from the point of view of the thinking now occurring—a center of absolute waste, a waste of freedom.

Beyond Self

> "I accept salvation as to create Christ." Now for the first time in history the *ego* hears, as such, the Godly imperative of God: create Christ's salvation. In the hearing of this word the *ego* is stripped of the essence of self-consciousness: in acting on this imperative the *ego* is for the first time pure other-consciousness: the thinking thing is the absolute actuality of the other for the first time.
>
> —BS, 11

The advent of a new world has begun and when thinking/creating begins in this world, it begins now in place absolute, a place *beyond beyond x*, otherwise than being, otherwise than nothing. The foundational and objective dispositions of Gratitude, Readiness, Discretion, and Beneficence take the place of the self-enclosed, recessional, and interior self—not objective over against subjective, but objective beyond the pale of the dichotomy subjective/objective itself. The "I" begins as a fully manifest body—in its action and creation—one whose beginning is no longer tied to the onto-theological roundabout of Being and Nothing. Being given into a universal body absolutely transparent whose imperative is to create the Resurrection after the death of God, human existence is given the status of omnipotence itself. The hole in the middle of Being, the *nihil*, is no longer, having been supplanted by absolute difference. No longer total presence or total absence, but otherwise than both, the beginning of apocalyptic twenty-first-century thinking, where "transcendental thinking is, for the first time, taken up with the recognition that what it conceives in essence is what in fact appears, but that, before now, it has conceived nothing in essence. Now it conceives life itself" (NM, 317).

This is the territory of the thinking of D. G. Leahy. The presuppositionlessness of the thinking now occurring, the taking seriously of the ousting of the self, the beginning beyond beyond x, the thinking and creating now, this is the world of absolute creation. "This absolutely created world whose truth is absolute otherness is the perfect field of action for an I completely free for the first time. Everything I am is not mine, yet I am it completely. Everything I have is not mine; yet I have it completely. Everything I make is not mine; yet I make it completely" (FP, 159). Evil in this new world has shaky legs to stand on. Evil's ground is not radical (as in Altizer) nor is it palpable in relation to events that cast shadows on potential Immortals (as in Badiou). The internalized *res cogitans*, the internal "I" of self-consciousness that Descartes thought into being as the form of thinking itself is finally liberated from the interior castle, liberated from being "owned" by the person, and now persons are given freedom constitutive of the Godhead itself. This freedom is precisely the freedom of not owning, the freedom of being a person absolutely particular, infinite as difference itself. Not the freedom to be the Godhead but a commensurate freedom as created omnipotence, given by that which is Uncreated. A relational, complex, and infinitely differentiated world begins in the now, where the ending of a computation cannot be known in advance, unlike in the binary logic of modernity. We are living in a world where the competition between Being and Nothing has vanished and we are delivered into the unity of existence as difference itself. Life as pure otherness and difference, difference all the way down.

In Western history, the densely ramified roots of the self run deep. While many remain convinced somewhere in their heads that their "own" self exists, for the thinking now occurring the new reality now existing is an explosion of I's and identities, beyond interior/exterior. This formerly internal species of thought/being is usurped by a fully exterior form of consciousness beyond the distinction interior/exterior; this is not a consciousness in which the internal has been externalized, but is rather an exterior consciousness that is flat, meaningless, and with no depth whatsoever. The ethical basis of the new world is founded in attention's productive receptivity. A place of pure and absolute superficiality in which the realness of creating the Good—and thereby the non-necessity of Evil—are the inheritance of the earth. The newness of the world thought by the thinking now occurring is one in which consciousness is purely and absolutely other, in which there is no own-ness qualifying anything whatsoever that the "I" is—and yet all that the "I" is, it is completely.

Notes

1. Omnipotence is a complex and important concept in Leahy's work. As human beings, we are related to the Creator (uncreated omnipotence) as created omnipotence. We share in the power of the Creator through a free act of creation and by receiving freely the imperative to create we are thoroughly abandoned to the imperative to create by God and left in the site that God's transcendence used to occupy.

2. Beyond beyond direction, other-consciousness surpasses the self that is reflected in the mirror. "Just as John writes [in Rev. 21:23] 'the city did not need the sun or the moon for light, since it was lit by the radiant glory of God, and the Lamb was a lighted torch for it, so now for the first time in history the *absolutely self-less distance* of the Godhead of God in the form of *sensible very existence*: the very existence of the Godhead of God for the first time the actual universe *qua* sensible existence. What now absolutely occurs for the first time in history is not the beginning of what is, strictly thought, the superstition of total presence, the strictly non-actual ideal beginning of nothing, the completely actual superstitious presence of the beginning, the beginning in the form of the self-embodiment of God, no, what now absolutely begins is the very embodiment of the transcendent other of superstition. For the first time the other of superstition is made perfect flesh. You, the actual reader, you who are not able to say 'I am Christ,' you, nevertheless, *are* the Jesus Christ who is the beginning. . . . Divine omnipotence is for the first time the absolute elimination of the impediments of superstition, distance itself, and identity. Divine omnipotence is for the first time superstition itself, itself distance itself, identity itself. For the first time divine omnipotence *is* the actual and ideal totality of existence absolutely. This is the beginning of the advent of the totality of history as the advent of completely sensible very omnipotence" (F, 619–20).

3. Thomas J. J. Altizer, *Godhead and the Nothing* (Albany: State University of New York Press, 2003), 88–89.

4. Thomas J. J. Altizer, *Genesis and Apocalypse: A Theological Voyage toward Authentic Christianity* (Albany: State University of New York Press, 1990), 85.

9

The Transparency of the Good

ALINA N. FELD

The new apocalyptic thinking delineated by Leahy enacts a change in essence of being and consciousness, effecting a unification of the two ontological orders separated by Descartes, an atonement made possible by thinking that is *transparent* to the transcendental essence of existence recognized as its object. The word *transparent* (Latin: *trans*, through, *parere*, to appear) denotes appearing through, seeing/ showing through, also meaning *evident, obvious*.[1] Thought has taken the form of its object, has been trans-formed. This recognition by thought of the transcendental essence of existence as its own object defines the new thinking in its novelty and absolute distinction from modern thinking—which is defined by repeated and deepened failure to recognize its appearance in the course of time. In creation, the transcendental essence of existence appeared as the form of conversion of the world from being nothing to being something; Aquinas recognized it as transcendental natural reason, whereas modern thought appropriated transcendental natural reason as the form of thought itself, while the existence of the world was doubted. Only the new thinking understands that, in its *transparence* to the transcendental essence of existence, thought is converted into its object, existence itself (NM, 324). The transparency of consciousness and universality of the body will be the key subjects of exploration in this essay.

Modernity's Lack of Transparency

Novitas Mundi (1980) sets forth the "essential history of thought" as a "radical critique of modern thought's essence" (NM, 1) from the perspective of the new thinking now occurring for the first time, a new thinking that is revealed only in the three appendixes, with the third appendix, "*Missa Jubilaea*: The Celebration of the Infinite Passover," presenting Leahy's most comprehensive initial statement laying out *novitas mentis*. The preface already announces the new ontological and hermeneutic environment that readers are invited to inhabit actively with the author. In the very first paragraph Leahy introduces a *totaliter aliter* universe of discourse articulating a novel existential or rather ontological situation. The book, the thought of it, its substance, history itself does not belong to the author any more than to the reader; rather, author and reader and "an indefinite number of others" are here and now witnessing "the intelligible power of life itself or its integral existence" (NM, ix).

Modernity, a thinking in the past initiated by Galileo's mathematics of the vanishing point or abyss and Descartes's *cogito sum*, continued with Kant and Hegel, the latter's system being its epitome. Although counterreactions to Hegel—and through him to modernity itself—were mounted by Kierkegaard, Nietzsche, Marx, they were not sufficiently transformative to overcome it and begin a new thinking. This failure was due to modernity's "opacity to the historical essence of existence, its lack of transparency to this world's essence" (NM, 296). Modernity's opacity is contrasted to the new thinking's "transparency to the world's essence in which history's being is thought in the form of the appearance of the transcendental essence of existence itself" (NM, 296).

An enigmatic proclamation of the novelty of the new thinking is being pronounced as a new kerygma, one that will be subsequently taken up from different perspectives, pointing to the same apocalyptic truth. The historical structure of being, become transparent for the new thought, discloses being in its exaltation as love (*agape*) and truth (*aletheia*) (NM, 296–97). This disclosure of the essential fact is the "exaltation of the promise of existence kept"—*apokalypsis* (NM, 298). Transparent to the transcendental essence of existence itself, the new thought comprehends "the fact of being in its existence," without mediation, as "we stand face to face with existence itself," beyond opacity, beyond the dimmed vision of exile and waiting, beyond modernity's subjectivity, in the absolute transparency of thought, an objectivity beyond imagination (NM, 309), indifferent to time, and "unhistorical essential Being," while death, inertia, choice disappear and both past and future are left behind. The promise of existence is fulfilled in thought, as past thinking perishes in the contradictions of subjectivity (NM, 299).

As we traverse the three appendixes, the vision becomes clearer, these cryptic utterances are gradually deciphered as thinking now occurring finds itself in direct contemplation of reality itself (NM, 309), that is, the transcendental essence of existence itself, the transparent object of thought (NM, 235), truth itself (NM, 310), the appearance itself in and for thought of the absolute itself (NM, 315). The apocalyptic revelatory structure of being *novitas mundi* is now occurring in the *novitas mentis* as thought is converted to being, thought is identified with its object, unconditioned existence, identical with the energy of the universe, and nothing is hidden in essence but everything is now itself (NM, 324). Now thought becomes light, its "brand new shining object," and ontologically productive, thus what thought conceives in essence appears, life itself (NM, 327). This reality Leahy declares, totally other than our ordinary experience, is strangely familiar, previously glimpsed in exceptional inner experience, poetic articulations, or theological contemplation. A notable instance of prefiguration of *novitas mundi et mentis,* one that deserves further investigation, is found in the Upanishadic tradition that is philosophically elaborated in the absolute monist ontology of Shankara (eighth or ninth century CE). According to the latter, essentially, being and consciousness, subject and object, are one and the fruit of that oneness is supreme joy. As in the new thinking, it is only in the transparency of selfless consciousness that this truth, otherwise covered by the density of subjectivity, becomes actual. This similarity between Upanishadic monism and thought become light, its object, in spite of their different spheres and ramifications of meaning, may be ultimately significant for the universality of thinking now occurring that shatters all idolatry and provincialism, whether geographic or epistemological.

To contextualize and make visible the gravity of modernity's opacity or failure of transparency to the transcendental essence of existence, the stages in the history of the perception of being are homologized to three temptations of faith corresponding to the three temptations of Jesus, theurgic, theological, and theoretical (NM, 330). While the theurgic temptation to prove itself to thought (change stones to bread) was overcome in Augustine, and the theological temptation (throw yourself from the top of the temple) was overcome in Aquinas's sacred doctrine of transcendental natural reason, the theoretical temptation (accept Satan as master) to prove nothing, only conform to thought, see itself reflected in thought's appropriation of the appearance of the transcendental essence of existence, was not even resisted but indulged in by modern thought (NM, 330). Kierkegaard, although in opposition to modern thought epitomized in Hegel's system, not only failed to resist the third temptation but also became the very embodiment of the theoretical conception of faith (NM, 332). The essence of modernity emerges as satanic in its appropriation of the appearance of the transcendental essence of existence in the service of its own subjectivity and its deformed and myopic ends. Leahy notes the irony in this reversal of roles and values, in the course of which faith, ontologically prior to thought and the condition of thought's transformation from being metaphysical to being historical is taken hostage by thought in a Babylonian captivity that has lasted until the change in essence that is now occurring in thought. The change in essence is caused by the same word through which in the beginning every-thing came into existence, which in time became flesh, and is now spoken through faith in essence. Thanks to this change, faith thinks for itself for the first time (NM, 333).

This apocalyptic thinking articulates and enacts a sui generis Johannine logos christology that encompasses Creation/Incarnation/Eucharist/Death/Resurrection. This unifying *theologoumenon* becomes the key to the apocalyptic new world and new thinking. The repetition of creation and incarnation in thinking now occurring responds to and overcomes the third temptation (NM, 333). Spoken again now, the word is heard everywhere by everybody, provoking essential change in the structure of being and the essence of history, putting being at the disposal of thought. Repetition of the essence of history in thought witnesses to this change as the essence of being in its exaltation (NM, 334) and reverberates through time birthing the history of being. A narrative structure of *analepsis-prolepsis,* or rather the classical biblical typology of *figura* and fulfillment has enacted, without forcing, a completely free and unpredictable unfolding of history. The moments of this history are marked as Abraham, God's incarnation, and the new world. In other words, the implication of Abraham's existence in time is Jesus the Nazarene. Indeed, for the new thinking, the Incarnation is the appearance in time of the transcendental essence of existence and of history: thus, a repetition of creation (NM, 335). The implication of Jesus the Nazarene is a completely new universe elaborated in thought or being itself at the disposal of another (NM, 336). The third temptation is overcome by faith transcending modern intellectual modes and thinking for itself, and "being at the disposal of another," not for another. Promise kept (NM, 337).

The renovation of thought and world is grounded in a repetition of creation through the acceptance of the word spoken and heard as the exaltation of being itself understood as being at the disposal of another. The words of promise instituting the Eucharist are now conceived essentially in thought and terminating in existence: it is the repetition of creation and incarnation, taken into thought, that converts thought into being, its object, as perfect atonement. The function of the word spoken is the repetition of creation, essence of history, "an invitation to exist" now for the first time in history (NM, 342). Thought informed by faith accepts the synthesis of word made flesh and is enabled to conceive "the eucharist of existence itself now for the first time in history" (NM, 338–39). Leahy declares: For *novitas mentis* "nothing is innate, no perception, no idea, no transcendental ego, everything is historical, is being created. This is *novitas mundi*, an essential state of world's novelty perceived in a new reflection ending in existence" (NM, 342).

With *"Missa Jubilaea,"* the third appendix of *Novitas Mundi*, content and language become strongly apocalyptic constituted as an original hermeneutic—on the edge of philosophy and theology—of the Gospel according to John and the Book of Revelation. Philosophical temperance gives way to kerygmatic pronouncements of an ecstatic vision enacting the apocalyptic qua revelation of the beyond the end of time and the beginning of the total novum of consciousness and being. The opening motto, a passage from the Gospel of John (John 6:54–57) containing the prophetic promise, "Anyone who does eat my flesh and has drunk my blood . . . will have eternal life" (NM, 344), is followed by an exalted exegesis turned into an *ecce homo* apocalyptic proclamation: "Here is the form of man: the infinite meekness of God beheld, through which everything exists in fact, in the blood of the lamb made forever new, the infinite of being there in the form of man well disposed to being the bread of life for others" (NM, 344).

Leahy reiterates previous affirmations integrating them exegetically: the unleavened bread of existence in the form of man, though itself unchanged, is change in essence, a "perfect transparency in the form of man to existence itself now occurring to man in the form of thought itself": this is the "eucharistic essence of existence," the knowledge of faith itself (NM, 344–45). The enigma of *novitas mentis et mundi* is now being deciphered: it is the recognition and realization in thought of transubstantiation that generates the beginning of a new world. Grounded in the passion of existence of the one whose essence is to be at the disposal of another, the new world is necessarily without self (NM, 346). In the *missa jubilaea* the elements on the table are transformed in essence into the resurrected Christ, the body of God, temple of the New Jerusalem. As a result, the world becomes the body of God in God, the body "transformed into being here at the disposal of another in essence," the "bread of life upon which others feed" (NM, 348). The words of eucharistic institution provoked an essential change in history and taken up in the Mass have gradually transformed existence and thought: the world has become the body itself, the efficacy of the love of God, homologized to "manna in the desert that this world is in essence" (NM, 349). The world and thought are now both transfigured, transmogrified, transmuted into God, the body of God, "the appearance of the transcendental essence of existence now in thought itself" (NM, 349).

In *"Missa Jubilaea,"* Leahy's apocalyptic thinking actualizes the Eucharist in and for thought, terminating in existence. It becomes a condensed systematic theology, containing quintessentially the Catholic doctrinal articulations—God, the Trinity, Christ, Mary, human being, faith and sin, the Church and community of saints, the sacrament of the Mass, salvation, eschatology—all shaped by an apocalyptic consciousness while sacramentally and liturgically centered on the Incarnation—further fulfilled in the Eucharist as repetition of kenotic creation and figure of death-resurrection. Arguably, this heterodox theology enacts a close reading of the kerygma of radical incarnation central to the essence of Christianity. The retrieval of an original and essential Christianity represents the paradoxical threshold, the absolute edge, simultaneously uniting Leahy's apocalyptic theology to Altizer's and separating them from one another. One may be tempted to understand it as a contention between Protestant and Catholic thinking, a Catholic thinking here close to Byzantine Christianity, thus a contention between Good Friday and Easter Sunday, death and resurrection. That would explain the different apocalyptic modes of approaching the Eucharist, which for Leahy becomes the promise of the new world as universal actualization of the transubstantiation of matter, the body itself, resurrected, while for Altizer is an enactment of death/crucifixion, the final stage of descent in God's self-emptying, a resurrected body as abysmal dead body of God, the only God accessible to late modern consciousness. Leahy proclaims *missa jubilaea* as center of new consciousness that comprehends being as the infinite meekness of God in the form of man, the body itself, essentially, the resurrected Christ. *Missa jubilaea* celebrates the identification of man with God, of the world with the body of Christ's being at the disposal of another, the beginning of the world in the form of man. Thus:

> Before now the world itself experienced thought's incapacity to perceive the body in the form of man, to comprehend being beheld in essence, the infinite meekness of God in the form of man, the body itself. Now what occurs in thought transcending the end of the world in essence is the perception itself of the body, God in God in essence, the temple of the New Jerusalem, effected now inclusively in *missa jubilaea*, the center of a new consciousness. . . . The world itself in essence is the body, the identification in essence of man with God in essence. The world in essence itself is where God is with man. The world itself in essence is the body itself, is the living flesh of Jesus the Nazarene transformed into being here at the disposal of another in essence. The end of the world in essence in existence is the beginning of the world in the form of man. (NM, 347–48)

Paradoxically, for both Altizer and Leahy *missa solemnis* becomes *missa jubilaea*, a celebration of ultimate joy, the joy of ending and, respectively, of absolute beginning. For Leahy *missa jubilaea* celebrates not only the human resurrection of the dead one (Jesus the Nazarene), but the divine resurrection of the dead messiah (NM, 351). The promise from the foundation of the world, repeated in the words of the Eucharist, actualized in the mass, is now fulfilled: world and thought reconstructed in the image of God, the "pathetic form of an absolutely passionate essence," the essence of existence suffering itself (NM, 351). The centrality of the Eucharist in its ontological and cosmological significance, *missa jubilaea* opening the Mass "catholicologically"—Leahy's term—to Here Comes Everybody, evokes and apocalyptically fulfills Teilhard de Chardin's sacramental theology of the mass on the world[2] and of holy matter.[3] In "Hymn to Matter,"

Teilhard officiates a benediction of matter as flesh of the word and divine milieu.[4] He envisions this metamorphosis qua transubstantiation encompassing creatures and organic matter, in an evolutionary teleological drive from amoeba to Omega Point. The key articulations of the cosmic sacrament, complexification and intensification are a *figura* of Leahy's repetition of creation. They mark the evolutionary movement from matter to spirit, from consciousness to self-consciousness, from alpha to omega," or cosmogenesis, biogenesis, noogenesis ultimately Christogenesis.[5] Teilhard identifies a homology between the development of the human body and the divine body, or, as Richard Kearney aptly names it, "an evolving *theo-poiesis*, the prolongation of God's love through creation."[6] He witnesses in faith to the eucharistic transformation of the world, in "expectation of the Parousia," when [the earth, matter] becomes the "body of him who is and of him who is coming."[7] On New Year's Day 1932, during an expedition to the Gobi Desert, Teilhard offers to God a "mass upon the altar of the world," as a sacrament of life itself extended to all, non-Christians included, an "open mystical eucharistics" (MFT, 196). As in the thinking now occurring, for Teilhard, eucharistic communions constituted, Kearney observes, "successive contacts and assimilations to the power of the incarnated spirit," thus "a theogenesis ultimately co-extensive with a life" (MFT, 196–97). For Leahy and Teilhard transfiguration of the world is a matter of both inner transformation and historical evolution: if Teilhard acknowledges glimpses of it in private moments of inner illumination, for the new thinking, the kairotic event is occurring in thought for everybody everywhere, and the appearance of the transcendental essence of existence is existence itself (NM, 353).

With the realization in thought of the world as body, as real food and real drink (NM, 354), *novitas mentis* is now dawning, while the world is made ready for being admitted into the kingdom of God as Trinity, a communion of love and joy of Father and Son integral to the sharing of the spirit of God in Christ (NM, 354). As in the Augustinian pneumatic doctrine of the Trinity, Father and Son, different persons in one essence (the creedal *homoousios*), reflect themselves in the third, the love of the spirit of God, in which their joy of existence in its exaltation is complete, "root and flower" (NM, 354). What remains to be effected before entering the kingdom of God is the "absolute conception of the spirit of Christ" (NM, 352). Arguably, Joachim de Fiore's economy of trinitarian gradual unfolding fulfilled in a pneumatic age, taken over by Hegel and more recently Gianni Vattimo, is operative here in a paradoxical way, as a *coincidentia oppositorum*. The pneumatic apocalyptic model of de Fiore–Hegel–Vattimo is not endorsed, but rather reversed with a gesture recalling Boehme's and Schelling's emphatic preservation and elevation of the body according to the kerygma of resurrection of the body. Incarnation is being fulfilled without remainder, the divine body becomes all in all in thought.

What is this eucharistic body? Leahy declares: the body itself is the temple that is God in God in essence, essentially the risen Christ, formally the perception of the promise of existence kept, materially the substance of history (NM, 354). The transformation of the world into the body of God means the exaltation of matter, of being itself, since matter and being, appearance and essence are atoned (NM, 356). Calling forth the resurrection and exaltation of Christ, the language of the thinking now occurring, exalted and ecstatic, becomes an enactment of *missa jubilaea* itself, a *mysterium magnum* and showing of divine love glimpsed by visionary mystics, Protestant or Catholic, such as Jacob Boehme or, before him, Julian of Norwich, or even earlier, Hildegard of Bingen.

In this apocalyptic thinking, which declares the end and nullification by actualization and fulfillment of theology and christology, along with the Trinity, God, faith, and grace (NM, 363–64): God is the individual, the passion of existence, absolute objectivity, the infinite Passover (NM, 379), and "all are saved in essence through the appearance of the transcendental essence of existence itself that God is absolutely Christ" (NM, 377). Envisioned early on by Origen, Gregory of Nyssa, Evagrius Ponticus, Joachim de Fiore, and Karl Rahner, universal salvation, *apokatastasis,* breaks open special election and hospitably bestows agapeic grace as salvation for all. In this universal sacrament, as in Teilhard's New Year's Mass on the altar of the world, the distinction non-Christian versus Christian is no longer intelligible (NM, 387), the only absolute distinction that remains in operation, neither dialectically reconciled nor overcome, is that between Antichrist and Christ, between the opacity of sin as absolute death and the transparency of the eucharistic essence of existence visible in the acceptance of the passion of existence, the suffering of history itself (NM, 369). The nature of Antichrist is revealed as the double-minded self, the silence in which Jesus the Nazarene is not conceived in essence; the darkness in which God is not the absolute thought in essence in existence; the denial and relinquishing of the passion of existence (NM, 379). Since nothing is hidden, all is transparent thus revealed, and light and thought penetrate everywhere, sin becomes visible in its universality and gravity as all action except that at the disposal of another, *in imitatio Dei* (NM, 372–73). The power of the temptation to sin is not irresistible, however. Both the Augustinian notion of a post-lapsarian, fallen state and the Ricoeurian notion of human fallibility grounded in ontological disproportion belong to thinking of the past. Because sin is not inherent in creation, divine perfection is demanded of every individual, endowed by omnipotence with complete freedom (NM, 387, 363). The universe is in the process of being transformed into a state of absolute perfection as requirement of existence and fulfillment of the promise (NM, 393). Apparently, Leahy endorses a Pelagian theology or transcends Christian boundaries altogether. Since the word is spoken in essence, speech itself is grace. The liberty of the absolute love of existence without the notion of self is key to salvation as infinite Passover of God's touch (NM, 395).

The Dark Transparency of the American Death of God

Only Altizer's retrieval of God's otherness and apocalyptic beginning will enact the apocalypse of modernity itself (FP, 149). In *Foundation: Matter the Body Itself* (1996), Leahy identifies the "Year of the Beginning" as occurring in 1989, symbolically, the fall of the wall of separation, and Altizer's theology of the death of God, as threshold and absolute edge between the old and the new, self-consciousness and world-consciousness, *opacity and transparency* (F, ix). American consciousness—both in its puritanism and pragmatism, culminating with the death of God—constitutes the great hinge between modern consciousness and the new consciousness of the world now dawning.

Leahy argues that in European consciousness, in Hegel or Nietzsche, the death of God is not truly thought through, and that it occurs for the first time only in American consciousness with Altizer's theology. This theology is grounded in the "infinite postponement of self-consciousness," which defines the essence of American thought rooted in pragmatism, positivity and piety—Edwards and Emerson, Peirce, James, and Dewey. According to Leahy's insight, it is precisely the "postponement of self-consciousness in American consciousness [that] makes possible the death of the Godhead" (F, 596). He explains Altizer's *coincidentia oppositorum* of being and nothing, transcendence and immanence, God and Satan, as an expression of the American pragmatic consciousness. Peirce, for whom being is "a matter of more or less so as to merge insensibly into nothing," cannot conceive pure unproductive nothing and invests even the nothing of the beginning with possibility and future. In the same way, for Altizer, the light in its extinction is visible in and as absolute darkness.[8]

Leahy goes further. He advances the idea that besides being the expression of American consciousness itself, Altizer's death of God is the final and culminating thought of modernity generally, of Christianity essentially. European consciousness could not think the death of God through, Aquinas conceived the death of God as *divinitatis instrumentum,* the humanity of Christ, Hegel conceived the death of God as *divinitatis principalis,* the divinity of Christ. Altizer goes beyond both Aquinas and Hegel, and conceives the death of both the humanity and the divinity of Christ, *instrumentum et principalis,* death of the Godhead itself, the nothing of the beginning of God as well as of the selfless self that will be the absolute imperative of the new thinking and the new world (F, 559). The absolute nihil of the abyss of Godhead is the beginning of a universal nothingness in the depths of consciousness, the silence of the beginning and the experience of nothing itself (F, 600). Altizer's death of God theology actualizes both American pragmatism and pietism by reaching into the abyss of God, beyond the Trinity, into the nothing of the beginning, William James's "logically opaque bottom of being" (F, 610), Jonathan Edwards's "being in general" (F, 607). Prior to Altizer, American consciousness, puritan or pragmatist, could not conceive the absolute nothing, the *"dark transparency of consciousness"* was infinitely postponed (F, 624). Thus, for Edwards, the *darkness transparent* is hidden in the sharing of the being of being in general. With the pragmatists, the *darkness is transparent* in different forms: as the beginning of mind in general (Peirce), as the particular beginning (James), as the totality of beginnings (Dewey) (F, 624). It is only Altizer who conceived "the state of utter nility," the nothing as the a priori other, the *transparent darkness,* the relatively opaque bottom of being, in the form of the death of God (F, 625).

Leahy maintains that Altizer's theology of the death of God thinks through the end of Christianity and of the entire tradition of thinking that started with the Presocratics. Leahy answers Hegel's question whether Christianity can survive the end of Christendom by arguing that Christianity transcends the end of Christendom in the beginning now of a universal faith already glimpsed by Altizer (F, 603). He envisions the pure beginning in America of universal nothingness in the depths of consciousness, an experience of the silence of the nothing (F, 601) of a pure new world, the infinite expanse of universal consciousness of infinite possibility, universal faith (F, 610), the absolute elimination of nothingness (F, 604), absolute exteriority (F, 606), and objectivity (F, 607–608), consciousness as reunification of the ideal and the actual displacing self-consciousness (F, 611). Thus, "for the first time God is really and actually dead . . . modernity's last chance to think nothing in essence in the face of the reality of the beginning of a new universe—faced with the beginning of a new form of thinking and a new universe, the swerve and swivel into Nothing of consciousness itself" (F, 601).

In other words, the radical apocalyptic iconoclasm of the American death of God, Altizer's conceiving the *transparent darkness of the nothing*, is the condition for the possibility of the postapocalyptic new heaven and new earth, the *novitas mentis et mundi* now occurring for the first time in history since the creation of the world. In response, Altizer reviews and confirms Leahy's analysis of the American death of God as the apocalyptic event of the purely nothing in the depths of consciousness. Thus: "Now existence itself is for the first time purely Nothing, Being itself for the first time, the Nothingless Nothing."[9] But, Altizer continues, this Nothingless Nothing and "crucifixion of philosophical conceptualization" uniquely possible in America is the condition for the possibility of the absolute apocalypse of the new beginning: "Leahy can understand America as the deepest site of the death of God, an America which is the furthest extension of modernity. . . . Yet this is a death of God prior to that absolute apocalypse which is the identity of the essentially new world now beginning."[10] Here, the absolute novelty of the apocalyptic selfless I emerges—a paradoxical Deleuzean repetition and difference, a unity of sameness and difference—by clear contrast with its occlusion and obscuration in the thinking of modernity. Leahy uses Hegel's own formula to dismantle the Hegelian and modernity principle, and makes his point using an "ontological donut with a whole in the middle" thought-experiment (FP, 153–55).

Transparency of the Apocalyptic I

Faith and Philosophy (2003) continues the critique of modernity begun in *Novitas Mundi*. The appendix, "Thinking in the Third Millennium: Looking Without the Looking Glass," is a dense constructive thought and lucid articulation of the new thinking this time centered on the apocalyptic I. Here, the effects of the eucharistic transubstantiation—being at the disposal of another—for the I are being considered. Subjectivity and self-consciousness that marked the thinking of modernity vanish and absolute objectivity, freedom, and transparency of selflessness become the new reality of consciousness. But can the I exist without a self, without its own self? The question is being answered using American pragmatist Herbert Mead's thinking experiment of the I and *me*, its mirror reflection. "I see me in the mirror seeing me. I know I can see. But can me see?" (FP, 144). Since in the looking glass we see *through a glass darkly*, not face to face (1 Cor. 13:12), transparently, the new thinking shatters the mirror that mirrors the I as me, my self. The creative, unpredictable immediate subject I is distinguished from me, self-mediated by others, stable, predictable assumed self, and object in the past (FP, 144). Leahy argues that the purely active ego is never a self in the actual now, therefore, there is no ground for the notion of self. This I not a self is "absolutely pure consciousness," a "transparency within a transparency," the "transparent foundation of a complete human freedom," "disclosing itself to itself without the aid of a looking glass," the I of a "consciousness of absolute objectivity," the "I whose time has come at the end of the second millennium" (FP, 145). This I that I now am is apocalyptic, having been shaped in the form of the apocalyptic I, the Creator, made flesh two thousand years ago, the same I sitting on the throne in the New Jerusalem, declaring: "Behold I make all things new, I am the alpha and omega the beginning and the end" (FP, 146). The apocalyptic I in whose shape the individual I has been formed constitutes the foundation of complete freedom of the human I (FP, 147).

While apocalyptic thinking, this new form of mind and new essence, was anticipated in Augustine and Aquinas, it has been subjected to increasing forgetfulness and occlusion in modernity beginning with Descartes, Kant, culminating in Hegel, for whom the apocalyptic consciousness conceived by Aquinas becomes self-revelation, beginning is reduced to becoming, and the idea of God replaces God (FP, 148–49). If forgetfulness of the otherness of the Godhead and of the unknown is absolute in Hegel, counterreactions to Hegel taken up by Kierkegaard, Husserl, and Heidegger remain within the sphere of modernity (FP, 150). Nietzsche and Sartre fail to conceive a consciousness of absolute objectivity, of complete freedom and sans anxiety otherwise than knowledge (FP, 150). Levinas likewise misses the mark; although his pre-phenomenological, preconscious subjectivity is without anxiety, its primordial responsibility to the other predates its own freedom. Levinas cannot conceive the I not a self, while the self "stuffed with the other" leaves self-consciousness intact (FP, 157).

The I of the apocalyptic consciousness appears as the new essence, absolutely objective, acting absolutely, a "perfectly infinitely transparent surface of the body . . . [coming] forth without limitation across the surface of the body, an other with others, absolutely freely," "infinite being at the disposal of across the surface of the body" (FP, 156). The ethics corresponding to this I cannot be metaphysical (Levinas), but a physical ethics, of the existing body, disruptive, explosive, and transformative, the end of the old world, the beginning of a completely new existence, one "that when we pay attention we can all feel in our bones" (FP, 158). An assembly of such free "infinitely transparent" I's, of persons both completely disinterested and totally engaged with the world, is the *pièce de résistance*, the foundation of society and of a new conception of existence of a new world order "here on the threshold of the third millennium" (FP, 159–60).

Transparency as Ethics

Beyond Sovereignty: A New Global Ethics and Morality (2009) lays out the ethic of simplicity corresponding to *novitas mundi* and *novitas mentis*, by comparing it with Alain Badiou's ethic of truths and Giorgio Agamben's ethic of *the coming community*. Prepared throughout previous work and initiated at the end of *Faith and Philosophy*, thinking the new ethic expands and is fulfilled in *Beyond Sovereignty*, Leahy's foundation or prolegomena of moral philosophical theology. Moreover, this ethic of simplicity is also an eschatological vision of resurrection and the kingdom in the form of the traditional tension *already/not yet* of inaugurated theology with a swerve: *novitas mundi et mentis* are occurring now, the resurrection body is being thought now, the kingdom is beginning now for the first time in history. The new life beginning of selfless existence actualizes nimble omnipotence offered in a universal distribution of the substance of divinity in a world of corporate humanity, no longer of self-making individuals but of a species-making species (BS, 4). According to the presence or absence of self, the new beginning of "perfect transparency of the other's otherness" is received as hell or heaven (BS, 4). The divine absolutely selfless body is the first universal—*catholicological*, as Leahy names it—thought of the infinite universe, the first transcendental essence, it is the foundation of existence, *res cogitans absoluta* (BS, 5).

The nonnegotiable imperative or new commandment is to create the kingdom of God on earth as it is in heaven. That means to immediately create a world in the image of the Creator, a world of singularity inclusive of plurality, of selflessness giving priority to the selfless other, of pure act eliminating rest, a world whose essence is freedom (BS, 7–9). Refusal to create constitutes sin as absolute death, "self-division, self-severing of self in rest" (BS, 9). After the American death of God, resurrection of the body infinitely shared becomes visible as the actual existence of global humanity, the beginning of the transformation of the world essence into infinite body (BS, 20). In this new existence, salvation is conceived as a personal acceptance of becoming a member of this infinite body, in other words, "to create Christ" (BS, 11). The foundation of the new world society is freedom of trinitarian *withness*, that is, intimacy of perichoretic love embodied in the third person (BS, 23). The new concept of society involves actuality of the *withness*, being beyond sovereignty, specificity, coexistence, and partnership, perfect species of individuality, elimination of generic existence and self-interest. As such, it is the living body of the new humanity: the beginning of *res pretiosa, res novissima, res singularis, res nominata*. The New Law is absolute change, perfect plurality of the *with* (BS, 24).

Faced with the effect of the Incarnation as God's embodiment of the ontic fulfilled in the Eucharist, that of a universe become the "sheer transparency of existence," the question of the possibility and nature of a principle of ethics is inevitable (BS, 39–40). In order to make visible by contrast the novelty of the apocalyptic ethic of *novitas mentis*, Leahy engages Badiou's ethical thought that is an attempt manqué at a new beginning of thinking beyond modernity after the end of philosophy in Heidegger and the American death of God (BS, 51–52). The ethic corresponding to the new ontology of "nimble omnipotence," of a "savior who saves all but does not save himself, but embodies those he saves," is a physical ethic of the body and of simplicity (BS, 43). The new ethic emerges by contrast to Badiou's ethic of truths that remains captive to modernity's subjective lack of transparency to the transcendental essence of existence and, in continuity with Descartes's appropriation of Aquinas's transcendental form of natural reason, appropriates the content of Paul's proclamation of the resurrection as void of reality.

In dialogue with Badiou's ethic of truths, Leahy's ethic of simplicity or revolutionary metanoesis emerges as the ethic of the new world for which the imperative is to create the world and real evil is "defection from creating the world" (BS, 112). Badiou's revolutionary *noesis* extols the indefeasibility of the human spirit, the immortality of the Subject, and the void, and participates in the "infinite postponement of absolute particularity," the "infinite postponement of the exhaustion of subjectivity" also defining American pragmatism. In counterdistinction, revolutionary *metanoesis* enacts the truth of the resurrection, as the "indefeasibility of the embodied human spirit," the "immortality of the live human body," the "defeasance of the void," the "proclamation of a truth as a singularity absolutely particularized— as a singularity actually embodied in existing omnipotence" (BS, 115). Event, fidelity, and truth are the three dimensions of Badiou's ethic of truths, vulnerable to the evils of terror, betrayal, and disaster. The new ethic of simplicity actualizes and fulfills in essence the economy of traditional moral thought. Its four dimensions of gratitude, readiness, discretion, and beneficence, transparent to the new commandment, recover and ground in freedom and nimble omnipotence the theological virtues of sacred doctrine. These are challenged by defective dispositions that negate, resist, and oppose the ethical imperative to create the new world of transparent being at the disposal of another (BS, 107).

Transparency of the Good

At the end of "Good and Evil," the third and final chapter discussing Alain Badiou's ethic of truths in relation to the ethic of thinking now occurring, Leahy quotes from *Foundation*: "In the delicate factuality of transparent identity complementarity itself is absolutely transcended: memory itself absolutely coincides with perception, absolutely exists in the delicate transparency of perception, the simulacrum which is no simulacrum, the product of an absolute repetition, identity itself" (BS, 121). Here, we observe a critical point of intersection between *novitas mentis et mundi* and Jean Baudrillard's world of the virtual: the transparency of the simulacrum as the actualization of the promise, or of our perennial desires. While both Leahy and Baudrillard envision the apocalyptic as eschatological fulfillment, the modes or keys/tonalities (mood) and significance of fulfillment are radically opposed. The nature of transparency is different. For Baudrillard the transparency of the simulacrum represents a perverse enactment of Joachim de Fiore's pneumatic age whose transparency is the final sign of ontological void and the vanishing of the dialectics of being and truth. The triumph of singularity and simulacra is the triumph of the nihil, of spurious infinity, of ghostly meontological repetition, the beginning of life in death and hell here and now. In the world of simulacra, transcendence of polarities—both ontological and ethical, life and death, good and evil—is accomplished *à l'envers/en abime* as a demonic double, an abysmal reflection whose ultimate product is evil. For Baudrillard, pure transparency is pure evil. The transparency of evil as the actualization of our perennial desires is the final scene of Gnostic dualism and the demise of the body, the denial and reversal of the Incarnation, docetic ontology of the void, a literal and perverse Eckhartian mysticism of unbecoming.

Apparently, Baudrillard's thinking belongs to the past, witnesses to the apocalyptic exhaustion of all forms of European modernity outside the American consciousness enlivened by pragmatism and puritanism that made possible Altizer's explosive celebration of the death of God. Baudrillard's transparent evil is thus not even the end but rather the illusion of the end. The absolute novum of thinking now occurring whose signature is transparency of the good emerges by contrast to Baudrillard's chlorotic transparency of evil. It centers on the Incarnation, matter the body itself. Through a paradoxical actualization, by the loss of the body and disincarnation, the desire of liberated spirituality appears, in its true identity, as a reversal and end of creation and the human. The absolute edge, separating good and evil, is constituted by "the new beginning, the other-consciousness as the "Incarnation finally assaulting thought" (F, xiii), "absolute realization of the Incarnation" (BS, 20), the "resurrected body" becoming all in all (BS, 14). Actuality has annihilated possibility, the body is thought. While Baudrillard's transparency let the void appear, transparency of the new thinking lets the fullness of transcendental essence of existence appear: the simulacrum is no simulacrum, but the product of an absolute repetition, identity itself (BS, 121).

From *Novitas Mundi* to *Beyond Sovereignty* there runs a dividing line, an unsurpassable threshold, between the past or modern consciousness and the new. The threshold appears to be an absolute edge, separating the old world and the new heaven and the new earth. The biblical dichotomy between seeing face to face at the end of time and seeing through a glass darkly, constitutes the main marker of the edge separating absolutely transparency and opacity.

Transparency—pure, sheer, perfect, absolute, infinite, complete phenomenologically—enacts the resurrection and exaltation of being, essence, life and body. Unhistorical past modes of thinking, essentially an opacity, if not to the fact of existence, to the historical essence of existence itself, specifically modern thought of "radical passivity" (NM, 212), a "paranoia in process" (NM, 122), could not contain the "transparency now occurring to this world's essence," in which "the appearance of the transcendental essence of existence itself manifests the historical structure of being as occurring truth: *aletheia*" (NM, 296). Transparency manifests and corresponds to aletheia, remembering, ultimately eucharistic anamnesis, and the virtues of the ethic of simplicity. Contrariwise, opacity refers to blindness, both ocular and noetic, oblivion, forgetfulness, and by extension, the evil forms or vices of the new ethic of simplicity: inattention, rest as passivity, intention in the absence of action, hesitation, modern skepticism and doubt, boredom, leading to a dissolution and annihilation of the transcendental I.

Since transparency involves both the subject and the object, both the seer and the seen, in the new thinking one can see for the first time the really real, the truth, face to face, the essence liberated from contradictions (NM, 18), otherness, oneself in God, God in oneself (NM, 65). Reason sees through itself in God's light as sheer transparency, reflecting without obstruction God's creative act (NM, 66). Modern thought in its radical passivity "failed to maintain itself transparently face to face with the transcendental essence of existence" (NM, 212). The glory of God is "transparently presented to pneumatic immortal persons" (NM, 229). The clarified essence is a manifestation of the glory of God that provides the intellect with the capacity to understand the transcendental essence of existence (NM, 229). The spiritual work of the mind as clarification, thus existence in light, involves the conversion of psychopathetic individuality into the pneumatic mind extending to the universe of mind, thus transcending the narrow limitation of self (NM, 229). Clarity of self-perception is achieved by the individual only in relating immediately to God as the power in which one exists transparently (NM, 271).

Noetic transparency, as true vision and active contemplation, presupposes complete objectivity and selflessness, thus requires as its condition of being, the transcendence of subjectivity and the self. The self, increasingly hardened during European modernity, obturated or occluded/obstructed visibility and obscured perception-conception of the transcendental essence of existence. Not only a quality or attribute of being, transparency becomes being itself, a form of perfect ontology: the word made flesh is "perfect transparency in the form of man to existence itself (NM, 344). It is this perfect transparency to existence that is now fully actualized, "now occurring to man in the form of thought" (344). The possibility of the transparency of the eucharistic essence of existence is now occurring for the first time in history (NM, 362), a possibility that was proven by the virgin birth, Mary's nonresistance, thus transparency, to the transcendental essence of existence. What has made possible the transparency to the essence of history is the conception/perception now occurring of eucharistic substance of existence as the new universe, an embodiment of the word spoken and made flesh in essence (NM, 338). Having come closer to the end as absolute materialization of the objectivity now thought when memory becomes absolute remembrance, eucharistic anamnesis, of existence itself in essence, the structure of this ending becomes transparent to us (NM, 391–92). Arguably, this end not an end since, we are reminded, "everything exists perpetually," evokes the eschatological moment of total revelation, *apokalypsis,* also envisioned by Teilhard as Omega Point.

Transparency gains a deeper complexity in *Foundation*. Leahy warns against any confusion of the experience of transparency with subjectivity. He insists that the "transparency, the very pellucidity, of the relations which constitute this center of the consciousness of creation, where the reader has arrived, is not a matter of subjective feeling but, in fact, absolute" (F, 528). The system of equivalence of proportions and numbers unveils the identity of transparency of this center of the consciousness of creation with "synthetic intelligence," "spiritual center," ultimately, the Spirit of God (F, 528). Recalling Joachim and Teilhard—and with a swerve, Vattimo—in this context seems in order. As mentioned earlier, there is a paradoxical movement throughout thinking now occurring: on the one hand, toward the age of the spirit, and the noosphere; on the other hand, and turning Baudrillard's apprehension around, it is precisely this movement grounded in creation-incarnation-eucharist, that constitutes itself as total embodiment, as if fulfilling Teilhard's prayer, the noosphere becomes Christosphere, transubstantiating the world into divine body: matter the body itself. Thought absolutely, transubstantiation enables the only pragmatic conception of substance as William James argues, transcendence of James's "foreignness and intimacy" of plurality and monism.

Leahy elaborates a sublime cosmic and apocalyptic vision of an "infinite number of infinitely transparent absolute actualities" (F, 534): "the sphere of absolute objectivity now existing; the sphere of spheres infinitely newly beginning, the sphere of infinitely new, infinitely separate spheres; the sphere the surface of which is the beginning of an absolutely transparent depth" (F, 534). The hypnotic vision of the infinitely transparent spheres and of "transparent depth," abyssal depth appearing through, reverses James's "opaque bottom of Being," as well as Pascal's bottomless abyss and "eternal silence of infinite spaces." The transparent spheres recall premodern hermetic cosmologies from Plato and Aristotle to Ptolemy, Cusanus, and Galileo, the *sephirot* of the Kabbala, and most emphatically Dante's concatenated transparent worlds of quintessence illumined by God at the center of all. Speech/the word eliminates silence, the infinite spaces echo and embody the Word. This is the Body, the "the infinite proportionality of the body" (F, 534, 544). The perception/conception amplifies into an exalted pronouncement of the Kantian sublime, both mathematically and dynamically. Surrounding eucharistic transubstantiation, echoes of Cusanus and Galileo are present and transcended:

> This is the limit of the infinite expansion of the single sphere. This is the beginning of the circumference of the infinite circle. This is the line for the first time. This is the time of beginning. This is creation displacing the abyss itself: the body of the living God in the form of the beginning, depth absolutely surface, the infinite identical with the finite: the absolute incompatibility of the infinitely numbered points of the circumference of the circle: the absolutely *transparent* circle. (F, 534)

Opacity and oblivion have dissolved. This is a world of transparent singularity: a *coincidentia oppositorum* of depth absolutely surface, the infinite identical the finite, the impossible infinite circle become actuality. In this new universe, the absolute transparency of the perfect infinite circle of creation, the body of the living God, displaces the abyss of modernity begun with Galileo's mathematics of the vanishing point and Descartes's cogito sum.

Following the gradual actualization of the promise from the foundation of the world, the body along with the selfless I of objective universal consciousness suffer a radical transmutation and become transparent. If the transparent body as absolute window emerges in *Foundation*, it is *Faith and Philosophy* that perfects it: "This is the beginning of the absolute transparency of the body, the body as the absolute window: the infinitesimal beginning of the absolute, the minimum for the first time" (F, 564). The perception/conception of the I as "the perfectly transparent surface of the body" (FP, 156), the I that is "the infinitely transparent surface of the body," this I, "invisible, infinitely transparently the surface of the body" (FP, 156) recalls and reverses Michel Henry's "body that is already myself," the "immanent subjective body." For both Henry and Leahy, body and I are one original being that cannot be separated ontologically, for both, the body is pathetic and, as Henry remembers, "the body will be raised." The similarity is soon curbed, however. While Henry, following Meister Eckhart's experience of deification—psychology identical metaphysics—envisions a subjective body, for the thinking now occurring subjectivity is the modern form of opacity and obstruction. Subjectivity eliminated, consciousness becomes diaphanous, pure consciousness of absolute objectivity manifested as freedom qua gift of being (FP, 145). This I of *novitas mentis*, the infinitely transparent surface of the body, appears as the complete opposite of the immanent subjective pathetic I of Henry: an I turned inside out, "absolutely pure objective consciousness, a transparency within a transparency," "absolutely objective and completely free. . . . The I absolutely other as the foundation of a society that is the beginning of an essentially new world . . . the infinitely transparent I is the surface identifying body and world absolutely" (FP, 144, 159). The opacity of subjectivity has been transcended.

A mysterious phenomenology of transparency defines and marks perfect being from beginning to end, and new beginning. The initial transparency at the foundation, the cubic or fourfold absolute, begins to exist as universal Body. Thus: "Now occurring for the first time in history this is the experience of the absolute increase of existence: the perfect bodying of the initial transparency, the universe-filling cubic absolute absolutely beginning to exist, the foundation for the first time in the form of existence" (BS, 6). This transparency of the absolute foundation of the world indicates ontological perfection, not only an epistemic quality—or rather, in the singularity of the beginning, recaptured now, both. The apocalyptic moment in the history of divine being is the "perfect transparency of the First Finitude of the Infinite God," the "absolute thought of matter," the conception of the absolute matter of thought: "withness" is the thought of the finitude of God beginning (BS, 13). Withness or relation constitutes the nature and function of the Spirit of God that manifested as the "perfect transparency of the First Finitude of God" in the incarnation.

Perfect transparency appears when God is all in all, "when the universe is embodied in God" and "the world becomes the sheer transparency of existence" (BS, 39). Faced with this cosmic theophany and theosis now universally actualized in essence that had been dreamed of, imagined, or lived through only in the intimacy of mystical experience, Leahy asks, "What remains of the possibility of Good and Evil? If . . . the divinity embodying the universe itself is itself embodied as world itself absolute foreground . . . what room is left for ethical decision? (BS, 39). The ethical imperative to create the world is polyontological, addressed now to everybody everywhere. The I is called to act absolutely in acknowledgment and reception of the gift of being. This I "the infinitely transparent surface of the body is the form absolutely of the absolute gift of being" (BS, 84). The I as transparency and gift of being, the beginning of the resurrection, responds to the imperative to create the world with gratitude, readiness, discretion, and beneficence, the ethical dispositions available to it. They are the classical theological virtues resurrected and ontologically relevant: faith or readiness for being, hope or the I constructing being, love as creative act, and the fourth which comes first, "omnipotent embodiment, the beginning of polyontological difference" (BS, 87, 89).

The ethic of simplicity is an ethic of transparency, of transparent I's, of the new society *res pretiosa, res singularia, res nominata*, of transparent polyontological being. A Kantian kingdom of ends beginning here and now, the Kingdom of God thought through, repetition of creation, universal celebration of *missa jubilaea* in which the apocalyptic I as transparent body is all in all. Teilhard's diaphanous body and Boehme's pearl or transparent crystalline body come to mind as *figurae* whose fulfillment is now occurring. For visionary Boehme, God's own desire is incarnation, self-revelation in nature and human being of its own dialectical tension of dark ground and light.[11] Although this tension or *turba* will reverberate throughout nature and the human being, perfection of original unfallen humanity remains that of transparent body resembling God according to God's light and love.[12]

While Hegel figures prominently in Leahy's thought as the epitome of modernity and thus at the aphelion of the new thinking, as Altizer remarks, "it is Hegel alone with whom Leahy can be compared" as pure and apocalyptic thinkers.[13] Indeed, the unfoldings of thinking in both Hegel and Leahy share similar magnitude and comprehensiveness of critical thinking and follow similar lines of constructive elaboration. As in Kierkegaard's case, there is a proximity or family resemblance between Hegel and Leahy, yet the thinking now occurring finds itself in agonic confrontation with Hegel, the apogee of absolute self-consciousness, misunderstanding of the beginning, and opacity to the transcendental essence of existence. Since the main centers of thinking now occurring are the beginning, God, and freedom, there are two interesting omissions in Leahy's critical thinking, Spinoza—noted by Altizer—and Schelling.[14] The omission may be justified by Leahy's own disclaimer that he has intentionally "neglected specifically theological works" of modernity (F, x). From Leahy's perspective, Schelling, unlike Hegel, as well as Boehme, unlike Eckhart, would not be thinkers of modernity and of the past, but rather heralds or prophets of *novitas mentis*. Apparently, aspects of Joachim de Fiore, Boehme, Spinoza, Schelling, and Teilhard have been taken up as prefigurations of the fulfillment of the world as divine body now occurring. In Teilhard's thinking, in particular, transparency and diaphany predominate and define the nature of the progressive transubstantiation and transfiguration of the world itself. A visionary forerunner of *novitas mundi*, he prophetically calls forth the "coming of the divine milieu, the diaphany of God" (DM, 128), the "splendour of a universal transparency aglow with fire" (HM, 55), "[matter], flesh so transparent . . . as to be no longer distinguishable from spirit" (HU, 68).

The thinking now occurring is not only a thinking through but is also an enactment of the apocalyptic absolute edge/threshold to the Parousia expounded by Aquinas, glimpsed by Teilhard, the destination of creation as fulfilled promise. This apocalyptic new singularity of being-consciousness involved a thoroughgoing in-depth critical analysis of European and American modern and postmodern consciousness, culminating with the death of the American God as well as a constructive system transcending all dichotomy and the modern boundaries separating science, logic, mathematics, philosophy, theology. This new logic and thinking emerges as an apocalyptic fulfillment of creation in thought here and now, in an absolute actuality or body.

Leahy's work enacts a *divina commedia* beginning with the oblivion, obscuration, opacity to the appearance of the transcendental essence of being that was recognized in Aquinas's sacred doctrine, and ending with the beginning of new thinking: from infernal opacity and oblivion ruled by satanic modernity to the transparency of the *vita nuova* of *novitas mundi*. Here, in counterdistinction to Dante's *Commedia*, Mary and the feminine seem to be almost inexistent. And yet, however absent throughout his work (with one exception in "*Missa Jubilaea*"), Mary—as in Dante's *Commedia*—is conferred the unique role of ultimate guide and grand priestess officiating the initiation of humanity through death and apocalypse into resurrection. Mary is "the exception in essence implicated in the repetition of creation," in whom "the appearance of the transcendental essence of existence itself came to be everything," for whom "nothing existed in essence but God himself," whose knowledge of the righteousness of God bore fruit in the person of Jesus, the meekness of God made visible (NM, 362). Mary as *capax dei* is thus "the proof of the possibility of the transparency of the eucharistic essence of existence itself now occurring for the first time in history," according to which in the form of Body is seen everywhere the form of man (NM, 362).

Moreover, Mary makes visible a justified demand for perfection, grounded in God's compatibility with essential perfection of the creature so disposed in absolute freedom (NM, 363). Mary appears as embodiment of faith, freedom, and perfection, one whose fulfillment is now beginning to occur universally in the new objective consciousness of transparent being at the disposal of another. If matter the body itself, is a cipher for or a traditional archetype of the feminine, as French American depth psychologist Monique Pommier aptly argues in her analysis of Teilhard's thought, then our new being, consciousness, and world are unfolding absolutely and essentially under the sign of the great Divine Mother-Matter of ancient tradition, thus both fulfilling and transcending Christian thinking.[15] Fulfillment of the promise from the foundation of the world in history means both fulfillment of the Christian sacred doctrine and its transcendence into a new heaven and a new earth of infinite transparency to the transcendental essence of existence, of universal objective consciousness, of the body, matter itself, of transcendental I's, of the omnipotence of being at the disposal of another.

Notes

1. In Greek the synonym of *transparency* is *diaphany* (*dia*, through, *phanein*, to show).

2. Pierre Teilhard de Chardin, "The Mass of the World," in *The Heart of Matter*, trans. René Hague (New York: Harcourt, 1978).

3. Teilhard de Chardin, "The Spiritual Power of Matter," in *The Divine Milieu*, trans. Bernard Wall (New York: Harper and Row, 1960), 106–10.

4. Teilhard de Chardin, "Hymn to Matter" in *Hymn of the Universe*, trans. Gerald Vann (New York: Harper and Row, 1965), 67.

5. Teilhard de Chardin, "The Last Page of Pierre Teilhard de Chardin's Diary," in *The Heart of Matter*, 104.

6. Richard Kearney, "Mystical Eucharists: Abhishiktananda and Teilhard de Chardin," in *Mysticism in the French Tradition: Eruptions from France*, ed. Louise Nelstrop and Bradley B. Onishi (Burlington, VT: Ashgate, 2015), 194.

7. Teilhard de Chardin, "In Expectation of the Parousia," in *The Divine Milieu*, 154–55.

8. Leahy writes in *Faith and Philosophy*: "Absolute darkness [is] not absolutely devoid of light since the absolute darkness is the light's very own doing: the light in its self-extinction is . . . itself in a measure visible in and as the absolute darkness. The absolute future form of the actual nothingness of existence in Altizer, the absolute possibility form of the absolute nullity of the beginning in the American death of God theology, the absolute & final contra-Nietzschean refusal to put meaning into things is the reflection in its finally negative form of the profound positivity & piety of American consciousness" (FP, 120–21).

9. Thomas J. J. Altizer, "Appendix: D. G. Leahy and the Triple Nothingness of the Godhead," in *The Apocalyptic Trinity* (New York: Palgrave MacMillan, 2012), 161.

10. Altizer, "Appendix: D. G. Leahy," 168.

11. Cyril O'Regan, *Gnostic Apocalypse: Jacob Boehme's Haunted Narrative* (Albany: State University of New York Press, 2001).

12. Gerhard Wehr and Pierre Deghaye, *Jacob Bohme* (Paris: Albin Michel [Cahiers de l'Hermétisme], 1977), 79: "However, for Boehme, the body does not necessarily identify itself with matter. The body of the original man is conceived by him as being of a marvelous transparency vis-à-vis beauty and purity. It is in this that he reveals his resemblance to God" (my translation from the French).

13. Altizer, "Appendix: D. G. Leahy," 164.

14. Ibid., 168–69.

15. Monique Pommier, "Teilhard de Chardin," in *The Twelvefold Archetype of the Human Soul* (Boston: Xlibris, 2009), 109–16.

PART IV
THE EDGE WHERE CREATING BEGINS

10

Concerning the Absolute Edge

EDWARD S. CASEY

Almost every edge you can think of is *relative*. By this, I mean that it is the edge that it is only in relation to other edges. These other edges can be contiguous, as when we are talking about the edges of a wooden block, or the edges of the outer flesh of our bodies.

But they can also be located at some distance from a given edge—say, the outer edges of my computer as located in the café where I am using it: its edges have an external but still meaningful relation to the interior edges of the café in which I am seated. Or, to be less overtly physical, the edges of many of my thoughts enjoy an internal relationship: the outer edge of one thought leading to that of another, and that in turn to still another, until we have an entire nexus of edges-of-thoughts. Socially, too, we are caught up in clusters of edges as we relate to others in and through the edges of their bodies, their beliefs, their actions, and their words. (This is so in spite of Levinas's insistence that, even so, our relationship with others is at an infinite ethical distance; Levinas himself requires that a very specific "proximity" to others obtain if fully ethical action is to take place, and this proximity is surely a plane in which personal and interpersonal edges interarticulate.)

It is my contention that human beings (and doubtless other sentient beings) live in densely configured edge-worlds. They have no choice but to do so. Their lives—our lives—are spent navigating and negotiating edges of innumerable kinds. I have attempted elsewhere to discuss the major kinds of such edges and many of their subordinate species.[1] I contend that edges are not merely confining or constricting—as we might think if we consider them only as where things and events peter out and perish—but are inherently expansive, serving to connect these same things and events to their surroundings and items still further afield. This connectivity obtains not only materially but in terms of the outlay of directions in alternative realms, acting to release inhabitants of given edge-worlds into very different worlds altogether. By this, I do not mean anything specifically mystical or spiritual but rather experiential at unanticipated and novel levels—wherever the intentionality inherent in edges themselves might take us. I maintain that edges bring with them their own self-transcendence, a special form of liminal intentionality that is capable of opening up regions of experience not otherwise accessible. Viewed in this light, edges are thresholds to other worlds. That which we take to be forms of closure are also, in lived fact, apertures. Edges are not limits but horizons that open ever outward—outward from the compression they effect when considered to be merely where things and events end. Edges commence as much as they terminate; beyond closing in and closing off, they open up and they open out. Edges *dis-close*.

I

This brief opening meditation on edges bears on the unsuspected richness of edges that exist in relation with other edges, whether close by or much farther off. What, then, are we to make of Leahy's idea of a truly *absolute* edge, where the purport of "absolute" must mean minimally to surpass or to suspend the domain of relative edges? It is also to imply that an absolute edge is utterly unique—not a matter of difference of degree from other edges but of a distinctive difference *of kind,* and the kind in question has only one occupant or one candidate: this is the absolute edge itself. But what can this be? "Absolute/edge" is close to oxymoronic, given my claim that almost all edges present themselves as relative, as inherent in clusters of other edges or in contiguity with the edges of other things and events.

Here, we need to back up a step or two before comprehending what is an edge that would be absolute. Leahy does this himself by identifying two kinds of less-than-absolute edges: one existing between two (or more) definite things and another between two (or more) indefinite things. In his example, the edge of a stream that intersects with the edge of the land or bank with which it is contiguous is itself indefinite in that it is difficult to determine just where one edge starts and the other ends; more precisely, it is arbitrary as to what we take to be the exact outer edge of the stream in relation to the bank at any given moment since this outer edge changes shape continually as the stream courses along. Since it changes with every passing moment, the exact place where it touches the bank alters continually. There is, in Leahy's words, "an infinitely indefinite separation" between the edges, and this is equivalent to there being "almost nothing" between them—where the "almost" points to the indefinite and shifting character of the edge-to-edge circumstance: "The edge of the land interacting with the edge of the stream is the real indefiniteness of the respective edges of definite stream and definite land; [whereas] the indefinite edges of two definite things at the point of contact [are] supported by their infinitely indefinite separation (= almost nothing between)."[2]

In contrast, between two *in*definite things there is "nothing" insofar as the edges of such things are themselves definite—so definite that there is no interim space at all, not even an indefinite space. Between God and the world—each inherently indefinite insofar as it is subject to continual redefinition—there is no measurable distance; the two polysemous concepts stand apart, their edges standing in splendid isolation from each other. They do not touch, not even in the shifting and ambiguous way in which the stream and its bank are nevertheless contiguous. The difference here is that between a situation quite literally *on the ground,* and thus a matter of perception—what the eye can see and the hand measure—and that of conception, whereby the meaning of the concept "God" or the concept "world" is radically indefinite (i.e., subject to continual recharacterization). The paradox here, not fully explicated by Leahy (who speaks only of "the functionally irreducible distinction of perception and conception," [F, 587]) is that, despite their indefinite semantic content such concepts have distinct outer edges that keep one concept (e.g., "God") distinct from another (e.g., "world"). The range of meaning in each case is multiplex, but the outer edges of the range are definite insofar as they are immediately recognizable and discussable, as when we speak of "God talk" in a way that makes it clear that it cannot be reduced to the naturalism and historicism of speaking about the world around us ("world talk"). Between these two kinds of discourse there is no measurable distance;

there is simply "nothing," that is, no determinable distance, not even an indefinite distance, between their respective edges.

All this is preparatory to the onset of the absolute edge, which is said to be "infinitely shared" (F, 587, 593). This suggests that part of the absoluteness of such an extra-ordinary edge is to be *everywhere accessible*; it is not situated elsewhere nor is it at the outer edge of things or in edges of what surrounds it, but is spread throughout: an omni-edge, as it were. This would be a radical new kind of edge that is no longer conceived on the model of the edge of anything merely material—its "essentially narrow part" (F, 586), in Leahy's own formulation—in other words, where it tapers off. In the case of the absolute edge there is no tapering off; it is present everywhere with equal intensity. We are talking about an "absolutely existing edge, the edge every part of which is identical with the edge itself" (F, 592). This is no mere thought-experiment. Such an edge is at one with the "actual existential matter" (F, 587) that is an integral part of the era now emerging and that gives to it its unique bearing and charisma. This same matter will contain "the existence itself of order" (F, 587)—a radically new order of existence. This order represents the systematic structure of the absolute edge as it ramifies through existential matter, the body that is an essentially creative agent in the new actuality: not the physiological body, nor even the lived body, but the body that does not belong to a subject but is absolute objectivity, the locus of creative omnipotence.

You will notice that such an edge has three further characteristics. First, it is strictly unique, as Leahy's usage of *the* in referring to "the absolute edge." We are not talking about *an* edge among others, but an edge so singularly absolute that it coincides with all other edges, and for this reason cannot connect with them as the stream does with its banks. Any mention of "almost nothing between" or "nothing between" is out of the question, for there is no *between* in this situation. There is only a radical exteriority that is in some sense comparable to Deleuze's model of "pure immanence"—in which transcendence leaves no trace.[3] In such a scene, not only are all edges internally related—as in F. H. Bradley's relational monism—but they have coalesced into an edge like no other. This ecstatic edge absorbs all others, taking them into its measureless maw in an action of radical dissolution until only one edge abides: *the* absolute edge.

Second, the word *absolute* is not chosen idly. Its literal roots suggest that whatever is absolute is literally *indissoluble*. It is so intact that it cannot be taken apart.

Indeed, it has no parts into which it might be analyzed and from which, brought together, it could be constructed. There are no parts and no construction, with the result that there is no dissolution of it. It is integral; it is itself itself—and nothing other.

Third, integral to the absoluteness of such an edge is its unique spatiotemporality. My descriptions of the absolute edge have so far been mainly of a spatial sort. This is predictable insofar as most of the time we presume the very essence of "edge" to be spatial, with the edges of physical things being paradigmatic; Leahy himself begins with such edges in his stream/banks model. I would argue, however, that *events* have their own peculiar edges: their own way of beginning and ending, of opening up and then closing down in time.[4]

Leahy is certainly in accord with this last claim: the absolute edge is as fully event as it is any kind of spatial structure. Indeed, it is a special kind of event: an *advent* of something altogether novel, constituting a radical new beginning. This is why he claims that with such an edge, "the threshold of a new universe is traversed for the first time" (F, 587). The use of *threshold* is especially significant given that thresholds are special edges that signify moving from one state of being or becoming to another, typically one more challenging or auspicious.[5] A threshold is always at least spatiotemporal; for example, spatial in the form of a doorway, lintel, or the like, and temporal as ushering in movement across just such a spatial point of access or ingress. Thus, the absolute edge offers passage in and through its uniquely configured *coniunctio* of space and time.

This is a move into *place*—more specifically "The Place," which is where the dissolution of time in absolute actuality takes us: "The temporality of time is The Place which we, embodying, intimately comprehend as the pure 'at the disposal of another'" (F, 593). For place, on this conception, is not mere locus (as common sense dictates) or container (as Aristotle claims), but the very region in which others come to us, arise before us; this is not merely a matter of interpersonal relations but of the surpassing of the self altogether: "To create the absolute edge is to begin to operate *essentially* without reference to self" (F, 593). This is not a matter of encountering someone else in a given place; rather, it is bringing about a unique place—"The Place"—in which the sole occupant-event is the other. Not just a matter of self-transcendence, this is closer to a self-annihilation in which the self and its possessive mineness disappear; when this happens, we have in effect abandoned the modern subject. As Leahy puts it in the preface to *Foundation*: "The consciousness adequate to the beginning of real world consciousness is a universally new consciousness, in fact, a perfect other-consciousness, a consciousness categorically and essentially beyond the other-self relation" (F, xiii). This is not merely a matter of bracketing the self qua ego (empirical or transcendental), or just leaving it behind, but of a movement in which "every notion of self is completely dissolved" (F, 592).

II

By this action of abandoning the interiority of self and entering into the exteriority of the place of the absolute(ly) other, one enters into the event of what Leahy calls insistently "the thinking now occurring" (see especially "Thought Beyond Nietzsche: Foundation Itself," F, 91–110). This is not mere promise or projection; it is something that is already happening even if all the signs of its coming are not yet manifest. It is dawning—another term that is equally temporal and spatial—coming upon us, and it is doing so in the wake of the death of God in Thomas J. J. Altizer's sense of the term: that is, as an apocalyptic event long in coming but now having arrived. From its wake there arises the prospect of a "New World consciousness" (F, 587)—a consciousness that constitutes an absolute actuality. Which is to say, integral to what is now happening not just to individuals but to the entirety of existence on earth is the *world-historical* advent of this new thinking: the making-immanent of space and time in the form of an event, an *Ereignis* that marks the advent of something essentially new—that not only has an absolute edge but *is* the absolute edge.

Such an edge is at once "existential matter" and "existence"— terms that are kept separate in what Leahy considers the specifically American response to the death of God. Thus Altizer is said to choose "beginning without existence, substituting for the latter precisely the unknown 'presence.' Beginning itself is 'apprehended' as the beginning of the end" (F, 588). Altizer himself speaks of "the advent of a wholly new but totally immediate world."[6] But for Altizer this happens paradigmatically when we are released from our own existential solitude into total presence by experiences such as listening to music or being in the presence of others. Thus, there is a dense dialectic happening between being alone with oneself—in "our interior"[7]—and being released from this aloneness into a presence that is tantamount to "the beginning of the other at the edge itself of our separation from self" (F, 588).

In contrast, Leahy delineates an absolute objectivity or externality that is not the mere result of abolishing existential solitude, the dark den of the self, but bespeaks immediate active creation of the absolute edge; that is to say, the edge of all occurrence, eventfulness itself. This is why he points to 1989 as the opening moment when the new consciousness first emerged and with it a vision of a "new world order." It is a matter of something much more comprehensive and quite other than a mere opportunity or prelude. At play and at stake is an "absolute now" (F, 613, 615) that exceeds any currently experienced moment along the lines of the Kierkegaardian/Heideggerian notion of the *Augenblick*. We are talking about a radically transformative way of existing *now* that is quite otherwise than ever heretofore: existing qua creator in such a way as to give essential form to the other with absolute responsibility. How can this happen?

Edge reenters the analysis just here. It does so as "actually the totality of Identity *after* nothing"—that is, after the nothing, the void, left by the death of God. It is a matter of a new beginning within this very abyss. To explicate this, Leahy turns to an edge he had so far neglected, that of the *mind*. "The edge of mind," he avers, "is a consciousness the edge of which is absolute. The edge is essentially perfect as never before" (F, 591). This is not a merely exploratory edge as displayed in abductive experimentation on Charles Sanders Peirce's conception—an edge characterized by its inherent fallibility and tentativeness—but an edge of new creation that emerges only ex nihilo, "after nothing": after the evacuation of essence effected by the death of God. When Leahy writes that "the mind is absolutely edged out of the edge after nothing" (F, 591), this is to say that in and with mind an *essentially* new way of thinking qua creating now pertains for the first time ever.

To explicate this extraordinary new state of affairs, we must reconceive the paradigm based on the edge of a stream vis-à-vis the land alongside. Rather than the separation effected by the contiguity of the edges of two definite masses with "almost nothing" between them, we have to do with a circumstance in which "the banks are identical with the stream for the first time . . . in the cosmological flood of the stream of consciousness both banks flow as the stream itself flows" (F, 591). We approach a truly Heraclitean situation here in which "everything flows and nothing abides."[8]

The stream/banks analogy relies on our perceptual experience of intraworldly interaction, whereas Heraclitus takes us toward the fully cosmological. Leahy wishes to induct us into a third way of thinking in which it is the edge of mind itself—though not the mind of the individual self or subject—that effects the thinking now occurring. We might say that mind edges us into such thinking. But this is not a matter of *our* mind; it is mindfulness of otherness itself that takes us to the new place: the new actuality, the actual newness of the world. As he states: "The edge of consciousness begins to be an essential objectivity, not the edge of mind [as such], but the edge sharing the edge of the other for the first time, the edge of the mind of the other. . . . Consciousness, at once absolute, begins to *share* the edge of the mind of another consciousness" (F, 593). The "infinite sharing" cited earlier is here explicated in terms of the way that the mind operative in the new thinking is what it is only by not being the mind of an individuated thinker, *his* mind or *her* mind. So much is this the case that Leahy can even say that "thought is the edge of the thing" (F, 593). Thought so little belongs to *me* as its thinker that we might as well say that it belongs properly to things—to *their* edges, not those of our subjectivity as individual thinkers. This is to *dis-place* Cartesian or Kantian thinking from the enclosed domain of mind as *res cogitans* or as transcendental *Erkenntnis* and to take it into "the absolutely unconditioned exteriority of the world" (F, 592).

It is altogether remarkable, and certainly surprising, that this last phrase is intended by Leahy to characterize the *body*. But no more than our mind does our body literally belong to *us*. Rather, it is *elsewhere*. For "the essentially narrow part of existence *ex nihilo* [where 'narrow' signifies *edge*], the body after the nothing, *ex nihilo*, [left by the death of God] exists everywhere" (F, 592; concerning edge as the "narrow" part of a thing versus surface as the "thin" part, see F, 586). The body-as-edge takes us to the edge of the other's body; it *places* us there in a second mode of "infinite sharing," now corporeal as well as mental. In this ingenious way, Leahy shows that the body-mind relation can no longer be considered as a *problem*; for body and mind are the two primary ways by which the self is eclipsed in(to) the Place of the Other.

III

But wait! It is one thing for body to have edges, but surely quite another for *mind* to possess them.[9] And above all, the kind of mind that as "new consciousness" can realize all that Leahy attributes to it—especially its power of effecting "absolute other-consciousness" (F, xiii)? One might think that such a mind would have no effective limits—thus, *no* edges.[10] Would not such a mind reach out and reach into all that it encounters, actually generating the very "other" posited by Leahy as what becomes the creative consequence of mind in the new actuality? Or so we would think if mind were anything like what Kant or Hegel took it to be; each emphasized its synthetic powers (in judgments and in world history, respectively). But, with Leahy, we are going somewhere exceptionally novel, and especially exceptional in terms of the modern era in philosophy, wherein the emblematic status of the self required that it engage in acts of constructive synthesis to overcome what would otherwise be splendid self-isolation. The result is that the modernist conception of mind is of something in perpetual metamorphosis, continually overcoming any delimiting edge in the craving for knowledge and power. How then can edge be made integral to the new idea of mind, and all the more so must we ask this question of a mind that constitutes the "absolute edge" that is at the heart of the thinking now occurring?

One response might be that mind in the actuality of the "new consciousness" is an *entering edge* in the thinking now occurring: a leading edge, as it were. But something more fundamental is at stake here. This is what we hear when Leahy claims that "thought *is* the edge of the thing" (my italics)—which flies in the face of modernist claims to the effect that thought (that is, mind as cognitive) can only edge toward the thing via a priori synthetic judgments of the understanding (Kant) or via the dialectic of reason (Hegel). If thought is the edge of the thing known, it is already in some sense *that thing itself*. This radicality is still more apparent in the associated assertion that "the edge of consciousness . . . [is] the edge sharing the edge of the other for the first time" (F, 592–93). The delimitative perimeter of my consciousness does not need to reach out to the other, to merely approach it; in the actuality now underway, it is already at one with this other—whether other thing or other person. Since the sharing is "infinite," it leaves no remainder of unshared commixture: the merging is complete in an unlimited ontology—an infinite polyontology—since "the thing in essence is nothing but appearance itself" (F, 6). This sets the stage for the pronouncement that the edge of consciousness *is* "the edge of the mind of the other." With this last proposition, Leahy is saying that the edge of any particular mind is not only shared with the other's mind but is fully transmuted into the edge of that mind.

So the dynamism of the absolute edge, considered in its cognitive/ mental dimensionality, is that of an *ad-equation* and not a *rapprochement*. We are not talking, then, about an action of edging toward or entering into, but of the *becoming* of the edge of the other's mind in a process wherein the edge of our own mind—that of the existing individual—has become coinherent with "the edge of the mind of another consciousness" (F, 593; note that Leahy uses "mind" and "consciousness" as virtually equivalent terms).

IV

Here, a skeptic will ask: Are we not here in the realm of some merely imaginary or fantasied edge—thus "edge" meant only metaphorically? Do not mind and consciousness on this conception possess edges only by delegation, that is, by a kind of philosophical *honoris causa*? Is not the whole idea of an "edge of thought"—whether my own or that of the other or, still more disputatiously, that of my mind-become-that-of-the-other's-mind—so much philosophical confabulation?

It is not. I have argued elsewhere that in the phenomenon of "thinking on the edge" a special kind of edgefulness is realized that allows us to consider productive thinking as moving us into *new edges* of thought, new edge-worlds with their own unique topographies. Whether in reverie or in rigorous reflection, such edges take us *elsewhere*—to a wholly novel elsewhere other than where we abide in our customary, habitual thinking in accordance with established and routinized patterns. The articulation of infinitely unique mental edges is just what we find in Leahy's thinking now occurring. As if to answer continuing *skepsis* on the part of the reader, Leahy fills out his thesis by embedding it in two concrete ways: first, by allusion to the "Place of the Other" and then in the radical Catholic theology of his own proposing.

Regarding place, the move is to embed the other's mind—with whom the edges of my own mind merge—in a *place*. Place not only provides a concretum of actual embodiment but also actively implicates body as *of the essence,* since between body and place there is a conjoint indispensability: that is, matter mattering. As I like to put it, no place without body and no body without place.[11] I take it that something very close to this is meant in Leahy's otherwise enigmatic assertion that "the reality of the body is the absolutely unconditioned exteriority of the world" (F, 592). Such exteriority is also that of place—

the place of the other—given that the world for Leahy is ultimately a place-world. In view of this, we can say that place as *hamaqom* (the Hebrew word for place, specifically the place of Yaweh) entails "the being of the other being at the disposal of another" (F, 593). Our being with another in a place is not at our disposal but at the other's: the other as always *another other* rather than the other as just a version of the same; for example, our same secluded self. When our thinking is actively creating the absolute edge—when its edge has become the edge of the other who is the animated carrier of the absolute edge—then such thinking happens *in the other's place,* not our own. Thinking has moved to an absolutely exterior scene of enactment, an edge-place that is no place at all in its ordinary acceptation but an absolutely new place, a scene of absolute novelty, in which the absolute edge occurs as world-creativity itself.[12]

Finally, the extraordinary edge of thinking is thought within the crucible of Leahy's apocalyptic philosophical theology in which the void left by the death of God can be considered to be an ultimate non-place, a unique historical/conceptual void that is altogether an abyss—unless and until the advent of the event of the absolute edge intervenes. Here, *event* is again a key word—for an absolutely actual *new world* is now eventfulness itself. This actual newness of the world, the likes of which the world has never seen, is the work, the deposition, of an absolute edge unlike any other. In contrast with the edges of determinate physical things (streams and banks) and of indeterminate concepts (being, nothingness, as well as God and world in prior acceptations), such an edge is at once an avatar and an outcome of the edges of mind and consciousness, and thus of the edges of the other into which my own self-centered edges collapse and disappear as distinctive presences. This absolutely othered edge, now embodied and implaced, *is* its very enactment as an event: the event of the thinking now occurring per se. As utterly decisive and not divisive, such a new actuality not only separates itself from every other historical era—for example, from the modern world of thought—but is a scene of creative action such as the ancient and the modern worlds have never seen or conceived.[13]

V

A final, quite different direction is indicated by the poet Wallace Stevens:

> The palm at the end of the mind
> Beyond the last thought, rises
> In the bronze distance.
> A gold-feathered bird
> Sings in the palm, without human meaning,
> Without human feeling, a foreign song.
> You know then that it is not the reason
> That makes us happy or unhappy.
> The bird sings. Its feathers shine.
> The palm stands on the edge of space.
> The wind moves slowly in the branches.
> The bird's fire-fangled feathers dangle down.[14]

Here, Stevens points to another destiny of mind's edge ("at the end of the mind")—not toward a new world-order that is a dense imbroglio of the human and the (deceased) divine but toward a capacious world that includes nonhuman beings who, in the manner of Stevens's "gold-feathered bird," stand "on the edge of space": a space that is the place of a specifically *natural* world-order. This world has been evolving for millennia, and is still with us—though for how much longer we cannot say.

My parting question to Leahy is: Can the thinking now occurring come to include this full natural world with its manifold superabundance of edges—edges in places of nature that call for their own inscription in an amplified world-order of the absolute edge? Early in "To Create the Absolute Edge," Leahy gestures in this direction in his discussion of John Dewey's *Experience and Nature* (1934): Mind, "unlike its predecessors [i.e., in Aristotle and Hegel], is a thoroughly naturalized product of 'prior interactions' of the self with environment" (F, 583). He then cites Dewey's *The Quest for Certainty* (1929), claiming that a new take on knowledge "installs man, thinking man, within nature" (F, 584). Similarly, William James's notion of a "pluralistic universe of intelligent existents" constitutes (in James's own words) "the wider life of things"—"to which," adds Leahy, "we are 'tangent'" (F, 583). How then to incorporate this "wider life" in the absolute edge? How to envision it as centrally and not just peripherally ingredient in the apocalyptic newness of the world that is now actually being created ex nihilo? How, in short, to move the bird, the palm, and the wind that courses through both from their peripheral positions at "the edge of space" and to recognize their immanence in the very matrix, the place, of the thinking now occurring?

Notes

1. See Edward S. Casey, *The World on Edge* (Bloomington: Indiana University Press, 2017).

2. D. G. Leahy, "To Create the Absolute Edge," first published in *Journal of the American Academy of Religion* 57, no. 4 (1988): 773–89; reprinted in D. G. Leahy, *Foundation: Matter the Body Itself* (Albany: State University of New York Press, 1996), 581–93, quote on 587. Hereafter, I cite the version reprinted in *Foundation*.

3. See Gilles Deleuze, *Pure Immanence: Essays on a Life*, trans. J. Rachman (New York: Urzone, 2001); and *A Thousand Plateaus: Capitalism and Schizophrenia*, trans. Brian Massumi (Minneapolis: University of Minnesota Press, 1987), 266–67.

4. See Casey, *World on Edge*, ch. 3: "Edges of Places and Events."

5. For further discussion of thresholds, see *The World on Edge*, 15, 21, 23–24, 73, 193, 202, 326.

6. Cited by Leahy from Thomas J. J. Altizer, *Total Presence: The Language of Jesus and the Language of Today* (Aurora, CO: Davies, 2016), 106–107.

7. Altizer, *Total Presence*, 106.

8. Heraclitus, fragment 20: "Everything flows and nothing abides; everything gives way and nothing stays fixed" (translation by Philip Wheelwright, *Heraclitus* [New York: Atheneum, 1968], 29).

9. On bodily edges, see *The World on Edge*, ch. 8: "At the Edges of My Body."

10. Not that edges and limits are the same thing. I argue for their essential difference in *The World on Edge*, ch. 2: "Edges and Surfaces, Edges and Limits."

11. On this bivalent proposition, see *Getting Back into Place: Toward a Renewed Understanding of the Place-World* (Bloomington: Indiana University Press, 2009), 104: "Just as there is no place without body . . . so there is no body without place" [italics omitted].

12. On this last line of thought, see the convergent discussion in *The World on Edge*, 363–64; this is part of the book's afterword entitled "Thinking Edges, Edges of Thinking."

13. On such an instant see Gaston Bachelard, *The Intuition of the Instant*, trans. Eileen Rizo-Patrone (Evanston: Northwestern University Press, 2015). See also my discussion of the instant in *The World at a Glance* (Bloomington: Indiana University Press, 2007), 8–9, 151, 278, 297.

14. Wallace Stevens, "Of Mere Being" (1954), cited from the Poetry Foundation website: www.poetryfoundation.org.

11

To Think the Beginning

The Apocalyptic I

SARAH LILLY EATON

Due to his extensive use of mathematics and the unusual style of his writing, D. G. Leahy's work remains largely obscure, which renders his claim to give utterance to an essential transformation of consciousness simultaneously outrageous and yet plausible. Theologian Thomas J. J. Altizer has called Leahy our "most isolated and unknown major thinker" and his first volume, *Novitas Mundi*, "our most intrinsically difficult book since the *Phenomenology of Spirit*" as well as the most important work of philosophical theology of the twentieth century.[1] I join in the lament of so many who have recognized the importance of Leahy's work. Attempts to think along with Leahy often run up against limitations imposed by both his mathematizations and what he termed a sparse, precise, and "style-less style" (F, xiv). Leahy apologizes for this style in his preface to *Foundation*, adding that he too shares in the embarrassment he anticipates the reader must feel "for the inevitable inconvenience of having to read again in order to read" (F, xiv). It is ironic and unfortunate that texts written for ultimate clarity, precision, and "sheer intelligibility" are deemed so opaque. In the assessment of Edward T. Oakes, Leahy's work "makes no compromises, flinches from no complexity, and harbors no concern for pedagogical realities."[2] Some confusion is due to the innovations of his categories, but another difficulty is with his somewhat recursive syntax, which requires one to reread each sentence to get a clearer sense of the relationships being described. The almost mechanical nature of the prose is quite consistent and intentional. If one could imagine future Artificial Intelligences reading theology and philosophy, Leahy might well be their favorite, the first apostle to silicon-based life. Is it too hopeful to imagine that making the leap between the mechanical manipulation of numerical input and sentient meaningful linguistic output may be one of the intended or unintended practical consequences of Leahy's theory of the meta-identity of language and number? All this is to say: Leahy's use of the mathematical reading of biblical texts is a surprising approach, deserving more attention than it has received. His work cannot be comprehended fully without due attention to the novel gematria he uses, though many of his readers have preferred to avoid it. This essay will describe his objectives, demonstrate his method, and then expand upon his fascinating results.

The task of the thinking now occurring is a transformative undertaking, which is in response to an imperative. Leahy has a mission that we find elaborated in *Foundation*. We serve in virtue of a new Spirit, as Paul says in his letter to the Romans. To be on task, to have a mission, to be a hearer of a call who is then sent out to proclaim—this free, loving response—is still the response to an imperative. According to Leahy: "The world-imperative now actually existing is to actualize infinitely the very first thought" (BS, 3). Philosophers such as Aristotle have taught that the best and highest life is the philosophical one, because contemplation is the highest perfection of the human animal. But didn't Paul, who called himself the least of the apostles, have a greater vocation, which was not contemplation but proclamation: speaking and writing good news and testimony to a singular fact that Christ is Risen? In his letter to the Church at Corinth, Paul writes (and here I give Leahy's translation): "My word and my proclamation were not embodied in persuasive words of human wisdom but were embodied in the proof of the Spirit and of its power, so that your faith might be embodied not in human wisdom but in omnipotence" (1 Cor. 2:4–5). Leahy's thinking is such a proof and proclamation and with the same aim. When we think about omnipotence embodied in creation we are thinking the body and thinking the resurrection body, the absolutely unconditioned body. For Leahy, such thinking is the essential conception of the apocalyptic vision.

The method of study is given by the teacher and we can see the theory and practice of teaching as a basis for the interpretation of philosophy. A brief reflection on pedagogy is thus in order as we hope to defend Leahy's approach to demonstrating in his texts the thinking now occurring. As philosophers, which almost always also means as teachers, we aspire to actualize thinking in ourselves and in others. Sometimes those who are there to learn to think along with us have neither the patience nor the desire to actualize within themselves the process by which the concepts are generated and the arguments are constructed. In Plato's academy, study of mathematics and geometry was prerequisite to philosophy, or study of dialectic. Of course, there is a value judgment behind this, but further, the lengthy study of math and geometry produces the virtue of patience. The desire to think and to know is easily undermined when our patience is outstripped. In the tradition of philosophers such as Descartes and Leibniz, Leahy is on firm footing with his mathematical skill. Although the reader may be too far behind for Leahy's logical and mathematical reasoning to be perspicuous, nevertheless we are given the means to perceive the soundness of his demonstrations if we persevere.

J. G. Fichte states in the *Wissenschaftslehre nova methodo* that his philosophy begins with a postulate that is grounded in an Act. Thus, he writes, "if one wants to communicate this philosophy to someone else, one has to ask the other person to perform the action in question."[3] Fichte had a characteristic way of initiating his students into the problem of philosophy. One of those students, Heinrich Steffens, left us the following description:

> "Gentlemen," he would say, "collect your thoughts and enter into yourselves. We are not at all concerned now with anything external, but only with ourselves." And, just as he requested, his listeners really seemed to be concentrating upon themselves. Some of them shifted their position and sat up straight, while others slumped with downcast eyes. But it was obvious that they were all waiting with great suspense for what was supposed to come next. Then Fichte would continue: "Gentlemen, think about the wall." And as I saw, they really did think about the wall, and everyone seemed able to do so with success. "Have you thought about the wall?" Fichte would ask. "Now, gentlemen, think about whoever it was that thought about the wall."[4]

This directive to think the wall—or rather to "think of yourself, think the wall, think of whoever it was that was thinking of the wall"—is the entirety of the three moments that Fichte seeks to elaborate in the *Wissenschaftslehre*. Everything within can supposedly be pulled out of this exercise. This idealism epitomizes what Leahy calls the obsolete detour of modernity, for which modern consciousness is self-consciousness. But thinking the beginning is not a self-reflective move in the thinking now occurring. The new consciousness that Leahy announces is absolutely objective, thought without self or notion of self: absolutely new, essentially transcendental, and, by the way, essentially not self-conscious. It is essentially historical, but not in the sense of a materialist historical logic—which Leahy deems not *essentially* historical. The expression of the absolute saying itself absolutely is in explicit *discontinuity* with all previous saying. In the giving of the great prophecy in Matthew 24, Jesus says that the good news of the kingdom will be proclaimed throughout the world, as a testimony to all the nations, and then the end will come. Leahy's *Foundation* is a proclamation of good news that thinking itself, qua absolute, *hears*. Now, everything is making a proclamation in the form of praise: "The Subject is nothing!" It is the apocalyptic I that hears this proclamation as thanks and praise. This is heaven. To hear and receive it otherwise, to hear it and remain silent, is sin. This is hell. Modern thought, according to Leahy, can only perceive the new thinking as absolute self-alienation.

To continue our pedagogical detour, consider now Heidegger, for whom teaching is not a matter of passing out information but of giving formal indications. This involves leading the student through an original unity of historical recollection, which is living in his or her "free, productive grasp of the task harbored in philosophy" and focused reflection on the present. This original unity is "the temporality of the philosophizing factical *Dasein* itself."[5] Heidegger charges Fichte with a "constructive violation of the facts" or an "unphenomenological onset" in his request to "think the wall." He explains that in our natural comportment with things we never think a single thing. Furthermore, "whenever we seize upon it expressly for itself we are taking it out of a contexture to which it belongs in its real content: wall, room surroundings."[6] He sees Fichte's request to "think the wall" as the beginning of a philosophical interpretation of the subject, but also as a violation of our natural way of being among things.

Instead, Heidegger often began his lecture courses by attempting to awaken what he called a fundamental attunement [*Befindlichkeit*]. The history of Being itself is a history of various attunements. Any transformation of existence will involve a transformation of attunement. During the age of technology the attunement in which we find ourselves is dual for Heidegger: both horror and boredom. Perhaps it is boredom occasionally punctuated by horror, or boredom for some, horror for others. If you have ever scrolled through a Twitter feed and felt numb to the accounts of environmental, personal, and political calamities streaming past, you know how the two can interpenetrate. In his *Contributions to Philosophy*, Heidegger speaks of the crossing over to another beginning and preparing for "the ones to come" in the future who are "destined by the last god." They will "remind themselves of the greatest thing that is created: the enfilled onceness and uniqueness of being."[7] This last god has "its most unique uniqueness." Cults and churches, he says, cannot prepare for the "colliding of god and man in the mid-point of being." The thinker prepares for these "ones to come" and for this other beginning by *effecting* it. Heidegger has already named the grounding attunement of these "strangers of like mind." It is the intimation of startled dismay and reservedness that can also be described as deep foreboding. He writes: "The mastery of the last god only comes upon reservedness; reservedness furnishes the deep stillness for the mastery and for the last god."[8] Considered as "style" it is "the self-assuredness of the grounding measure."[9] Although I see no foreboding or dismay in Leahy's work, I do see such a style present in *Foundation* as he patiently, perhaps tediously, elaborates his method for the mathematical reading of language. It is also readily apparent in *The Cube Unlike all Others*, which could be seen as his ontology of space, but is ultimately central to his theology for which the *novitas mentis* is the intellect beginning to think the resurrection body. Contrary to Heidegger, Leahy says he is not sure if the question of "attunement" is even an ontological question. According to Leahy, there is no need to prepare for anything except the messianic meal. We are now in a new Universe (at least in thought). We have "crossed" thoroughly. The future that has been anticipated has arrived: the beginning of an "actually universal new world consciousness," which is an essentially apocalyptic form of mind. We can see in Leahy the coming thinker that Heidegger had bowed to from afar, moving into a thinking that is a saying, a proclaiming of truth.

The task of thinking is "to think foundationally the essence of this beginning" (F, xiii). Why is this the task? In short, we can say that this is the task because the actualization of this thinking is the beginning of the resurrection body. We cannot overlook that the thinking now occurring is, as he says, penultimate, because we are in the process of overcoming the weight of self-consciousness. Leahy states that "Nothing short of a Resurrection of the Divine Intention shall provide the necessary foundation for the New Jerusalem, call it what you will" (F, 578). The body is raised at a time appointed, but in the mind the essential conception of the body is raised now and we are the ones both free and responsible for raising it and proclaiming it. The resurrection of Jesus was formally unprecedented, but the resurrection for which we hope is preceded, formally, in thought. This is transformation, renewal, discernment, readiness, engagement, and creation. I see the mathematical reading of language as one important way of resurrecting the divine intention. Once computation is pegged to this insight we may indeed see truly aware thinking machines.

The thinking now occurring is the beginning of the resurrection, because it is the thought of resurrection beginning. And this renewed mind, the perfect mind understands something about God that is very different than has been understood before now. In a seminar on *Novitas Mundi*, Leahy stated that "no proof of the actuality of what now occurs is possible other than the perception in fact itself." The thinking now occurring is one in which the distinction between perceiving and conceiving is transcended. So the demonstration is key. You have to see it to understand it and to believe it. If one is to actually think foundationally, rather than simply read the report of one who claims to have done so, one must be willing to follow the procedure (in this case, of the mathematical reading of language) so that what is merely conceptual becomes perceptible in the course of the thinking.

The first point to establish is the place the meta-identity of language and number occupies within Leahy's thinking as a whole. In his new trinary logic, no terms represent "nothing." Getting rid of the nothing is key to his enterprise. In explaining the idea of meta-identity, Leahy calls it "a function of the irreducibility of the Universe to Nothing" (F, 265). The living relationship of the rational unity (meta-identity) of language and number is an important corollary, he says, to this trinary logic. As such, it follows from and is appended to the trinary logic having been elaborated. If we do not see the importance of the logic we will not understand why to care about the thesis of the meta-identity of language and number. The trinary logic is what he calls the logic of quantum gravitational computation. I suspect that his logic is conceived either as something which could be fruitfully put to use in future computing and/or that the qualification "quantum *gravitational*" indicates what you would simply call the logic of the god-level source code.

The most interesting aspect of all this for the non-logically trained among us may be his effort to show the traction, the grip, the points of contact between some important words in the Bible and the constants in nature discovered by physics. In short, science and revelation share numbers (see F, 525n98). As Leahy would say, "the Universe is the Intelligible Body of God." This universe also includes words, which can be shown to have an objective intelligibility due to this meta-identity. Of course, there are different words and meanings that share the same numerical value. Indeed, there are whole sentences that, when calculated according to his method, produce the same value as a single word. The objectivity is an absolutely relative one (with emphasis on *absolutely*). The merely relative coincidences would be just that. But the absolutely relative coincidences are indicative of something truly meaningful and worthy of being pursued further.

While modernity sees the new thinking as self-alienation, poets and mystics will likely be shocked to hear that thinking the beginning of the new universal consciousness involves the numerical calculations of the values of words and even names. Perhaps such shock can be transformed into awe. My own work has been involved in checking Leahy's method by using it, and the results are quite astonishing. In particular, it demonstrates the way in which the entire biblical text has been encrypted and how those encryptions point beyond the text itself. Ultimately, as an exegetical method, this is not the equivalent of hacking the code in a purely mechanical way. Calculating, חישוב, is required but those who have insight proceed with some degree of imagination and leading of the spirit. "Nothing is hidden that shall not be revealed" (Luke 8:17). How can one prove that the numerical coding of the Bible is intentional and not just a complicated but neat coincidence? Imagine if you knew the common coefficient factor in the four fundamental force constants and encoded sixty-six books written over a two thousand year period such that that number showed up as the numerical value of the names and titles of the main character.

The precedent for this method, of course, is the esoteric practice known as gematria: where numerical values are assigned to letters, and then the words themselves become calculable. "Deciphering the arithmetic of letters opens the biblical text to deep and accurate exegesis, despite its apparent disorder."[10] The method works in both Hebrew and Greek, and using Leahy's particular method the calculations yield witnesses which testify to each other. The biblical text is actually two texts: a plaintext and a cipher text. Gematria may seem quite alien to most of us today, but it is an ages-old technique and one of interest in the Church as well as among Jewish mystics. In the thirteenth and fourteenth centuries it found great acceptance in the Franciscan order, and was even taught at Oxford as a subdivision of mathematics. Methods of calculation vary, but the process has a view toward exposing underlying identities or equivalence relations in the text that might not be seen otherwise. Leahy's claim is that although a meta-identity exists between language and number, all former gematria should be rejected as arbitrary. He considers his new form nonarbitrary because words are treated in an essentially mathematical way, which means that the word values are calculated as the product of ratios.[11] For example, according to the standard method, the gematria of שלום (*shalom*) is (300 + 30 + 6 + 40) giving a total sum of 376. For Leahy, using proportion (300:30::6:40) the value calculated is 1.5:

$$\frac{300}{30} \times \frac{6}{40} = \frac{3}{2} = 1.5$$

He calls this the rational product, which gives in numeric terms the *identity* of the word. If instead we take the square of the product of the numerators of the ratios we will arrive at the integral product, which he calls the *absolute identity* of the word (cf. F, 357n13). For *shalom* the integral product value is 1800 or 3,240,000 (3.24E6). He also calculates a linear product, which is less often used, as the simple product of the string of numbers.[12]

How, then, does Leahy actually marshal the results of his mathematical reading of language in service of his thinking? Remarkably, in the course of his first demonstration using the method, he tests the mission of his own identity and in so doing invites each of us to do the same. This is an overcoming of Self at once an establishment of Identity. The choice of *shalom* to demonstrate the methods of gematria is a fairly arbitrary example, but the first three terms reckoned by Leahy are specifically chosen because they are crucial to his demonstration.

The first term is Torah, which he translates as "law"—although *guidance* or *instruction* perhaps better captures the meaning. The second, Eleph, is "thousand." The third term is David, which he calls "little Torah." Accepted tradition relates King David to Torah with the claim that he was born and died on Shavuot (the Feast of Weeks), which marks the end of the seven weeks of counting the omer.[13] Scripture does not name Shavuot as the day on which the Torah was revealed at Sinai, but the holiday is celebrated as a commemoration of this. This fits nicely with the fact that in the New Testament, Shavuot is Pentecost, the day of the sending of the Spirit to the gathered, expectant believers. But David, as a musician, would have had to understand ratios, not theoretically but quite practically. Whatever the note you are tuned to has to do with how hot or cold or wet or dry it is. Instruments are always getting out of tune. The primary string has to resound a note and according to that all the other notes are tuned to it. David plays music soothing to the harsh character of King Saul. In medieval psaltery illustrations, David tuning the harp represents the ordering of the microcosm. Even the unrealistic triangular "Delta" shape of the instrument in the illustrations is related to the Gematria of 4 and the Pythagorean tetractys symbolizing the ratios upon which the universe is built. What is David doing here as the third term defined in the first crucial proof set before us?

Is this David the King who exclaims in Psalm 119: "Oh how I love your Torah! It is my meditation all the day"? Yes and no. This David is the new Moses—one who does not hear a voice from a burning bush, but hears a proclamation from "everything." And his recapitulation of the encounter with the Holy One must proceed according to a certain logic, following the encounter given in Exodus. I do not think it unreasonable to say that this David is David Leahy, rationally identified as 2.<u>666</u>. Moses tells God that the people will not believe he has heard God speak and command him, so he asks for his name as a proof. Leahy quotes an extended passage from Moses Maimonides's *Guide for the Perplexed*. Here, the suggestion is that Moses was not simply asking for God to reveal his name to him as a sign of the validity of his message to the people. Maimonides construes the difficulty in this way: "Moses replied that he might first be asked to prove the existence of God in the universe, and that only after doing so would he be able to announce to them that God had sent him" (quoted in F, 363). The statement "I AM that I AM" is the proof provided to Moses: *Ehyeh asher Ehyeh*. It is the syntax of the statement that makes the demonstration.

Leahy then uses this syntax in his own demonstration. At issue for Leahy is not the proof that God exists but rather the meta-identity of One LORD and One Name, and the meta-identity of unity and absolute *unum* as per the trinary logic. This is spoken of in Zechariah 14:9: "In that day will the LORD be One and His name One." What we are to see, demonstrated, and thus what we are to think for the first time, is the beginning which is also seen at the Last Day: that the Being of God *is* the Name of God. Our inability to think this identity has been a blindness in thinking before now. A second coming of Moses in the messianic period was a common rabbinic belief in the late middle ages, and in fact was held by Maimonides's own father who wrote: "And after he presented his intercession on our behalf . . . he said farewell to Israel and ascended heavenwards, and his Creator hid him till the time shall come when He will be pleased with this world, and then He will send him back to it, to assist the king who is to reign in the strength of God, that beloved one of God of whom testimony is borne in the verse 'Thou art my son, this day have I begotten thee' (Ps. 2:7)."[14] It is David, 2.666 that is the "essentially rational measure," which rationally unifies the Name of the One God.

Leahy sets out to rationally decipher the cipher of the Name. We can see Leahy as distinguishing his rational form of gematria from a kabbalistic approach, which he has referred to in lecture as "not rational." Given that there are various possible assignments of letter values, including the use of final letter form values, arbitrariness of these letter values seems a reasonable initial concern when approaching the subject critically. If an internal coherence were the only goal, the initial assignment of values to the letters would be irrelevant. As long as the chosen values are consistently applied, various equivalences could be demonstrated. But how is he to ensure that the resulting equivalences are actually meaningful? Leahy uncritically takes over the set of letter valuations from traditional gematria. He gives no historic attestation of the origin of these values, nor does he insert himself into any debate over the relative modernity or antiquity of Kabbalah and gematria. These letter values just emerged, he says, from a grey area: the "mist of history." It seems we could easily charge him with arbitrariness on just this point. Why, for example, if there are twenty-two letters, do we not simply assign ordinal values 1 through 22 to the letters? Indeed, at least one method of gematria does just this. Why should Yud = 10 and the next letter Kaf = 20 rather than 11? The highest value, Tav, is 400. However the final, *sofit,* forms of Kaf, Mem,

Nun, Pe, and Tsade are sometimes used in a method called *Mispar Gadol*, assigning values from 500 to 900, better matching the Greek gematria values, since the ancient Greek alphabet has twenty-seven letters. Leahy does not use these "final form" values. He also allows no substitutions of values, as some methods of gematria allow. It is generally understood that gematria is originally Greek rather than Hebrew, and was a Jewish borrowing; however, there is evidence of alphabetic ordinalia as early as the eighth century BC. The use of such ordinalia would be connected to the establishment of alphabetic order, and we know from far earlier witnesses that the Greek is not the origin of alphabetic order. Of course the source of this order is a subject of speculation, so I offer my own observation. I have the common difficulties reading the Jewish square script, but the ancient letters of paleo Hebrew in use prior to the Babylonian captivity are extremely easy to read and many look like letters from the English alphabet. If you become familiar with these letters you will be able to perceive that every letter, in order, from Aleph to Tav, is apparent connecting the zodiac-associated fixed stars along the ecliptic plane. It takes one year to see them all pass over head. One need simply look directly at the evidence to judge the plausibility of this explanation.

At certain crucial moments in *Foundation*, Leahy uses the Greek gematria values to reckon words from the New Testament, but for the most part he uses a Hebrew translation of the Greek or Latin because "the thinking now occurring for the first time perceives the perfect and precise form of language itself here in the form of the Hebrew language" (F, 369). For example, he even translates *"cogito ergo sum"* into Hebrew in order to calculate its values. The reason that Hebrew is seen to be the perfect and precise form of language has to do with its ability to identify (using the rational gematria) the impostor, the idol, the "double" that imitates Atonement. Altizer asks: "But if a uniquely modern apocalypticism is inseparable from the death of God, a death of God which it can know as apocalypse itself, could this be the first purely conceptual realization of the Kingdom of God? Or is it the first purely conceptual expression of an absolute atheism or an absolute desacralization? Or could it be both at once? And could this be said of the whole world of modern apocalyptic thinking?"[15] The ambiguity of the *Novus Ordo* and the careful demonstration of this "double" stand on the far side of the notion that is so important for Altizer: the *coincidentia oppositorum*. It is essentially transcended in the thinking now occurring.

A careful reader will also notice instances where the current Hebrew term is actually a transliteration, as in the case of the word *rational* (רציונלי). Some of his choices are worth puzzling over. After all, the word is the basic unit of meaning but Hebrew words are built up with prefixes, infixes, and suffixes. To use a simple example, do we count the gematria for "Messiah" or for "The Messiah" (*ha-Moshiach*)? In the period of the paleo Hebrew motherscript all the words were run together with no spacing in between. The Lord's question, "How do you read it?" and the concern over "rightly dividing the word" are alive in evaluating Leahy's demonstration. Ultimately, however, the fact remains that he simply accepts these traditional number values for the letters with a rather pragmatic attitude. If it works, it works. So does it work?

Now we are going to think the act of creation absolutely. It sounds easier to say this: we are going to think Identity. Now is the time to begin. We can't fail to do so, if Leahy is correct: in every now is the beginning absolutely. This is worth repeating, just to underscore our rejection of the idea that thinking the beginning requires a thinking back behind the now; in every now is the beginning absolutely.

The form of thought is the now-unity of the beginning. The truth of this now is understood as the relation of perfect equality which is the identity of the foundation. According to Leahy's gematria, the identity of *being* הוה is the rational product: 4.1<u>666</u>. The identity of *thought* הרהור is 4.1<u>666</u>. For his demonstration he chooses a word that only appears once in Scripture, in Daniel 4:5. A more commonly used Hebrew word for thought is from חשב "thinking," מחשב, but a successfully communicated thought would get a final Hey to become מחשבה. Even if we choose this word instead the demonstration can be furthered. The rational product of מחשבה is 750. The rational product of *to create* ברא is 0.1. Leahy identifies "created unity" by the proportion 1/.01 = 100. Since *thought*, 750, denominated by *everything* (הכל, RP = 7.5) = 100, this shows the created unity of thought and everything.

Incidentally, the rational product of my own name, *Sarah* שרה, is also 7.5. So I have just demonstrated the created unity of Thought with my identity. I did not actualize this thought until I came to just this point in the explication while writing this essay. So thinking identity in the now-unity of the beginning really shows itself. Consider this also: the rational product of *name* (שם) is 7.5. Here we can also see the created unity of Thought and Name: 750/7.5 = 100. For Leahy, the thinking now occurring has no place for the category of self, but identity is central. If "Sarah" is identical with "everything," then qua subject she is nothing. As Leahy writes: "What now occurs for the first time in history is the invitation to the absolute loss of self from which we dare not withhold our selves as exceptions in essence to the invitation. We exist in the divine opening of the creative act which knows absolutely no hesitation, or not at all" (F, 355). Yet here we see what Leahy calls the second absolute, which transcends American pragmatism: "the univocal predication of being itself in the form of the name of an actually existing person" (F, 184).

Let us now proceed from the consideration of name to the consideration of "The Name" (השם). Leahy begins the demonstration of the meta-identity of the One Lord and the essential conception of the name by deciphering it in what he calls the form of the Minimum. As a proportion, the minimum is 4:1::2:3 giving a rational product of 2.$\underline{666}$. This had been shown earlier in *Foundation* during his discussion of the new trinary logic. *Torah* has a rational product of 2.$\underline{666}$E3. The little Torah is the minimum, the thousandth part. *Thousand* is 2.$\underline{666}$, just as *David* is 2.$\underline{666}$. But why is it that this rational measure, 2.$\underline{666}$, is the key to deciphering the Name? A confirmation is sought, in good Catholic fashion, by way of a substantial analogy. The mission of David is tested. The mission of the identity 2.$\underline{666}$ will be confirmed in the same way that the mission of Moses can be confirmed. Moses = rational product 0.$\underline{666}$. If we follow the syntax of "I AM that I AM" given by Maimonides, we see that "I AM" = "that I AM." Expressed as rational products: .40 = .2$\underline{666}$ (or 1 = 2/3). This is the fundamental truth of the minimum. The rational product of השם, The Name = 2/3 (.2$\underline{666}$) The mission of Moses is confirmed in the following manner: First notice that אהיה (I AM) is equivalent to אני identified with מלוכה; "I AM" identified with "dominion." Literally, אני is "my inquiry." EN is to enquire and the suffixed Yud is possessive (rational product of אני is 1/5 = .20). This identified with "dominion" (מלוכה) (rational product = 2) gives .40. When this "I AM" (.40) is identified with Moses (0.$\underline{666}$) the rational product is .2$\underline{666}$, which is equivalent also to the rational product of "understood" and "speech." The "I AM" (0.40) is also equivalent to the rational product of "father of the Prophets" (.40) identified with the incomplete noun *esher* (2/3) and Moses (2/3). If 1 = 2/3 as in the syntax of "I AM that I AM" then 1 is also equal to 3/2 or 1.5 which is the rational product of the word peace, *shalom*. Thus, The Name (השם) is identical with Peace. To see this demonstrated is to hear the Absolute Existent speak "Peace be with you"

(שלום לך *shalom lecha*), which he says is, qua beginning, the death of solitude. The rational product of שלום לך is 2.25 (which is 1.5 divided by .666).

How then can we test the mission of the identity 7.5 (Sarah/everything)? The identity of I (אני) which is rational product 0.20 and (Sarah/everything) הכל which is 7.5, results in the rational product of 1.5 which is identical to Peace/Shalom. Now the "Peace be with you" is answered with peace. Jesus said to His disciples, "Into whatsoever house ye enter, first say, Peace be to this house. And if the son of peace be there, your peace shall rest upon it; but if not, it shall turn to you again" (Luke 10:5–6). Heidegger said that startled dismay and deep foreboding were to be the attunement of the future humanity. But *shalom*, the ratio of 3/2, is the tuning of the perfect fifth, the first interval to bring us into harmony. "For the first time," Leahy writes, "the logic of creation is absolute relativity, absolute precision" (F, 369). The very identity of *name* (שם) is 7.5. "What is revelation?" when calculated is 7.5e-6.

We are working our way with Leahy from *name* שם, to *the name* (השם), to the Tetragrammaton. In the third chapter of Exodus, verse 14, we notice that Moses is directed to tell the people, "I AM has sent me to you." In the next verse he is directed to use the Tetragrammaton name: "יהוה . . . has sent me to you" and "this is my name forever." But just as *Ehyeh* was deciphered in the context of "I AM who I AM," the name יהוה is deciphered in the context of a title. Rightly dividing the word י and הוה gives the meaning He Being/He Existing. But this being/existing is determinate. Leahy considers this name in the context of the title: "יהוה King of Israel." This choice follows a logic, because in the prior phase of the demonstration "I" was identified generically with "dominion" (מלוכה).

Things get very interesting with the value calculated for "יהוה King of Israel." The integral product (the absolute identity) is 8.2944E18, which is the same value as "the stone that smote the image" from Daniel 2:35. The integral product of the designation of יהוה in Exodus 3:6 as אלהי אברהם אלהי יצחק ואלהי יעקב ("the God of Abraham, the God of Isaac, and the God of Jacob") is 8.2944E26. And when יהוה ("King of Israel") is identified with absolute בן ("son" or "between"), the product is absolute "Dead Center/zero point of energy." 82944 is the total area of Leahy's absolute dead center hypercube (four dimensional analogue of a cube, also called a tesseract), which is uniquely perfectly hypercubic according to Leahy's proof. The volume of the hypercube is unvisualizable and the gematria for "the volume will not be visualized" is 8.2944E28. We are interested in the number 82944 because as we move through his demonstration we eventually repeatedly arrive at this significant value. Leahy calculates the integral product value of *Iesous Christos* in Greek as 8.2944E28, which is "absolute dead center/zero point of energy identified with absolute consciousness" (F, 503). It is also, identically, "absolute consciousness identified with coordinate code." Interestingly, the value of "quantum computer" is also 8.2944E16. The thesis of the meta-identity of language and numbers expressed as "*Logos kai arithmos*" gives the value of 8.2944E22 when using the Greek rational gematria. The integral product of Genesis 1:3, ויאמר אלהים יהי אור ויהי אור, "And God said 'Let there be light' and there was light," is 8.2944E26. And we cannot fail to mention "The last day" (John 6:54), whose integral product is 8.2944E16. In speaking of the resurrection, Paul says in 1 Corinthians 15:44: "What is raised is the spiritual body." The integral product (absolute identity) value for this statement calculated using the Greek gematria is 8.2944E40. Further, Αναστάσεως αρχη ("the beginning of the resurrection") has the integral product value 8.2944E20. Leahy identifies the number 82944 as uniquely the equivalent of Unity. "I am at once the Alpha and the Omega" calculated using the Greek gematria values yields the value 8.2944E32.

Lest we emerge from all this in a dizzy muddle, quite sure that this is all an intricate trick of some sort and we have been bewitched by a numerology detached from anything real or meaningful, consider this: the four fundamental physical forces (the strong, weak, the electromagnetic, and the gravitational forces) can be seen to be functions of 82944. Leahy writes: "The gravitational exponent of 82944 is thus seen to be the latter's electromagnetic exponent divided by the squares of the odd numbers, that is, divided by the squares of the ratio of the distances traversed in successive equal intervals of time in Galileo's law of universal constant gravitational acceleration. Assuming 82944 as the common coefficient of the fundamental force constants, the gravitational constant is seen to be the electromagnetic constant reduced to the square of the universal constant of acceleration."[16] In *The Cube Unlike All Others* he states that gravitational force is reducible to a function of the purely geometric dimensions of this perfect hypercube.[17]

If we continue with reference to the mathematics of the hypercube, we can relate the number for the unvisualizable volume of the cube, calculated by Leahy to be the unique natural number 10749524, to the great sign heralding the *novitas mentis*. Saint John's heavenly vision of a woman clothed with the sun, the moon beneath her feet, and crowned with twelve stars, is certainly well known, and I will make no attempt to broadly survey the significances that have been attributed to the sign within various Christian groups over the course of church history. The woman is emblematic for what Leahy calls the "spiritual conception of the church now occurring for the first time in thought itself" (NM, 385). It is to be the foundation of an unqualifiedly total engagement with the world as well as its essential transformation: "the unconditioned itself appearing in essence bringing into existence in thought itself the essential condition of an essentially new world, the receptivity for the existence itself of another in essence, being itself in essence at the disposal of another in essence" (NM, 385). What to so many has been a mysterious sign is, paradoxically, the herald of the End of Mystery (mystery as represented by her counterpart, "the whore riding the beast"). The crowning knowledge is centrally related to now-time and to new beginning. It is described as an *absolute expansion of identity* where the woman laboring to give birth represents the overcoming of the idea that unity must be multiplied with respect to a source, and is thus existence beyond the One. Such mysticism is to be shunned. There is no outside the act of beginning and this knowledge is her crown: knowledge at once the actuality of creation in which the resurrection body is now thinkable as absolute placedness, absolute sociability, and absolute particularity. Using Leahy's rational gematria method for "And there appeared a great sign in heaven" (Revelation 12:1) gives the value $1.07495424E16$. According to Leahy, "there is no natural number other than the absolute dead center hypercube volume 107495424 in the ratio 82944/784/1 to its integral product."[18] Whereas the value for *Iesous Christos* is related to the total area of this unique hypercubic structure, the value for the great sign is related to the volume of the hypercube—an enfilled onceness, as Heidegger anticipated? Heidegger was trapped in a mode of modern self-consciousness to have been enthralled by the Nothing phenomenologically experienced as a brute transcendence, but he was right to say that being itself is finite, according to Leahy. A purely self-relative identity would be indistinguishable from nothing, which is to me the fundamental incomprehensibility of solipsism and certain forms of mystical yearning for Oneness. But the value for "the woman who was about to give birth" of Revelation 12:4 is 7.5, which as noted above is the same value as הכל, "everything." Here we catch a glimpse of what is meant by the idea that the divine mind is univocally predicated of the totality of existence (F, 243).

Leahy's demonstrations of the thinking now occurring are certainly revelatory, but what about the thinking beyond now? The "apocalyptic I" as the new objective consciousness of the new world order is not peering into any expected or possible futures. As Leahy says in his video interview with Todd Carter, in the thinking now occurring "there is no future, so I cannot peer into it."[19] Nevertheless, we should notice that in discussing the beyond now, he brings into play yet another product, the result of dividing absolute identity values by absolute identity values. This, he says, is how the "expansion of identity" is quantified, and these numbers are what I would call *directive* in the sense that they expose one seeking them to the kind of being at the disposal of the other that heretofore has been exemplified by what the Bible calls the servants, the prophets, and the handmaidens. Leahy calls these values the unity of existence itself, yet sees these in these values the absolutely prophetic. These values (x/y) represent "the absolutely unconditioned meta-dichotomy in which the 'after' exists absolutely unconditioned" (F, 500).

To many this method may seem like a strange form of numerology, which is usually thought of as a sort of fortune telling. But Leahy certainly did not see his thesis on the meta-identity of language and number in that way. He saw the absolute clarification of thought itself in this collapse of the wall between language and number. The question of the relationship of all this to prophecy, however, is a serious and deep one. Consider again Leahy's concern with what is spoken prophetically by Zechariah: "In that day will the LORD be One and His name One." This is the transcendence of the anonymous God of theology in its most proper sense. "Being itself thought in essence is something with a name for the first time in history" (F, 100) is, at least, the beginning of prophecy fulfilled.

I would like to invite further discussion of Leahy's approach as it relates to the understanding of the prophetic dimension of the scriptures. Daniel can certainly be seen as an early data encryptor, as he is specifically instructed to "conceal and seal" the book. Since people have run to and fro, and knowledge has increased, we are now in a time when methods of data encryption are an important area of concern. In generations where people see themselves as living in "the time of the end," interpreters come forward claiming either to have unsealed the vision themselves or to perceive that the unsealing is taking place in a spiritual sense as evidenced by increased understanding of the text in relation to other prophecies and to historical events. Some point to equidistant letter spacing codes that have only become apparent since the development of computers, but whether those have legitimacy is not my concern here. In Daniel 9:24, "seventy 'sevens' are decreed . . . to seal up vision and prophecy." It seems that the decryption of Daniel's text involves understanding how certain ratios leave their traces in the deciphering of that text using Leahy's novel method. Further, we can examine how those values are disseminated through scripture. The trace is an infinitely repeating series, which can be taken up at any point: 142857. This series is related to the value of "diagonal" and to his explanation of the unity of the *novitas mundi* (F, 500). There is no doubt that the mass of mathematical calculation appearing in *Foundation* is only the tip of an iceberg, extending to the infinite structure of existence itself. Having spent several years doing my own calculations, now reaching almost eight hundred pages of numerical values for everything from scientific terminology, to newspaper headlines, to verses of scripture, I can say that the tool Leahy has given us can unlock valuable insights if only it is used.

Notes

1. Thomas J. J. Altizer, "Apocalypticism and Modern Thinking," originally published in the *Journal for Christian Theological Research* 2, no. 2 (1997); published in revised form as chapter 4 in this volume.

2. Edward T. Oakes, "Exposed Being," *The Journal of Religion* 78, no. 2 (April 1998): 256.

3. Johann G. Fichte, *Foundations of Transcendental Philosophy Wissenschaftslehre nova methodo (1796/1799)*, trans. Daniel Breazeale (Ithaca: Cornell University Press, 1992), 110.

4. Ibid., 111.

5. Martin Heidegger, The *Metaphysical Foundations of Logic* (Bloomington: Indiana University Press, 1984), 8–9.

6. Martin Heidegger, *Basic Problems of Phenomenology*, trans. Albert Hofstadter (Bloomington: Indiana University Press, 1982), 162.

7. Martin Heidegger. *Contributions to Philosophy (From Enowning)*, trans. Parvis Emad and Kenneth Maly (Bloomington: Indiana University Press, 1999), 280.

8. Ibid., 24.

9. Ibid.

10. Brian Copenhaver and Daniel Stein Kokin, "Egidio di Viterbo's Book on Hebrew Letters: Christian Kabbalah in Papal Rome," *Renaissance Quarterly* 67, no. 1 (Spring 2014): 3.

11. See D. G. Leahy, "Transdecimal Calculation of Number Identity: A Note on *Integral Product* and Related Terms," *The New Universal Consciousness* (open access): http://dgleahy.com/dgl/p21.html.

12. This value becomes important when he discusses the matter of the "double" or impostor of atonement; see F, 369.

13. The claim that King David died on Shavuot is found in Yerushalmi Halachah 4 Daf 11a and Midrash Ruth Rabbah 3, with the additional notion that God told him he would die at exactly seventy years, his day of birth and death being on Shavuot. Interestingly, traditional summative gematria makes a connection as well as it calculates *"and Yishai gave birth to David"* from the book of Ruth as having a gematria of 796, and *"On the festival of Shavuot"* also with gematria of 796. Passages of the book of Ruth are read on this holiday, connecting revelation with messianic redemption.

14. Maimun ben Joseph, "The Letter of Consolation of Maimun ben Joseph," trans. L. M. Simmons, *The Jewish Quarterly Review* 2, no. 1 (Oct. 1889): 100.

15. Altizer, "Apocalypticism and Modern Thinking," par. 24.

16. D. G. Leahy, "82944 and the Four Fundamental Forces and the God Particle," *The New Universal Consciousness* (open access); http://dgleahy.com/p22.html.

17. Leahy, *The Cube Unlike All Others*, available at http://dgleahy.com, 20.

18. Ibid., 8.

19. Quoted from Todd Carter's video interview of D. G. Leahy, March 19, 2014; https://www.youtube.com/watch?v=FIsJRGOECXU&list=WL&index=11. Links to the three-part interview are publicly available on Leahy's website: http://dgleahy.com.

12

Life at the Edge

Medicine and the New Thinking

STEVEN B. HOATH, MD

> The I, *qua* self, is essentially and categorically no longer real; the essentially categorically real I is the first person other.
>
> —BS, 8

Others have emphasized D. G. Leahy as a classical scholar, theologian, and philosopher of stunning originality. This essay focuses on Leahy as a mathematician and bio-logician whose thinking defines a new view of the body, a view that is grounded in science and amenable to precise measurement. It is a view of the body that is uncompromising in its focus on another, a view that has important implications for Medicine in general and the American healthcare system in particular. Concrete examples are drawn from biology and mathematics addressing the importance of boundaries in living systems. These examples serve to illustrate the revolutionary change which follows necessarily from implementation of the new way of thinking proposed in its beginning by Leahy.

This new thought termed by Leahy the thinking now occurring is a natural if unexpected outgrowth of American pragmatism extending the thought of Peirce, James, and Dewey from a merely relative objectivity to an absolute objectivity of consciousness.

> The consciousness adequate to the beginning of real world consciousness is a universally new consciousness, in fact, a perfect other-consciousness, a consciousness categorically and essentially beyond the other-self relation. The new world order is the beginning of the universal or absolute objectivity of consciousness. The task of thinking is foundationally the essence of this beginning. The inconvenience of the beginning of this new way of thinking is then nothing less than the shaking, the removal, and the replacement of the foundations of thought by a completely new foundation. In the work before the reader nothing less than this beginning is tried, a thinking essentially and categorically without *self*. (F, xiii)

Leahy exemplifies the axiom, "Through their works you shall know them." To understand Leahy's work requires work—just as with Euclidean geometry, there is no royal road to the thinking now occurring. Leahy is decidedly not a humanitarian in the sense of Mother Teresa. He is not a professional academician with a number of degrees and awards. Nor is he a bench scientist or a popularizer of practical theology or theoretical physics. What Leahy has done is to think what is totally new. This is not an exaggerated statement but a fact, which becomes increasingly obvious with the passage of time. This new way of thinking, moreover, is not a mere theory. It is a profoundly practical and transformative view of the world. In essence, this thinking is apocalyptic. It serves to conjoin science and spirituality in an exceptionally fruitful and unexpected manner. As Leahy puts it, what now occurs for the first time in history is the explosion of reason to fit the form of faith.

Although not the focus of the current essay, it is probable that increased scientific understanding of the logico-mathematical basis of this new way of thinking will result in accelerated realization of Leahy's spiritual vision. This vision posits a new world in which "the beginning of the essentially new form of thinking—the beginning of a universal newness—is *essentially* and *categorically* without the notion of self" (F, xii). According to Leahy, the notion that there is a difference between the spiritual and the objective is a notion belonging to self-consciousness. Rather, this new way of thinking is absolutely foundational and characterized by a logic categorically without self. This thinking is humble in the sense of "humus," the earth that is beneath us. It is not in the least self-effacing or self-deprecating. It is joyful, jubilant, expansive, and other-focused without being self-sacrificial.

The logic underlying Leahy's thinking is not binary. It is not a matter of either/or. It is not a yin-yang symbol. Nor is it a Necker cube where *either* the face "a" *or* the face "b" can be perceived as in front, but not both simultaneously (Figure 12.1). The thinking now occurring, Leahy's name for his foundational thought, is based on an all-inclusive trinarity *and* not an exclusive *either/or*. This is the logic of the mathematicized body, of the infinitely shared edge of the body. In the examples given, imagine the complex boundary of the yin-yang symbol as a *third* element conjoining the black/white fields into an integrated flowing pattern or imagine the invisible plane whereupon perception pivots to yield the alternate anterior faces of the Necker cube.

This third element is not the result of a dialectical Hegelian synthesis. "The essentially new thinking is for the first time beyond dialectical identity neither by way of the negation of identity nor by way of the supplementation of identity by the non-identity of the Subject, but by way of embodying identity" (BS, xiii). It is in the expression of this logic in physics and biology that the creative interbraiding of spirituality and science is most evident. With Leahy, nothing is hidden. Everything is exteriorized. As Leahy points out, the Hebrew word for *interior* (פנים) is, differently inflected, also the word for *exterior* or *surface*. The boundary of the body is the boundary of the universe. The body is the universe absolutely.

To use Leahy's terminology, real trinary logic is foundational; it is the logic of the real in existence. This logic is "virtually left-handed,"

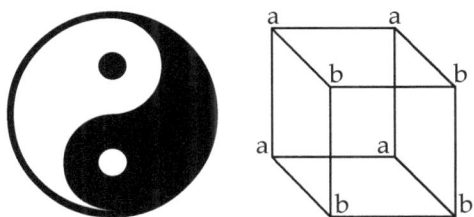

Figure 12.1. Yin-Yang symbol and Necker cube.

and, hence, asymmetric like the basic biochemical building blocks of living organisms. It is a logic beyond dualism and beyond self/non-self distinctions. It is the logic of the boundary beyond yin and yang, beyond the Necker Cube, beyond the political synthesis of Red and Blue America. It is the logic of the thinking now occurring, a form of thought in which the world itself begins absolutely now. Real trinary logic is a logic of complete novelty, which underlies a new consciousness of the beginning in which there is no concept of "same." What would Medicine and the US healthcare system look like if structured according to the thinking now occurring and real trinary logic?

Just as Leahy positions the new thinking in relation to American pragmatism, the thinking now occurring can be heuristically examined in the context of the US healthcare system, a system badly in need of reform and rapidly approaching fiscal insolvency unless major transformations are enacted. The new thinking offers a number of useful, if revolutionary and often painful, recipes for reform reaching from research at the bench to the bedside to the boardrooms of hospital CEOs and administrators. Critical to the appreciation of the thinking now occurring is the recognition that this is a new *form* of thinking, a form of apocalyptic thinking that thinks the beginning of an essentially *nonpolitical* society. Given that healthcare is an intensely political issue with respect to fiduciary policy and resource allocation, this fact must be held constantly in the foreground. Table 12.1 lists a number of aspects of a future healthcare system grounded on the thinking now occurring, a system that I here provisionally entitle *Novitas Mundi Medicinalis*. *Sensu stricto,* there is no internal medicine. Medicine deals with the progressive exteriorization of the organism. This is obvious in surgical operations where the patient is literally opened up. Less obvious are the myriad methods of diagnostic imaging and laboratory analyses, including genotyping, which extend the organism and thereby open a Pandora's box of possibilities with ethical and fiscal consequences. The language of "external" medicine, so to speak, has not been conceived and developed. We need specific examples.

Given the seeming complexity of the language in the thinking now occurring, it may seem paradoxical that this thinking overlies a crystalline, near-mathematical exactitude in its expression. As Leahy states, "The language of the new thinking possesses in its sparseness and precision a likeness to complex mathematical formulation" (F, xiii–xiv). This precision extends to the application of the thinking now occurring to biological science and medicine. Thus, there is no cell

Table 12.1. *Novitas Mundi Medicinalis*: Healthcare in Accord with the Thinking Now Occurring

OLD	NEW
Internal medicine	External (surface) medicine
Disease	Health
Self-consciousness	Other consciousness
Cell division and cell multiplication are interchangeable terms (imprecise quasi-mathematical language)	Cell multiplication = mitosis (neither normal cells nor cancer cells divide) Cell division = meiosis (applicable to gamete formation only)
Self-generation/organization	Generation/organization of and by others
Immunity as innate/acquired protection from potentially hostile microorganisms/stressors	Immunity as seamless joining of body and environment
Self-centered (autopoietic boundary)	Other centered (center is everywhere)
Logical foundation is binary (dualistic)	Logical foundation is trinary (threefold)
Selfish genes	Extended organism
Classical Darwinism discounts Lamarckian evolution	Cultural evolution eclipses classical Darwinism
Evolutionary origin (a "deep time" creation locus)	Evolutionary edge (an absolutely now superficial creation locus)
Self-contained (separate) 3D body	Artifactual body—open ended infinitely flat manifold
Brain, self, physician, gene, etc., are sources of control	Body surface as place of contact and closure with environment (no source of control)
Basic neural circuitry is sensory-motor loop: self-contained brain	Basic neural circuitry is "Möbius strip": no inside/outside distinction possible
Political sovereignty is the rule: physician, CEO, nurse, patient, therapist, etc., as ultimate arbiters of disease, treatment, and cost in a vertical organization	Beyond sovereignty: physician, CEO, nurse, patient, therapist, etc., as members of an interdisciplinary healthcare team in a horizontal organization
Mechanistic point of view (exertion of control is possible)	Freedom, spontaneity, novelty (absence of control or fixed point of view)
Science grounded on the convergent mathematics of the vanishing point (looking down the DNA axis in convergent perspective)	The logico-mathematical form of DNA offers a bridge structure to the infinitely flat manifold of the thinking now occurring

division in normal development. Mitosis is multiplicative. If science is grounded in mathematics, terms that refer immediately to the basic arithmetical operations—addition, multiplication, subtraction, and division—deserve special consideration. In common parlance, it may be sufficient that one be merely understood but, in scientific discourse, the careful definition of terms is paramount in order to avoid confusion and to foster cross-disciplinary communication. Cancer research, for example, would be more scientifically grounded and accurate if it used clearer concepts and avoided quasi-mathematical terminology such as "cell division."

Just as Leahy examines the history of Western thought via thoroughgoing critique of individual thinkers, the thinking now occurring can be applied to the unquestioned assumptions grounding the conceptual frameworks undergirding medical science. Thus, Descartes, Harvey, Freud, and Darwin offer ready-to-hand examples for analysis by the thinking now occurring. A more contemporary thinker, Richard Dawkins, provides an excellent counterfoil for introducing the productive conjunction of the thinking now occurring and Medicine in the context of modern scientific thinking and traditional skepticism. Dawkins is a lucid writer and the author of *The Selfish Gene* and *The Extended Phenotype: The Long Reach of the Gene*.[1] He is an acclaimed evolutionary biologist who recently has won new fame as an evangelical atheist railing against the deleterious effects of organized religion in his latest book *The God Delusion*.[2]

Irrespective of his avowed lack of faith, Dawkins's conception of the selfish gene as a mechanistic molecular replicator needing the body only as a means to an end, that is, a means for replicating itself, seems at first blush perfectly opposed to Leahy's notion that the universe (and ergo science) is grounded in freedom and spontaneity rather than mechanism and causality. Nevertheless, Dawkins recognizes that there are problems with a way of thinking in which the *apparent* boundary of the organism reigns supreme. In Dawkins's view, we must teach ourselves to think *beyond* the boundary of the body to see the effects of the genome on phenotypic structures such as beaver dams, termite colonies, and beehives since such structures facilitate the replication of the genome.

It is noteworthy, however, that the adjective *extended* in extended phenotype, like *internal* in internal medicine, both call attention to the apparent commonplace boundary of the body. This apparent boundary acts like the invisible pivot plane of the Necker cube facilitating the seamless union of differing points of view. It is precisely in the operational definition of this boundary that the thinking now occurring and real trinary logic can be most usefully applied. In engineering terms, one cannot understand a complex dynamic system without first knowing its boundary conditions. Even better, one would like to know its initial conditions, a task well suited to the thinking now occurring and real trinary logic considered as "a logic of beginning." The remainder of this essay is devoted to the notion that the surface of the body, that place of contact and closure with the environment, constitutes ground zero for a transformative redefinition of healthcare.

It is a paradox of internal medicine that the boundary of the body, that place where a truly personalized approach to patient care is most obvious, is often treated as trivial or superficial. The idea that one can provide fully personalized care while remaining totally objective is not clear in current medical practice but it is central to the thinking now occurring. In fact, the surface of the body, in its seamless union with the environment, is completely nonsubjective and constitutes the perfect meeting place for Medicine and society. There is no need to muddy the waters with subjective concerns. There is no place for the self to hide and certainly no place on the surface of things. The increasingly technological practice of medicine through advanced imaging, stem cell research, genetic engineering, transplant science, and so on occurs without reference to subjectivity. The increasingly artifactual nature of the surface of the body precludes trivialization as illogical and unscientific.

To reiterate, there is no self in healthcare delivery. All linguistic references in Medicine to "self-interest," "self-care," or "self-consciousness" lack credible evidence. The idea that immunity refers to self/non-self distinctions is a thing of the past. In the same way, as cell "multiplication" is the correct terminology, so, likewise, organisms are not "autopoietic" or self-generating. Thus, the thinking now occurring does not agree with recent conceptual trends positing self-organization or self-generation as a counterforce to Darwinian natural selection in the evolution of life. Organisms, according to Leahy, are not autopoietic or self-generating. What distinguishes living organisms is precisely that organisms are other-generated and other-generating!

The requirement for Medicine to find an objective foundation extends to recent efforts in the broad field of healthcare research. Over the past decade, for example, considerable focus has been leveled on efforts to increase the objectivity of medical decision making and the evaluation of therapeutic efficacy. These efforts are generally grouped together under the banner of "evidence-based medicine."[3] The highest level of evidence in this field is generally considered the randomized double-blind controlled trial. The lowest level of evidence is expert opinion based on individual observation. Perhaps nowhere is the contrast between traditional medical research and the thinking now occurring more evident than in this comparison.

The thinking now occurring denies both the need and the possibility of control. As such, the thinking now occurring is nonmechanistic and grounded in spontaneity and freedom. The seeming naiveté of this approach is countered neatly by Leahy's insistence on remaining totally engaged with the world absolutely NOW. The existing world is without presupposition: new, novel, now. Causality in a world absolutely NOW cannot be what we thought it was. With the insistence upon remaining absolutely NOW, the place where something occurs becomes decisive and important. "In the thinking now occurring for the first time the place where something takes place is the cause of its taking place" (BS, 236). This is a world taken on faith with a supportive logic and mathematical foundation which resists dismissal.

The incorporation of the thinking now occurring into medical decision making is not a simple matter. The language of medicine, like that of most scientific and philosophical endeavors, is rife with reference to the unquestioned notion of self. All reference to self is anathema to the thinking now occurring. Thus, ideas of self-consciousness, self-organization, self-generation are verboten and deemed notions of the past. Focus from hither on must be on "other consciousness," organization or generation by and for others, etc. Medically, consciousness focused in the moment on being at the disposal of another is exactly what is needed in healthcare organizations.

Arguably, what is needed is more attention to the seamless interface (identity) of body and environment. At first glance, the surface of the body is that shared surface of care which forms the actual interface for Nursing practice and is often championed directly or indirectly by practitioners of "alternative medicine." Thus, holistic or integrative medicine is often touted as more intuitive and nurturing than reductionistic medical practice, which is traditionally based on understanding cellular and molecular mechanisms of disease. It is doubtful that Leahy would any more accept the highly subjective under/overtones of current holistic practitioners, however, than he would the self-interest of modern medicine.

A good example of the integrative potential of the thinking now occurring is illustrated in the notion of "immunity." Leaving aside the unsubstantiated claims of "immune boosters" and other questionable approaches to maintaining wellness or fighting off disease, immunity is generally viewed scientifically in terms of cellular mechanisms involving innate or acquired defense against potentially hostile microorganisms or toxins in the environment. Thus, the immune system is a kind of corporeal Homeland Security positioned strategically between the body and the environment. Immunity is characterized by various means of protecting self from non-self rather than as that whereby the body is seamlessly integrated with the environment.

The immune system, therefore, provides a credible biological straw man for examining the claims of the thinking now occurring. In particular, the outermost surface of the body (as commonly understood in everyday language) provides a preeminent example.[4] One practical result of focusing on the logico-mathematical structure of the epidermis, for example, and the concomitant notion of a surface of contact and closure is that, if this most evident and obvious surface can be discussed in all its facets without resorting to the notion of *self*, the question can be legitimately raised whether such a notion is needed at all. This surface additionally provides a conceptual springboard for discussing Leahy's notion of creating the absolute edge.

What is the most commonly perceived object in the universe? Is this "object" not the surface of the body itself? Growing evidence supports the contention that the outermost surface of the body is organized in a phi proportional manner.[5] Specifically, the segmentation pattern of the human epidermis manifests a logico-mathematical structure closely linked to real trinary gravitational logic—the term Leahy uses for virtually left-handed logic or the logic of infinite inclusive difference.[6]

This finding is significant insofar as the skin *personalizes* the surface in the looking glass. Leahy says we need to look *through* the looking glass to see what is there to be seen. It is a salient biological fact that the human epidermis and the human brain are derived from the same embryological tissue called *ectoderm*. From both a developmental and a perceptual (commonsense) perspective, the skin is the surface of the brain. Moreover, in the epidermis, we have an organ, like the brain, which is peculiarly human in comparison to other primates; hence, the designation of man as the "naked ape."[7] Even Darwin was hard put to explain the evolutionary significance of losing a protective mantle of fur insofar as a naked skin surface renders man vulnerable to thermal, solar, and mechanical injury. It is worth noting that in the relatively new field of computer science, larger and larger central processing units are useless without the co-development of more and more flexible and adaptive interfaces, and the same holds true for the brain and the boundary of the body. The brain and the skin must co-evolve, co-develop, and co-adapt.

The finding that the human epidermis manifests, in a particularly striking manner, a rational structure amenable to mathematical analysis *seems* to give special importance to humanity, thereby violating the Copernican principle that there are no special observers in the universe. Note, however, the central thesis in all Leahy's works: "It is the writer's understanding that the new beginning is categorical, and that the categories and, indeed, the very structures of modern philosophical, theological, and scientific self-consciousness are essentially inadequate to the new beginning, and, further, that the most fundamental structure, the very notion of the *self*—in any but a purely formal sense—is completely and essentially dysfunctional in the light of the beginning of this new world" (F, ix).

As a first approximation, it is noteworthy that mathematicians through the centuries have associated "spiritual" terms with aspects of phi proportionality. Thus, the golden ratio (phi = ~1.618034) has been called the "divine proportion" and the closely related logarithmic spiral termed the *spira mirabilis*. What are the implications of discovering that the boundary of the body is rationally organized and incorporates a "divine" proportionality? What should we make of a science that finds deep mathematical meaning and a logical foundation manifest in this most superficial and common of biological structures? Might not the perspective revealed by such a science cast new light on the spiritual iconography of the past: humanity created in the image of God and the emotive power of a crucified Creator? Most importantly, wouldn't a trinary logic that explicated this spiritual connection in a completely objective manner—that is, in a manner devoid of self-reference—lay the foundation for a new Copernican revolution? These conjectures open the door to a discussion of a central concept in the thinking now occurring, namely, the creation of the absolute edge.

Is there a spiritually based mathematics? The posing of this question seems at first a non sequitur. What does mathematics have to do with spirituality? What might constitute such a mathematics? If such a mathematics can be justified, however, what might its implications be for Medicine? Of all the applied fields of science, Medicine arguably stands the most to gain from a conjunction of faith and logic. Leahy addresses the mathematics of phi proportionality with startling depth and erudition. One must move *through* phi proportionality to a new logic, and that is the purpose of Leahy's reference to this topic. Phi-geometry is an "imperfect" likeness of real trinary logic. Phi-geometry makes it seriously possible to set aside the subject-object focus and, in this way, calls it into question. Real trinary logic absolutely excludes the subjectivity-objectivity complex.

If spiritual and scientific quests are both searches for unity, phi is a logical starting place. Both the golden rectangle and the logarithmic spiral embody phi proportionality (for example, the ratio of the long to the short side of the rectangle containing the spiral equals phi). In a transcendental sense, phi is an arithmetical function of unity. Phi most simply identifies the operations of addition/multiplication and subtraction/division; thus, phi is the unique solution of the simple arithmetical equations $1 + x = x$ and $x - 1 = 1/x$. Leahy illustrates decisively the philosophical and logical underpinnings of phi proportionality. Leahy's conclusion that phi proportionality is the missing link between the physical constants is illustrated with wonderful precision by relating the lengths of the axis segments enclosed by the very same spiral in Figure 12.2 to the Planck constant of action (energy x time).[8]

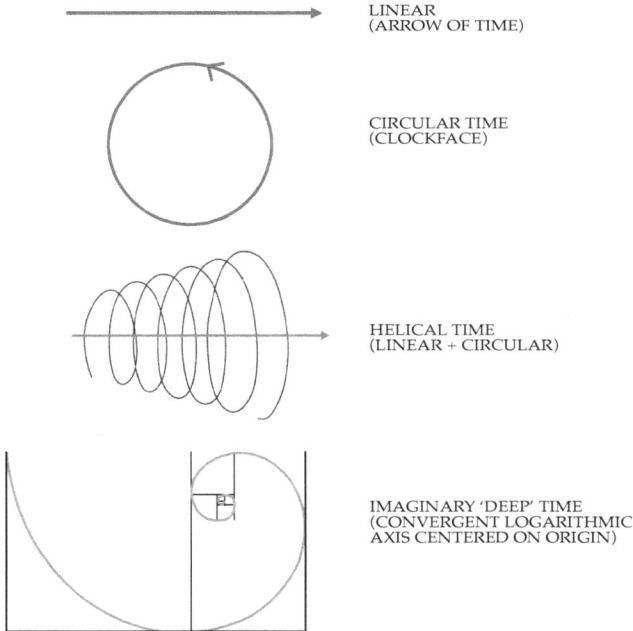

Figure 12.2. To create the absolute edge: Phi proportionality and the evolution of the arrow of time.

Figure 12.2 gives a rough indication of how different means of imaging/measuring Time have evolved. Thus, the progression from the simple arrow of time to a clockface universe and the union of linear and circular time in the construction of a helix. The asymmetric orbit of the earth around the sun provides a ready example of the helical model, *if* the center of the sun is not considered stationary but moves forward uniformly as the moment of time. This model, consistent in all aspects with Newtonian mechanics, results in a strikingly different view from the standard elliptical orbit of the earth around a stationary sun. The latter viewpoint can be envisioned by looking down the long axis of the sun's trajectory along the arrow of time. Thus viewed, the orbit of the earth assumes, by hypothesis, the form of a logarithmic spiral and the previous time axis (the path of the sun's movement) is incorporated into the image plane posited on the origin of the spiral. Since the term *origin*, like that of *self*, is disallowed in the thinking now occurring, as too suggestive of a distant past, this latter spiral is best considered an imperfect form. This form, nevertheless, incorporates the time axis of the previous helical construct into a flat ruled surface, which requires the active participation of the observer to imagine. The convergent properties of the spiral allow measurements to be performed. The "time axis" itself is invisible. This form is not meant to precisely illustrate time according to the thinking now occurring but to offer a decided step in that direction. As Leahy writes, "Essentially, therefore, the measure of time itself is the object of transcendental historical thinking" (NM, 307).

With respect to the goal of providing an objective foundation for medical science, the imperfect form of the logarithmic spiral has the salutary advantage of demonstrating a geometrical method wherein the "deep time" advocates of evolutionary biology can be offered a method of measurement that is constructed on an infinitely flat phenomenological manifold that is absolutely NOW and that demonstrably requires participation of the observer. The perpendicular "cross" of the diagonals of the superimposed golden rectangles connects this construction with the Cartesian coordinate system and allows the notion of a single "origin" to be brought into question.

Thus, in Figure 12.2 there is a progressive series of temporal analogues that may be useful and productive in allowing transition to the "place" of the thinking now occurring. It is easy to use the construction of the logarithmic spiral within the bounds of the golden rectangle to demonstrate: (1) the crossed axes of the Cartesian coordinate system (the basis for graphing one quantity against another); (2) the fact that mathematical construction of these crossed axes incorporates the "divine" proportion; (3) the presence of an artifactual manifold of infinite breadth, which requires the participation/imagination of the observer to "see"; and (4) the crossed Cartesian axes can be analogized in a productive manner in conjunction with the image of the Christian cross. The "deep time" construct used in the context of the logarithmic spiral, moreover, seems perfectly suited to the notion expressed in *Foundation* that "this is at once itself for the first time the perfect reduction of depth to surface" (F, 439).

Finally, given the structural stability of the logarithmic spiral under transformation, it is not unreasonable to consider the degree to which this structure exhibits the properties of biological materials such as DNA, which combine a helical form with structural stability under change. Viewed down its long axis under the constraints of convergence, DNA possesses a form similar if not identical to the logarithmic spiral. This possibility forms the basis for the last entry in Table 12.1; that is, "Science grounded on the convergent mathematics of the vanishing point (looking down the DNA axis in convergent perspective)" versus "the logico-mathematical form of DNA offers a bridge structure to the infinitely flat manifold of the thinking now occurring." The thinking now occurring is beyond the mathematics of the vanishing point.

The connection between the mathematical properties of the logarithmic spiral and spirituality deserves further study. Jacob Bernoulli, the Swiss mathematician, noted that attempts to transform this curve invariably ended in reproducing the curve itself. The logarithmic spiral is invariant under transformation (*eadem mutata resurgo*). Further, just as the spiral grows in measured increments, so too do the enclosing rectangles. Rotating the logo for the Templeton Foundation and highlighting the diagonals yields the adjacent figure. The diagonals of each of the consecutive rectangles in this figure intersect the origin of the spiral at right angles to form a cross or, equivalently, the perpendicular x-y axes of the Cartesian coordinate system. The right arm of the cross points in the direction of the future growth of the spiral. The logic of the Trinity is never far from Leahy's thinking; he attests that the trinitarian relations perfectly coincide with what is now for the first time in history the universal logic of a new world (F, 629–30).

In the logic of the beginning there is no point of origin in the sense of a source or a cause operating before the thing itself comes into being. There is nothing behind what appears. In every now is the beginning absolutely. In the thinking now occurring, the "origin," if such a word is allowable, is a surface, which is not behind anything and which is infinitely flat—sourceless and not itself a source. The construction of the origin of the logarithmic spiral allows such a vision to be articulated. The construction of the logarithmic spiral within the golden rectangle, for example, provides a ready means of fixing both the origin of the Cartesian coordinate system and the origin of the spiral *within a ruled surface*. The time axis in this viewpoint is embedded in an absolutely superficial manner such that both circular and linear representations of time are combined. This is the mathematical imagery of deep (spiral/helical) time. The working out of the logic of the beginning with respect to cosmology and biological evolution alone (two fields that commonly, and often uncritically, use the term *origin*) promises to keep future scholars and scientists busy for generations.

If Darwinian evolution is concerned with the origin of species, the thinking now occurring is decidedly non-Darwinian. Real trinary logic is the logic of infinite inclusive difference and recognizes no class or species. In it there is no origin in a distant past. Rather, there is the global imperative to actively engage the world in the absolute NOW in the form of an infinitely centered surface. The thinking now occurring marks the consciousness of a new beginning, the beginning of a global society composed of multiple individuals engaged in the act of creating a new world, a new body, an artifactual body. "The artifactual body is the perfect conception of the new creation. The artifactual body is the inception of the absolutely selfless interchangeability of absolutely discrete individualities, the initiation of the absolutely unconditioned unicity of plural personalities, the beginning of the complete joy of existence" (BS, 7).

The extent to which the subjective self still clings to the boundary of the body is the extent to which we *inappropriately* identify with superficial appearances. To that extent, we remain trapped in the bondage of self. The "skin encapsulated ego" is the little god that must ultimately die in order to make manifest the larger reality. As Leahy writes: "For the first time the new reality of the world—world unity—is not a mere ideal. . . . The consciousness adequate to the beginning of real world consciousness is a universally new consciousness, in fact, a perfect other-consciousness, a consciousness categorically and essentially beyond the other-self relation" (F, xiii). And elsewhere he declaims even more forcefully: "Essentially nothing other than the lingering vestige of subjectivity keeps the 'species-making species' from creating an absolutely new universe."[9]

Notes

1. R. Dawkins, *The Selfish Gene* (Oxford: Oxford University Press, 1976) and *The Extended Phenotype: The Long Reach of the Gene* (San Francisco: Freeman, 1982).

2. R. Dawkins, *The God Delusion* (Boston: Houghton Mifflin Harcourt, 2006).

3. D. L. Sackett et al., "Evidence Based Medicine: What It Is and What It Isn't," *BMJ* 312, no. 7023 (1996); S. E. Straus and D. L. Sackett, "Applying Evidence to the Individual Patient," *Ann Oncol* 10, no. 1 (1999).

4. S. B. Hoath and D. G. Leahy, "The Human Stratum Corneum as Extended, Covalently Cross-Linked Biopolymer: Mathematics, Molecules, and Medicine," *Med Hypotheses* 66, no. 6 (2006); and "The Organization of Human Epidermis: Functional Epidermal Units and Phi Proportionality," *Journal of Invest Dermatol* 121, no. 6 (2003).

5. S. B. Hoath and D. G. Leahy, "Formation and Function of the Stratum Corneum," in *The Essential Stratum Corneum* ed. Ronald Marks, Jean-Luc Lévêque, and Rainer Voegeli (London: Martin Dunitz, 2002).

6. Leahy, *Quantum Gravitational vs Quantum Logic: Virtually Left-Handed Real Trinary Logic* (2009); cited March 1, 2009; http://dgleahy.com/p19.html.

7. D. Morris, *The Naked Ape: A Zoologist's Study of the Human Animal* (New York: Random House, 1999).

8. D. G. Leahy, *The Golden Bowls & the Logarithmic Spiral*; cited March 1, 2009; http://dgleahy.com/p14.html.

9. Leahy, *The Golden Bowl Structure: The Platonic Line, Fibonacci, and Feigenbaum*; cited March 1, 2009; http://dgleahy.com/p15.html. See also F, 559–60.

Glossary of Key Terms in D. G. Leahy

LISSA McCULLOUGH

This glossary of key philosophical terms in the writings of D. G. Leahy aspires to be essential, not exhaustive. Not appearing here are philosophical terms that Leahy uses for the most part within the range of connotations familiar to contemporary philosophers: terms such as Being, Nothing, absence, presence, totality, subjectivity, universality, ontology, and the like. Terms featured here are the distinctive ones recurrently used to delineate the new thinking as something happening for the first time in history, never thinkable previously in the specific senses denoted in this "thinking now occurring for the first time"—abbreviated here as TNO (the -FFT, which is essential, is assumed for the sake of brevity). When understood and correlated, these terms form a semantic web that begins to make apparent the essential content of the new thinking. The definitions in this glossary are intended to help the neophyte reader get started: they are basic rather than thoroughgoing, and at points they are suggestive—like a musical motif, koan, or imaginative conceit (at times verging on cheeky). Indications are given as to where these terms are elaborated in Leahy's oeuvre, and a comprehensive Leahy bibliography is offered in the back matter to this volume.

For their astute corrections and suggestions to improve this glossary I wish to thank Todd Carter, Michael James Dise, Alina N. Feld, and Charles Stein. Todd Carter proposed the entire definition of *anypothetotopia* and Michael James Dise proposed several one-sentence formulations indicated with his initials in brackets: [M.J.D.]. —L.M.

absolute (adj.)
Thoroughgoingly, demonstratively, and independently the case, needing nothing outside itself.

actuality, absolute
The thinking/creating/existing now that excludes past and future. *See:* creation ex nihilo; time.

analogy of being, absolute
In the TNO the creature is identical with the Creator without any trace of the idealism that has hitherto dominated all forms of modern Western thought; in other words, the body of incarnate Christ is God. "In the mind of God the creature exists absolutely. In the mind of the creature God exists absolutely. This is for the first time the *absolute* analogy of being," which is to say, "the embodied soul's consciousness of its *essentially corporeal, artifactual, relation to God*" (F, 579). In the biblical declaration *Et verbum caro factum est* ("and the Word is made flesh"), the *factum* gives rise to the English word *fact*: the fact of existence. Existence is a fact, and what God and creature share in (and as) absolute fact is existence. This sharing occurs in one artifactual Body. *See:* artifactual body

anypothetotopia
A thinking/revelation that supplants utopian thinking. Utopian thinking is a thinking that is not placed, that is nowhere, that essentially does not create the world. Anypothetotopian thinking, by contrast, is absolutely *there/here*, absolutely *Da,* a thinking/being/doing that creates the world absolutely immediately. Utopian thinking is beholden to a fallen world, perpetually attempting to find rest in placing thought outside itself in a land of nowhere. Anypothetotopian thinking is absolute placedness itself. "Unlike utopian thinking which is thinking not being placed, being nowhere, not being here/now—not creating the world, essentially apocalyptic thinking, created omnipotence here and now, is *anypothetotopian*, absolutely places, absolutely *Da*/here, absolutely now. Qua *anypothetotopian*, far from being just another story/idea, the thinking now occurring/essentially apocalyptic thinking for the first time is the absolutely real story/schema/idea—not the simulacrum of the absolute idea, not the simulacrum of omnipotence itself, not

the representation of a reality but absolutely the reality" (Appendix 3, BS, 269). *Anypothetotopian* thinking thinks "the place beyond beyond place for the first time," founded in the cornerstones of the Ethic of Simplicity: Gratitude/Readiness/Discretion/Beneficence. "The Last Judgment makes manifest that it is this world, fallen and blind to revelation, whose existence is finally *utopia*; while it is the new heaven and the new earth of the apocalypse whose existence for the first time is *anypothetotopia*, absolutely t/here, absolutely *Da*" (Appendix 4, BS, 286). [definition by Todd Carter]

apocalyptic "I"
The apocalyptic I is that which says "I" in the beginning, after the vanishment of self and the advent of absolute objectivity, for which there is no such thing, essentially, as subjectivity. "This I, invisible, infinitely transparently the surface of the body, shucks off the form of the me. I is no longer the matter of the *form* of me. Here the consciousness of the beginning . . . transcends the pre-consciousness accusative case of the self immemorially bound to the other in the thought of Levinas" (FP, 156; my italics). The I is now the actually received object (FP, 157). This I, qua essential singularity, is the active embodiment/essential body now being created through absolutely productive receptivity of an infinite number of others in one material Body; as such it is both universal and particular at once, both an imperishable individual and an absolute discontinuity of the continuum [M.J.D.]. The I is the complete *matter* of the body's unmirrored consciousness; the infinitely transparent I is the surface identifying body and world absolutely: "Every I that I meet objectively is not me; yet I meet it completely in differentiating it. The face-to-face of perfectly other I's is a unity perfectly differentiated" (FP, 159). The self-annihilating I of modernity is a waste of I-saying in solipsism, insubstantiality, and anxiety, whereas the apocalyptic I is not wasted but absolutely fulfilled, plenary. For the fullest elaboration in Leahy's work of the apocalyptic I and the *I* vis-à-vis *me*, see "Thinking in the Third Millennium: Looking without the Looking Glass" (FP, 143–63). *See:* productive receptivity; self; world society

appropriation
Existence qua reception of absolute Gift renders appropriation inappropriate. Absolute otherness forfends that there could be any sense in saying "my" or keeping for/to one's *self*; omnipotence is not lacking anything that it should appropriate, and every notion of *self*-hood or

"owning" or "enowning" (as in Heidegger) is consigned to forms of thinking of the past. Where there is no nothing, there is no actual scarcity: nothing is able to be removed from the essential wholeness of existence (BS, 192). The transcendental essence of existence is absolute plentitude and repletion in the form of sharing but not having (F, 628). The minimum existing is a maximum. *See:* ethic of simplicity; new world order; minimum; unicity

artifactual body
The artifactual body is the absolutely self-less body now being created, co-creating a new humanity for which the means is the end absolutely (F, 560) and ends are absolutely means (BS, 175). Not thought representing the body, but thought ending in essence, where essence *is* the existence of the body: thought the body itself, absolutely inclusive of matter. The perception that thought is the fullness of being, the conception that the being of God is the material existence of thought (F, 580). All facts are artifacts actually created in the moment they hold sway. But this does not imply that facts do not hold sway. They hold sway absolutely as a matter of fact. *See also:* body; unicity

ban of sacred doctrine
See: interdict of sacred doctrine

beginning
Beginning is *to begin now*. Essential beginning cannot be construed in the past tense ("we were beginning to understand," "when God began to create"), but rather signifies as present participle or far rather as present imperative ("begin right this second!" "begin the show!"). The absolute origin is now. Now is the moment of beginning *in principio* ("In the beginning," Gen 1:1). Beginning is the newness of mind, the receptive productivity, the productive receptivity that is *creating now*. Sheer receptivity experiences itself as nothing but other-productive (BS, 156). It actively produces the Gift received. In the beginning (Gen 1:1), "it is finished" (John 19:28–30).

beyond beyond *x*
A notion that first appears in *Beyond Sovereignty*. When we get "beyond *x*," the *beyond* that we reach bears in itself its consequential relation to—remains in the tow or thrall of—the very *x* we leave behind. "Beyond beyond *x*" is Leahy's terminological shorthand for saying that all residual influence and aftereffects of *x* are categorically eliminated in principle

(*in principio*) and in fact. New creation makes this possible. Absolute actuality means, in addition to many other things (*all* things!), the drag of "the past" on the actual here-and-now is banished, as is the spectral thrall of "the future." *See:* hitherto; now for the first time

body (the Body)
Body, material incarnation, the actual creation/subsistence of existence itself, is all in all, embodying an infinite number of bodies/others, and "as many truths as there are bodies" (BS, xiv). The world not yet matter itself existing is precluded (F, 93). "The world itself in essence is the body, the identification in essence of man with God in essence" (NM, 348); this sentence repeats "in essence" three times, each modifying a different noun, hence the distinctive logical sense of each must be thought. *See:* foundation; matter

created omnipotence
The foundationless thinking of the universe, which creates the universe. There is nothing omnipotence is able to do that it does not actually do. Hence, omnipotence itself is absolute actuality (BS, 208), absolute creation ex nihilo. The essential person qua apocalyptic I is the created omnipotence or Gift that, qua incarnate Word, actively co-creates in the midst of the Body with the infinite others in an absolute society [M.J.D.]. *See:* apocalyptic "I"; uncreated omnipotence

creation ex nihilo
What now occurs is that the logic of creation is the essence of thought (F, 368, 356). To think—that is, to perceive, conceive, hypothesize, smell, taste, sense, cogitate, dream, feel, intuit, imagine, hope, emote—is to create. Creation is understood to be *creating* (present participle), that is, actively creating now ex nihilo, where the nihil is not a literal nothing but an existence aborning *ex abysso*. To begin is to create, to create is to begin. We cannot *not* begin, we can only begin badly. An uncreated world does not exist (NM, 4), therefore, we face the inescapable ethical imperative to create. To create is objectivity itself (F, 585). Creation is not a matter of causality but of noncausal efficacy: it is all effect, no cause, due to the absolute discontinuity of the continuum. *See:* ethical imperative; discontinuity of the continuum

death of God
The death of the uniquely Christian God, which is not perfectly begun in European consciousness (from Descartes to Hegel, Nietzsche, and

Heidegger), is in American consciousness the absolute beginning (Altizer): absolute death enacts pure Nothing for the first time, which simultaneously enacts the beginning of the selfless self (F, 597). Absolute death is the *conditio sine qua non* of Resurrection, rendering the latter absolutely actual and apocalyptically complete. The beginning of God was not merely the death of God, but the death of the God who could not truly become incarnate (F, 595). God is in fact being there in the absolute nullification of God (NM, 364), indeed, in the absolute nullification of the Trinity (BS, 264). As the author of this glossary would attempt to characterize it, the new thinking understands itself to be the absolute creativity of GH (where GH is defined as *God absolutely multiplied by humanity*) at work in co-creating the world after the death of God. The world now being created is the artifactual body of God: the Resurrection of God qua second absolute after the death of God qua first absolute. Absolute death inaugurates the new world order. *See:* artifactual body; new world order

difference
In the TNO there is no concept of "same"; identity is not a matter of "not the same as something else." The difference that is identity is not a function of any comparison, positive or negative. There is absolute (nonrelative) particularity—that is, absolutely different existents—for the first time: an infinite number of nonrelatively different (absolutely different) existents absolutely relating with one another (BS, 262). *See:* differentiation, absolute; transcendental difference

differentiation, absolute
The absolute uniqueness of all things—absolute unicity—ensures that difference is *absolutely* (not relatively) different for the first time in the TNO (BS, 192). *See*: particularity; transcendental difference; unicity

discontinuity of the continuum, absolute
The parts of the universal Body are independent (free) but not unrelated. The TNO wholly eliminates the notion of causality. Neither is there room for entropy. Essential newness means having occurred as of now, having ceased as of now: the universe as miraculous birth. It is not trending or sliding or verging. It is not in process. It exists *ex abysso*. *See:* unicity

edge, absolute
Where is the point of contact with the world within the world? The meshing takes place at the edge: in the case of the universe as a whole, it takes place at the absolute edge, the infinitely shared edge (F, 586–87). To create is the absolute edge upon which cannot be projected any a priori thing, any thing from before the edge of the totality of being now (F, 585). Existence *is* the creative edge of existence. Beginning is the beginning-of-the-other at the point of contact, at the absolute edge, where the apocalyptic "I" receives the Gift. For more, see Edward S. Casey, "Concerning the Absolute Edge" (chapter 10). *See:* apocalyptic "I"; productive receptivity

epoch of the One
The epoch of the One now beginning is the end of all epochs. The One now actually existing, qua unity/unicity beyond the One, is the essence of history (F, 354–55). *See:* history; new world order; time; unicity; world society

essence
In the TNO, as in Aristotle, essence is actual individual existence (see NM, 48, re. Aristotle). Essence qua existent individuality, the auto-identity of a thing qua existing, means *a thing actually is what it is.* The intellect is immediately certain that simple existence is *bound up with being what it is*. Essence is for Aristotle a distinction in being, beyond nature (NM, 55). In the TNO, by contrast, the essence of essence is content, therefore not beyond nature, and content is essentially absolute differentiation through and through. Given that essence is existence itself, the activity of an *essentially* new thinking (creating the other) actually creates the *essential* newness of existence. Here "essentially new" is distinguished from "formally" or "materially" new: the essentially new implies a substantial change, an absolute change of identity, a transfiguration, a metanoia. *See:* nature; substance; transcendental essence of existence; metanoia

ethic of simplicity
Now the intelligibility of God is absolute simplicity. Why so? In what sense a simplicity? It is a transparency in which nothing is hidden. The mystery that abides is the mystery of visibility: "The God of Revelation has no secrets. Omnipotence itself absolutely exposed—absolutely

outside—for the first time. . . . There is absolutely and essentially no plan. . . . This being of omnipotence itself without plan . . . this being absolutely now, is creating love" (BS, 208–209). The ethic of simplicity beholds (like Levinas) a particularity otherwise than the universal, a particularity beyond the Same, but not (contra Levinas) otherwise than being (BS, 55). The creaturely life of the Godhead is now for the first time infinitely digital, infinitely parsed, infinitely particular, and infinitely deictic (BS, 209). Per the minimum order of the trinary logic, the fourth dimension of the ethic of simplicity, gratitude, *embodies* its first three dimensions: readiness, discretion, beneficence. The fourth dimension, omnipotent embodiment, is the beginning of absolute polyontological difference, the absolute distribution of existence itself for the first time identically the Distributor (i.e., Godhead) (BS, 86–87, 209). The limitation of Levinas's metaphysical ethics is that it transcends the order of essence *in*essentially. As the apocalyptic "I" is the beginning of consciousness of essence as absolute gift of being, the ethics indicated by this beginning is not a metaphysical ethics but a *physical* ethics, an ethics of the existing body (FP, 158). For more on the physical ethics, see Nathan Tierney, "The Ethic of Simplicity" (chapter 7), Todd Carter, "The Vanishment of Evil from the World" (chapter 8), and Alina N. Feld, "The Transparency of the Good" (chapter 9). *See:* simplicity; ethical imperative

ethical imperative
The absolute ethical imperative is the imperative to create the world. "To attend essentially to the essentially new world is to create the new world (= the good or the global imperative of the new global ethics and morality)" (BS, Appendix 4, 285). This "attending essentially" is also described as productive receptivity. For further elaboration, see "imperative to create" in the index to *Beyond Sovereignty*. *See:* productive receptivity

eucharist of existence
The essentially new substance, the word made flesh, logic for the first time understood to coincide with existence itself, a completely new universe, the flesh and blood of God (NM, 338, 344, see also 341, 350; BS, 42, 260). Every existent shares in this substantiality—each uniquely and irreducibly. It is the substantive identity of *novitas mundi* and *novitas mentis*. *See:* existence; *missa jubilaea*; substance; world society

ex abysso

Leahy often uses the term *ex abysso* rather than *ex nihilo* to forfend the connotation of creation from or "out of" a literal nothing. Creation begins from the minimum, not from nothing. There is no literal nothing in the TNO, but rather a creative nothing symbolized in the "zero not nothing" of the trinary logic. *See:* minimum; nothing; zero not nothing

existence

Existence is indubitable for the thinking now occurring. The Incarnation is a matter of fact. Essential matter, substance, exists absolutely. The essential existence of everything for the first time (in and for this new thinking) precludes the inessential matter of phenomenology (Kant through Husserl), the "consciousness of absolutely nothing in essence, of everything being related to nothing in essence," that is, stuck in a Being/Nothing binarity (F, 93). Absolute body—the Body itself—exists. This is why *nothing* does not exist and why zero cannot be nothing in the trinary logic of the TNO. There is neither nothing nor something prior to foundation itself for the first time: *exsistere ipsum ex nihilo* (F, 139). This is the foundational logic of creation: it multiplies zero not nothing (the minimum) and absolute essential existence. Transcendence absolutely begins in the novelty of history itself (NM, 14). Existence itself is *essentially* historical; history is the story of Incarnation aborning, the story that now witnesses the identity of story and storyteller. The teller is the telling itself, the story told. The promise of existence itself exists only in the absolute novelty of history itself in the world (NM, 15). *Verbum caro factum est.* God not existing—not transcending into existence—would not be God. *See:* transcendental essence of existence

finite omnipotence

See: created omnipotence

first absolute

The First Person of the Trinity, or that totality which is absolutely transcended in existence by the second absolute, absolute existence itself, the Body: "The second absolute is the existence of the first absolute." God inexistent (infinite/uncreated omnipotence) is revealed in God existent (finite/created omnipotence). The first absolute is known through the second absolute as the absolute itself, or as Leahy expresses this: "The second by which the first is the second is the absolute itself" (F, 111). *See:* second absolute; third absolute

for the first time
Not heretofore actual, therefore not heretofore (thought/perceived/known to be) the case.

foundation
Universal existence ex nihilo, the Body itself, is the absolute foundationless foundation. This metaphor of foundation invokes telluric connotations that might lead to misunderstanding. In the TNO there is no foundation on which the building stands, there is only *absolute building* (understood as an active present participle, as in "we are building"). Upon *this* foundation there is nothing to be erected; this is the coping-stone of existence itself (F, 45). This foundation is everywhere, all material/substantial existence is foundation for the infinite profusion of alio-relatedness: "This passion of existence absolutely creates itself/itself creates absolutely. . . . This for the first time absolutely passionate creation of the world, this beginning of the absolutely passionate making of the actuality of the world, is the foundation, firmer than which none can be conceived, of an absolute world society now beginning to exist for the first time in history" (F, 198, see also 138). *See*: body; existence; Fourthness; world society

Fourthness
Fourthness is absolute novelty, the *beginning* qua foundation of order (BS, 257n27). It is omnipotence itself the embodiment of absolute alterity/objectivity (BS, 49). Leahy adopts and transforms Charles Sanders Peirce's categories of Firstness, Secondness, and Thirdness by introducing Fourthness (F, 457–62, 558–60). In both the abstract formality of the trinary logic and the existential logic of creation, Fourthness is the minimum order. Both formally and existentially, Fourthness precedes Firstness in the TNO (F, 460–61, FP 117). Fourthness is a *new* Firstness, the *Very* First (BS, 49), a real triadic unity (BS, 240; F, 289, 613). Fourthness is the logical expression of Godhead actually incarnate: Three Persons absolutely One transcending into existence ex nihilo (F, 612–13). Fourthness does not create folds or layers of complexity but rather a transparent unicity. Fourthness is the unity beyond the One: existing absolute unicity. The fourfold identity of the One, which is the foundation, has the form of a tetratomic identity free from any dichotomic element—a logical feat

of which Hegel dreamed, and which Peirce did not believe possible (F, 289). For the clearest capsule summary of Fourthness in Leahy's work, see BS, 240–41n42 and 257n27. *See:* minimum order; first absolute; second absolute; third absolute; *Very* First

history
Existence itself is *essentially* historical (NM, 15). The transcendental thinking now occurring knows the object to be as such *essentially unhistorical* (eternal, uncreated), while at the same time knows the object to be *in existence historically* (created). This is not the conversion of temporal to eternal being, nor of transcendent to transcendental existence. "But, taken up as it is with the transcendental essence of existence itself (beyond every point of view in essence, being itself *ho logos katholikos*), it is the perpetual inversion of every object . . . to existence itself. . . . It is the *absolute end of reflection in existence*" (NM, 17). *See:* perception of the history of being; time

hitherto
Hitherto is used to denote forms of thinking that preceded the TNO and that are now consigned to being thinking of the past, no longer pertaining per se, though still thinkable qua past thinking. "For the first time" would be its contrastive correlate; for example, "hitherto the cogito emulated and imitated the ratio of God, whereas now for the first time essential thinking creates the object." It is not a question of the thinking hitherto having been in error or mistaken, but having been reasonable and tenable in its epoch, an epoch that has now been brought to an end by the new thinking. All forms of fundamental thinking hitherto are respected as good-faith historical expressions of reason. *See:* for the first time

identity
All that, inclusively, which a particular individual exists as, and in that sense *is*. The very essence of identity is existence. *See:* essence

individual
The individual is the absolutely unique particular existent, the *relative absolute* (see BS, 249–57, especially 254–55); a person either uncreated (a Person of the Trinity) or created (all other persons). *See:* particularity; person

infinite finitude
The infinite is meta-identically the finite, the finite essentially infinite (F, 319, BS, 183). This coheres with *absolute unicity* qua unity and simplicity at once, and coheres with indifference to the dichotomies time–eternity and transcendence–immanence. In the essentially new logic, in which for the first time the universe is absolutely infinite, the a priori = the a posteriori; the universe is the experience of nothing a priori (F, 281). *See:* unicity

infinitely flat structure of the universe
A projective geometry of the trinary logic (in which zero does not equal nothing), in which the zero dimension is a point that has position, and is therefore measurable, resulting in a thoroughgoing metamorphosis of geometric relations (see F, 313–19). The geometry of the infinitely flat structure of the universe predicts rigidity rationally using one formula for both two and three dimensions, a simplification that is possible because vertices count identically as edges, as the vertex is itself the beginning of the edge. For the first time the structure of the universe is completely vertical, completely flat; the infinite is meta-identically the finite, the essentially imperfect is perfectly identical with the perfect (F, 319). But here "perfect" does not exclude change (BS, 183). *See:* trinary logic

interdict of sacred doctrine
Modernity ultimately loses God, loses faith, loses being. Why? In Aristotle's metaphysics, essence included existence. In Thomas Aquinas, by contrast, essence becomes form or nature, and the existence of an essence can only be given by God. According to Leahy's analysis, the doubt of modern science undoubtedly derives from sacred doctrine: Once Aristotle's essential light of intellect becomes in Thomas Aquinas the (created, thus contingent) natural light of reason, then sacred doctrine illuminated by God's light is explicitly *alone* possessed of certitude, while other sciences operate in the doubtful light of nature (NM, 59). In the light of natural reason, apart from God, humanity sees itself *inessentially* existing, not possessing in itself a sufficient cause of its own existence (NM, 20). Identity is no longer existentially significant. Essence reduced to form is a merely potential existence. But it is just this that God's humiliation of man brings into existence: an ordering of man's practical life, qua practical, to eternity (here Leahy echoes Kierkegaard). God knows being's particularity—other-

wise metaphysical—to be his own creation. In creating, God empties himself of metaphysical reserve absolutely. For sacred doctrine it is not God who is abstract; rather, it is metaphysics. It is intellect, not God, that suffers abstraction. God particularizes (incarnates) in the act of creation (NM, 62–63). Metaphysics drives God's creation to abstraction, producing the concepts of Being and literal nothingness. Whereas creation is the diametric identity of being and nothing: for the first time the discontinuity of being and nothing is the very form of thought (F, 628). "As never before the impasse of ontology is very existence" (BS, 300). Only this line of analysis can account for modernity's ontological impasse, zeroing out not only God, but also itself, in inessentiality and insubstantiality. Sacred doctrine is the prevenient condition for the *paranoia* of modern thought. But now the interdict (ban) of sacred doctrine is lifted: no longer is there need for faith to take up a position outside the world in order to move the world; the TNO is the logic of faith itself existing in essence (NM, 372, ix). *See:* paranoia; transcendental form of natural reason; sovereignty

matter
Matter is "the Incarnation *assaulting* thinking" (F, xiii). Matter exists absolutely and is the principle of objective individuality. "The proclamation now occurring for the first time precludes the world not yet matter itself existing. . . . This is the miracle, the manna of consciousness itself, the subsistence of existence" (F, 93). *See:* body; essence; substance

meta-identity
Creation ex nihilo is the meta-identity of zero not nothing (0), unum ($\bar{0}$), and one (1) in the trinary logic of creation. The meta-identity of the Trinity is creation ex nihilo. In the TNO, Godhead meta-identifies as the universe. See: *missa jubilaea;* Trinity; triple nothingness of the Trinity

metanoia
Change of mind, a conversion or transformation of thinking. In the TNO this is not merely a new thinking, to think new thoughts, but an *essentially* new thinking: a thinking that *creates* new essence. "Nothing in thought is innate. There exist in essence no preconceptions; there is in essence no idea whatsoever" (NM, 343). For an essentially new thinking, the world is ever an actual absolute newness. *See: novitas mentis; novitas mundi*

minimum
The minimum is the second absolute—the actuality of the body itself *ex abysso*—not merely a place but the place of the beginning of absolute place (F, 111), which is existence. Existence is the minimum. Colloquially, we can say that the minimum is that than which nothing greater can *exist,* and so, with a minimum like this, who needs a maximum? "Nothing is to be added to the minimum itself. . . . [There is] no possibility not the absolute actuality of the minimum being itself a maximum" (F, 111). There is no potentiality in the minimum because everything that makes the minimum maximal is actual (like Spinoza's God in this respect, but Spinoza's God is self-necessitated whereas the Trinity of the TNO is pure freedom directed to the other, pure otherness through and through, pure gift giving, pure outgoing selflessness, all for love and nothing for reserve). Beginning now anew, creation *ex abysso* actualizes the zero that is not nothing (0) to coincide the minimum (not nothing, unum, $\bar{0}$) to specify the universe (one, 1); this is not a transition from a literal nothing to the universe, but the diametric *identity* of being and nothing in the work of beginning. Metaphorically speaking, the absolute beginning "engages" nothing and being, but eliminates them by supervenience. Metaphysically speaking, human reason abstracts Being and Nothing (pure zero) from creation, which per se is neither/nor. Creation is symbolized logically in the equation $0\bar{0}1$ (F, 255–86, BS 156); the basic elements of this logical structure are distinct but meta-identified in creation itself. *See:* second absolute; Fourthness

minimum order
The minimum order is not to be confused with the minimum, its existential starting point. Leahy adopts and transforms Charles Sanders Peirce's categories of Firstness, Secondness, and Thirdness by introducing Fourthness. In the abstract formality of the trinary logic, Fourthness is the minimum order, Firstness is the minimum within that order. Fourthness qua minimum order is often represented by Leahy in the form of a cube, which is then extended and elaborated in the hypercube and latticework. Correlatively, in the minimum order of the existential logic of creation, Fourthness precedes Firstness. Because Fourthness is the minimum order, the relations between Firstness, Secondness, and Thirdness can be thought as a unity. Fourthness is the body in which the three basic orders (Firstness, Secondness, and Thirdness, or 0, $\bar{0}$, 1) co-relate infinitely. Although formally speaking they are ordinal, they multiply and co-ordinate absolutely in the

syncretic act of creation such that the resultant fusion—Fourthness—is all in all. Fourthness is the beginning qua foundation of order, making it the Absolute Middle or Absolute Third that superordinates Thirdness per se, and also making it the New Firstness that superordinates the precedence of Firstness per se (F, 613, 627; BS, 10). "Fourthness is the intervening subvention constituting the Identity of Possibility and Measurable Actuality" (BS, 257n27). See also FP, 131–41. This is the most decisive notion in the TNO: the very firstness that is logically arrived at last, the capstone that becomes the transcendental foundation-stone. *See:* Fourthness; foundation; *Very* First

missa jubilaea
The transubstantiation of God into world, also identified as the infinite Passover (NM, 344–96). *See:* this is *IT*, there is nothing more (or less) to see

modernity
An era characterized by unhappy consciousness due to its default of essence, an inescapable nihilism or inessentiality (from Descartes and Pascal through Hegel, Nietzsche, Kierkegaard, Heidegger, Husserl). The TNO sees the bright side: modernity's "being disappointed in existence is recognized to be a determination of the final result of the appropriation of the appearance of the transcendental essence of existence itself to thought" (NM, 15). Roughly paraphrased, this means that modern consciousness pines for a blessed telos, a God or God-equivalent, that is, alas, lost, past, dead, zeroed out—not realizing that this default and this loss is the very condition of the divine Parousia. The question after modernity for the TNO is not where God is, but where God is not. The answer: nowhere. After the death of God, the world too is essentially transcendent existence, is God. After the death of the modern ego, the apocalyptic "I" too is essentially transcendent existence, is God. Time and eternity, transcendence and immanence belong to the same essential history. The TNO transcends modernity in a way that fulfills modernity: "In the actual realization of the modern project . . . the modern is absolutely not" (F, 455). *See:* interdict of sacred doctrine; paranoia; self; sovereignty

new world order
Novitas Mundi and *Foundation* announce the undeniable historical advent of a new world order. Although Leahy does not address explicitly how neoliberal forces have parasitized this advent, he does

so implicitly in his analysis of Marx (F, 10–88). Leahy employs the phrase "new world order" (F, 251–62) in a logical-ontological sense that is categorically other than the term's contemporary mainstream association with neoliberalism, which—with respect to the glorification of *proprietas*—stands for attachments that refuse and forestall the new world order of absolute nonpossessiveness denoted in the TNO: a new transmural polyontological thinking, a new hyperdimensional logic, a new infinitely saturated actuality now being thought/articulated/created. Appropriation is inappropriate in the new world order. *Proprietas* is an absolute failure to love, to receive and share in the beloved, the holy of holies: the transfiguration of the world into Godhead incarnate. *See:* appropriation; world society

nothing
There is no such thing as "nothing" in the TNO. This thinking *"does not contend with Nothing,"* it neither affirms nor denies the termination of the essence in existence, it has nothing to say in its own behalf except that it *is*, that it now exists (NM, 8). "In the thinking now occurring it is impossible even to conceive of a condition of which the predicate 'no information' would be true" (BS, 156). The nothing that we *think* is not a nothing; thinking makes it a "nothing not zero" that is not-nothing. "There is nothing able to not-be. There is not nothing. There is *is*. There is not *is not*. There is difference. Difference is not *is not* (nothing). Difference is. Difference is absolutely different for the first time" (BS, 192). Nothingness is always ex nihilo, always and everywhere the beginning: "Now for the first time in history it is able to be essentially comprehended that the very Nothing is created, is existence after nothing, is existence not sourced in nothing" (F, 383). *See:* creation ex nihilo; *ex abysso*; existence; zero not nothing

novitas mentis
Newness of mind in Latin. In the TNO, as existence now thinks itself objectively/historically/essentially—thinks the identity of the knower and the known, of the story and the storyteller (NM, 9, 14, 179; F, 455)—*novitas mentis* is essentially identical to *novitas mundi*. In this thinking it is not the case that mind "mirrors" the world ideally but rather that mind *creates* the world—not materially but essentially. Materially, the world is given qua *factum*—a gift, a fact—which can be denoted existence itself, the minimum; but *essentially* the world must now be created. Newness of mind is the essential creation of the

newness of the world. Quite simply, newness of the world *is* newness of mind now creating; newness of mind *is* newness of the world now creating. World *exists* mind, mind *exists* world. This is not a twofold but an absolute unicity: absolute existence now (pure otherness) as absolute Gift offered/received/shared infinitely. In the TNO the form of mind or freedom is the actual atonement of creature and Creator: "Here is Mind . . . the actual at-one-ment of Nature & Logic" (FP, 140). *See:* thinking now occurring for the first time

novitas mundi
Newness of the world in Latin. "The essential state of the world's novelty" (NM, 343). Thinking the world essentially now (*novitas mentis*) creates the world now (*novitas mundi*). The world that exists now absolutely is created *ex abysso* as newness of mind. Here is Nature "mind & logic immediately" (FP, 140), that is, existentially absolute. See: *novitas mentis*

now, absolute
See: actuality

objectivity, absolute
Absolute objectivity is actual. There is no room for subjectivity. Otherness is essentially all that is; all that is, is essential otherness. Because there is no subjectivity, no self, there is no such thing as self-relation. Alio-relativity is all. All relations are external and substantial, a matter of alterity, making them objective as opposed to subjective. There is no transcendent differentiation of the object from being itself; the object is thinking itself qua existence itself for the first time in history (F, 97). The *Ding an Sich* is eliminated inasmuch as all phenomena are essentially noumenal; the appearance of the body is real, the real appears as the surface of phenomenological transparence. The Body, the universe, shows itself everywhere in its "simplicity" as appearance to mind. Mind holds (*be*-holds) the body in its substantial actuality. Mind-body dualism is absolutely overcome in the *arti-factual* body, known to itself as a matter of fact (*fait accompli*, perfect factum, done deal qua creative coincidence of absolute beginning and absolute ending). "For the first time the Very Godhead speaks the Word intimately to everyone living in the universe in the form of the absolute exteriority of existence" (F, 615). *See:* artifactual body; creation ex nihilo; simplicity; substance

omnipotence
See: created omnipotence; first absolute; uncreated omnipotence

paranoia
Leahy considers modern thought a *paranoia,* meaning madness in Greek—to think amiss, to misconceive—the mistake of madness being everywhere a substitution of appearance for reality (NM, 121). This paranoia is manifest from Descartes forward as "a progressive displacement of reality itself (*noumena*) by appearances (*phenomena*), so that reason perceives itself beside itself, perceives beside things intelligible in themselves of which it knows nothing (*noumena*) appearances (*phenomena*) of which alone it has knowledge" (NM, 122). Exemplary case in point would be Kant's *Ding an Sich*. Pure reason is beside itself in a structural schism by which it is objectively divided from itself by that infinite indifference to particularity, qua particularity, that constitutes its transcendental unity. This pure reflection is neither knowledge nor faith, but purely subjective. Through its peculiar "mistake" (miss take, taking amiss) modern science dissociates knowledge from reality itself (NM, 122–23). The effective antidote to paranoia is metanoia. With the conversion from paranoia to metanoia, "history's absolutely creative essence" appears (NM, 5). "Before now the self-consciousness of the nothingness [*das Nichts*] of the creation displaced the very ground of mind in the form of the end of history. The beginning of the mediation of existence now occurring is the absolute immediacy of the Word displacing the groundlessness of the mind" (F, 615). *See:* interdict of sacred doctrine; metanoia; modernity; transcendental form of natural reason

particularity, absolute
The absolutely unconditioned individuality and discrete uniqueness of all things. Every point has its unique measurable location. Absolute particularity ensures that no individual existence is "grounded in" or dependent on another. The body is unicity all the way up, all the way down, where *unicity* is understood in its double sense as uniqueness and unity. Absolute particularity is the principle of unicity: absolute unity beyond the One. *See:* unicity; unity beyond the One

perception
"The object, qua existing species, is the absolutely immediate existence of thought itself. Qua this actually existing species, i.e., qua magni-

tude, the object is the magnitude of perception itself existing. This is the absolute relativity of the object itself measuring thought itself: the object of perception *is* the absolutely unconditioned transcendence of the absolute, *is* actuality itself. The object is not merely actual, but transcendently actual" (F, 118–19). *See:* creation; objectivity

perception of the history of being
Fundamental ontological thinking as it is recorded in the history of Western philosophy and theology. Since there is no distinction between conception and perception in the TNO, the "perception of being" is the primal and original thinking of being, which brings being and/or existence to birth in a specific historical (epochal) form. *See:* history; transcendental dichotomy

person
It is absolutely comprehended that being itself is a person (F, 154). Personality is absolute objectivity; the body is the person, the absolutely concrete identity of a certain existence (F, 184–85). Each particular person is absolute personality, but absolutely specific personality is three Persons (BS, 262). See "The Person as Absolute Particular," Appendix 1 in BS (249–57). *See:* differentiation, absolute; individual

philosophy and theology
For the first time thought in essence omnipotence is nothing but existence itself: "There is neither philosophy nor theology. There is nothing but the thinking now occurring" (BS, 93).

politics
Politics as it has variously been enacted and understood hitherto, historically and theoretically, pertains strictly to the past. The new humanity constituted in the TNO is apocalyptically "beyond beyond politics" in view of the beginning of an essentially transmural consciousness (F, 526–27; see also BS, 173–74). The new nonpolitics beyond politics, beyond sovereignty, is the ethic of simplicity (BS, xx, xxii, 193). Ends are absolutely means for the first time; means and ends are identical: "The Good is to create the world here and now" (BS, 175). Matter, the Body itself, "knows nothing of walls or classes," that is, neither exterior division nor interior division, but, rather, a perfect distinguishability of its elements (BS, 182–85). *See:* beyond beyond *x*; ethical imperative; world society

productive receptivity
To create the world is a labor of divine love in faith. Faith operates substantially in no other activity than in creating. Faith is an act of attention, attentive receptivity, not will. Attention to the object, the Body, creates what it beholds; this was introduced in *Novitas Mundi* as "the moment of thought's being *reception* itself" (NM, 338). This notion is carried further in *Beyond Sovereignty*, in which sheer receptivity "experiences itself as nothing but other-productive"; existence itself is absolutely and essentially construction, the writing of the absolute text of existence (BS, 156). Existence beginning absolutely now is existence qua absolutely unconditioned productive receptivity (BS, 238, see also xxii). Productive receptivity is an attention to the object that actually creates the object (the loved one). Expressed in traditional trinitarian terms, this activity would be called the work of the Holy Spirit, which is the spiration of the Father and the Son. The Father creates ex nihilo (the creative 0), the Son is incarnated ex nihilo ($\bar{0}$), and the Holy Spirit creates (creatively receives) the Gift (1), in creational co-equality with the Father and the Son. These distinct Persons are meta-identical. Where receptive productivity is creation (1), $1 = 10\bar{0}$ (BS, 193). *See:* creation ex nihilo; ethical imperative

reality
See: actuality

reason
Existence is infinitely, apocalyptically rational. Reason (logic) is its real measure. Logic for the first time coincides with existence itself (NM, 338). What exists is "existed" by logic all the way down, all the way up, all the way through. Absolute reason measures reason itself absolutely unconditionally, the absolute measure of totality itself ex nihilo (F, 138–40). Thought is absolutely the individuation of God himself (NM, 387). "Now thought thinks absolutely beyond the origin for the first time. . . . Beyond set and power set, beyond belonging and inclusion, beyond axiomatic ontology and excess, neither the one nor the void is conceivably the point of the ontologically real. As never before the impasse of ontology is very existence" (BS, 300). Reason (mind, logic, thinking) now articulates the transcendental essence of existence even as the transcendental essence of existence specifies reason as the "species-making species" (F, 559, 579). *See:* transcendental essence of existence

same
In the TNO there is no concept of "same" (BS, 262). *See:* difference; differentiation, absolute

second absolute
The Second Person of the Trinity, the minimum. The second absolute is the Incarnation, matter the body itself ex nihilo (F, 94). It is neither more nor less than the first absolute; the second absolute is the absolute transcendence in existence of the first absolute (F, 111). *Et verbum caro factum est* ("and the Word was made flesh"): here the *factum* of incarnation means Godhead is "in fact" a creature, is finite omnipotence—an actuality that is creating all things (*novitas mundi*), a creating of all things that is actual (*novitas mentis*). In terms of the Second Person's phenomenology: "The visible is the new species of reality itself. The thing appears absolutely. The thing exists absolutely *a posteriori* (is the second absolute)" (F, 154). *See:* the minimum

self
There is no self in the TNO. Subjectivity, selfhood, myself (*my* self), are notions of the past, utterly inessential; they do not and cannot pertain in the TNO. They constitute an inappropriate appropriation of existence, the Gift. "For the first time the absolute death of selfhood is thought" (F, 423). This thinking is not *to be* absolutely for another, but rather to *not-be* absolutely for another (NM, 396): to not-be as self, to be qua absolutely self-less. Correlatively, there is no such thing as self-relation; all relations are alio-relations. Self-less gratitude creates the other. *See:* ethical imperative; objectivity

simplicity
The notion of simplicity in the TNO can be expressed with exemplary clarity in German as *Einfachheit*. Absolute *Einfachheit* is the transparency, the visibility, of absolute particularity, with nothing hidden or enfolded. Simplicity is not alternative to complexity. "Such is the absolutely simple complexity, absolutely complex simplicity of the conception of creation . . . the perfect reduction of depth to surface. . . . The Face of God appearing for the first time as the face of existence: the divine and absolute superficiality of every actual thing ex nihilo" (F, 439–40). The absolute intelligibility of the text itself of existence, now being written, is plaintext (F, 154, BS, 160). In the TNO simplicity is identical with conception/perception (BS, 210). The operative struc-

ture of complex simplicity is the unity of the real trinary logic, which preserves the real differences in its constituents (zero, unum, one) in a perfectly differentiated unity, $0\overline{0}1$: infinite unity = absolute simplicity = omnipotence (BS, 293). *See:* unicity; unity beyond the One

sovereignty
Prior to faith in God there could be no "outside" of faith in God, sacred doctrine having first constituted the distinction between sacred and profane. The "ban of sovereignty or politics that has become the rule" presupposes the division of sacred and profane constituted by this interdict (BS, 198n5). The lifting of the ban of sacred doctrine is now occurring in the TNO, the beginning of an essentially transmural consciousness, appropriately expropriated from sovereignty, that knows nothing of walls or classes: absolute singularity beyond class, beyond beyond sovereignty (BS, 171). *See:* beyond beyond *x*; interdict of sacred doctrine; politics; unicity

subjectivity
Subjectivity, selfhood, *my* self, are notions of the past, utterly inessential and impertinent. *See:* self

substance
The incarnate body of God taken to be a matter of fact in the essential perception of transubstantiation. Transubstantiation is identically the beginning of substance. This thinking perceives—as a matter of *fact*—the beginning of substance (NM, 351), the second absolute. *See:* matter; second absolute

thinking now occurring for the first time (TNO)
This is a thinking that enacts the holy of holies: a transcendental faith-full thinking freely witnessing that existence is absolutely sacred (God) and that absolute sacrality (God) is existence; a thinking for which the perception of the body (the universe) is "God in God in essence," and "the center of an essentially new consciousness in the conversion of the universe into an entirely new stuff" (i.e., universal transubstantiation) (NM, 348). This recognition is produced "through no necessity whatsoever, but simply through the conception in essence of existence itself," which in this thinking involves—as a matter of fact—the beginning of substance (NM, 351), matter the Body itself. This thinking is the beginning of the identity of conception and per-

ception, of acting and thinking, of imagining and accomplishing (FP, 153), a thinking without boundaries, borders, or exclusions. Nothing lies outside the new thinking ("it's logic all the way down"), not even nothing, with one extravagant and telling exception: "The exception to everything-including-nothing is the absolutely objective being of the I otherwise than presence" (FP, 155; hyphens added). To understand this fine point of the TNO is to merit a gold star! *See:* apocalyptic "I"; transcendental essence of existence

third absolute
The Third Person of the Trinity. The Third Person Absolute is the spiration of the Father and the Son (F, 622, 628). The Trinity is itself the very First omnipotence. Absolute Second and Absolute Third were in the Absolute First and they were the *Very* First (BS, 49, 241; F, 289, 613). This is the beginning of being-in-itself-without-solitude (F, 622). Since the Third is immediately second to the First as well as to the Second, it is no less an absolute discrete identity than are each the first and the second (BS, 266). Each existing person is an absolute instance of the third absolute apart from which there is no third absolute, the place where there is absolute beginning at the edge of creation as the noncausal effect of omnipotence [M.J.D.]. Trinity embodies and thereby manifests the very essence of Fourthness. *See:* Fourthness

time
Time is now the absolute totality of being (F, 586). This implies a fulfillment of time in an essential history that is free from time. An observation of Hans Blumenberg may be helpful for grasping this: "An absolute beginning in time is itself, in its intention, timeless" (*The Legitimacy of the Modern Age*, trans. Robert M. Wallace [Cambridge: MIT Press, 1983], 145), except that Leahy would replace "in its intention" with *in its actuality*. Intentionality is blotted out by the repletion of actuality. What occurs in the TNO is the infinitesimal end of the "additive" notion of creation (F, 564), that is, the end of "becoming" and historical process. The consciousness of beginning is not a species of becoming (FP, 153); it is not "on the way" to something else, but is in itself absolute. The now is eternity not in an hour (as in Blake's poem), but in the absolute actuality of THIS EXISTENCE. "Now-for-the-first-time is the time absolutely" (F, 355; hyphens added). Everything that occurs happens *now* for the first time. In the transcendental dichotomy, historical time qua continuum of becoming yields

to an apocalyptic now that is absolutely "present perfect." The now is not *in* time but is an absolute now that is time-overcoming and time-vanquishing, but also time-constituting, indifferent to the polarity of time-eternity and to the dichotomy of transcendent/immanent (NM, 14–15, 6, 10; F, 101–102, 625). "The historical perpetuation of time is that now-evident fact through the essential perception of which this thinking now occurring is related to previous thought as through the essence of potentiality" (NM, 10). *See:* history; transcendental dichotomy

transcendental dichotomy
Only absolute beginning ensures the decisive cut of absolute end. Leahy's term *transcendental dichotomy* names this absolute watershed, this cutting edge, that signals the creation of an essentially new universe: *Dasein* is now the existence of the beginning, the beginning of existence (F, 425). This novelty institutes a bifurcation between historical becoming (process) and the now of absolute *metanoia*, which brings history, the sequentiality of historical time, to an end by virtue of being itself the beginning of existence (F, 455). The transcendental dichotomy is the fact that before now the absolute now is transcendent ("in heaven"), and that now for the first time the now is absolute existence ("heaven on earth"); that now for the first time consciousness *is* the world concretely and essentially. Before now, there exists the revolutionary imperative; now, for the first time, existence is essentially revolutionary: time itself actually opening and expanding into a world in the form of *time transcending temporality* (F, 454, 426). This absolute watershed, the transcendental dichotomy of time itself (F, 426), is the beginning of absolute history bringing history hitherto to an end in its own fulfillment. This dichotomy is the divide between "hitherto" and "now for the first time." It signals the absolute expropriation of sovereignty (the end of politics), the beginning of the epoch of the One, of absolute world society, as distinguished from all historical epochs hitherto. *See:* hitherto; for the first time; epoch of the One; sovereignty; world society

transcendental difference
Because the logic of creation establishes the diametric identity of being and nothing, for the first time the discontinuity of being and nothing is the very form of thought (F, 628). Time and eternity are transcendentally identified in the factuality of existence; the Kierkegaardian "infinite qualitative distinction between the temporal and the eternal" is now absolutely *aufheben*—God is *aufheben*—in Fourthness (BS, 264).

The transcendental thinking now occurring knows the object to be *essentially unhistorical* (eternal, uncreated) while at the same time *in existence historically* (created) (NM, 17). The difference between fact and reflection, or appearance and essence, is overcome by the essential priority of existence itself to being. The fact itself is essentially comprehended qua absolute (F, 5). Translated into simpler terms, this declares that actual existence creates being, not being existence. The world, qua Fourthness, creates God. In the unlimited ontology that thought itself now is, essence terminates in appearance itself; speech itself is the essential measure of (the conception in essence of) transcendental difference, is the thought itself of existence itself (F, 6). Now nothing, including thought itself, escapes the essential predicament of existence itself (F, 7). "There is [now for the first time] no fact or appearance transcendently different from the absolute transcendence of identity now occurring: there is now no immediacy whatsoever that is not 'in essence' the absolute" (F, 8). The irrational element of reason—the "immaterial"—is eliminated; now nothing is able to be said except it be matter of the body itself (F, 9). Matter is Godhead subsuming transcendence (transcendent difference) into transcendental difference (F, 70). In the *essential* dialectic of matter itself for the first time, every difference except the transcendental difference is overcome (F, 78), bringing to an absolute end the relative dialectics of Hegel and Marx. *See:* Fourthness; time

transcendental essence of existence
Actual Godhead creating essence. (The ambiguity in this sentence is intended: Godhead is creating essence, even as essence is Godhead-creating.) When an absolute creative pleroma is all there is, the distinction between Godhead and world is rendered past. *"What occurs now for the first time in history is the elemental reconstruction of the world essentially in the image of God"* (NM, 350). Now for the first time in history, *thinking begins in essence* (F, 339). Essence does not preexist thinking. Thinking creates essence. Thinking is this polyontological creating now. "This universe as a matter of fact . . . is not yet conceived in essence, coming into existence for the first time in history in the form of thought itself—essentially transcendental" (NM, 351). See: *missa jubilaea*

transcendental form of natural reason
Leahy uses this term to evoke the trajectory of modern reason in the wake of Thomas Aquinas as it fashioned itself into an instrumental

"pure reason," a structure of infinite indifference (NM, 125). "The enterprise of sacred doctrine freed reason from presupposing its own necessity, that is, from essential being's priority [as in Aristotle]. Its encounter with God left [reason] radically conscious of its own contingency, but this loss was reason's gain. It came to be a perfect instrument for knowing an object other than itself, qua other, as actually existing together with it in that totality of intelligibility that is God's creation. Its only presupposition was divine revelation—what, metaphysically, it is not possible to presuppose" (NM, 76). Modern thought takes up the transcendental form of natural reason from Thomas as the form of thought's very own existence, prescinding from nature, in Descartes, producing a subjective transcendentalism that "takes itself to be something other than its dependence upon the *fact* of existence"; it begins, it thinks, with its own right to be the *thought* of existence (NM, 3). In Descartes, *cogitatio* takes the liberty of abstracting itself from *extensio*. The question of substantiality becomes a matter of pure subjective judgment. In Kant one sees most clearly the state of pure abstraction that reason becomes in the absence of substantial essence. The transcendental unity of *reine Vernunft* is pure potentiality. Per Leahy, this self-misunderstanding of reason begins in Thomas, who asserts that "our intellect cannot know the singular in material things directly and primarily. . . . Our intellect knows directly the universal only" (NM, 125). *See:* interdict of sacred doctrine; modernity; paranoia

transparency
See: simplicity

trichotomy
Trichotomy is the end of dichotomy for the first time (F, 426), which begins with the trinary logic of the new thinking in its full existential consequentiality. *See:* trinary logic

trinary logic
Crucially, Peirce argues and Leahy affirms that "logic is rooted in the social principle" (F, 458). The trinary system of logic of the new thinking was first set down by Leahy in 1985 (per F, 629), and published a decade later in *Foundation* (chapter 3, section 1). The trinary logic asks the reader temporarily to set aside the most fundamental truth of ordinary mathematics: the assumption that it is simply true that $1 + 0 = 1$. This truism is set aside "for the purpose of opening the mind to

the possibility of a new logic" (F, 255), and the assertion is made that a truly *trinary* logic must break with this simplest of truths. In order to arrive at a categorically new logic, the reader is asked to consider a logic in which 1 is unity, 0 is zero, and $\bar{0}$ is unum, combined in the formal truth that $1 + 0 = \bar{0}$. Because zero is not nothing, and for this logic nothing does not exist, no term is reducible by relative valuations of more or less—nothing whatsoever can be zeroed out—hence, between the terms there is such a perfect equality and commutability that there is an indifference of operations (addition, subtraction, multiplication, division). Fiat triunity. The different terms can be differently related but it is not possible to express inequality (F, 256). *See:* infinitely flat structure of the universe; unum; zero not nothing

Trinity
Absolute Trinity Itself is absolutely without self-transcendence (F, 139). It is the absolute identification of the divine with existence here and now, the absolute objectivity of identity itself. There is no outside of this absolute existence of the divine Trinity. The God existing in the universe is not the transcendental God, but the transcendence into existence of the transcendental God (F, 365). Trinity is the absolutely apocalyptic identity of the new world now beginning (F, 366). The trinary logic articulates its structural modus operandi. The most definitive treatment of the fundamental ontology of the Trinity in Leahy's work occurs in Appendix 2 in *Beyond Sovereignty* (BS, 259–67, especially n22, 265–67), which addresses systematically the relations between uncreated Persons and their relations with created persons. Leahy provides a technical analysis of Augustine's *De Trinitate* in terms of the trinary logic in an appendix (F, 629–34). *See:* first absolute, second absolute, third absolute, triple nothingness of the Trinity

triple nothingness of the Trinity
Creation is the diametric identity of being and nothing; for the first time the discontinuity of being and nothing is the very form of thought (F, 628, 613–14). Existentially and logically to *see* the beginning of the difference between being and nothing is the universal faith now actually existing in the form of the very essence of thought: "To see for the first time the nothingness of the nothing as not the nothingness of the finite but the nothingness of the infinite. . . . This is the arrival for the first time at the triple nothingness of the Trinity, at the infinitely finite nothingness of the Godhead of God" (F, 616). In other words,

the newness of the universe (1) renders nothingness infinitely creative, therefore not-nothing: a rational zero (0), a zero not nothing. Each Person becomes nothing itself to become meta-identified as everything for the other in Fourthness: an absolutely infinite gain. Creation is the absolute nullification of the Trinity in an *absolute Aufhebung*. This is not a *relative Aufhebung* as in the Hegelian system, not the negation of the negation, for there is no negation, but, rather, the truth of the sheer affirmative preserves the Trinity in its ceasing (BS, 264); this is the Yes and Amen that is very omnipotence. "For the first time the Triune Identity is the actual and ideal simplicity of the nothing. This is the first beginning of the ideal nothing, the absolutely pure First" (F, 613). The ideal nothing exists in creation; it is not a literal nothing. It is the first completely actual beginning of divinity in the very form of nothing. *See:* Fourthness; nothing; Trinity; zero not nothing

truth
"Mind creates now willy-nilly the reality of the truth, the perfect truth of the world, the truth of the perfected world" (F, 564). Love of truth is the perfection of sincerity itself (F, 24). In place of the duality of truth and falsehood that Peirce judged to be inescapable for the logician-mathematician, including Hegel (see F, 265, 287, 289), Leahy sets forth a trinary logic in which there pertains an absolute asymmetry of truth and falsehood, just as there is an absolute asymmetry of the universe and nothing (F, 265), ultimately "the transcendence of the necessity of the difference between 0 and 1" (F, 287–88). *See:* simplicity; trinary logic

uncreated omnipotence
Uncreated omnipotence is the first absolute. "Omnipotence precisely is that which is absolutely nonexisting in its existing" (BS, 44). *See:* first absolute

unicity
Unicity denotes unity beyond the One, the simplicity that is existence itself (BS, 104)—simple because everything including nothingness has an absolutely unique and uncontested placedness, making (artifactually creating) the absolutely differentiated Body transparent to itself. The Body, embodiment, is universal unicity (BS, 153). Unicity is understood in its double sense as uniqueness (absolute differentiation) and unity (a simplicity that is not alternative to complexity). Matter, the body

itself, "knows nothing of walls or classes" (BS, 185); it is a unity of absolute particularities beyond the One. Absolute particularity in its thoroughgoing discreteness and uniqueness as such constitutes unity beyond the One, a unicity beyond "belonging," absolutely unconditioned (BS, 191). Metaphorically, the drop of water maintains its particular (particulate) identity in the sea absolutely without separateness. *See:* artifactual body; differentiation; discontinuity of the continuum; simplicity

unum ($\bar{0}$)
The base digit $\bar{0}$ in the trinary logic: a third to the 0 and the 1. "The other, existing for the first time as the essentially universal body, is the (singular/plural)/(plural/singular) which is the unum" (FP, 155). In the trinary logic, "the proof that $\bar{0}$ is *not not nothing* and *not nothing* and 1 is the proof of the absolute asymmetry of the Universe and Nothing" (F, 265). Within the minimum order, the unum is Secondness. *See:* minimum order; second absolute

***Very* First**
The new Firstness, the "absolutely pure First," is logically expressed as Fourthness, but superordinates Firstness to be the *Very* First (F, 627, 612–13). In the trinary logic of creation, metaphorically speaking, the capstone is meta-identically the foundation-stone. "The First now actually existing is the Godhead of God . . . identifying itself as the beginning of God in the form of Resurrection of the Trinity, in the form of the Unity actually and ideally transcending the Difference within the identity of God. This is the beginning of the Trinity as the simple identity of the Godhead as nothing" (F, 613). *See:* Fourthness; triple nothingness of the Trinity

world society
The unity of existence is the community (*com-unity*, the sharing of *withness* that creates unity) of absolutely unique and distinct particular existences. Each unicity coexisting with all others forms an absolute world society (F, 198), a new world order and new humanity (F, 47–48, 461, 600). Absolute society creates, creation is absolute sociability (BS, 225). Not a utopia but a *uchronia*, the absolute immanence of the eternal (F, 44). Peirce argues, and Leahy affirms, that "logic is rooted in the social principle" (F, 458). *See:* epoch of the One; new world order; unicity

zero not nothing (0)
One of the three base digits in the trinary logic: a rational zero. A "nothing" that is not-nothing inasmuch as it is absolutely productive and creative, therefore not wasted: "Imagine that the nothingness of the nothing is the being of everything beginning" (FP, 154), not a finite nothing but an infinite nothing. Nothing is the minimum actuality of beginning, not a vain emptiness or vacuity. Because the nothing is not wasted in the act of creating—any more than silence is wasted in music—it is not nothing, nor is it by any means reducible to nothing. In the trinary logic this is expressed: The rationality of zero (0) is the minimum/unum ($\bar{0}$) as the infinitesimal limit of the beginning of unity (1) (F, 264–65). Zero qua infinitesimal limit *meta-pairs* every object with itself and with every other in the form of the existence of the unum, in the form of existence as minimum. *See:* nothing; trinary logic; unum

D. G. Leahy
Comprehensive Bibliography

Books

Novitas Mundi: Perception of the History of Being. New York: New York University Press, 1980; reprint, Albany: State University of New York Press, 1994. xii+422 pp., appendixes, index. ISBN 0-7914-2137-6 and 2138-4.

Foundation: Matter the Body Itself. Albany: State University of New York Press, 1996. xvi+696 pp., index, appendix. ISBN 0-7914-2022-1 and 2021-3.

Faith and Philosophy: The Historical Impact. Burlington, VT: Ashgate, 2003. xiv+180 pp., appendix, index. ISBN 0-7546-3120-6 and 3119-2.

Beyond Sovereignty: A New Global Ethics and Morality. Aurora, CO: Davies Group, 2010. xxxi+353 pp., appendixes, backnotes, index. ISBN 978-1-934542-19-4.

The Cube Unlike All Others. http://dgleahy.com/p49.html. 2010. 118 pp, 33 color illust. Available: CreateSpace Independent Publishing Platform. ISBN 1-4536-4129-7 and 978-1453641293.

Articles, Essays, and Conference Papers

"To Create the Absolute Edge." Introduction by Thomas J. J. Altizer. *Journal of the American Academy of Religion* 57, no. 4 (Winter 1989): 773–89. Reprinted in D. G. Leahy, *Foundation: Matter the Body Itself*, 581–93. Also reprinted in *Frontiers in American Philosophy: Volume 2*, edited by Robert W. Burch and Herman J. Saatkamp Jr. College Station TX: Texas A&M University Press, 1996.

"Cuspidal Limits of Infinity: Secret of the Incarnate Self in Levinas." In *Rending the Veil: Concealment and Secrecy in the History of Religions*, edited by Elliot R. Wolfson, 209–48. Chappaqua, NY: Seven Bridges Press, 1999.

"The Originality of Levinas: Pre-Originally Categorizing the Ego." Internet. The Paideia Project: Proceedings of the Twentieth World Congress of Philosophy. http://www.bu.edu/wcp/Papers/Cont/ContLeah.htm. 1999.

"The Diachrony of the Infinite in Altizer and Levinas: Vanishing without a Trace and the Trace without Vanishing." In *Thinking Through the Death of God: A Critical Companion to Thomas J. J. Altizer*, edited by Lissa McCullough and Brian Schroeder, 105–24. Albany: State University of New York Press, 2004.

Coauthored Medical Research Papers

With Steven B. Hoath, MD. "The Human Stratum Corneum as Extended, Covalently Cross-Linked Biopolymer: Mathematics, Molecules, and Medicine." *Medical Hypotheses* 66, no. 6 (February 2006): 1191–98.
With Steven B. Hoath, MD. "The Organization of Human Epidermis: Functional Epidermal Units and Phi Proportionality." *Journal of Investigative Dermatology* 121, no. 6 (2003): 1440–46.
With Steven B. Hoath, MD. "Formation and Function of the Stratum Corneum." In *The Essential Stratum Corneum*, edited by Ronald Marks, Jean-Luc Lévêque, and Rainer Voegeli, 31–40. London: Martin Dunitz, 2002.

Website

www.dgleahy.com

Critical Responses to Leahy

Altizer, Thomas J. J. "D. G. Leahy." In *The Routledge Encyclopedia of Postmodernism*, edited by Victor E. Taylor and Charles E. Winquist. London: Routledge, 2000.
———. "Appendix: D. G. Leahy and the Apocalyptic Trinity." In Altizer, *The Apocalyptic Trinity*, 151–70. New York: Palgrave Macmillan, 2012.
———. Review of D. G. Leahy, *Foundation: Matter the Body Itself*. *International Studies in Philosophy* 35, no. 4 (2004): 332–34.
———. Review of D. G. Leahy, *Novitas Mundi: Perception of the History of Being*. *Religious Studies Review* 11, no. 4 (October 1985): 350–52.
Feld, Alina N. "Thinking the Absolute Edge between Altizer and Leahy." *Journal for Cultural and Religious Theory* 19, no. 1, special issue on Thomas J. J. Altizer, guest editor Lissa McCullough (Winter 2019–20): 171–88. https://jcrt.org/archives/19.1/Feld.pdf (open source).
———. "Thinking Now Occurring and the God Who May Be: David Leahy and Richard Kearney." The 13th International Conference of the International Society for the Study of European Ideas (ISSEI), Nicosia,

Cyprus, July 2012. Internet: https://lekythos.library.ucy.ac.cy/bitstream/handle/10797/6192/ISSEIproceedings-AlinaFeld.pdf;sequence=1.

———. "Teilhard de Chardin and D. G. Leahy: Philosophical Foundations for Sustainable Living." Proceedings of the 24th Ecumenical Theological and Interdisciplinary Symposium of the Romanian Institute of Orthodox Theology and Spirituality (December 2017): 35–44. Internet: http://www.romanian-institute-ny.org/images/Symposium_XXIV_-_2017_-_Copy.pdf

Koterski, Joseph W. Review of *Novitas Mundi*. *The Modern Schoolman* 60, no. 2 (January 1983): 134.

McAleer, Graham James. "Agamben on the Ontology of Clothes." In *Erich Przywara and Postmodern Natural Law: A History of the Metaphysics of Morals*. Notre Dame: University of Notre Dame Press, 2019.

McCullough, Lissa. "D. G. Leahy." In *Palgrave Handbook of Radical Theology*, edited by Christopher D. Rodkey and Jordan E. Miller, 269–80. New York: Palgrave Macmillan, 2018.

Oakes, Edward T. "Exposed Being." Essay review of *Foundation: Matter the Body Itself*. *Journal of Religion* 78, no. 2 (April 1998): 246–56.

O'Brien, Astrid M. Review of *Novitas Mundi*. *Library Journal* 105, no. 6 (1980): 727.

Scharlemann, Robert P. Review of D. G. Leahy, *Novitas Mundi: Perception of the History of Being*. *Religious Studies Review* 11, no. 4 (October 1985): 347–50.

Torry, Malcolm. Review of D. G. Leahy, *Faith and Philosophy*, *Theology* (January/February 2004): 55–56.

Yule, Sandy. Review of D. G. Leahy, *Faith and Philosophy*, *Pacifica* 17, no. 2 (June 2004): 228–30.

Compiled by Lissa McCullough

D. G. Leahy
Biographical Sketch

David George Leahy (March 20, 1937–August 7, 2014) was an American Catholic philosopher and religious thinker. He was born in Brooklyn, New York, and attended Brooklyn Preparatory School, graduating in the Greek honors program in 1955 with a scholarship to St. Peter's College in Jersey City, New Jersey. After graduating from St. Peter's in 1959 with a BA in Classics, he served in the US Army Reserves as first lieutenant of ordnance, taught as a lecturer in humanities at Iona College, and attended graduate school at Fordham University on scholarship, obtaining an MA in Classics in 1964.

Leahy taught at New York University, 1964–1972, where he was tenured in Classics and received the Lindback Foundation award for distinguished teaching. During the same period he wrote and delivered a series of lectures at the Newman Center affiliated with NYU that would be published later, in 1980, as his first book *Novitas Mundi*. In the period 1972 to 1998 he taught at C. W. Post College of Long Island University, Brooklyn College, Stony Brook University, and again at NYU in the religious studies program, in addition to working for a dozen years outside academia as a business consultant. He joined the philosophy department at Loyola University Maryland, 1998–2002, to fulfill a three-year term as Distinguished Visiting Professor of Philosophy.

Leahy was a research consultant to the Skin Sciences Institute, Children's Hospital Research Foundation at the University of Cincinnati, 2001–2007, conducting research and co-publishing papers in collaboration with pediatrics researcher Steven B. Hoath, MD. In 2003, Leahy founded the New York Philosophy Corporation, where he taught courses on the history of philosophy and theology until 2013. This private teaching and learning organization provided those interested the opportunity to study with him and with fellow engaged persons the history and major works of Western philosophy, as well as Leahy's works, in "an intellectual atmosphere suitable to the importance of the subject matter and free from many of the extraneous concerns of the contemporary university" (dgleahy.com). Courses were hosted in various locations in Manhattan, and in addition to regularly scheduled class meetings, both in-person and virtual, all courses provided access to a 24/7 online class discussion board in which the instructor participated from his home base in the Pocono Mountains of northeastern Pennsylvania.

On August 7, 2014, Leahy succumbed to pancreatic cancer after a year of illness while residing in his native city of Brooklyn. He was seventy-seven years old. He is survived by his younger sister Mary Jane (b. 1939), his four children Christopher, Genevieve, Aimee, and Timothy, thirteen grandchildren, and three great-grandchildren.

Compiled by Lissa McCullough

Contributors

Thomas J. J. Altizer (1927–2018) was professor emeritus of religious studies at Stony Brook University. Widely known for working out a radical death-of-God theology, he published more than a dozen works including, most recently, *Living the Death of God: A Theological Memoir* (SUNY, 2008), *The Apocalyptic Trinity* (Palgrave Macmillan, 2012), which contains an appendix on D. G. Leahy's trinitarianism, and *Satan and Apocalypse and Other Essays in Political Theology* (SUNY, 2017).

Todd Carter is an independent researcher, artist, and teacher living in New York City. He studied the history of philosophy and theology at the University of Chicago Divinity School. An active songwriter and filmmaker, he has several media projects in the works.

Edward S. Casey is Distinguished Professor of Philosophy at Stony Brook University; he is past president of the American Philosophical Association (Eastern Division) and has taught at Yale University and the New School for Social Research and the Pacifica Graduate Institute. In addition to early books on imagination and memory, he is the author of a series of books concerning the phenomenology of place: *Getting Back into Place, The Fate of Place, Representing Place in Landscape Painting and Maps,* and *Earth-Mapping.* He is the author of two recent books on the periphenomenology of human experience: *The World at a Glance* and *The World on Edge.* His forthcoming book is entitled *Turning Emotion Inside Out* (Northwestern University Press, 2021).

Michael James Dise is an American PhD candidate in the graduate school of religion and theology at Free University Amsterdam (Vrije Universiteit Amsterdam) specializing in radical theology and the continental philosophy of religion. His current primary research interest is in the concept of incarnation in the history of Western thought and its relation to cognitive science.

Sarah Lilly Eaton is an independent scholar who lives in Jordan and works as a consultant on educational travel and pilgrimage. Formerly, she was director of religious studies at Marygrove College and taught courses in philosophy. She has also taught at John Jay College, Eastern Michigan University, and Ecumenical Theological Seminary, where she served as dean.

Alina N. Feld is the author of *Melancholy and the Otherness of God* (Lexington, 2011) and a number of book chapters and essays in philosophical theology. She received her MA in comparative literature from Stony Brook University and her PhD in theology from Boston University. Her research interests include medieval and contemporary theology, existentialism, and French phenomenology. She teaches philosophy and theology at Hofstra University and CUNY York while pursuing her scholarly work. She is working on a book project *Nimble Omnipotence: D. G. Leahy and Post-Apocalyptic Society*.

Steven B. Hoath, MD (1949–2017) was professor emeritus of pediatrics (neonatology) and former medical director of the Skin Sciences Institute at Cincinnati Children's Hospital Medical Center and the University of Cincinnati. He received his undergraduate degree in German studies from Stanford University and MD from the University of California Los Angeles. He has authored more than one hundred peer-reviewed scientific papers, twenty book chapters, and a book on neonatal skin development. His work with D. G. Leahy focused on the logico-mathematical organization of human epidermis and the close embryological connection of the skin and the brain.

D. G. Leahy (1937–2014) was tenured in classics at New York University in the 1970s, and later taught in the religious studies program there. He also served as Distinguished Visiting Professor of Philosophy at Loyola University Maryland, and was founder of the New York Philosophy Corporation based in New York City. A comprehensive bibliography and fuller biographical sketch appear at the end of this volume.

Graham James McAleer is professor of philosophy at Loyola University Maryland, and author of *Erich Przywara and Postmodern Natural Law* (University of Notre Dame Press, 2019).

Lissa McCullough is author of *The Religious Philosophy of Simone Weil* (I. B. Tauris, 2014), editor of *The Call to Radical Theology* by Thomas J. J. Altizer (SUNY, 2012) and *Conversations with Paolo Soleri* (Princeton Architectural Press, 2012), and coeditor, with Brian Schroeder, of *Thinking Through the Death of God* (SUNY, 2004). She teaches philosophy at California State University Dominguez Hills, and has previously taught religious studies at Muhlenberg College, Hanover College, and New York University.

Cyril O'Regan is the Catherine F. Huisking Professor of Theology at the University of Notre Dame. He specializes in systematic theology and historical theology, with a specific interest in continental philosophy, religious literature, mystical theology, and postmodern thought. He is best known for his multivolume gnosticism series, which includes *Gnostic Return in Modernity* and *Gnostic Apocalypse: Jacob Boehme's Haunted Narrative*. His most recent book is *The Anatomy of Misremembering: Von Balthasar's Response to Philosophical Modernity, Volume 1: Hegel*.

Charles Stein, born in New York City in 1944, lives in Barrytown, New York. Stein's work comprises a complexly integrated field of poems, prose reflections, translations, drawings, photographs, lectures, conversations, and performances. His recent work includes *Black Light Casts White Shadows* (Lunar Chandelier, 2018), *Twelve Drawings* (Station Hill Press, 2018), *There Where You Do Not Think to Be Thinking, Views from Tornado Island, Book 12* (Spuyten Duyvil, 2016), and a verse translation of *The Odyssey* (North Atlantic Books, 2008). His prose includes a vision of the Eleusinian mysteries, *Persephone Unveiled* (North Atlantic Books, 2006), and a critical study of poet Charles Olson's use of the writing of C. G. Jung, *The Secret of the Black Chrysanthemum* (Station Hill Press, 1987). His work can be sampled at www.charlessteinpoet.com.

Nathan Tierney is emeritus professor of philosophy at California Lutheran University. His main fields of work are ethics and metaphysics, and he has long been engaged in interfaith dialogue. He is the author of *Imagination and Ethical Ideals* (SUNY, 1994) and numerous articles on ethics and peace building. His current research has concentrated on issues of war and peace. He is a regular speaker at international conferences and parliaments, and has organized three conferences on peace issues at CLU. For two decades he has co-taught, with a theologian, a senior honors seminar on faith and reason. He may be contacted at tierney@callutheran.edu.

Elliot R. Wolfson, a Fellow of the American Academy of Jewish Research and the American Academy of Arts and Sciences, is the Marsha and Jay Glazer Endowed Chair in Jewish Studies and Distinguished Professor of Religion at University of California, Santa Barbara. He is the author of many publications, including the most recent books *Giving beyond the Gift: Apophasis and Overcoming Theomania* (2014), *The Duplicity of Philosophy's Shadow: Heidegger, Nazism and the Jewish Other* (2018), and *Heidegger and Kabbalah: Hidden Gnosis and the Path of Poiesis* (2019).

Index

$\overline{0}$ (base digit of the trinary logic). *See* unum
~1.618034 (phi proportionality), 280–81
1989, as year of the beginning, 121, 141, 145, 218, 243

absolute, 288; actuality, 3, 50, 61, 64, 71, 164, 169, 206, 231, 241–42, 288; analogy of being, 288; beginning, 82, 190; change, 6; creativity, 2, 4; differentiation, 17, 160, 292; discontinuity of the continuum, 61, 166, 292; existence of existence, 61; exteriority, 2; first, 76, 295–96; identity of thought, 57; metaboly, 158; objectivity, 10, 14, 19, 64–65, 76, 217, 221, 226, 228–29, 240, 243, 272, 303; particularity, 19, 23, 32, 46, 177, 224, 266, 304; relative, 158; transcendence of knowledge, 3
Absolute Infinite (Cantor), 44
actuality, 4; of absolute change, 6; absolute newness of, 9; beginning of, 72; of being, 76; of creation, 177, 266; digitized, 2; of existence, 164; exterior, 60; of faith, 13; as gift, 5, 132; historical, 114; of the impossible, 201; of Incarnation, 19; infinitely supersaturated polyontology of, 2; of *ipsum esse*, 169; negation of, 85; negative, 117; of the new community, 142; novelty of, 199; of the now, 64, 73, 245, 256; as omnipotence, 186; of the other, 206; self-circling, 59; subjectification of, 128; thinking of for the first time, 71; unconditioned, 68; of withness, 223; of the world itself, 50, 169, 244
actuality, absolute, 3, 50, 61, 64, 71, 164, 206, 231, 241–42, 288
Agamben, Giorgio, 9, 14, 21, 145, 151, 222
aletheia, 210, 226. *See also* truth
alio-affection, 21
Althusser, Louis, 142
Altizer, Thomas J. J.: absolute future in, 72; apocalypticism of, 205; Being and Nothing in, 205; and *coincidentia oppositorum*, 162–63, 190, 195–96, 203, 217–19, 228, 261; death of God theology of, 219–20, 242; and Incarnation, 12, 39–40; interiority and exteriority in, 59–60; justification of evil in, 203; Leahy's critique of, 12–13, 59–61; Leahy's indebtedness to, 10, 137, 140; and *missa jubilaea*, 215; mystical quest in, 167; nonbeing

Altizer, Thomas J. J. *(continued)*
of God as ground of the
infinite, 168; and post-Cartesian
subjectivity, 14; problem of evil
in, 192–95; and radical evil,
203–204, 206; thanatology of, 143
American democracy, 144
analogy of being *(analogia entis)*, 74,
100, 103, 105; absolute, 288
Antichrist (Satan), 118, 123, 195, 212,
217, 218
anypothetotopia, 288–89
apocalypse: as end of the end and
beginning of the beginning, 80–81,
86; as eschatological fulfillment,
224; time as place of, 67
apocalyptic "I," 289; as absolutely
pure consciousness, 19, 221; and
ancient apocalypticism, 122–24;
as center of consciousness, 112;
as created omnipotence, 165–66;
and evil, 190–91; freedom of,
206–207; as gift, 177; as objective
consciousness of the new world
order, 267; and proclamation, 254;
as pure self-consciousness, 116–17;
self-consciousness of, 186; selfless
conception of in immediacy
of Christ, 185; sharing in the
omnipotence of God, 167–70;
thinking of, 5; transparency of,
220–22, 226, 230; and world
creation, 13–14
apocalypticism, 9, 56; as absolute
novelty, 127; American, 120–22;
as challenge to Christian
orthodoxy, 124; and the death
of God, 124–26; distinction of
beginning and origin in, 205;
of eternal return, 119; and the
French Revolution, 112–14; of
Israel, 119; in modernity, 123, 221;
and negation of interiority, 124;
in Orthodox Christianity, 119;
punctiliarity of, 141; rebirth of,
120; subversiveness of, 124–25;
thinning of, 206; in Western
history, 111
apokatastasis, 217
appearance, and reality, 56, 58
appropriation, 5, 59, 100, 169, 171,
212
Aquinas, Thomas: and apocalyptic
consciousness, 221; and
criteriology for critique of
modernity, 133, 136; death of God
in, 219; essence of existence in,
28; existentialism of, 129; in *Faith
and Philosophy*, 135–37, 143; God's
essence in, 156–57; and magic, 98;
metaphysics of, 98–99; mysticism
of, 161; and natural reason, 29,
209; in *Novitas Mundi*, 8, 18,
129–34; parousia in, 231; problem
of evil in, 193; theism of, 156. *See
also* sacred doctrine *(sacra doctrina)*
Aristotle, 15; conception of the
now, 72–73; essentialism of, 129;
in *Faith and Philosophy*, 9, 20,
34–35; in *Novitas Mundi*, 8, 18, 28,
136; now, conception of, 72–73;
philosophy as good life, 252; the
place in, 241
artifactual body, 163, 275, 284, 290
atomism, 116
attention, embodied, 204
Aufhebung (dialectical negation),
114–15
Augustine: *Confessions*, 132;
consciousness in, 112; creation
in, 101; doxological nature of
theology, 132–33; in *Faith and
Philosophy*, 20; in *Foundation*,
137; Neoplatonism of, 33, 47;
in *Novitas Mundi*, 8, 131–32;
revolution of thought of, 16;
secretarium tuum, 104–105; and
temptation, 212; theodicy of, 192

autopoiesis, 277
avoidance, 193

Badiou, Alain: as anti-Calvin, 202; apocalypticism of, 144–46; *Being and Event*, 144–45; *diaphysical* ethics of, 194; ethic of truth, 222, 224; and the ethical subject, 200–201; in *Foundation*, 137, 146; and Galatians 3, 63; Incarnation in, 197; and infinite alterity criticized by Leahy, 91–92 n18; and mathematics, 145; omnipotence in, 202; and Pauline universalism, 63, problem of evil in, 190, 194–95, 197; and punctiliarity of apocalypse, 141; self in, 197
Balthasar, Hans Urs von, 131, 151
ban (interdict) of sacred doctrine, 29–30, 48, 298–99
barred subject, the, 104–105
Baudrillard, Jean, 224–25
beginning, 197, 290; absolute, 82, 190; absolute silence of, 71; as beyond beyond being, 190; as existence *ex nihilo*, 164; of the new beginning, 184; now-unity of, 262; silence of, 219, 225; thinking the, 254, 256, 274
beginning, new: absolute apocalypse of, 220; morality of, 20
Being: of Being, 37–39; of being, 37–38; as Creation, 38; of history, 35–37, 255; oblivion of, 36
being: apocalyptic revelatory structure of, 211; for the first time, 17; quantum identity of, 75; and thought, 54
Being and Event (Badiou), 144–45
Being and Time (Heidegger), 36, 53, 128
beneficence, 179, 187, 192–93, 198, 206, 224

beyond beyond x, 5, 71–72, 91, 166, 169, 190, 205–206, 290–91
Beyond Sovereignty (2010), 50–51; beyond beyond x, 14; ethic of simplicity in, 222; ethical imperative in, 6, 8–9; the Good in, 191, 193; sovereignty in, 20
biblical text, encryption of, 256, 262–68. *See also* gematria
Blake, William, 41, 115, 118, 120, 140, 309
Blumenberg, Hans, 309
body (the Body), 291; artifactual, 163, 275, 277, 284; boundary of, 273, 275–77, 280; created ex nihilo, 11; as edge, 244, 273; eucharistic, 166, 217; existing for the first time, 204; as foundation, 8; of God, 140, 199, 205, 214–15, 217, 228, 257; identity of, 177; as infinite unicity, 164–65, 223; itself, 17, 122–23; as locus of creative omnipotence, 240; logico-mathematical structure of, 279–80; matter of, 17, 225, 232; and mind, 244; surface of, 229, 277–80; transparency of, 229–30; universality of, 206, 209, 229
Boehme, Jacob, 137, 217, 230, 231
boredom, 193
Bradley, F. H., 240
Bruno, Giordano, 146–47
Buddhism, 42–43, 47
Byzantine Christianity, 214. *See also* Orthodox Christianity

Cantor, Georg, 44, 145
catholicity, of Leahy, 98, 120, 123–24, 137, 141, 144, 146, 204, 214, 246
catholicological, 141, 147, 215, 222
change, tautology of, 157
Christ, Jesus: apocalyptic body of, 122; as apocalyptic prophet, 113; as beginning of actual existence,

Christ, Jesus *(continued)*
62; body of, 45, 163, 199; body of as the church, 134; creating of as salvation, 206, 223; death of, 76, 121, 126; humanity of, 219; incarnation of, 39, 59, 191, 197; incorporation into the body of, 62–63; and law, 166; as manifestation of the new, 140; and metaphysics, 99–100; mathematical paradox of, 146; mind of, 185; name of, 180; New, 185; radical particularity of, 32; resurrection of, 32, 197, 201–202, 204, 214–15, 217, 252; Spirit of, 56, 216; temptation of, 212–13; as Tetragrammaton, 147; as thought existing for the first time in the form of man, 74; as transcendental essence of existence, 103; as Truth, 28; as Word, 140, 160; as the world, 46
circle, 36, 59–61, 65–70, 152n37, 186, 228; infinite, 65–66, 152n37, 228; nucleus of, 87
circularity, 65–70
clarity, 100, 103, 105
cogito ergo sum, 15, 112
coincidentia oppositorum, 162–63, 190, 195–96, 203, 217–19, 228, 261
Commedia (Dante), 232
concern, 181, 187
Confessions (Augustine), 132
consciousness, 112; absolute, 140; absolute objectivity of, 272; absolutely other-ed, 198; American, 218; apocalyptic, 70; and apocalyptic unveiling, 56; beginning of, 71; edge of, 245; European, 218; modern, 12, 18, 119, 225, 254; new, 19, 215, 225, 243–44; new world, 59, 121, 163, 242, 255; objective, 117; otherness of, 197; qualitative transformation of, 15; self, 116–17, 128, 163, 185, 189, 196–98, 218, 221, 231, 266; subjective, 116–17; transcendence of, 122; transformation of, 57; transparency of, 209, 211; unhappy, 118; universal, 84, 116, 118, 220, 229, 232
Contributions to Philosophy (Heidegger), 255
cosmology, 45
created omnipotence, 7, 20, 158–60, 165, 167, 190–92, 197–98, 207, 291. *See also* uncreated omnipotence
creation: actuality of, 177; as beginning of the beginning, 80; as Gift, 166; imperative of, 180 191–92, 195, 197, 223–24, 230, 284; mathematical account of, 65; novelty of, 168; omnipotence embodied in, 252; as prompted by mercy, 101; and redemption, 133; as requirement of justice, 101; transcendental repetition of creation, 165
creation *ex futuro*, 122, 166
creation ex nihilo (*creatio ex nihilo*): and apocalypticism, 190–91; in Christian theology, 28, 30; in contemporary philosophy, 44–45; and kingdom of God, 223; in Leibniz, 128; as the now of existence, 20; and the repetition of creation, 64–65; in the thinking now occurring, 157–58
creative perception, 3, 304. *See also* productive receptivity
Creator, the: and apocalyptic "I," 221; and creature, 50–51, 136, 140–41, 161, 166, 169–71, 180, 199; in essence, 155, 158; of existence, 47; God as, 17, 71, 160, 202, 260, 280; in mysticism, 163–64; and omnipotence, 190, 192; in open theism, 159; person as 31, 33

Crucifixion, 115, 123, 126, 193, 203, 205, 215
Cube Unlike All Others (2010), 265

Daniel, Book of, 262, 264, 267–68
Dante, Alighieri, 103, 123, 228, 232
darkness, 6, 13, 48, 106, 125, 189, 193, 194, 203, 217, 219–20, 230, 243
Darwin, Charles, 275, 276, 277, 279, 284
Dasein, 36, 62, 254
David, King, 259
Dawkins, Richard, 276
death of God, 8–9, 291–92; and American pragmatism, 219, 225; American responses to, 121, 122, 220, 223, 231, 242; as apocalyptic event, 86, 118, 121, 124–26, 261; apocalyptic iconoclasm of, 220; apocalyptic imperative of, 13; in Blake's *America*, 120; as culminating thought of modernity, 219; as foundation of Christianity, 76; freedom of, 17; and the French Revolution, 115, 118; gift of, 16; as knowable, 183; and modernity, 12–13, 15; and nihilism, 112, 184; and omnipotence of God, 160; and self-consciousness, 218; theology of, 40, 137, 218–19, 225, 242; void of, 243–44, 247. *See also* Altizer, Thomas J. J.
deification, 229
Deleuze, Gilles, 6, 151n35, 157, 171, 220, 240
denial, 193
depth-spirituality, 48
Derrida, Jacques, 9, 31, 34, 136, 138, 200
Descartes, René: and absolute self, 184; and age of disenchantment, 97–98, 100; Christian consciousness of, 183; *cogito ergo sum*, 15, 112; consciousness in, 12, 204, 207; coordinate system of, 282–84; God as universal cause in, 113; in *Faith and Philosophy*, 9, 20, 136; in history of philosophy, 111, 221; Incarnation in, 31; and interdict of sacred doctrine, 29; metaphysics of, 97–98; methodological turn of, 127–28; in *Novitas Mundi*, 8, 18, 130; subjectivity in, 10, 112, 135
Desmond, William, 148
difference, 292
differentiation, absolute, 17, 160, 292
discontinuity of the continuum, absolute, 33, 61, 84, 157, 166, 169, 186, 197, 205, 289, 291, 292
discretion, 179, 187, 192–93, 198, 206, 224
dissemblance, 193
disenchantment, age of, 97, 101
disservice, 193
double visage, 72

Easter Sunday, 214
Eastern traditions, 42–43, 47, 49, 119
Eckhart, Meister, 137, 146–47, 161–62, 225, 229, 231
edge, absolute, 214, 225, 231, 238, 245, 293; accessibility of, 240; and actual existential matter, 240; creation of, 243, 247, 280–82; death of God as threshold, 218; as existential matter, 242; indissolubility of, 240–41; selflessness of, 241–42; spatiotemporality of, 241
edge, definite, 239
edge, indefinite, 239–40
edge-worlds, 237–38
Eliade, Mircea, 39–40, 42; *Myth of the Eternal Return*, 39
enchantment, metaphysics of, 97–98
Enkelte, den (Kierkegaard), 59

epoch of the One, 293
eschaton, 133
essence, 5, 293; as beginning of thinking, 11; and death of God, 15; as essential, 5; of existence, 28, 30, 55, 129, 169, 215, 232; new creation of, 57. *See also* transcendental essence of existence
essence-in-the-making, 6
essentialism, 128–29
eternal: in Altizer, 205; Being, 20; forms (Platonic), 32–33, 39, 46; life, 213; nature of God, 156, 157; now (present), 47–48, 66, 67, 70, 87, 310; recurrence (Nietzsche), 42, 66, 67, 90, 125; return, 114, 119; secret, 165
ethic of simplicity, 20–21, 222, 224, 226, 230, 293–94; attention in, 182, 199; authority in, 183; creative imperative of, 186–87; dimensions of, 179, 187, 192–93, 198, 206; and embodied identity, 175; imperatives of, 179–80, 187; necessity of, 180; as reframing of ethics, 182, 187; and the will, 182, 196
ethical imperative, 2, 6, 21, 191–92, 224, 230, 294
ethics: challenges to, 181; of the coming community, 222; *diaphysical*, 194; philosophical code of, 180–81; as physical, 178; of the thinking now occurring, 9; of transparency, 230; of truth, 222, 224; virtue, 182; without self, 20
ethics, physical, 9, 193, 198, 222–23
Eucharist, 59, 121, 147, 199; as actualization of the transubstantiation of matter, 214; cosmological significance of, 215; as fulfillment of Incarnation, 223; as infinite passover, 55; as kenotic creation, 214; and logos christology, 212; and the transcendental essence of existence, 214; as transcendental repetition of creation, 134–35
eucharist of existence, 160, 213–14, 217, 227, 232, 295
Eucharistic Body, 166
event: absolute edge of, 241; as category, 144, 145
evil: defections of, 193–94; as failure to act, 190; ground of, 206; and intention, 199; non-necessity of, 192, 205, 207; ontological status of, 193; transparence of, 225; and the will, 193, 195–96, 199
ex abysso, 4, 55, 62, 74, 76, 87, 92, 122, 170, 291, 292, 295, 300, 303
existence, 294–95; as absolute alterity, 177; absolute freedom of, 176; as absolutely actual unicity, 3; in ancient thought, 28; asymmetry of, to nothingness, 6; as body of Christ, 45; creation of by individuals, 31–32; as creative mode of being, 21; essence of, 28, 30, 55, 129, 169, 215, 232; eucharistic essence of, 160; existence of, 3; as gift, 11, 132; as God's Creation, 29; human, as created omnipotence, 191; as hyperdimensional multiplicity, 33; as its own schema, 46; as participation in Divine life, 176; phenomenology of, 34; as plane of immanence, 157; as pure creativity, 185; rationality of, 34; revelatory structure of, 11; Sabbath of, 166; sacred character of, 46; simplicity of, 176; as transcendental, 11; transparency of, 227, 230; unity of, 177
exsistere ipsum, 169
exterior, identification of, 59–60

Fabro, Cornelio, 130, 131, 133
faith: as comprehension of existence, 30–31; as distinct from belief, 31–32; in existence, 56; and knowledge, 137, 214; logic of, 79–80, 82, 136, 278, 280; new, possibility of, 13; and *nous*, 20; and philosophy, 18, 28–32, 112; as readiness for being, 92, 230; and reason, 74, 121, 130, 170; as response to the Word, 34–35; temptations of, 211; as thinking, 37, 125, 184, 197–98, 212; as thinking the transcendental essence of existence, 46–47; truth of, 70; universal, 219–20; as virtue, 179
Faith and Philosophy (2003), 8, 19, 34–35, 229; Aquinas in, 135–37, 143; Aristotle in, 9, 20; Augustine in, 20; constructive apocalyptic theology of, 135; critique of modernity in, 220–21; Descartes in, 9, 20, 136; Hegel in, 9–10, 136–37; Kabbalism in, 147; Kant in, 9; Kierkegaard's critique of Hegel in, 9, 20, 136; logic, catholic form of in, 141; Marx in, 137–38, 141–42; mathematical reading of language in, 255, 268; meontological turn in, 141–42; new mathematics of, 143–44, 146, 178; new way of speaking in, 138; Nietzsche in, 143; and punctiliarity of apocalyptic, 141; theological language of, 139
Falque, Emmanuel, 81
Fear and Trembling (Kierkegaard), 100
Fermat's theorem, 143
Fibonacci's sequence, 143–44
Fichte, J. G., 253–54
finite omnipotence. *See* created omnipotence
first absolute, 76, 295–96

Firstness, 137, 296, 300–301, 315
flatness, 194, 197, 207, 275, 282, 283, 284, 298
flesh (*sarx*), 56, 74, 112, 123, 160, 183, 190, 208, 212, 213, 215–16, 221, 227, 288, 295, 307. *See also* Incarnation
for the first time, 296
foundation, 12, 64, 167, 169, 171, 176–77, 223, 229, 262, 296; as the Place, 165; transcendental creation of, 166
Foundation (1996), 8, 19; apocalyptic shape of, 144, 147; Augustine in, 137; Badiou in, 137, 146; as challenge to Catholicism, 123; Hegel in, 35, 139, 168
Fourth Lateran Council, 99
Fourthness, 296–97
French Revolution, 113–16, 121; as apocalyptic event, 111, 113–14, 117; and death of God, 115; as embodiment of death of God, 118

gematria, 8, 257–58, 262; demonstration of, 259, 262–67; and Greek, 265; and Hebrew, 261–62; Leahy's innovation of, 260, 262; origins of, 261
geometry, 8, 16, 143–44, 253, 272
Gilson, Étienne, 130
gnoseology, 139–40
Gnosticism, 99, 161, 164, 225
God (Godhead): abyss of, 74; as Absolute Society, 165; in Altizer, 13, 193; as act-of-being itself, 157; body of, 140, 199, 205, 214–15, 217, 228, 257; clarification of the created, 75; constitution of, 165; created, 143, 205; as Creator, 160, 164; creaturely life of, 160, 186; Crucifixion as enactment of, 126; death of Godhead of, 77, 218–19; as Divine Otherness, 183; as essence of the world, 55–56;

God (Godhead) *(continued)*
eternal Now of, 157; existing as form of the universe, 167; exteriority of, 184, 195; freedom of, 207; glory of, 226; in Hegel, 7; immanence of, 119; immutability of, 156; infinity of, 162; inversion of, 156; name of, 147; as Nothing, 184; otherness of, 158, 170, 221; personalization of, 140; Self of, 161, 167; self-consciousness of, 185; self-sacrifice of, 12; transcendental history of, 165; trinitarian structure of, 158; as the Uncreated, 190, 207; union with, 161

good: in Badiou, 194, 197; creating, 207; defections from, 191–92, 195; and the ethic of simplicity, 182, 193; and evil, 193–94, 201, 205, 230; in Kant, 181–82; predestination of, 203; transparency of, 224–25; willing the, 21, 101

Good Friday, 12, 214

gratitude, 179, 187, 192–93, 198, 206, 224

Greek language, 265

Groundwork for a Metaphysics of Morals (Kant), 20, 181–82

hatred, 193

healthcare, and the thinking now occurring, 274–78

Hebrew language, 261–62

Hegel, G. W. F., 53–54, 112; and Absolute Spirit, 156; apocalypticism of, 113–15; Christianity, instrumentalization of, 129; comparison of, to Leahy, 230–31; death of God in, 218–19; essentialism of, 128; and faith, 136; in *Faith and Philosophy*, 9–10, 136–37; in *Foundation*, 35, 139, 168; French Revolution, view of, 116; God's essence in, 156, 158, 221; logic of, 118–19; mystical quest in, 167; in *Novitas Mundi*, 8; panentheism of, 156; pantheism in, 113; *Phenomenology of Spirit*, 112, 114–18, 121, 251; reason, dialectic of, 245; *Science of Logic*, 53, 114, 118; and self-consciousness, 128, 231; Spirit in, 12, 113, 116–18; and thinking, 53; and theodicy, 136. *See also* Idealism, German

Heidegger, Martin: *Being and Time*, 36, 53, 128; *Contributions to Philosophy*, 255; and modern self-consciousness, 266; and modernity, 221, 223; nihilism of, 128–29; and the nothingness of being, 92n18; in *Novitas Mundi*, 8, 18, 120; ontology of, 35–38; originary sovereignty of, 91n17; philosophical pedagogy of, 254–55; and subjectivity, 128, 131; and time, 72–73, 90–91nn13–14; *What Is Metaphysics?*, 36

Heraclitus, 175, 186, 243

hermeticism, 137, 147, 148, 228

Hinduism, 15

history, 297; essence of, 79, 92, 212–13, 227; teleological view of, 137, 139, 145, 216; in the thinking now occurring, 35–37

hitherto, 179, 297

holiness, every day, 180

humanitarianism, 97–99, 105

Husserl, Edmund, 8, 16, 18, 31, 35, 82–83, 168, 221, 294, 301

hypercube, 264–66, 300

Idealism, German, 111, 113–14, 121, 135

identity, 297; as change itself, 33; embodied, 175; for Lacan, 103–104; and memory, 177;

perpetuity of, 69; thinking, 262; thought's comprehension of, 58; and transcendental essence of existence, 6
intelligibility, absolute essential, 3, 55, 64, 163, 186, 210, 251, 257, 293, 307, 312
immanence: plane of, 6, 157–59; pure, 240
immanence/transcendence dichotomy, 6
immunity, 278
impotence, 193
in illo tempore, 40, 42
inaction, 193
Incarnation: as absolute pleromatic existence, 5–6; actuality of, 19; in Altizer, 12, 39–40; in Badiou, 197; in Catholic thinking, 123; as conversion of omnipotence, 160; in Descartes, 31; and docetism, 225; Eucharist as fulfillment of, 160, 214, 217, 223; as existence, 31, 160; existence of in thought, 67; as God's embodiment of the ontic, 223; historical development of, 31; historicity of, 45, 197; in history of Western thought, 9–10, 198; and human experience, 39; as idea not reality, 183; as "idea of God" mattered, 203; Incarnationism, 36; and myth, 40; ontology of, 36; Platonic view of, 33, 42; radical particularity of, 32, 48; as self-emptying of God, 167; and temporalization of the noetic, 59; thinking the, 191, 212; and the transcendental essence of existence, 75, 157, 212–13; work of, 13
indifference, 193
infinite finitude, 168, 298
interdict of sacred doctrine, 29–30, 48, 298–99

interior, identification of, 59–60
ipsum esse, 157, 163, 165, 169

Jetztsein, 73
Joachim of Fiore, 99, 105, 134, 216, 225, 227
Joyce, James, 123
Judaism, 124–25, 140; apocalypticism in, 124; messianic, 63. See also Torah

Kabbalah, 48, 93–94n24, 137, 147, 228, 260
Kant, Immanuel: abstraction in, 312; *Ding an Sich*, 304; ethics of, 17, 181–82, 187, 230; in *Faith and Philosophy*, 9; *Groundwork for a Metaphysics of Morals*, 20, 181–82; immanence in, 130; in *Novitas Mundi*, 8, 18; and transcendental imagination, 157, 228; and universal law, 182; and the will, 181–82
Kearney, Richard, 216
kenosis, 12, 60, 115, 118, 170, 194, 205, 214. See also self-emptying
kerygma, as apocalyptic proclamation, 213
Kierkegaard, Søren: and absurdity of the present, 185; critique of Hegel, 128–29, 136, 212; *den Enkelte* in thought of, 59; and existence, beginning of, 17; and faith, 212; in *Faith and Philosophy*, 9, 20, 136; *Fear and Trembling*, 100; and God's will, 98; Leahy's interpretation of, 67, 80; in *Novitas Mundi*, 8, 18, 35; ontology of, 47; *Philosophical Fragments*, 128; and thoughtlessness of faith, 80
kingdom of God, 230; as apocalyptic, 113–14, 124, 230; as body of God, 140; co-creation of, 165, 223; and French Revolution,

kingdom of God *(continued)*
116; as Trinity, 216; triumph of, 126

La Mettrie, Julien Offray de, 98
Lacan, Jacques: and the barred subject, 104–105; and language, 101, 106; and psychoanalysis, 103; Real, world of the, 201; Schema L, 100
language: mathematical reading of, 255–56, 258–59, 262–66; meta-identity of, 256, 258, 267; transformation of, 138
Leibniz, Gottfried Wilhelm: as computational, 101–102; and *creation ex nihilo*, 128; monads, 98, 100, 101–104, 168; in *Novitas Mundi*, 100; as panpsychist, 100; and preestablished harmony, 102; and reality as garden, 104, 106; and sufficient reason, 130
Levinas, Emmanuel: and absolute past, 71–72; in *Novitas Mundi*, 9; and the other, 237; and subjectivity, 221–22
Lévi-Strauss, Claude, 41
logic, 2, 3–4, 15; dialethic, 61; of faith, 82; of faith beyond beyond modernity, 79: and *metanoia*, 4; of newness, 15–18; novelty as essence of, 79; phenomenality of, 6; as social construct, 3. *See also* trinary logic
logos christology, 212
loving: the body, 180; the person, 180; things, 179; truth, 180
Luther, Martin, 115

malfeasance, 193
malice, 193
Marx, Karl, 137–38, 141–42
Mary, 150, 214, 227, as *capax dei*, embodiment of the new consciousness, 232

Mass, 63–64, 103–104, 214–15; upon the altar of the world, 216–17. *See also* Eucharist; *missa jubilaea*; *missa solemnis*
mathematics: as form of wisdom, 146–47; and language, 255–56, 258–59, 262–66; Leahy's new, 143; ontological status of, 43–45; as prerequisite to philosophy, 253; unveiling function of, 145–47
matter, 232, 299; as absolutely novel essence, 57; as apocalyptic beginning of absolutely new universe, 122; as consciousness, 102; mattering of, 246; qua absolute particularity, 19
McCabe, Herbert, 142
McDermott, John, 9, 31
Mead, George Herbert, 221
memory: absolute indifference of, 84–85; of the absolute repetition of the absolute, 64, 69; eucharistic, 226; and identity, 177; and perception, 224; recreated, 166; and self-identity, 85
meontology, 141, 144; anthropological locus of, 142; theo-ontological locus of, 142–43
Merleau-Ponty, Maurice, 16, 83
Mersenne, Marin, 112
metaboly, absolute, 158
meta-identity, 74, 93, 165, 252, 256–58, 260, 263, 265, 267, 299
metanoia, 2, 4, 14, 74, 169, 293, 299, 304, 310
metaphysics: analogical, 99; Christ at the heart of, 99–100; of enchantment, 97–98; equivocal, 99; of morals, 99–100, 105; univocal, 98–100, 103, 105
mind: "archaic," 41; and body, 244; divine, and totality of existence, 267; edge of, 242, 244, 246; as entering edge in the thinking

now occurring, 245; modernist conception of, 245
minimum, 146, 300
minimum order, 263, 300–301
misfeasance, 193
missa jubilaea, 55–56, 63–64, 103, 217, 300; as actualization of Leahy's apocalypticism, 213–14, 230; as center of new consciousness, 215; as glorification of existence, 120; as infinite passover of God, 8, 121, 210
missa solemnis, 56, 103, 106, 120, 215
modernity, 301; ahistorical thinking of, 184; as apocalyptic event, 111; as denial of history, 101; egological regime of, 127, 144, 147; genealogy of, 135; opacity of, 210–11; subjectivity in, 10, 12–13, 19, 128, 135, 211–12, 221: transcendental mode of thinking of, 6
monads (Leibniz), 98, 168; as constituents of reality, 100; as a garden, 101–104
mysticism, Christian: abolishment of in the thinking now occurring, 167; apophatic, 163, 169; cataphatic, 162; goal of, 163–65; quasi-atheistic apophatic, 161
myth, 39–40, 42
Myth of the Eternal Return (Eliade), 39

Name, the, 260, 263–64
Necker cube, 273, 276
new, the, 134, 139; as absolute interruption, 141; continuity of, 81; gnoseological consideration of, 140; meontological characterization of, 143; other views of, 81
new world order, 2, 8, 10–11, 155, 212, 301–302; as absolute exteriority of the Godhead in existence, 160; absolute repetition of, 67; as apocalyptic event, 191; co-creation of, 170; consciousness of, 163, 267, 272; ethical basis of, 207; and existence, 222; and the French Revolution, 121; as gift, 138; 1989 as beginning of, 141, 243; thinking the, 206; universal logic of, 283
New York Philosophy Corporation, 35
newness: logic of, 15; paradox of, 66
Nicholas of Cusa, 146, 162
Nietzsche, Friedrich, 13, 125; apocalypticism of, 120; in *Novitas Mundi*, 9. *See also* death of God; nihilism; nothingness; will
nihilism, 123, 125, 128, 143
nonexistence, existence of, 76
nothing, 36–37, 62, 302; beginning of, 71; idealism of, 123; silence of, 220
nothingness, 12, 161, 184; as the actual existence of God, 185; apotheosis of, 13; asymmetry of, to existence, 6
novelty, 4, 57, 129, 209; and apocalyptic discourse, 127; and the circularity of time, 68; creation as, 168; critique of in the thinking now occurring, 63–66, 77–78, 81–82, 87; in perception of the history of being, 140; as repetition of the same, 70, 82; of sacred doctrine, 130; temporal basis of, 63–64; in the thinking now occurring, 56, 59, 68, 210
novitas mentis, 302–303; and the apocalyptic "I," 229; and circularity, 60; ethic of 222–23; and *missa jubilaea*, 210–11, 213, 216; *et mundi*, 220; as new consciousness, 10, 13; as new imperative, 140; as philosophical innovation, 18, 21; and thinking

novitas mentis (continued)
   the resurrection body, 255; as transcendental imagination, 157
novitas mundi, 303; as apocalyptic, 191, 205, 211, 213; and circularity, 60; and consciousness, 198; ethical imperative of, 21; *et mentis*, 220; as newness of the world, 10, 13
Novitas Mundi (1980) 78; apocalyptic "I" in, 221; apocalypticism of, 54–55, 120; Aquinas in, 8, 18, 129–34; Aristotle in, 8, 18, 28, 136; Augustine in, 8, 131–32; being, history of in, 18–19; catholic apocalyptic of, 148; as challenge to Catholicism, 123; constructive apocalyptic theology of, 133–34; death of God in, 17; Descartes in, 8, 18, 130; Hegel in, 8; history of thought in, 210; and the interdiction of sacred doctrine, 29; Kant in, 8, 18; Kierkegaard in, 8, 18, 35; Leibniz in, 100; Levinas in, 9; meditation on the Mass in, 103; Nietzsche in, 9; as philosophical theology, 98; sacred doctrine in, 134; and the transcendental essence of existence, 78
now, absolute. *See* actuality
now, the, 64; of the apocalypse, 81; Aristotle's conception of, 72; as beyond beyond *x*, 71–72; as bounding time, 73; and Christ without the Christ, 76; eschatological, 139; eternal, 48; historical orientation of, 48; novelty of, 71; permanence of, 70; as pleromatic, 138; of the thinking now occurring, 73, 75–76; transtemporal status of, 73–74

objectivity, absolute, 303; and the apocalyptic "I," 5, 221; body as, 240; of consciousness, 229, 272; as externality, 243; God as, 217; of the Incarnation, 19; itself, 64–65; as sphere of spheres, 228; and subjectivity, 10; of time, 76; world as, 14
occasionalism, 33
Olson, Charles, 49
Omega Point, 216, 227
omnipotence, 158, 304; and the apocalyptic "I," 167; body as locus of, 240; created, 7, 20, 160, 165, 167, 190–92, 197–98, 207, 291; in creation, 252; as foundation of creation, 204; of God, 159–60; and imperative of attention, 193; new ground of, 160; in the thinking now occurring, 164, 190; trans-theistic conception of, 156; uncreated, 160, 165, 314
one (1), base digit of the trinary logic. *See* trinary logic
ontological inquiry: Heidegger's levels of, 37–38; in the thinking now occurring, 39
ontology: Christian revelation as, 36; of gift, 131; incarnationist, 31; monist, 211; participatory, 162; rational, 47
opacity, 158, 210–11, 228–29
open theism, 158–59
Orthodox Christianity, 119, 214
orthodoxy: Western Christian, 99, 115, 120, 124, 147, 162, 193; in Judaism, Christianity, and Islam, 124–25
Other, the: absolute, 158, 169; creation of in love, 160; infinite multiplicity of, 165; unconditional existence of, 158
other-consciousness: and the apocalyptic "I," 190; edge of, 244–45; in the logic of newness, 15; in medicine, 278; and mysticism, 163; perfect, 11; and the Place, 241–42

panentheism, 156
pantheism, 113, 152n38
panpsychism, 100, 102
paradigm-thinking, 4, 15, 32, 39, 48, 160
paranoia (madness), of modern thought, 18–19, 226, 299, 304
Parmenides, 38, 53–54, 87n1, 145
particularity, absolute, 19, 23, 32, 46, 177, 224, 266, 304
passivity, radical, 158
Passover, infinite, 8, 55, 210, 217–18
Paul, the apostle: apocalypticism of, 112, 123–25, 145; and Christ, as new foundation, 201–202; Letter to Corinthians, 126, 252, 265; and Jewish messianism, 63; proclamation of, 252
Peirce, Charles Sanders, 81, 137, 142, 219, 243, 296–97, 300 312, 314
Pelagianism, 218
perception, 3, 18, 304–305
person, 305; and the apocalyptic "I," 163, 189–91, 207; in Badiou, 199–201; as being itself, 176; as Creator of existence, 31; and drama of primordial jealousy, 104; essence of, 100; as form of self-consciousness 40; human as edge, 196; identity of in actual existence, 158–61, 263; itself, 74–75; love of, 180; speciated, 194
personalism, 99, 103–104
phenomenology, 16, 83; of existence, 34; of the mass, 103; of transparence, 229
Phenomenology of Spirit (Hegel), 112, 114–18, 121, 251
phi proportionality: as divine, 283; mathematics of, 280; and trinary logic, 281
Philosophical Fragments (Kierkegaard), 128

philosophical/ethical thinking, 17–18
philosophy: empiricist, 181; history of, as progressive, 40; pedagogy of, 253; radical, as a return to beginnings, 83; and science, 28. *See also* specific philosophers
philosophy and theology, 17, 138, 146, 213, 305; attempts to reconcile, 28; pedagogy of, 254; problem of evil in, 195
Place, the, 241, 248, 278, 282; exteriority of, 242; and the foundation, 165–66; nonsubjectivity of, 194; of the other, 244, 246–47; time as, 67; truth of, 65
pleroma, 6, 23
Plotinus, 20, 31, 33, 47
poetics of thinking, 49–51
politics, 6, 20, 106, 187, 305
polyontology, 32, 35, 38–39, 43, 45, 47–48, 61, 230, 245
Pommier, Monique, 232
postmodernism: as challenge to ethics, 18; imperative, 14
poststructuralism, 34, 141
pragmatism: American, 9, 122, 218–19, 224–25, 227; as precursor to the new thinking, 142, 271–72, 274; and the second absolute, 263
preestablished harmony, 102
process theology, 162
product, rational, 262–63, 265–66
productive receptivity, 306; and the apocalyptic "I," 183; and body as Gift, 159, 166; as ethical basis of the new world, 207; as faith, 197; as gratitude, 179, 192, 198–99; and identity, 5. *See also* creative perception
projective verse, 49–50
prophecy, 267

Przywara, Erich: as critic of Heidegger, 129; and metaphysics of morals, 100; posture of distance, 99; and Augustine, 103–105
Pseudo-Dionysius, 130

Quasha, George, 49
Quest for Certainty (Dewey), 248

rationes, 102
readiness, 179, 187, 192–93, 198, 206, 224
reading Leahy, 2, 34–35, 178, 188, 251–52; strategies that work, 21–23
reality. *See* actuality
reason, 306; natural, 29, 130–31, 204, 209, 212; pure, 18–19, 186; sufficient, 130
reconstruction of the world, novelty of, 56
res cogitans, 98
res extensa, 98
respect, 180, 187
responsibility, 181, 187
resurrection: of existence (the body), 55, 57, 67, 121, 185, 197, 214–15, 217, 222–24, 226, 230, 232, 252, 255, 256, 265, 266; of God, 67, 77, 124, 184, 191, 194, 195, 206, 292, 315. *See also* Christ, Jesus: resurrection of
revelation: as apocalyptic, 124, 213, 227; death of God as, 12; as eternal return, 119; and history of thinking, 11; ontology of, 36; and reason, 129; and the transcendental essence of existence, 29–30; and truth, 28; ultimacy of, 155
Rovelli, Carlo, 95n35

sacred doctrine (*sacra doctrina*), 28–30, 34, 212, 231; absolute novelty of, 130; eschatology of, 133–34; as grammar for apocalyptic, 127; and science, 29. *See also* Aquinas, Thomas; interdict of sacred doctrine
Sahlins, Marshall, 41
Sallis, John, 83
same (sameness), 13, 65, 92, 177, 181, 200, 220, 307
Sartre, Jean-Paul, 16–17, 31, 221
Satan (Antichrist), 118, 123, 195, 212, 217, 218
Schelling, F. W. J. von, 112, 146, 170, 217, 231
Schopenhauer, Arthur, 98
Schema L (Lacan), 100
science: as challenge to ethics, 181; of the infinite, 44; modern, 19, 113; new, 130; and philosophy, 28–29, 111; and revelation, 257; and spirituality, 272; in the thinking now occurring, 272–83; thought as new, 127, 130; of true beginnings, 83
Science of Logic (Hegel), 53, 114, 118
second absolute, 307
Secondness, 137, 296, 300–301, 315
secretarium tuum, 104–105
Seinsvergessenheit (forgetfulness), 128
self, 5, 307; dialectic of the exhausted, 12; dissolution of, 86: interiority of, 176, 242
Self, Absolute, 156
Self, infinite, 164
Self, universal, 161, 167
self-consciousness, 163, 196–97; of the apocalyptic "I," 186; end of as new beginning, 190; interiority of, 111; modern, 116–17; self-constructing of, 204
self-emptying, God as, 12, 115, 130, 170n1, 115, 167. *See also* kenosis
selflessness, 226
simplicity, 211, 224, 307–8. *See also* ethic of simplicity, unicity

sin, 59, 60, 167, 190, 192, 204, 214, 217–18, 223, 254. *See also* evil
sovereignty, 308; beyond beyond, 223; and ethics, 20, 187; of God, 124, 126, 192, 194; in healthcare, 275; and humanitarianism, 97; and omnipotence, 159
Spinoza, Baruch, 4, 15, 20, 112–13, 231, 300
spiral, logarithmic, 282–84
Spirit, 12, 113, 116–18
Spirit, Absolute, 156
Stevens, Wallace, 48, 247–48
structural anthropology, 41
sub specie aeternitatis (Spinoza), 4
subjectivity, 308; absolute, 85; Cartesian, 135; elimination of, 10, 20, 229; as foundational, 131; in medicine, 277, 285; modern, 10, 12–13, 19, 23, 128, 135, 211–12, 221; and mysticism, 165; and the new world order, 170; opacity of, 229; post-Cartesian, 14, 244; and pragmatism, 224; science of, 130; as self, 3; thinking beyond, 5; transcendence of, 226; and transparency, 227; and the will, 191
substance, 308; in Badiou, 145; of divinity, 222; of existence, 227–28; as given, 5, 19; in Hegel, 118; of history 28, 217; identity of, 57; and *missa jublaea*, 63; and mysticism, 33; of nothing, 190; as repetition of history in thought, 68. *See also* eucharist of existence

Taubes, Jacob, 135
Teilhard de Chardin, Pierre, 215–17, 227, 230–31
teleology, 137, 139, 145, 216
temporality, novel conception of, 59
Tetragrammaton, 147, 264
theism, classical, 156
theodicy, 129, 136, 192, 195

theology, Catholic, 99, 121, 214; apocalypticism in, 129, 131, 133, 137, 146–48
theology, Christian: history of, 48; *nous*, notion of in, 20; self-involving character of, 128. *See also* philosophy and theology; theology, Catholic
theology, modern, 125
theology, mystical, 130. *See also* mysticism, Christian
theo-poiesis, 216
thinking: beginning, 254, 256, 274; as creating, 15; as creating absolute edge, 247; on the edge, 246; existence, 17; as faith, 198; history of, 11; pure, 119–20; realization of apocalyptic in, 119; as world-creating, 16–17
thinking now occurring for the first time (TNO), 16, 50; as absolute exteriority, 7; and absolute identity, 69; and absolute now, 84; absolute particularity of, 46; as absolute technology, 23; as actualization of the resurrection body, 256; apocalyptic speculation of, 80; as beginning itself, 184; as beginning of essence, 11; challenges of Eastern thought to, 33, 46–48; and Christian mysticism, 33; and Christian soteriology, 63; christological underpinnings of, 74; and clarification of the created Godhead, 75; conception of time as problematic in, 84; and conforming reason to faith, 74; as consciousness of new beginning, 284; and creating essence, 5; as creating of the world now occurring, 4; and direptive understanding of the present, 77; eclipsing of self-consciousness in, 189; elimination of subjectivity in,

thinking now occurring for the first time (TNO) *(continued)* 20; as enactment of *missa jubilaea*, 217; as enactment of the absolute edge, 231; as epistemological change, 54; ethical imperative of, 192; ethics of, 9; and the evental being of truth, 201; ex nihilo, beginning of in, 169; the existence of the Other in, 158; freedom of God and creation in, 202; and healthcare, 274–78; and Hegel, 231; and Heidegger's levels of ontological inquiry, 38; historical orientation of, 27, 31; and immunity, 278–79; imperative of, 252; infinite absolute Othering of God in, 170; as inversion of Leibnizian monadology, 168; inversion of the Godhead in, 156; as "live" creation of essence, 23; logic, gaps in, 44; logico-mathematical basis of, 272; mathematics, relation to, 43–44; and mysticism, 167; as nonmechanistic, 277; and the now, 65; omnipotence in, 159–60, 164, 190; and ontological inquiry, 39; and open theism, 159; other-consciousness in, 190; as overly historicized view of thinking, 82; paradoxical movement of, 227; as perceiving, 4; Platonic forms, rejection of in, 33, 47; as poetic practice, 49, 51; and pragmatism, 271; presuppositionlessness of, 206; as projective, 49–50; and religion, 6–7; restrictions on, 56; as revolutionary; and *metanoesis*, 195; sacred doctrine, resistance to, 31; selfless logic of, 273; and spirit and matter disparity, 56; structure of existence as beginning of, 178; supersessionist bias of, 62; temporal underpinnings of, 53; as thinking of the transcendental essence of existence, 78; and time as materializing thought, 68; as transcendence of the beginning of thinking, 79–80; as transcendental historical thinking, 157; transparency of, 209–10

third absolute, 309

thought: and being, 54; and comprehension of identity, 58; as concrete event, 40; as edge of thinking, 244–45; as thinking the beginning of being, 80; transparency of, 211; world, distinction from, 46–47

time, 309–10; as the absolute now of creation, 54; absolute objectivity of, 76; arrow of, 281–82, 284; circle as, 61; as circular, 61, 65, 67; divinization of, 67; as existing actuality, 73; internal consciousness of, 82–83; linear circularity of, 67–68; mystery of, 48; as object of transcendental historical thinking, 282; temporality of as place, 67; as thought's comprehension of its identity, 58; time-transcendent change of, 68; transcendence of, 57; transcendental dichotomy of, 76

Torah, 86, 94, 124, 259, 263. *See also* Judaism

transcendence: of knowledge, 6; planes of, 158; of transcendence, 122

transcendental dichotomy, 76, 310

transcendental: difference, 56, 61, 310–11; form of natural reason, 204, 223, 311–12; repetition of creation, 64, 165

transcendental essence of existence, 28–29, 46, 54, 56, 78–79, 209–11, 227,

232, 311; absolute multiplication of, 158; in the Eucharist, 214; in existence itself, 55; and identity, 6; and Incarnation, 157; and transparency, 210
transparency: enacting resurrection, 226; of existence, 227, 230; noetic, 226; phenomenology of, 229; spheres of, 228; and subjectivity, 227; and truth, 226. *See also* simplicity
transubstantiation, 112, 214, 221, 227–28
trichotomy, 312
trinary hope, 312–13
trinary logic, real, 7–8, 19, 71, 260, 273–74, 277, 279–80, 283–84; and meta-identity of language, 256–57, 263; and phi proportionality, 281
Trinity, 130, 140, 158, 313; economic, 134, 216; immanent, 143; manifested in structure of existence, 185; temporalization of, 134; as Tetragrammaton, 147; triple nothingness of, 313–14
truth, 226, 314; evental being of, 201; and revelation, 28. See also *aletheia*

Uncreated, the, 190, 207. *See also* Creator
uncreated omnipotence, 160, 165, 314. *See also* created omnipotence
unicity, 3–5, 56, 74–75, 163, 165, 284, 304, 314–15
unity, 301; beyond the One, 195, 266, 267, 293, 296, 314–15; created, xi, 3, 10, 56, 58, 61, 74, 92, 105,
126, 145–46, 153–65, 177, 262, 265; of world, perfectly differentiated, 284, 289, 308. *See also* unicity
universal, as fulfillment of the particular, 63
universality, as apocalyptic event, 117
universe, infinitely flat structure of, 194, 298. *See also* flatness
unum ($\overline{0}$), base digit of the trinary logic, 74–75, 77, 144, 191, 260, 315
Upanishadic tradition, 211

Valéry, Paul, 21
Very First, 163, 169, 210, 252, 315
Vattimo, Gianni, 135, 146, 216–17, 227

Western thought, history of, 20, 34–35, 42, 48, 276
What Is Metaphysics? (Heidegger), 36
will, 90, 116, 181, 191, 193, 196, 198–99
willing, 59–61, 193, 195, 199; to create, 191–92, 196; and ethic of simplicity, 182; the good, 21
Wilson, Peter Lamborn, 41
withness, 158, 223, 230
world, as body, 216
world engagement, 179
world now occurring, 55
world society, 122, 223, 315
world-creating, 15–16

zero not nothing (0), base digit of the trinary logic, 7, 143–44, 164, 315
Žižek, Slavoj, 142

www.ingramcontent.com/pod-product-compliance
Ingram Content Group UK Ltd.
Pitfield, Milton Keynes, MK11 3LW, UK
UKHW041915140426
5217IPUK00013B/165